Families, Risk, and Competence
➤◆◄

Families, Risk, and Competence

Edited by

Michael Lewis

Candice Feiring

Institute for the Study of Child Development
Robert Wood Johnson Medical School

LEA LAWRENCE ERLBAUM ASSOCIATES, PUBLISHERS
1998   **Mahwah, New Jersey**   **London**

Lawrence Erlbaum Associates, Inc., Publishers
10 Industrial Avenue
Mahwah, New Jersey 07430

Cover Design by Kathryn Houghtaling Lacey

Library of Congress Cataloging-in-Publication Data

Families, risk, and competence / edited by Michael Lewis,
Candice Feiring.
      p. cm.
  Includes bibliographical references and index.
  ISBN 0-8058-2344-1 (hardcover : alk. paper). — ISBN
0-8058-2345-X (Pbk. : alk. Paper)
  1. Family. 2. Child development. I. Feiring, Candice.
II. Title.
  HQ734.L4984 1998
  306.85—dc21
                                          97–37790
                                          CIP

Books published by Lawrence Erlbaum Associates are
printed on acid-free paper, and their bindings are chosen for
strength and durability.

Printed in the United States of America
10 9 8 7 6 5 4 3 2 1

CONTENTS

PART II: FAMILIES AT RISK

PREFACE

The newborn human infant enters into the world of its family. The family varies in its numbers of different people. Historically, the family has been defined in any number of ways: to include only the mother on one hand, and on the other hand, all the people living under one roof. Although it is recognized that the child enters into a complex nexus of people and functions (Lewis & Feiring, 1978, 1979), it is the mother–child relationship that has received the most attention. Spurred on by attachment theory, which limited the earliest and prototypic relationships to the mother, the research literature is relatively limited when it comes to studying the family influences in the child's development. This is especially the case for research on infancy and early childhood. Although we tried to argue for the importance of observing the family system for understanding the child's social and emotional development, the impact of attachment theory and the difficulty of studying families have made the progress slow.

The problems of studying families arise from the difficulty in studying systems in which there are multiple elements interacting with each other and the child. One question is "How should this system's interaction on the child be described when the child is not a member of the dyad?" Still other problems have to do with what we have called *indirect effects*, namely the influence of a particular dyad. Although we all agree that the mother–father relationship has important bearing on the child's development, exactly how to study this, especially using observational techniques, remains a problem. Although progress in studying the family has been slow, there is no question that an increase in interest in family systems, as opposed to the mother–child relationship, is taking place. This results in an increase in research on families and their effects.

This volume, written by some of the leading figures in the study of families, attests to the growing sophistication of our conceptualization and measurement techniques for understanding family processes. This volume grew out of a conference sponsored by the Center for Human Development and Developmental Disabilities, an interdisciplinary effort of the Department of Pediatrics, Robert Wood Johnson Medical School at the University of Medicine and Dentistry of New Jersey, and the State of New Jersey, Department of Human Services, Office for Prevention of Mental Retardation and Developmental Disabilities. In addition to the participants represented in the chapters, Myron Gessner, David Mandelbaum, Mary Osborne, Barbara Snyder, and Margaret Sullivan also attended and contributed to the volume through discussions. This volume is the third in a series that aims to address topics that are relevant to developmental problems and to developmental disabilities and retardation. This volume is divided into two parts. In Part I, "The Nature of Family Environments," basic family processes and approaches for describing family dynamics are presented. It deals with these issues from a broad perspective including studying families at dinner, studying families in different cultural contexts, and understanding family in nonhuman primates.

Part II, "Families At Risk," looks at family processes in the service of studying at risk families. The risk factors include poverty, malnutrition, and developmental delay and retardation. The study of family processes in these contexts provides data on both family dynamics and how these dynamics affect children's developing competence.

We hope the volume is informative for researchers, clinicians, and educators from a variety of disciplines and settings. Our aim is to bring a greater clarity to issues concerning the family lives of children and to highlight new research and possibilities for intervention. In addition to the participants, we wish to thank Cynthia Tucker, Ruth Gitlen, and Despina Laverick for their help in arranging the conference and in typing and editing the manuscript.

—*Michael Lewis*
—*Candice Feiring*

I
▼▼▼▼▼▼▼▼▼▼

THE NATURE OF FAMILY
ENVIRONMENTS

In order to study the child and its family, we need to go beyond the dyad and the study of the parent–child interaction. Because we recognize that children are born to families made up of a varying number of people and functions, we are confronted by multiple ways, perspectives, and methods with which to describe the family. Lewis and Feiring (chap. 1, this volume) discuss how a systems approach is helpful in describing families. This approach, allowing for multiple elements, each interacting and influencing others, provides a framework for what they called a "social matrix system" (Lewis & Feiring, 1979). In their chapter, they focus on how different members of the family provide different functions directed to the goals that families set for themselves. Of particular interest is their concern for both direct and indirect interactive effects and how indirect effects are necessary to consider when studying a multielement system.

In chapter 2, Ramey and Juliusson provide a unique opportunity to understand the family from multiple perspectives: direct videotaped observations of interactions over multiple occasions, family members' perceptions of these videotaped interactions, self-reports of family members' experiences in the family, as well as observers' ratings of family dynamics. Of particular interest are the similarities between married families and divorced single-mother families. Quite striking from this research is the support for the notion of families as dynamic systems in which multiple paths are available in achieving a homeostatic balance.

Implicit in the study of families is the belief that studying the family system is likely to provide greater coherence in its effect on the child's development than studying elements in isolation. Feiring and Lewis (chap. 3, this volume) explore this question by studying how aggregating family views, rather than examining the views of individual members alone, is related to school competence. They examine family views by looking at the aggregate of beliefs about the family's intellectual environment within the family and also by looking at the disagreement between family members. By addressing the question of whether multiple family members' perspectives at the individual, dyadic, and entire family level are related to adolescent competence, they offer a multilevel approach for describing family systems and their impact on child development.

Although the context of other members of the family or group is likely to influence the child's development, Rosenblum (chap. 4, this volume), working with nonhuman primates, argues for the more traditional view of the major importance of the mother for the baby monkey's development. Recognizing the effect of the environment surrounding the mother–infant dyad, however, Rosenblum forcefully argues that although the maternal–child dyad is influenced by exogenous factors, it is still the dyadic relationship itself that supports, alters, and forms the competence of the developing infant. He sees the mothers' primary function in three areas: the modulation of arousal, the mitigation of environmental uncertainty, and the mediation of kinship relations.

Parke et al. (chap. 5, this volume) consider how the family is a central context for the socialization of skills and knowledge in social contexts outside the family. They present findings that examine a three-tiered model that suggests the modes by which parents may influence their children's peer relationships. Parents are viewed as affecting peer relationships through childrearing practices and interactive styles, a mode of influence that is often indirect. Parents also directly influence peer relationships in their role as educators by giving advice on managing relationships and by acting as gatekeepers to specific types of friends and settings for interaction.

In order to understand how families operate, it is necessary to observe how they function in different cultures. Lamb, Leyendecker, and Schölmerich (chap. 6, this volume) explore family differences in Euro-American and Central American families. Although there are major differences between these cultures, there are many similarities in the mother–infant interaction. One important difference between the cultures is the different everyday experiences of the infants; daily life is quite structured and predictable for the Euro-American infants, whereas the daily lives of the Central American infants are less routinized. The study of cultural differences is clearly a valuable way to explore how families affect children's development.

How the developing child forces a reconsideration of the factors important for a home environment that facilitates competence, as well as issues of measurement, are addressed by Bradley and Whiteside-Mansell (chap. 7, this volume). To promote optimal development, family systems must function to sustain viability, stimulate skills, support the child's self-sustaining capacities, and control inputs to maximize the fit between the child's and the other's social agendas. How families carry out these functions and how to measure them varies as the child ages and depends on cultural, socioeconomic, and ethnic considerations.

In general, the chapters in this volume share the common premise that families have multiple functions and that their structure and processes have important consequences for the child's development. Although a variety of theoretical and measurement models are offered, there remains much work to be done; of particular importance is the need to understand and articulate those measures of family functions best related to children's competence.

1

▼▼▼▼▼▼▼▼

The Child and Its Family

Michael Lewis
Candice Feiring
Robert Wood Johnson Medical School
New Brunswick, NJ

The newborn human infant enters a world filled with networks, the most immediate and important of which is the family. Soon, the infant's network includes significant others beyond the family including friends, teachers, and eventually mates. Moreover, the first network is embedded in other networks that form larger reference groups such as a clan, social class, or religious group. Still larger networks can be imagined that are made up of geographical regions and countries or cultures. These networks are interconnected and exert influence on each other. They form the ecology of development (Bronfenbrenner, 1986). Each of these separate networks, as well as the entire system of networks, operates under general systems principles and therefore, possesses the characteristics of systems (Von Bertalanffy, 1967).

It is to this changing array of people, institutions, behaviors, and goals that the infant is born, and it is in this array that the development and socialization of the child takes place. As we noted (Lewis & Feiring, 1978), the socialization of the infant is the process of learning to become a member of these different networks. The task of the socializer(s), then, is to teach the child the rules of membership. This teaching can be carried out through a variety of procedures, some of which are direct, as in didactic information exchange, and some of which involve more indirect interaction, such as modeling, imitation, and referencing (Feinman & Lewis, 1983; Feiring, Lewis, & Starr, 1984; Lewis, 1979b; Lewis & Feiring, 1981).

In order to study the child and its family, we need to go beyond the dyad and the study of the mother–child relationship (e.g., Lewis, 1984; Lewis &

Rosenblum, 1974). As soon as we realize that the child develops in a social nexus rather than in just the mother–infant dyad, we are confronted by how to talk about the family. The nature of the family requires that we consider a systems analysis. A corollary to this problem is the issue of how to describe the forces acting on and being acted on by the child. When we discuss interactions that involve more than two actors, we are forced into a consideration of what we called "direct and indirect forces or effects" (Lewis & Feiring, 1981, 1992).

In this chapter, we first discuss a general systems approach to family life, including in it what we learned about the child's social nexus. In the next section, we focus on the forces, both direct and indirect, that must exist when multiple family members, rather than the mother–child dyad, are considered. Using information from families at dinner, we give examples of both these direct and indirect effects that act on the children in the family setting.

A SYSTEMS APPROACH

Systems, in general, and families, in particular, can be characterized by a number of features: (a) there are more than two elements or family members; (b) those elements are interdependent; (c) the elements are nonadditive and thus, the sum of the individual elements does not equal the total system of family; (d) elements of the system change and yet maintain the system; and (e) systems and families are goal-oriented.

Elements

Systems are composed of sets of elements. In the family, an element represents each individual member—mother, father, child—or it can represent dyads— mother–child, father–child—or even triads when there is more than one child in the family. When considering units larger than the family, families themselves can become the elements of the system. In a family of 4 (2 children), there are a total of 4 simple elements, 6 dyads, and 4 triads, or a total of 14 possible elements. The potential array of different social elements that infants experience that can influence them, and are influenced by them, is large. Unfortunately, there are almost no data on the changing number of different social contacts and their frequency and intensity as a function of the child's age (Lewis, Young, Brooks, & Michalson, 1975). This scarcity of data applies to other potentially important figures. For example, there are few data as to the number of grandparent, aunt, or uncle experiences, and there is no real count of sibling contacts. Information regarding these relationships is also missing. Clearly, the number of others the child interacts with needs study, especially in the light of changing childrearing practices. We collected data on the social networks of over 117 three year olds (Feiring & Lewis, 1988). The children in our sample had approximately 5.8 friends. In addition to mother, father, and siblings, the children came in contact with an average of 9.6 relatives, including grandparents, aunts, uncles, and cousins. Mothers reported that these children came in contact with almost all the people the mother would include as important in her social network, including her friends. The number of adults other than family that the child made contact with was 7.1. On the average, 3.2, 4.4, and 4.4 relatives, friends, and adults (other than parents) are seen at least once a week. These data reflect what we observed at that time. Given the changes in the social structure of the society in the last two decades, these figures are likely to have changed. Nevertheless, for some infants the only significant relationship may be between the mother and infant, whereas for others, it may include fathers, caregivers (as in daycare), siblings, peers, and relatives such as grandparents. Having considered multiple significant relationships, it is now possible to ask which ones exist, how they differ, and what are their potential consequences.

People in the Child's Network

Mothers are the primary focus in attachment theory, but children form important relationships and attachments with individuals other than their mothers. In this section, we introduce other figures such as fathers, siblings, grandparents, and peers. The role of mothers in young children's lives need not be discussed in detail. Mothers are the primary caretakers, even today when many fathers take an active role in childrearing and many mothers hold jobs outside the home. It is the mother who usually buys clothes for the child, arranges for child care (whether it be hiring a babysitter or taking the child to a child-care center), makes medical appointments, and takes the child to the pediatrician's office. Also, even when the child is under someone else's care, the person who normally takes the mother's role is usually someone else's mother.

Fathers. The research literature, although still dominated by studies of mother–child, brought into focus some of the roles fathers play in children's lives. Four questions were directed toward the father–child relationship. Each of these is discussed, albeit briefly.

1. Can fathers do what mothers do? One important question raised about fathers is whether there is any biological difference between mother and father care for the very young. Perhaps mothers take care of infants better than fathers? Parke and O'Leary (1975), in their work with fathers and newborn infants, demonstrated that fathers' care—the interaction patterns between fathers and children—is similar to mothers' care. Thus, one would

say that fathers care for their very young infants. Although fathers provide care, it is apparent that, in general, they do not, especially in the case of a young infant under 9 months or so. Even the increased multiple roles assumed by the mother (mother, worker out of the home, wife) does not seem to lead to a major increase in fathers' involvement (Feiring & Lewis, 1984; Russell & Russell, 1987).

2. What do fathers do that is different from mothers? Although fathers have been shown to be equally capable of caring for the young, there are differences in their interaction patterns that distinguish them from mothers. Whereas maternal interactions are likely to center around child-care activities such as feeding, changing diapers and clothes, bathing, and other caregiving and maternal activities, fathers' interactions are more likely to include physical playful activities. Studies have shown fathers engage in more rough and tumble, bouncing, and tickling activities than do mothers (Lamb, 1976; Lewis & Weinraub, 1976; Parke, MacDonald, Beitel, & Bhavnagri, 1988). Although mothers play with their young children, their play is likely to be less active and arousing than that of father. Moreover, as the children become older, the father's role is likely to increase, mostly as a function of the declining need for caregiving activities and the increasing needs for exploration, play, and self-initiated action or efficacy vis-à-vis the physical environment. Mackey (1985) showed that across many cultures fathers' interactions with young children in public places are quite different than those that can be seen in the home. Although not sufficiently studied, fathers' involvement with their children is probably considerably greater in public than at home, whereas mothers' involvement may be the reverse. This change in roles by situations, with mothers dominating in the home, may be responsible for our rather limited view of fathers' interaction patterns. By studying children in their homes, we inadvertently reduced the paternal role.

3. What are the direct versus the indirect effects of the fathers? In exploring the roles of fathers and mothers, most studies observed the interactional patterns of family members. Such patterns, which directly involve the child with the father, are called "fathers' direct effects" (Lewis & Feiring, 1982). Of these, we already mentioned that play and exploration are major areas of interaction. It is also interesting to note that fathers, more than mothers, were influenced by the sex and birth order of their children. In studying families at dinner, Lewis and Feiring (1981) found that the father talked more to first- than later-born and more to male than female children at the table. Fathers also affect their children's lives indirectly by impacting the lives of their wives (Lewis, Feiring, & Weinraub, 1981). These indirect effects include emotional support of the mother. The interdependent nature of the child–parent and parent–parent subsystems are amply demonstrated (Belsky, Rovine, & Fish, 1988; Belsky & Volling, 1987; Christensen & Margolin, 1988). Some research indicates that variation in the quality and func-

tioning of the marital relationship is more systematically related to fathering than to mothering (Belsky et al., 1988). Thus, it is important to recognize that mothers affect their infants' lives indirectly by affecting the lives of their husbands.

4. Are the children attached to their fathers? The answer is: Of course, children are attached to their fathers (Belsky, 1981; Fox, Kimmerly, & Schafer, 1991; Lamb, 1977a,b). Moreover, Lewis and Ban (1974) and Lewis and Weinraub (1974) looked at children's behavior toward their mothers and fathers and found that children directed equal social behavior to each, the only difference being that fathers received somewhat more distal behavior.

Siblings. Very early in a child's life, a sibling can affect the child's behavior (Abramovitch, Corter, & Lando, 1979; Dunn, Kendrick, & Mac-Namee, 1981) and the child's relationship with and view of the family (Stocker, Dunn, & Plomin, 1989; Volling & Belsky, 1992). Even children's views of themselves are affected by siblings (Greenbaum, 1965; Tesser, 1980; Yamamoto, 1972). Siblings protect and help one another. Many mothers note that when they are punishing one of their children, the other protects that child even if the punishment concerns a sibling conflict. Dunn and Kendrick (1979, 1982) studied sibling behavior in regard to communication, social interactions, and teachings and found that even young siblings (14 months of age and younger) are capable of turn taking as well as empathic and teaching behaviors. Siblings provide important social models for each other. Children learn how to share, cooperate, help, and empathize by watching their siblings. Siblings spend their early lives sharing a variety of objects, experiences, and people.

Siblings show strong affective bonds, and these relationships show continuity over time (Pepler, Abramovitch, & Corter, 1981; Stillwell & Dunn, 1985). The attachment of siblings to one another has received some attention. Lamb (1978) showed that, whereas older siblings (20–40 months older) showed little attachment to younger siblings, younger siblings showed inordinate interest in, and were influenced by the older sibling. This earlier attachment, at least by the younger toward the older sibling, persists through time. In a 3-year follow-up study of siblings, the older siblings' verbal descriptions were remarkably related to the kind of behavior they had shown toward their younger siblings (Stillwell, 1984). Such findings of sibling attachment appear in the Western child, where the sibling role is somewhat different than that in other cultures. Whiting and Whiting (1975) showed that in some cultures, the older sibling may be one of the principal caretakers of the child. One would expect that in such cultures, the attachment relationship between siblings would be even stronger. The degree to which siblings become attached to each other should be a function of the value of the family, the cultural expectations, sex, age, spacing of siblings, and more.

Even so, many siblings show a strong attachment toward one another that lasts a lifetime. Cicirelli (1982), for example, found that siblings, especially sisters, are very likely to live together in their old age.

Perhaps one of the most striking qualities of sibling relationships is their dual nature of positive and negative attributes. It has been argued that sibling relationships are among the most volatile of human relationships because they are rooted in ambivalence (Pfouts, 1976). On the one hand, sibling rivalry is seen as the basis for most of the negative aspects of sibling relationships such as emotional struggles involving issues of sibling anger, identity, and competition for recognition and approval from parents. On the other hand, there are the positive features of closeness, supportive caregiving, and companionship.

Interviews and questionnaire responses of children, adolescents, and young adults indicated support for the idea that sibling relationships have a good deal of both positive and negative qualities (Buhrmester & Furman, 1987, 1990; Furman & Buhrmester, 1985). Siblings characterized sibling relationships in terms of such attributes as intimacy, companionship, quarreling, and competition. Four factors appeared to capture individuals' perceptions of their sibling relationships: relative status and power, warmth and closeness, conflict, and rivalry.

Older siblings are more likely to perceive themselves as nurturant and dominating, whereas younger siblings are more likely to report being nurtured and dominated (Buhrmester & Furman, 1987). Brody and colleagues (Brody, Stoneman, MacKinnon, & MacKinnon, 1985; Stoneman, Brody, & MacKinnon, 1984) distinguished a coherent set of roles that children use when interacting with their siblings: helper, helpee, teacher, learner, manager, managee, and observer. Not surprisingly, the older sibling was more likely to assume the roles of teacher, helper, and manager. A similar set of roles in siblings was also identified across early to late childhood (Vandell, Minnett, & Santrock, 1987). Although these roles become less extreme with age, there is evidence that they continue to characterize sibling subsystems into adolescence and adulthood (Furman & Buhrmester, 1992; Searcy & Eisenberg, 1992).

Grandparents.   The failure to consider the possible role of the grandparents in children's development is surprising given the obvious facts that parents of parents exert strong influence on children's development if for no other reason than that they influence the parents. Even the term *grandparent* should make it obvious that such a role carries with it importance for both child and grandparent. Tinsley and Parke (1984) suggested three important reasons for neglecting the study of grandparents: the focus on only the nuclear family, the focus on only the mother as the important social agent in the child's life, and the limited interest in exploring the full life-span development.

To these we should add a fourth reason: the focus on only direct effects on the child's development. Clearly, if grandparents do not live in the same home as the child, how can we focus on only direct effects? As Tinsley and Parke (1984) made clear, however, grandparents exert both direct and indirect effects on their grandchildren. It is clear that the lack of study of influence of grandparents on development reflects a culture that does not value age, that is highly age segregated, and in which intergenerational learning is not encouraged. In cultures, such as Japan today, in which many grandparents, parents, and children live together, the role played by grandparents is more obvious. Even in our culture, the direct effects of grandparents should be considerable given that grandparents generally have contact with their adult children (the parents of the child) at least once a week (Shanas, 1979). Lewis, Feiring, and Kotsonis (1984) reported that grandparents are most often seen when compared to other relatives. Indeed, on a weekly basis, at least one of the grandparents is seen once by these 3-year-old children.

Aunts, Uncles, and Cousins.   There is little research literature about the role of aunts, uncles, or cousins in the development of the child. In anthropology and animal behavior, the role of these others is well-recognized. In many groups, such as lion prides, for example, the social structure of the group includes the female relatives: mothers, aunts, daughters, and female cousins (if such terms can be used in this context). The data we collected 15 years ago about contacts indicate that aunts, uncles, and cousins are present in the child's life (Lewis et al., 1984). Given that the previous generation's siblings maintain life-long contacts, it should come as little surprise that parents' siblings (aunts and uncles) should be a part of the social fabric of the young children. The same reasons for neglecting grandparents apply to these relatives.

Because aunts and uncles are in close contact, their children (cousins) should also be in close contact. In fact, for many children, their first peer contacts, which are long lasting, are with cousins. Thus, cousins are likely to play an influential role, and the social network data indicate a considerable rate of cousin contact. Cousins are viewed as so close, at least genetically, that in many states, there exist laws against marriage between them.

For aunts, uncles, and cousins, differences similar to those already reported for grandparents and siblings are likely to appear. Mothers' siblings, aunts, uncles, and children's cousins are more likely to be in contact than fathers' kin, a finding previously reported (Lewis et al., 1984; Oliveri & Reiss, 1987). Female cousins and aunts are more likely than male cousins and uncles to maintain contact, a sex-role difference that should appear throughout the social network structure. Moreover, the role of grandparents in the maintenance of sibling contact is probably important. That is, aunt and uncle (and therefore, cousin) contact is more likely in some families than in others.

The exact nature of the relationship that facilitates this is not well-understood.

Clearly, the relationship of aunts, uncles, and cousins is related to sibling contact across the life cycle. As we come to focus on these aspects, the role of these other relatives becomes more obvious. Nonetheless, given our limited knowledge of sibling relationships over time, it is reasonable to include these relatives as important for the child's social development.

Peers.   Beyond family members there are various social entities that play important roles in children's development. Peers are surely the most important, for it is in peer relationships that most of adult social life exists. For this reason, of all social entities other than mothers, early peer relationships have been most studied.

The failure to examine peer relationships in very early childhood was based on the beliefs that children are intellectually incapable and emotionally uninterested in peer contact and relationships. Moreover, the role of peers in the child's early life was not explored. These factors are now recognized to be untrue or in need of considerable modification. Piaget's (1952) view on social development argued against early peer interactions; for example, he viewed egocentricity as resulting in parallel play and in the lack of empathy that prevented peer interaction. More recent evidence suggests that egocentric behavior is overstated for the early life cycle. Young children engage in interactive play as early as the first year of life, although it is not until the second year that more complex play is observed (Mueller, 1972; Mueller & Lucas, 1975). Moreover, young children appear capable of empathetic behavior (Borke, 1971; Zahn-Waxler, Radke-Yarrow, & King, 1979). In terms of perceptual–cognitive ability, infants are capable of discriminating social objects as a function of age, learning age-related terms easily, and showing that they possess some rudimentary forms of social roles (Brooks-Gunn & Lewis, 1981; Edwards & Lewis, 1979; Lewis, 1984). Thus, social skills and perceptual–cognitive abilities are in place quite early to facilitate peer interactions.

The belief that infants had no social or emotional interest in peers, due in part to the widely held view that the social–emotional life of the child primarily involved only the mother, also prevented the study of early peer relationships. Whereas the role of the mother is recognized, the role of peers proves to be equally important as it is encouraged or inhibited by the social structure. In some cultures, peers are given more direct roles in child care (Brown, 1971; Whiting & Whiting, 1975), and given the significant increase in group care, there are now more and earlier peer emotional–social interactions than when group child care was not a part of the culture.

Peers show interest, enjoyment, and emotional involvement from the earliest opportunities provided in the first year of life. Peer attachment is proven to exist especially in the absence of adults (Freud & Dann, 1951; Gyomrai-Ludowyk, 1963). Recently, the issue of intersubjectivity, the ability of the subject to realize the separateness, but interconnection between self and other, has been suggested to take place in the first 2 years; some research suggests even earlier (Stern, 1985; see also Bischof-Köhler, 1991; Bretherton, 1985; Lewis & Brooks-Gunn, 1979). All of these facts argue for the importance of peers, even in infancy.

Like siblings, peers perform both positive and negative functions. Peers are good for play (Lewis et al., 1975) and for modeling one's behavior because they share equal or nearly equal abilities and are most like the self. They are also good at teaching, especially somewhat older peers, because their abilities do not differ too markedly (Edwards & Lewis, 1979) and can facilitate the development of social competence (Furman, Rahe, & Hartup, 1979; Suomi, 1979). Peers protect each other, and most important, peers are capable of forming attachments to each other.

The negative features of the peer relationship revolve around the lack of adult perspective. Thus, for example, whereas an adult may be able to give up a need for the sake of a child, such behavior may be beyond the ability of young peers. Disputes, therefore, are often settled by power status variables, such as strength, age, and gender, rather than by true prosocial behavior. Aggressive behavior between peers represents another negative feature, with high physical interaction and direct aggression being two noticeable examples (Kochenderfer & Ladd, 1996; Olweus, 1993). Clearly, the lack of adult perspective affects levels of knowledge, history, and cultural rules, and this lack should affect the nature of peer interactions. Given that peer relationships themselves are embedded in the cultural rules, the study of peer behavior needs to be considered in the context of the entire social network.

Teachers, Daycare Personnel, and Babysitters. Even during the first few months, infants are exposed to nonrelated adults who care for the child while the mother is at work, in school, or at play. Given the large number of mothers who now work outside the home and the continuing change in the family structure, there are large numbers of children who are cared for daily by people other than relatives. The lack of study of children's attachments to other adult caregivers may rest on our general bias, which adheres to the importance of a single adult attachment figure. Even though there is some recognition that the human infant is capable of multiple attachments, research to support such a view is rarely performed. Cross-cultural research, such as that of Konner (1975), shows that even in the first few weeks infants interact with many adults, including nonrelatives to whom they may become attached. Recent evidence makes clear that, at least in the opening years of life, children raised in day-care settings show no adverse effects in their social and emotional development (Belsky & Rovine, 1990; Roggman, Langlois, Hubbs-Tait, & Rieser-Danner, 1994; Weinraub, Jaeger, & Hoffman, 1988).

Interconnection of Elements

Systems are characterized by a set of interrelated elements (Monane, 1967). In the family the interaction of elements can be at several levels. At the simplest level, the infant can affect its parents (Lewis & Rosenblum, 1974), the parents can affect the infant, and the parents can affect each other. Such effects come about through the direct interactions between family members. Moreover, elements are not only individuals, but may also be dyads or even larger units. When larger elements are considered, the study of the interrelation of elements becomes more complex. For example, a child can affect not only each parent separately, but also the parental interaction. Likewise, the father can influence the mother and child individually as well as the mother–child interaction. Many different effects of this complex nature have been observed. Several investigators studied the effect of the father on the mother–child relationship (Clarke-Stewart, 1978; Feiring & Lewis, 1987; Lamb, 1977b; Lewis & Weinraub, 1976; Parke, 1978). Cicirelli (1975) looked at the influence of siblings on the mother–child relationships and Dunn and Kendrick (1979) studied the effect of a newborn child (sibling) on the other child–mother relationship (see Dunn & Kendrick, 1980; and Lewis & Rosenblum, 1977, for a review of such studies).

Lewis (Lewis & Feiring, 1982, 1992; Lewis & Weinraub, 1976), Bronfenbrenner (1986), Lamb (1977a, 1977b), and Parke, Power, and Gottman (1979) discussed some of the various ways that elements in a system may influence each other. Direct and indirect effects were identified as belonging to two major classes (Lewis & Feiring, 1981; Lewis & Weinraub, 1976). These are discussed later because indirect effects in particular are important for any discussion of the family as a system. In short, the infant must adapt to a family containing elements that vary in number and complexity and that influence the infant both directly through their interactions with the child and indirectly through their interactions with each other. The child establishes relationships in a network of already existing relationships.

Nonadditivity

Families also possess the quality of nonadditivity; that is, to know everything about the elements that comprise a system does not reveal everything about the operation of the whole. In the family, the way a person behaves alone can be quite different from the way that person behaves in the presence of another. Because observation of a person alone is nearly impossible (and unethical), the study of individual behavior is difficult. More frequent is the observation of a dyad alone or in the presence of a third member. For example, Clarke-Stewart (1978) observed mothers, fathers, and children in dyadic (parent–child) and triadic (mother–father–child) interactions and showed that the quantity and quality of behaviors in the mother–child sub-system in isolation are changed when the mother–child subsystem is embed-ded in the mother–father–child subsystem. The mother initiated less talk, played with the child less, and was also less engaging, reinforcing, directive, and responsive in her child–directed interactions when the father was present than when she was alone with the child. Pedersen, Anderson, and Cain (1980) reported that, although the father and husband frequently divides his behav-ior between child and spouse in a three-person subsystem, the mother and wife spends much more time in dyadic interaction with the child than with her husband. The child also exerts influence on the parent system. Rosenblatt (1974) found that the presence of one or more children reduced adult–adult touching, talking, and smiling in selected public places such as the zoo, park, or shopping center. Lewis and Feiring (1982), looking at interactions at the dinner table, found that the number of children at the table affects the amount of mother–father verbal interactions as well as the amount of positive affect between the parents. A study by Parke and O'Leary (1975) illustrates the qualities of interdependence and nonadditivity in the family system. When mothers were with their husbands, they were more likely to explore the child's body and smile than when they were alone with the child. In addition, when mothers were with their husbands, they tended to touch their sons more than their daughters, whereas this difference was not evident when the mother and child were alone.

This rule of nonadditivity presents an obstacle for the study of interactions and relationships. There is some comfort in believing that the interactions one observes between two people remain the same or are invariant across situations or across changing social structures. The rule of nonadditivity suggests that this is not the case. The evidence that the relationships between elements are dependent on the set or subset of elements present suggests the relative nature of interactions. The effect on relationships is not known, although it might well be the case that, although interactions may vary, relationships do not. The relative nature of dyadic interactions makes the study of social behavior more difficult. Indeed, if the rule of nonadditivity is correct, the very act of observation (which introduces another element, the observer) must alter the behavior of those observed.

Steady State

The term *steady state* describes the process whereby a system maintains itself (e.g., its values or goals) while always changing to some degree. A *steady state* is characterized by the interplay of flexibility and stability by which a system endeavors to maintain a viable relationship among its elements and its environment. *Social systems* are defined as goal-oriented, and steady-state processes are directed toward goal achievement. However, the same general goal may be served by different patterns of behavior as the system changes to adapt to its environment. In the family, such processes appear essential because one major change that must occur is the development of the child. Because children's skills, knowledge, and behavior continually change, these changes must be accounted for by maintaining stability. That is, whereas the particular behaviors serving the relationship undergo change, relationships are likely to remain the same.

The child's functioning in the family is described by adaptation (steady state) and by development of new behavior patterns (flexibility) in the service of prior goals (stability). For example, Dunn and Kendrick (1980) found that firstborn children's independent behavior increased with the birth of a sibling. Although independent behavior occurred, was encouraged by the mother prior to the birth of the second child, and was a developmental goal, the amount, kind, and opportunity for independent behavior changed as the family system changed to include a new member. This consistency in the midst of change has to be an important factor in development that bears on relationships and feelings. This principle of steady states allows for continuity in a changing structure as well as in a changing developmental system where new behaviors and new situations are observed.

Goals

The family system is generally thought to exist in order to perform certain functions or goal-oriented activities that are necessary both to the survival of its members and to the perpetuation of the specific culture and society. Family functions are often enumerated as procreation and child rearing, which suggest that the family is the principal agent of these societal goals. Beyond this level of generality are numerous other ways of describing and defining family functions (Lewis & Feiring, 1978; Parsons & Bales, 1955).

The attachment model not only has restricted the number of the family attachment relationships available to the young child by focusing more or less exclusively on the mother, but also has limited the types of activities or goals engaged in by the other family members. If only caregiving functions or goals are considered, then it makes some sense to study the mother as the most important (and only) element. However, other functions in the child's life include, for example, play and teaching, which may involve family members other than the mother.

The issue of functions, needs, and goals is quite complex. In order to create a list of functions or goals, one could utilize Wilson's (1975) adaptive functions or Murray's (1938) need functions. We also defined some of the functions important for the infant (Lewis & Feiring, 1979). These include protection, caregiving, nurturance, play, exploration or learning, and social control. *Protection* includes protection from potential sources of danger, including both inanimate (e.g., falling off trees or being burned in fires) and animate sources (e.g., being eaten by a predator, taken by one who is not kin, or attacked by another). *Caregiving* includes feeding and cleaning at the least and refers to a set of activities that center around biological needs relating to bodily activities. *Nurturance* is the function of love or attachment as specified by Bowlby (1969). *Play* refers to activities with no immediately obvious goal. These activities are engaged in for their own sake. *Exploration or learning* involves the social activity of finding out about the environment through either watching others, asking for information, or engaging in information acquisition with others. *Social control* represents the restriction of the infant's behavior because it interferes with the behavior of others or because it is useful in teaching specific rules. It differs from exploration or learning in that its major function is to restrict the infant's ongoing behavior. More functions can be considered, but the discussion is limited to these in order to proceed to the connection between which people do which things and the possible outcomes, given that certain people do certain things.

Any analysis of the family must consider the range of functions and the nature of the different members who satisfy these functions. Although different family members are generally characterized by particular social functions, it is often the case that persons and functions are only partially related. Consequently, the identity of the family member does not necessarily define the type of range of its social functions. Whereas caregiving (a function) and mother (a person) have been considered to be highly related, research indicates that fathers are equally adequate in performing this function. Play, another function, appears to be engaged more by siblings and fathers than by mothers (Clarke-Stewart, 1978; Lewis & Ban, 1974; Parke & Sawin, 1980). A family member may perform several functions within the context of the family system although different family members may be more associated with certain functions than with others. Thus, parents may do more caregiving and teaching, but other children do more play. The relative amount of interaction time spent in different activities would certainly be expected to influence the child's development.

SOCIAL–COGNITIVE SKILLS RELATED TO SYSTEMS

Having shown the necessity to consider the wide number of people who inhabit the infant's social network, it is important to consider how the child might conceptualize them. One way to look at this problem is to consider that the young child may be able to construct its social space through the use of a limited number of dimensions, which when taken together, generates the wide variety of people who inhabit the family. The construction of the child's social world is possible if we allow for the use of only three dimensions. Three dimensions—age, familiarity, and gender—are attributes of the self and of the social world that the child acquires early. These three attributes may be used by the young child as a means to differentiate the social array.

Figure 1.1 presents this three-dimensional space along with the placement of some of the more common social objects in the child's life. As these dimensions become more differentiated (i.e., larger than a two-category system), one can add additional persons. Whether the infant uses these three dimensions to help create the social array is still to be determined. However, the ability to construct such an array from just three dimensions indicates that it may be possible. From a structural point of view, it appears to be an interesting possibility that should be further explored.

Data exist that support the proposition that very young children have knowledge about such dimensions as age, familiarity, and gender. For example, Bronson (1972) showed that familiarity in the social world is acquired early and becomes a salient dimension of the child's cognitive structures.

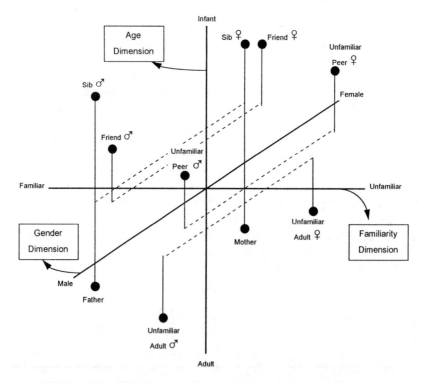

FIG. 1.1.   The child's social world conceptualized on the three dimensions of age, familiarity, and gender.

Children respond differentially to familiarity in terms of their social inter-action, although the literature on attentional processes supports the notion that children are responsive to familiarity soon after birth. Gender knowledge and gender identity appear quite early and indicate that infants are responsive to gender (e.g., Huston, 1983). Responses to age have been repeatedly shown to live subjects (Brooks & Lewis, 1976) and to pictures (Brooks-Gunn & Lewis, 1981; Lewis, 1985). These and considerably more data could be used to support the argument that the dimensions of gender, age, and familiarity are available for the construction of the social array and that these dimen-sions are concepts that come into use early in the child's life. Unfortunately, although some evidence exists for the demonstration of knowledge of each of these dimensions of the array, there is no information to allow us to conclude that these dimensions in combination are used. Even so, by allowing for the consideration of the cognitive ability of the young child to organize the considerable and diverse number of social objects and by using a struc-tural analysis such as the one presented, we have the start of a theory of social cognition based on the complex structure of the social world.

INDIRECT AND DIRECT EFFECTS IN THE FAMILY

Children's social and emotional growth is dominated by the attachment model that argues for the impact of a single adult (usually mother) on the child's development. This direct effects model is based on the premise that Person A (e.g., mother) interacts with Person B (e.g., child), and through Person A's behavior toward Person B, Person A influences Person B's be-havior or personality. Thus, for example, the mother's speech patterns toward her young infant are used to predict the child's subsequent language behavior. This model suggests both a dyadic view of social behavior and the idea that children's language acquisition is the result of mother's behavior directed toward them. Such a model assumes that mother and child constitute the only people in the child's social world and that children's development is a consequence of only those maternal behaviors directed toward them.

Such a limited view of the organism's development as a function of the dyad is predicated on biological and educational models as well as on methodologi-cal limitations. In the biological model, the emphasis on the mother–infant dyad is based on the belief that this dyad constitutes a biological unit endowed with characteristics that are essential for infant survival (Rosenblum & Moltz, 1983). Moreover, the teacher–pupil relationship also represents another pow-erful model of a dyadic interaction. Focusing on information exchange, this educational model argues for information dissemination in a single teacher–learner unit. Both the biological and educational models suffer from the bias of utilizing the dyad as the unit of measurement. This bias is perpetuated by the exclusive focus on one specific dyad (i.e., teacher–child, mother–child) because once we begin to consider other dyads (e.g., father–child, pupil–pupil), the need for expanding our view to a larger social context becomes more obvious. Nevertheless, the focus on only two-person systems, regardless of the diversity in membership of the dyad, results in a restriction of interactions and effects considered to be direct ones. It neglects to consider the impact of each member's behavior on others not in the dyad under study. Indirect effects do not operate through the direct interaction of one person with another. Indirect effects usually involve influences that result from social situations or contexts that involve more than one person. One such indirect effect, taken from our language example, would be a child's observation of parental conversation at dinner influencing the child's expressive language skills. These indirect effects (something we return to in more detail later) are understudied.

Definition of Direct and Indirect Effects

Direct Effects.   Direct effects have been defined as those interactions that represent the effect or influence of one person on the behaviors of another when both are engaged in mutual interaction. In the study of social behavior, direct effects are usually observed in dyadic interactions, but could occur in polyadic groups such as when a teacher instructs a class of students. Direct effects may involve information gathered from participation in an interaction with another person or object, and always involve the target person as one of the focused participants in the interaction. For example, a child learns about how puzzles work by playing with puzzles or develops an aggressive interaction style from being picked on by a sibling.

Indirect Effects.   Indirect effects refer to two classes of events. In the first class, indirect effects are those sets of interactions that affect the target person, but that occur in the absence of that person. These sets of interactions affect the target person, but may best be described as influences that play their role in development, as they affect direct effects (or interactions). More important for the present discussion is the second class of indirect effects that refers to interactions among members of the system that occur in the presence of the target person even though the interaction is not directed toward or does not involve that person. These kinds of indirect effects are those effects that are based on information that is gathered from sources other than the direct interaction with another person or object. These effects may be the result of an observation of another's interaction with persons or objects or may be the result of information gathered from another about the attitudes, behaviors, traits, or actions of a third person.

In the examples to follow, these two classes of indirect effects are presented. The first class, indirect influences, has been discussed in more detail elsewhere, especially as they refer to the role of the father and are only presented to show the various forms of indirect influence (Lewis et al., 1981). They included marital satisfaction, support, and arrangement of the environment. The second class has to do with phenomena discussed most often under the rubric of identification, observational, vicarious, and incidental learning, imitation, or modeling. These are presented in more detail because it is toward a general theory of these kinds of indirect effects, in combination with the direct effects, toward which we are interested in focusing our attention.

Indirect Influences. One important indirect effect is the relationship between mother and father. Parental indirect effects are discussed in terms of two parameters: marital satisfaction and self-esteem. From a marital satisfaction point of view, the parents are capable of better parenting if certain other needs are met, in particular, if their adult social relations are satisfactory. The praise of one's spouse for the other's work in caring for the child also has an effect on paternal self-esteem. For example, the mother, in her relationship with the father, may make him feel good about himself as a husband and as a father. The father's good feeling about his competence influences his responsiveness to the child in a positive way, making him more likely to praise the child's attempts to master the environment. Consequently, the child's development is indirectly influenced by the mother. The child is not present when the wife praises her husband and compliments him. If caregiving constitutes an important activity for the father, his success in this activity serves to foster feelings of competency and high self-esteem, which in turn, should positively affect the father–infant interaction. Although research has only started to explore such influences, there is some suggestion that they do play an important role.

The financial burden is currently more equally shared between mother and father, and there has been an increase in the father's sharing of household tasks. Although sharing financial and household duties may be important ways a couple supports the family and each other's functioning, a most important support function relative to the role of parenting must be in the ability of two adults to discuss the problem of child care. The sharing of tasks, responsibilities, information, and philosophies around child care between parents (or other caregivers) is an important indirect influence that has received too little attention, but nevertheless influences the child's development (Lynn, 1974).

Children learn about their environments through materials that have been provided by parents. Parents arrange the environments of their children. Parents indirectly affect children's development by providing opportunities for them to interact with varied objects and people. Arrangement of the child's physical and social environment is a kind of indirect influence the parent has on the child, which does not directly involve parent–child interaction.

This class of indirect influences is most broad in that it involves all those factors that have affected and continue to affect the parent(s), but do not directly affect the child. A dyadic interaction cannot be fully understood until one can specify the various factors that influence each member separately. Both parent and child enter an interaction with a set of influences that have an impact on that interaction. In general, a person's current state, past experience, knowledge, development level, and many more factors must affect a person's interactive interchange with another, and these need to be considered if the meaning and course of the interaction is to be understood.

There is another class of indirect effects: those effects that occur in the presence of the child, but that do not focus on the child. Indirect forms of information acquisition have been considered under a wide rubric that includes identification, modeling, imitation, and incidental, vicarious, and observational learning. Although a distinction between these terms is beyond the scope of this discussion, it should be clear that a discussion of forms other than direct kinds of information acquisition have received considerable attention (see, e.g., Bandura, 1973; Lewis, 1979a; Parke et al., 1979; Piaget, 1951).

In a study by Lewis and Feiring (1992), we examined the effects of direct and indirect question asking around the dinner table on the child's overall IQ. Work by Sigel and his colleagues (e.g., Sigel, 1991; Sigel, Stinson, & Flaugher, 1993) suggests that question asking, part of a distancing strategy, is important in the child's cognitive development. Question asking directed toward the 3-year-old child constitutes the direct effect, whereas question asking by other family members to each other constitutes an indirect effect on the 3-year-old child. For the sample as a whole, direct effects accounted for 11.6% of the variance, whereas the indirect effects accounted for only 2.3% of the variance of the 3 year old's IQ scores. Family size effects were found for a family size of four, with the direct factor accounting for 20.3% and the indirect factor accounting for only 1.0%. However, for a family size of five, the direct and indirect factors each accounted for 84.6% of the proportion of variance due to each factor with the other removed.

Examining family vocalization data, rather than question asking, and target child IQ data for the total sample, we found that direct vocalization accounted for 5.3% of the child's IQ variance, whereas the indirect vocalization accounts for 15.2%. For a family size of four, the partial correlations yielded a variance estimate of 21.2% and 1% for the direct and indirect factors, respectively. In a family size of five, the target child's IQ and the direct factor shows that 7.8% of the variance is accounted for, whereas for the indirect factor, the variance is 4.0%.

Similar analyses were performed, examining the family's and child's vocalization amounts. For the sample as a whole, direct vocalization to the child with the indirect factor removed accounted for 28.1% of the variance, whereas indirect vocalization with the direct factor removed accounted for 6.3% of the variance. As with question asking, family size appeared to be related to the direct and indirect factors' vocalization on the child's vocalization. For a family size of four, the variances for children's vocalization are 31.4% for the direct factor and 9.0% for the indirect factor. For a family size of five, the direct factor yielded a variance estimate of 10.9%, whereas the indirect factor yielded 17.6%.

These results support our belief that children's behavior, both specific behavior in a given context (i.e., dinnertime interaction) and more general outcome variables (i.e., child IQ), are influenced both by what family members directly do to the child and by what they do to each other in the child's company. Moreover, it appears reasonable to suggest that, across all families, the direct factor is a more powerful determinant of outcome than the indirect factor. The valences of the correlations between direct and indirect effects and outcome considerably fluctuate and are related to family size. As family size increases, the indirect factor becomes increasingly important. We can only speculate as to why this may be the case. One possibility is that in families with more people, the number of indirect possibilities increase. It may be the case that the large number of possible indirect effects makes them increasingly salient relative to direct effects.

Response-facilitating effects of exposure to a model occur in a situation in which the model's responses serve as discriminative stimuli for the observer (Bandura, Grusic, & Menlove, 1966). This discriminative-stimulus function of a model's responses facilitates the occurrence of similar responses in the observer. Thus, the child's tendency to babble and vocalize may be facilitated by observing the parents talking. Response-facilitating effects are considered less novel than the other two effects previously described because the child already has the responses in his or her repertoire. Response-facilitating effects may be a most important indirect influence in socialization as a prevalent process for conveying which behaviors are socially acceptable. Another example of response-facilitating effects involves young children's reactions to strangers. Children's positive social behavior is directed toward strangers through observation of their mother's positive behavior to the same stranger (Feinman & Lewis, 1983; Feiring et al., 1984).

As the foregoing examples and discussion indicate, indirect effects, whether we call them imitation, modeling, identification, or vicarious or observational learning, are probably of central importance for the development of social knowledge and relationships. It would not be in error to assume that a large degree of culturally appropriate behavior, knowledge, and values are transmitted on the basis of these types of indirect effects.

CONCLUSION

As the child's social interactions with various other people become more relevant for a theory of social development, both singly as in dyadic interactions and in groups of "$N + 2$" interactions, the need to consider the role of indirect effects becomes clear. Although the literature on identification, modeling, imitation, and vicarious, observational, and incidental learning have already suggested the role of indirect effects, little attempt has been made to develop a model of social interactions that articulates the impact of both direct and indirect influences. The heuristics of such an approach reside in the focusing on the various components and their joint as well as single influences. The social nexus or the interconnection of the child's social relationships requires conceptualizations that go beyond the dyad, and with it, the study of direct effects. The degree to which the child is embedded in a social network of many people who know the child and who know each other is the degree to which such indirect effects must be considered to influence development. The formulation presented here, concerning both the notion of a family system with many individuals, as well as the need, therefore, to consider direct and indirect effects, makes clear that infants' social, cognitive, and affective experiences are influenced through the interaction of the child with his or her social world, as well as the interaction of the child with significant others who, in turn, interact with others.

REFERENCES

Abramovitch, R., Corter, C., & Lando, B. (1979). Sibling interaction in the home. *Child Development, 50*, 997–1003.

Bandura, A. (1973). *Aggression: A social learning analysis.* Englewood Cliffs, NJ: Prentice-Hall.

Bandura, A., Grusic, J. E., & Menlove, F. L. (1966). Observational learning as a function of symbolization and incentive set. *Child Development, 37*, 499–506.

Belsky, J. (1981). Early human experience: A family perspective. *Developmental Psychology, 17*, 3–23.

Belsky, J., & Rovine, M. (1990). Q-sort security and first-year nonmaternal care. *New Directions for Child Development, 49*, 7–22.

Belsky, J., Rovine, M., & Fish, M. (1988). The developing family system. In M. R. Gunnar & E. Thelen (Eds.), *Systems and development: The Minnesota symposia on child psychology, Vol. 22* (pp. 119–166). Hillsdale, NJ: Lawrence Erlbaum Associates.

Belsky, J., & Volling, B. (1987). Mothering, fathering, and marital interaction in the family triad during infancy: Exploring family system's processes. In P. Berman & F. Pedersen (Eds.), *Men's transition to parenthood: Longitudinal studies of early family experience* (pp. 37–64). Hillsdale, NJ: Lawrence Erlbaum Associates.

Bischof-Köhler, D. (1991). The development of empathy in infants. In M. E. Lamb & H. Keller (Eds.), *Infant development: Perspectives from German-speaking countries* (pp. 245–273). Hillsdale, NJ: Lawrence Erlbaum Associates.

Borke, H. (1971). Interpersonal perception of young children: Egocentrism or empathy. *Developmental Psychology, 5,* 263–269.

Bowlby, J. (1969). *Attachment and loss: Vol. 1. Attachment.* New York: Basic Books.

Bretherton, I. (1985). Attachment theory: Retrospect and prospect. In I. Bretherton & E. Waters (Eds.), *Growing points of attachment, theory and research. Monographs of the Society for Research in Child Development, 50,* 3–38.

Brody, G. H., Stoneman, Z., MacKinnon, C. E., & MacKinnon, R. (1985). Role relationships and behavior between preschool-aged and school-aged sibling pairs. *Developmental Psychology, 21,* 124–129.

Bronfenbrenner, U. (1986). Ecology of the family as a context for human development. *Developmental Psychology, 22,* 723–742.

Bronson, G. W. (1972). Infants' reactions to unfamiliar persons and novel objects. *Monographs of the Society for Research in Child Development, 37* (pp. 1–45).

Brooks, J., & Lewis, M. (1976). Infants' responses to strangers: Midget, adult and child. *Child Development, 47,* 323–332.

Brooks-Gunn, J., & Lewis, M. (1981). Infant social perception: Responses to pictures of parents and strangers. *Developmental Psychology, 17*(5), 647–649.

Brown, C. (1971). *Manchild in the promised land.* New York: Signet.

Buhrmester, D., & Furman, W. (1987). The development of companionship and intimacy. *Child Development, 58,* 1101–1113.

Buhrmester, D., & Furman, W. (1990). Perceptions of sibling relationships during middle childhood and adolescence. *Child Development, 61*(5), 1387–1398.

Christensen, A., & Margolin, G. (1988). Conflict and alliance in distressed and nondistressed families. In R. A. Hinde & J. Stevenson-Hinde (Eds.), *Relationships within families: Mutual influences* (pp. 263–282). Oxford, England: Clarendon.

Cicirelli, V. G. (1975). Effects of mother and older sibling on the problem solving behavior of the younger child. *Developmental Psychology, 11,* 749–756.

Cicirelli, V. G. (1982). Sibling influence throughout the lifespan. In M. E. Lamb & B. Sutton-Smith (Eds.), *Sibling relationships: Their nature and significance across the lifespan* (pp. 267–284). Hillsdale, NJ: Lawrence Erlbaum Associates.

Clarke-Stewart, K. A. (1978). And daddy makes three: The father's impact on mother and young child. *Child Development, 49*(2), 466–478.

Dunn, J., & Kendrick, C. (1979). Interaction between young siblings in the context of family relationships. In M. Lewis & L. Rosenblum (Eds.), *The child and its family: The genesis of behavior, Vol. 2* (pp. 143–168). New York: Plenum.

Dunn, J., & Kendrick, C. (1980). The arrival of a sibling: Changes in interaction between mother and first-born child. *Journal of Child Psychology, 21,* 119–132.

Dunn, J., & Kendrick, C. (1982). Siblings and their mothers: Developing relationships within the family. In M. E. Lamb & B. Sutton-Smith (Eds.), *Sibling relationships: Their nature and significance across the lifespan* (pp. 153–165). Hillsdale, NJ: Lawrence Erlbaum Associates.

Dunn, J., Kendrick, C., & MacNamee, R. (1981). The reaction of first-born children to the birth of a sibling: Mother's reports. *Journal of Child Psychology & Psychiatry, 22,* 1–18.

Edwards, C. P., & Lewis, M. (1979). Young children's concepts of social relations: Social functions and social objects. In M. Lewis & L. Rosenblum (Eds.), *The child and its family: The genesis of behavior* (Vol. 2, pp. 245–266). New York: Plenum.

Feinman, S., & Lewis, M. (1983). Social referencing and second order effects in ten-month-old infants. *Child Development, 54,* 878–887.

Feiring, C., & Lewis, M. (1984). Changing characteristics of the U.S. family: Implications for family relationships and child development. In M. Lewis (Ed.), *Beyond the dyad* (pp. 59–89). New York: Plenum.

Feiring, C., & Lewis, M. (1987). The ecology of some middle class families at dinner. *International Journal of Behavioral Development, 10*(3), 377–390.

Feiring, C., & Lewis, M. (1988). The child's social network from three to six years: The effects of age, sex and socioeconomic status. In S. Salzinger, J. Antrobus, & M. Hammer (Eds.), *Social networks of children, adolescents and college students* (pp. 93–112). Hillsdale, NJ: Lawrence Erlbaum Associates.

Feiring, C., Lewis, M., & Starr, M. D. (1984). Indirect effects and infants' reactions to strangers. *Developmental Psychology, 20*, 485–491.

Fox, N., Kimmerly, N., & Schafer, W. (1991). Attachment to mother/attachment to father. A meta-analysis. *Child Development, 62*, 210–255.

Freud, A., & Dann, S. (1951). An experiment in group upbringing. In R. Eissler, A. Freud, H. Hartman, & E. Kris (Eds.), *The psychoanalytic study of the child* (Vol. 6). New York: International Universities Press.

Furman, W., & Buhrmester, D. (1985). Children's perceptions of the personal relationships in their social networks. *Developmental Psychology, 21*, 1014–1024.

Furman, W., & Buhrmester, D. (1992). Age and sex differences in perceptions of networks of personal relationships. *Child Development, 63*, 103–115.

Furman, W., Rahe, D. F., & Hartup, W. W. (1979). Rehabilitation of socially-withdrawn children through mixed-age socialization. *Child Development, 50*, 915–922.

Greenbaum, M. (1965). Joint sibling interview as a diagnostic procedure. *Journal of Child Psychology & Psychiatry, 6*, 227–232.

Gyomrai-Ludowyk, E. (1963). The analysis of a young concentration camp victim. *Psychoanalytic Study of the Child, 18*, 484–510.

Huston, A. C. (1983). Sex-typing. In P. H. Mussen (Series Ed.) and E. M. Hetherington (Vol. Ed.), *Handbook of child psychology: Vol. 4: Socialization, personality, and social development* (4th ed., pp. 387–468). New York: Wiley.

Kochenderfer, B. J., & Ladd, G. W. (1996). Peer victimization: Cause or consequence of school maladjustment? *Child Development, 67*, 1305–1317.

Konner, M. (1975). Relations among infants and juveniles in comparative perspective. In M. Lewis & L. Rosenblum (Eds.), *Friendship and peer relations: The origins of behavior, Vol. 4* (pp. 99–130). New York: Wiley.

Lamb, M. E. (1976). Interactions between 8-month-old children and their fathers and mothers. In M. E. Lamb (Ed.), *The role of the father in child development* (pp. 307–327). New York: Wiley.

Lamb, M. E. (1977a). The development of mother–infant and father–infant attachments in the second year of life. *Developmental Psychology, 13*, 639–649.

Lamb, M. E. (1977b). Father–infant and mother–infant interaction in the first year of life. *Child Development, 48*, 167–181.

Lamb, M. E. (1978). Interactions between eighteen-month-olds and their preschool-aged siblings. *Child Development, 49*, 51–59.

Lewis, M. (1979a). The self as a developmental concept. *Human Development, 22*, 416–419.

Lewis, M. (1979b). The social determination of play. In B. Sutton-Smith (Ed.), *Play and learning* (pp. 23–33). New York: Gardner.

Lewis, M. (Ed.). (1984). *Beyond the dyad.* New York: Plenum.

Lewis, M. (1985). Age as a social dimension. In T. Field & N. Fox (Eds.), *Social perception in infants* (pp. 299–319). New York: Academic Press.

Lewis, M. (1992). *Shame, The exposed self.* New York: The Free Press.

Lewis, M., & Ban, P. (1974). Mothers and fathers, girls and boys: Attachment behavior in the one-year-old. *Merrill-Palmer Quarterly, 20*(3), 195–204.

Lewis, M., & Brooks-Gunn, J. (1979). *Social cognition and the acquisition of self.* New York: Plenum.

Lewis, M., & Feiring, C. (1978). The child's social world. In R. M. Lerner & J. D. Spanier (Eds.), *Child influences on marital and family interaction: A life-span perspective* (pp. 43–69). New York: Academic Press.

Lewis, M., & Feiring, C. (1979). The child's social network: Social object, social functions and their relationship. In M. Lewis & L. Rosenblum (Eds.), *The child and its family: The genesis of behavior* (Vol. 2, pp. 9–27). New York: Plenum.

Lewis, M., & Feiring, C. (1981). Direct and indirect interactions in social relationships. In L. Lipsitt (Ed.), *Advances in infancy research* (Vol. 1, pp. 129–161). Norwood, NJ: Ablex.

Lewis, M., & Feiring, C. (1982). Some American families at dinner. In L. Laosa & I. Sigel (Eds.), *The family as learning environments for children* (Vol. 1, pp. 115–145). New York: Plenum.

Lewis, M., & Feiring, C. (1992). Indirect and direct effects and family interaction at dinner. In S. Feinman (Ed.), *Social referencing and the social construction of reality in infancy* (pp. 111–134). New York: Plenum.

Lewis, M., Feiring, C., & Kotsonis, M. (1984). The social network of the young child: A developmental perspective. In M. Lewis (Ed.), *Beyond the dyad: The genesis of behavior, Vol. 4* (pp. 129–160). New York: Plenum.

Lewis, M., Feiring, C., & Weinraub, M. (1981). The father as a member of the child's social network. In M. Lamb (Ed.), *The role of the father in child development* (2nd ed., pp. 259–294). New York: Wiley.

Lewis, M., & Rosenblum, L. (1974). Introduction. In M. Lewis & L. Rosenblum (Eds.), *The effect of the infant on its care giver: The origins of behavior* (pp. xv–xxiv). New York: Wiley.

Lewis, M., & Rosenblum, L. (1977). Introduction. In M. Lewis & L. Rosenblum (Eds.), *Interaction, conversation, and the development of language: The origins of behavior* (pp. 1–8). New York: Wiley.

Lewis, M., & Rosenblum, L. (Eds.). (1979). *The child and its family: The genesis of behavior, Volume 2*. New York: Plenum.

Lewis, M., & Weinraub, M. (1974). Sex of parent × sex of child: Socioemotional development. In R. C. Friedman, R. M. Richart, & R. L. Vande Wiele (Eds.), *Sex differences in behavior* (pp. 165–189). Huntington, NY: Krieger.

Lewis, M., & Weinraub, M. (1976). The father's role in the infant's social network. In M. Lamb (Ed.), *The role of the father in child development, Volume 1* (pp. 157–184). New York: Wiley.

Lewis, M., Young, G., Brooks, J., & Michalson, L. (1975). The beginning of friendship. In M. Lewis & L. Rosenblum (Eds.), *Friendship and peer relations: The origins of behavior* (Vol. 4, pp. 27–65). New York: Wiley.

Lynn, D. B. (1974). *The father: His role in child development*. Monterey, CA: Brooks/Cole.

Mackey, W. C. (1985). *Fathering behaviors: The dynamics of the man-child bond*. New York: Plenum.

Monane, J. H. (1967). *A sociology of human systems*. New York: Appleton-Century-Crofts.

Mueller, E. (1972). The maintenance of verbal exchanges between young children. *Child Development, 43*, 930–938.

Mueller, E., & Lucas, T. (1975). A developmental analysis of peer interaction among toddlers. In M. Lewis & L. A. Rosenblum (Eds.), *Friendship and peer relations* (pp. 223–258). New York: Wiley.

Murray, H. A. (1938). *Explorations in personality*. New York: Oxford University Press.

Oliveri, M. E., & Reiss, D. (1987). Social networks of family members: Distinctive roles of mothers and fathers. *Sex Roles, 17*(11/12), 719–736.

Olweus, D. (1993). Bullies on the playground: The role of victimization. In C. H. Hart (Ed.), *Children on playgrounds* (pp. 85–128). Albany, NY: State University of New York Press.

Parke, R. D. (1978). Perspectives in father–infant interaction. In J. Osofsky (Ed.), *Handbook of infancy* (pp. 549–590). New York: Wiley.

Parke, R. D., MacDonald, K. B., Beitel, A., & Bhavnagri, N. (1988). The role of the family in the development of peer relationships. In R. DeV. Peters & R. J. McMahon (Eds.), *Social learning and systems approaches to marriage and the family* (pp. 17–44). New York: Brunner/Mazel.

Parke, R. D., & O'Leary, S. (1975). Father–mother–infant interaction in the newborn period: Some findings, some observations, and some unresolved issues. In K. Riegel & J. Meacham (Eds.), *The developing individual in a changing world: Vol. 2. Social and environmental issues.* The Hague, The Netherlands: Mouton.

Parke, R. D., Power, T. G., & Gottman, J. M. (1979). Conceptualizing and quantifying influence patterns in the family triad. In M. E. Lamb, S. J. Suomi, & G. R. Stephenson (Eds.), *Social interaction analysis* (pp.). Madison: University of Wisconsin Press.

Parke, R. D., & Sawin, D. B. (1980). The family in early infancy: Social interactional and attitudinal analyses. In F. A. Pedersen (Ed.), *The father–infant relationship: Observational studies in a family setting* (pp. 44–70). New York: Praeger.

Parsons, T., & Bales, R. F. (1955). *Family socialization and interaction process.* Glencoe, IL: The Free Press.

Pedersen, F. A., Anderson, B. J., & Cain, R. L. (1980). Parent–infant and husband–wife interactions observed at age five months. In F. Pedersen (Ed.), *The father–infant relationship: Observational studies in the family setting* (pp. 71–86). New York: Praeger.

Pepler, D. J., Abramovitch, R., & Corter, C. (1981). Sibling interaction in the home: A longitudinal study. *Child Development, 52*, 1344–1347.

Pfouts, J. H. (1976). The sibling relationship: A forgotten dimension. *Social Work, 21*, 200–204.

Piaget, J. (1951). *Play, dreams, and imitation in childhood* (C. Gattegno & F. M. Hodgson, Trans.). New York: Norton. (Original work published 1945)

Piaget, J. (1952). *The origins of intelligence in children.* New York: Norton.

Roggman, L. A., Langlois, J. H., Hubbs-Tait, L., & Rieser-Danner, L. A. (1994). Infant day-care, attachment, and the "file drawer problem." *Child Development, 5*(65), 1429–1443.

Rosenblatt, P. C. (1974). Behavior in public places: Comparisons of couples accompanied and unaccompanied by children. *Journal of Marriage and the Family, 36*, 750–755.

Rosenblum, L., & Moltz, H. (1983). *Symbiosis in parent–offspring interaction.* New York: Plenum.

Russell, G., & Russell, A. (1987). Mother–child and father–child relationships in middle child-hood. *Child Development, 58*, 1573–1585.

Searcy, E., & Eisenberg, N. (1992). Defensiveness in response to aid from a sibling. *Journal of Personality and Social Psychology, 62*(3), 422–433.

Shanas, E. (1979). Social myth as hypothesis: The case of the family relations of old people. *Gerontologist, 19*, 3–9.

Sigel, I. E. (1991). Representational competence: Another type? In M. Chandler & M. Chapman (Eds.), *Criteria for competence: Controversies in the conceptualization and assessment of children's abilities* (pp. 189–207). Hillsdale, NJ: Lawrence Erlbaum Associates.

Sigel, I. E., Stinson, E. T., & Flaugher, J. (1993). Socialization of cognition: A family focus. In M. Lewis & C. Feiring (Eds.), *Families, risk, and competence* (pp.). Mahwah, NJ: Lawrence Erlbaum Associates.

Stern, D. N. (1985). *The interpersonal world of the infant.* New York: Basic Books.

Stillwell, R. (1984). *Social relationships in six-year-olds as viewed by themselves, their mothers, and their teachers.* Unpublished dissertation, Cambridge University, Cambridge, England.

Stillwell, R., & Dunn, J. (1985). Continuities in sibling relationships: Patterns of aggression and friendliness. *Journal of Child Psychology & Psychiatry, 26*, 627–637.

Stocker, C., Dunn, J., & Plomin, R. (1989). Sibling relationships: Links with child temperament, maternal behavior, and family structure. *Child Development, 60*, 715–727.

Stoneman, Z., Brody, G. H., & MacKinnon, C. (1984). Naturalistic observations of children's activities and roles while playing with their siblings and friends. *Child Development, 55*, 617–627.

Suomi, S. J. (1979). Differential development of various social relationships by rhesus monkey infants. In M. Lewis & L. Rosenblum (Eds.), *The child and its family: The genesis of behavior, Volume 2* (pp. 219–244). New York: Plenum.

Tesser, A. (1980). Self-esteem maintenance in family dynamics. *Journal of Personality and Social Psychology, 39,* 77–91.

Tinsley, B. R., & Parke, R. D. (1984). Grandparents as support and socialization agents. In M. Lewis & L. Rosenblum (Eds.), *Beyond the dyad: The genesis of behavior, Volume 4* (pp. 161–194). New York: Plenum.

Vandell, D. L., Minnett, A. M., & Santrock, J. W. (1987). Age differences in sibling relationships during middle childhood. *Journal of Applied Developmental Psychology, 8,* 247–257.

Volling, B. L., & Belsky, J. (1992). The contribution of mother–child and father–child relationships to the quality of sibling interaction: A longitudinal study. *Child Development, 63,* 1209–1222.

Von Bertalanffy, L. (1967). *Robots, men, and minds: Psychology in the modern world.* New York: Braziller.

Weinraub, M., Jaeger, E., & Hoffman, L. (1988). Predicting infant outcome in families of employed and nonemployed mothers. *Early Childhood Research Quarterly, 3,* 361–378.

Whiting, B. B., & Whiting, J. (1975). *Children of six cultures: A psychocultural analysis.* Cambridge, MA: Harvard University Press.

Wilson, E. O. (1975). *Sociobiology.* Cambridge, MA: Harvard University Press.

Yamamoto, K. (1972). *The child and his image: Self concept in the early years.* Boston: Houghton Mifflin.

Zahn-Waxler, C., Radke-Yarrow, M., & King, R. (1979). Child rearing and children's prosocial imitations towards victims of distress. *Child Development, 50,* 319–330.

2

▼▼▼▼▼▼▼

Family Dynamics at Dinner:
A Natural Context for Revealing
Basic Family Processes

Sharon Landesman Ramey
Halldor Kr. Juliusson
Civitan International Research Center,
University of Alabama at Birmingham (UAB)

Understanding family dynamics is a complex endeavor. *Family dynamics* can be conceptualized in terms of the transactions that occur among family members (actual behavior), the reactions of family members to these transactions (including behavioral, cognitive, and emotional reactions), and the encoded memories of both transactions and reactions. To document family dynamics well requires a strategy for data collection that gathers and integrates both objective and subjective data on all family members. Ideally, such data creates a clear and compelling picture of how different types of families and individual family members participate in family dynamics. Gathered prospectively, such data provides a basis for studying how family dynamics contribute to the development of individual family members and to the family as a unit. In addition, family dynamics reveal how families respond to challenges and changes, from both intrafamilial or extrafamilial sources.

The research presented in this chapter builds on two decades of ethological research about children and adults with special needs (primarily those with developmental disabilities, although linguistically precocious children have been studied as well) in a variety of naturalistic settings, including homes, schools, work settings, and social and recreational environments. This research emphasizes the fact that the collective behavior observed in groups of key individuals is a powerful predictor of an individual's behavior, both in the observed setting itself and in terms of developmental advances in social and adaptive behavior (e.g., Landesman, 1987; Landesman & Ramey, 1989; Landesman-Dwyer & Berkson, 1984; Landesman-Dwyer & Butterfield, 1983;

Landesman-Dwyer, Stein, & Sackett, 1978; Sackett, Landesman-Dwyer, & Morin, 1981). The research presented in this chapter is drawn from an ongoing longitudinal study of a population-based sample of 400 middle-class families with typically developing school-age children. For these families, the construct of *risk* is defined in terms of family demographic variables and psychological dimensions of the family. The direct observations have been gathered to complement many types of self-reports and direct assessments of children and parents.

THE IMPORTANCE OF DIRECT OBSERVATION OF FAMILY DYNAMICS

The rationale for gathering quantitative observations during dinnertime, across multiple occasions, is threefold. First, directly observing a naturally occurring family event is likely to reveal typical interactional patterns, thus providing objective evidence about family dynamics per se. Second, obtaining objective data about the multiple (and often simultaneous) interactions that occur in the family provides an empirical basis for testing hypotheses about the factors that are involved in transforming behavioral events (in this case, social interactions during dinnertime) into experiences and subsequently, into memories. In other words, direct observations are essential in studying the processes involved in social experience—that is, how individuals perceive what has occurred. Third, behavioral observations can estimate the degree to which certain family characteristics, risk factors, and developmental changes manifest themselves in an observable fashion during routine family events such as dinnertime.

DINNERTIME: ITS SIGNIFICANCE FOR FAMILIES

Both cohort and culture contribute to shaping the events that families engage in as a collective unit. Eating together regularly is one of a few family events that transcends many cultures and cohorts. In almost all societies, consuming food assumes a dual function—namely, a survival function and a social function. Although the societal and psychological significance attached to family meals is likely to vary as a function of family, culture, and cohort variables, we have yet to study a family in which everyone was not eager to tell us a lot about the dinner hour in their home!

In the United States, the family dinner hour has been a normative event for several centuries. Over the years, many customs changed, such as when dinner is served, whether very young children join the family for the meal, who prepares and serves the meal, and the formality of the meal. The American family dinner hour is widely perceived as on the decline in frequency, duration, and centrality to the family. Many demographic changes contributed to the presumed changes in the frequency of the family dinner hour, including increases in the proportion of mothers of young children in the work force, the number of households headed by a single mother, the amount of time parents work outside the home, and extrafamilial activities of children and parents. Collectively, these changes are likely to result in fewer hours available for key individuals to plan and participate in the family dinner hour and an increased absence of family members from everyday dinners.

Lewis and Feiring (1982, 1992; Feiring & Lewis, 1987) studied the family dinnertime for nuclear families. They concluded that "one important function of the dinner meal for families is maintaining the family system through the exchange of information between members (elements of that system). This function of information exchange may be an example of a steady-state process whereby family members maintain continuity in their family relationships" (p. 125). Similarly, Dreyer and Dreyer (1973) viewed the family evening meal as an important family ritual for understanding how family members function together and the differentiation of roles among family members. Theoretically, the amount and types of social engagement during dinnertime are likely to reflect family values and priorities, how individuals support one another, and ways the family functions as a whole.

THE CONCEPT OF RISK FOR MIDDLE-CLASS FAMILIES

Even in middle-class families, there exists a continuum of normative risk. Family characteristics that may affect developmental risks are: parental physical and mental well-being, the parents' relationship to each other, parenting competence, family configuration (particularly the combined effects of birth order and number and spacing of children), social support to the family unit, and external stressors. A family's day-to-day interactions are assumed to help or hinder achievement of family goals (Landesman-Dwyer, Jaccard, & Gunderson, 1991). Understanding how family characteristics, such as marital status, family size, and parenting knowledge, relate to behavioral interactions may elucidate why some children from middle-class families are at risk for nonoptimal development.

DIVORCE AND FAMILY BEHAVIOR

Over the last 20 years, parental divorce followed by living in a single-mother family environment for an extended period of time has become a common childhood experience (Dornbusch & Gray, 1988; Shiono & Sandham Quinn,

1994). Between 50 to 75% of all children born in the U.S. are predicted to live in a single-parent household before the age of 16 (Furstenberg, 1990). This prediction raises concerns because many studies have reported poorer outcomes on developmental measures for children in single-parent versus two-parent families (e.g., Amato, 1994; Amato & Keith, 1991; Hetherington & Clingempeel, 1992; Wallerstein, 1987).

Recent reviews of children's adjustment to divorce (Amato, 1994; Chase-Lansdale & Hetherington, 1990; Hetherington & Clingempeel, 1992) support three major conclusions: (a) when differences are detected, children from divorced families fare worse than those from intact married families; (b) typically, boys show greater negative effects than do girls; and (c) the effects of divorce are most pronounced during the first 2 years after the divorce. Remarkably, the likely factors mediating these observed effects of divorce have rarely been studied directly.

An implicit assumption in divorce research is that divorce alters children's social support and pattern of daily interactions. In contemporary family research, family is viewed as a system comprised of several subsystems, including the parental subsystem, the parent–child subsystem, and the sibling subsystem (e.g., Belsky, 1981; Bronfenbrenner, 1979; Landesman, Jaccard, & Gunderson, 1991; Lewis, 1987; Minuchin, 1974, 1988). A change in the parental subsystem, such as that created by divorce, is hypothesized to alter relationships in other subsystems, especially the parent–child subsystems and potentially the sibling subsystem. A reasonable expectation is that the absence of a parent—typically the father—from the child's primary residence increases the children's social contact with the custodial parent. The absence of one parent in the home also reduces the overall group size, which might heighten the rate of dyadic social interactions among remaining family members. Hetherington, Cox, and Cox (1982) postulated that, "Divorce can be viewed as a critical experience that affects the entire family system, and the functioning and interactions of the members within that system" (p. 233). Research evaluating these potential changes in social interactions in two-parent and divorced, single-mother families is needed to understand the social processes that mediate the effects of divorce on children's development.

Almost all research about children's adjustment to divorce is based on parental self-report, primarily that of mothers. The work of Hetherington and her colleagues (Hetherington, Cox, & Cox, 1982) and MacKinnon (1989) provided two notable exceptions. Both studies observed social interactions in divorced and married families, and although the magnitude of effects was not large, family interactions differed in ways consistent with adverse developmental outcomes. Moreover, these effects decreased over time and interacted with ex-spousal conflict. Both studies used samples of only moderate size and samples of convenience (i.e., not population-based). Also, both studies used a structured situation for observing interactions and did not include a naturally occurring family event to observe likely typical patterns of family interactions.

NUMBER OF CHILDREN AND FAMILY BEHAVIOR

The relationship between family size and a number of developmental out-comes—notably, intelligence and achievement—is well-established (e.g., Cirelli, 1978; Terhune, 1974). As an explanation, Anastasi (1956) theorized that family size affected cognitive development by influencing the quantity of adult contact with the child—specifically, the larger the family, the less contact parents had with each child. A similar assumption underlies Zajonc's *confluence model*, which hypothesizes that a child's intelligence decreases when there are more children in a family and when they are closer in age (Zajonc, 1976; Zajonc, Marcus, Berbaum, Bargh, & Moreland, 1991). Inter-estingly, the literature on family size does not empirically address the fact that divorce typically leads to a decrease in family size (i.e., one less parent in the home) with a corresponding change in the ratio of adults to children.

Lewis and Feiring (1982) related family size to family interactions during dinnertime. They observed social interactions during dinner for 33 white, middle-class, two-parent families with one to three children. The target child in these families was 3 years old. Family dinners were videotaped and the types and durations of verbal interactions and family functions among all dyads were scored. In these married families, family size did not affect how long dinner lasted or the overall amount of verbal interaction. The duration of dyadic verbal interaction, however, between parents and the target child did decrease with more children. In families with one or two children, mothers spent over 50% more time talking to their 3-year-old children than did fathers. In larger families, however, this role difference between parents disappeared and fathers interacted as much with their children as did mothers. In addition, with more children present, maternal caregiving per child declined, whereas fathers' caregiving increased. These results are consistent with the view of fathers as a supplemental caregiver, who responds only when need calls. This possibility is especially interesting regarding parental caregiving in one-parent families. It suggests that father absence has relatively few effects on family dynamics during events such as dinnertime, except for larger families where additional assistance is needed.

We hypothesized that compensatory mechanisms may operate in divorced single-mother families to facilitate achieving a new homeostasis in the family system—especially after the initial adjustment period (2 years) following the divorce. Specifically, to protect children from a decrease in the amount and quality of interactions with a parent, divorced single-mothers are likely to increase the amount of time they interact with their children and possibly to alter the content of their social exchanges to achieve a desired homeostasis. To the extent that divorced single-mother families effectively compensate for the daily absence of a father (but not necessarily total father absence from the child's life), the daily interactional consequences for children are diminished or minimal. (Note that in our study, as most others, effects associated with divorce per se versus the single-parent structure of the family cannot be differentiated definitively.) Although including a never-married group of mothers and their children would have been highly informative, we were unable to locate a sufficient number of such families who were also middle-class and stable in terms of residence and family composition.

THE WASHINGTON FAMILY BEHAVIOR STUDY: DINNERTIME IN THE CONTEXT OF FAMILY LIFE

The data presented here are from a population-based longitudinal study of middle-class families—the Washington Family Behavior Study—that focuses on factors mediating the cognitive and social development of school-age children in married and divorced single-mother families. The data include direct observations of social exchanges among family members during repeated occasions of a routine family activity—the family dinner—and perceptions of both parents and their children about social support. The key questions concerned how parental presence (one- versus two-parent families) and number of children (only child, two children, three or more children) related to family dynamics. Other variables, such as child gender, child age, and family attitudes toward single-parent families, were also taken into consideration. In addition, the dinnertime observations provided an opportunity to study the individuality of families in the broader context of family life.

The families were obtained via a population-based survey of interviews conducted with 18,000 middle-class families. Families invited to participate met the following criteria: a target child between 6 to 12 years lived in the home; income was above poverty level; there was no change in marital status, family composition, or residence in the past year; parents were born in the United States; and no family member had a major physical or mental health problem. Over 83% of eligible families volunteered to participate. For the present analyses, 339 families with complete data sets were included. Mothers who were widows, had never married, had separated, or were living with a partner were excluded from analyses reported here because the focus was on divorced, single-mother families. In addition, 30 families with guests at dinner or important family members missing at dinner were excluded.

Table 2.1 summarizes the study design. Target children included 118 boys and 153 girls, 86% White/non-Hispanic and 14% were African American. (Note that 21% of the African-American children have mothers who are White/non-

TABLE 2.1
Design of Washington Family Behavior Study

	Number of Children in Family			
	1	2	3 or more	Total
Married*	38	53	57	148
Divorced Single	37	53	33	123
Total	75	106	90	271

*All parents in the married families are the parents of the target child. Of these, 4% had a previous divorce, but not to parents of the target child.

Hispanic.) Children's mean age was 9.5 years ($SD = 1.65$ yrs). Mean time since divorce of the single-mother families was 4.8 years ($SD = 2.8$ yrs) and the mean age of the target child at the time of divorce was 5.2 years ($SD = 2.9$ yrs).

Objective Versus Subjective Sources of Data

Families were visited on three occasions within 4 weeks by trained research associates matched to the family's ethnicity. Parents and the target 6- to 12-year-old child participated in both structured and open-ended interviews about family background and functioning and completed questionnaires and self-administered tests, thus yielding multiple types of subjective data. In addition, families were observed during family dinner on each home visit, providing objective measures of social transactions, complemented by direct assessment of family members in the areas of cognition and linguistic development.

The *Observation of Family Functioning* is a group code developed for quantitative observations during dinner (Landesman, 1984). It has several distinctive features: (a) it permits simultaneous coding of the behavior of all family members, (b) it records behavior of each person using mutually exclusive and exhaustive codes, and (c) it is suitable for testing hypotheses about sequence, duration, and responsiveness of behavior. Each entry includes three primary types of information: who interacts with whom, the direction of the interaction (i.e., who initiated the exchange), and the content of the social exchange. Specifically, the content codes are active listening, the exchange of information about family management, general factual information exchange, positive social interaction, controlling, corrective behavior, or both, personal emotional support, negative social interaction, meal-related behavior, and other social behavior. In addition, emotional tone also was coded with a 5-point scale ranging from 1 (*very negative*) to 3 (*neutral*) to 5 (*very positive*). This group code provided a means for studying family dynamics beyond the usual dyadic level. In particular, the code itself was based on a systems theory framework in which alternative means could be used to achieve functional equivalencies within and across families, regardless of family composition per se. Observers were trained to achieve high interobserver reliabilities. Reliability of social exchange categories for multiple raters (Cohen's kappa) ranged from .84 to .99, with a mean of .94. For the ratings of affect, the kappas ranged from .89 to .99, with a mean of .99.

The findings present an impressive portrait of current American family life. Foremost, the family dinner hour remains a central and highly valued routine for these middle-class families. Although divorce has contributed to some differences, these effects appear to be relatively small from the child's perspective, while being more substantial from the mother's perspective. Just as important, the direct observations affirm some of the central principles of family system theory, especially that there is fundamental interdependence among the subsystems of the family and that the whole is greater than the sum of its parts (i.e., what makes a family distinctive is more than just the family members as individuals). These key findings are elaborated in the following section and in Table 2.2.

Frequency and Duration of Family Dinners.   First, somewhat unanticipated, was that 85% of the families dine together more than 4 days per week, and 35% of the sample eat dinner together every night. Both married and divorced single mothers highly value family dinner as part of their family life (Landesman & Lewis, 1984). Nonetheless, on a 10-point scale with 10 as the highest rating, twice as many married mothers rated the importance of dinner in their family lives as 9 or 10 compared to divorced mothers. Married mothers also reported that their families dine together slightly more often (about half a day more per week) than did divorced single mothers. Not surprisingly, significantly more married mothers (70%) reported they were moderately or highly satisfied with the dinnertime help they received from other family members than did divorced mothers (less than 50% were comparably satisfied). Finally, over 75% of married mothers rated their family's dinner experience as being a typically American dinner (ratings of 8, 9, or 10), compared to less than 50% of divorced single mothers who perceived their dinners to be typical.

Second, objective measures indicate that dinnertimes lasted a mean of 20 minutes. Married families dined significantly, but only slightly, longer than did single-mother families—22 versus 19 minutes, respectively. The number of children present did not affect the duration of dinner. Interestingly, maternal employment also had no significant impact on how long dinner lasted. When we explored the possibility that the presence of an observer and a video camera might have decreased the time spent at dinner, both parents and children emphatically said, "no." In fact, because family members were instructed to discuss what they had done that day, it is possible that the dinnertime was somewhat extended by the study protocol. Anecdo-

TABLE 2.2
Family routines at dinner and their significance: Mothers' perspectives

	Marital Status		
	Married families[a]	Divorced single-mother families	P values
Maternal attitudes toward married and single families:			
Number of days per week family eats dinner together	$M = 5.66$ (0.15)	$M = 5.04$ (0.16)	$p < 0.001$
Family eats dinner at same time every night	43% (0.05)	44% (0.04)	
On a scale of (1) low to (10) high:			
How important does mother feel family dinner is in family life?	$M = 8.51$ (0.15)	$M = 7.96$ (0.11)	$p < 0.001$
How satisfied is mother with help from other family members at dinner?	$M = 6.6$ (0.19)	$M = 5.9$ (0.18)	$p < 0.001$
How typically American does mother feel family dinner is?	$M = 6.6$ (0.20)	$M = 6.0$ (0.21)	$p < 0.001$

Note. [a]Married families do not include any step parents (i.e., these are intact married families)

tally, we noted that meals tended to be simple in preparation and service (hot dogs were served more often than any other main dish, followed by spaghetti). Thus, the widely held belief that the family dinner hour has changed, may reflect a shift to shorter, less elaborate mealtimes, rather than a true diminishing in their occurrence or their perceived importance. Without comparable historical data, however, such inferences remain speculative.

Social Engagement Rates. A major finding is that dinnertimes are characterized by remarkably high rates of social engagement among all family members. In divorced single-mother families, each family member engages in social interaction nearly 70% of the time ($M = 67\%$, $SD = 13\%$). In married families, this rate is significantly lower, with each person spending about 60% of dinnertime interacting with others. With increasing number of children in the family, the average rates of social engagement per person decreased significantly and substantially ($M = 72\%$ for only child families; $M = 64\%$ for families with two children; $M = 54\%$ for families with three or more children). The most dramatic effect of family size was seen for divorced single mothers who have only one child, where social engagement rates were extremely high—interacting more than 75% of the time with each other.

In both married and divorced single-mother families, there was evidence of high reciprocity or mutuality of social exchanges among family members. That is, each person initiated about the same amount of social behavior to other family members as he or she received from those people. In married families, for example, parents spent approximately equal amounts of time interacting with each other (mothers engaged fathers 26% of observed time, while fathers engaged mothers 24%). Parents also directed equal amounts of social behavior toward the target child as the target child directed toward each of them: married mothers engaged target children 24% of observed time, whereas target children engaged married mothers 23% of observed time; similarly, fathers engaged target children 16% of the time, whereas the children engaged their fathers 15% of the time. Comparably high levels of reciprocity between mothers and target children occurred in the divorced, single-parent homes. Also, target children in both married and divorced single-mother families initiated approximately equal amounts of social interactions toward their siblings as their siblings initiated toward them. This remarkable reciprocity appears to be one means by which well-functioning families establish and maintain their family as a system of interdependent elements.

Across married and divorced, single-mother families, however, there were differences in select aspects of particular dyadic relationships. Figure 2.1 displays social initiations of mothers to their target children and of target children to their mothers for married and divorced families. Figure 2.2 shows social initiation for families with one, two, and three or more children. Most strikingly, social engagement rates between married mothers and their children ($M = 43\%$) were significantly and markedly less than those observed

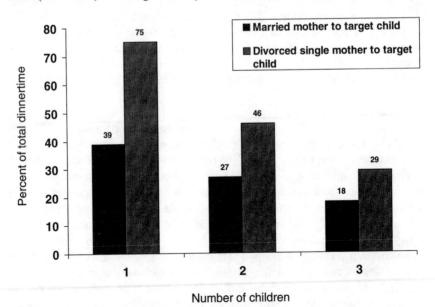

FIG. 2.1. Amount of mother–child engagement during dinner as a function of marital status and number of children.

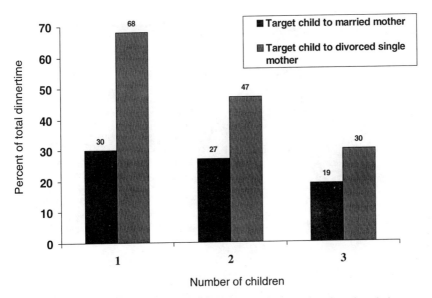

FIG. 2.2.   Children's social interactions with mothers as a function of marital status and number of children.

in divorced single-mother families ($M = 76\%$). Similarly, children initiated interactions with their mothers in married families ($M = 41\%$) at more reduced rates than they did in divorced single-mother families ($M = 76\%$). With an increasing number of children in the family, regardless of marital status of parents, the amount of parent–child dyadic interactions decreased.

If our study only concentrated on mother–child dyads, as most family research does, we would have overlooked a major aspect of family dynamics. However, because we scored all social exchanges between and among family members, we were able to assess the contribution of fathers' behavior to children's social experiences during dinnertime. Figure 2.3 presents a markedly different summary of what occurred during dinnertime as a function of one or two parents in the home. When the target child's interactions with both parents is considered, the large differences detected at the dyadic level between married and single-mother families essentially disappear. That is, the proportion of time married parents interact with their children is almost identical to that observed between mothers and children in divorced, single-mother families. From a family systems perspective, the parental subsystem appears to be operating at similar levels across family types, although a particular dyad—namely, the mother–child dyad—functions differently in order to create this similarity. The only exception to this finding is in the only child families, in which a divorced single mother and her only child still interact significantly more than do both married parents with their only child.

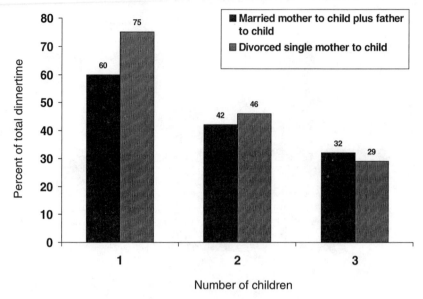

FIG. 2.3.   Amount of parent–child engagement during dinner: Family level.

Figure 2.4 shows the social engagement among siblings in married and divorced single-mother families. Children in divorced single-mother families interact almost twice as much among themselves as do siblings in married families. Interestingly, sibling social exchanges in divorced and married families do not increase when more children are present, at least for the range of family sizes included in this sample.

The Content of Social Interactions.   Looking at the content of social interactions among family members (i.e., what they are doing and saying during dinner) reveals a parallel set of findings about the relationship of marital status to family dynamics. As Fig. 2.5 summarizes, the amount of mother–child interaction across all types of social exchange categories is about twice as high in single versus married families. These marked differences essentially disappear again, however, when the interactions of fathers are considered, as Fig. 2.6 shows. This strongly refutes a view that fathers are essentially functioning as a passive support person for mothers. Rather, fathers of 6- to 12-year-old children are clearly assuming about half of the parenting and socialization responsibility in the context of dinnertime, a highly frequent family event. Married fathers' contributions are essentially the same as married mothers' in the areas of general positive exchanges (58% fathers, 57% mothers), family management (19% fathers, 20% mothers), meal-related behavior (10% fathers, 12% mothers), corrective behavior (6% for both fathers and mothers), personal emotional support (2% fathers, 1% mothers), and factual information exchange (5% fathers, 3% mothers). Also, all family

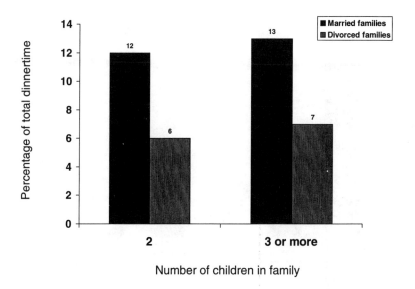

FIG. 2.4. Sibling interactions during dinner as a function of marital status and number of children.

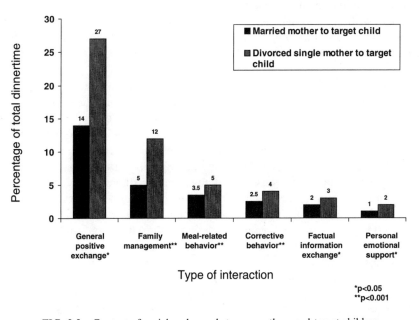

FIG. 2.5. Content of social exchange between mothers and target children.

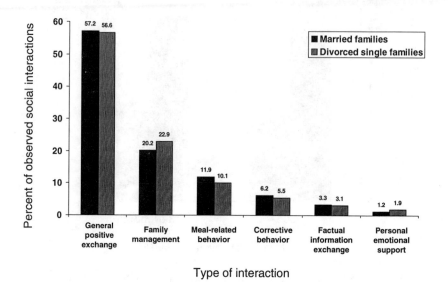

FIG. 2.6.   Content of social exchange between all family members and target children.

members demonstrate a remarkable reciprocity in the content of their social exchanges with one another. Essentially, today's American middle-class families show a balanced distribution in the types of exchanges that occur between parents, between parents and children, and between siblings.

Emotions at Family Dinnertime.   In over 95% of all exchanges during family dinners, the observed affective tone accompanying social exchanges was coded as *neutral*. Positive affective tone was coded for only 4% of the interactions and negative affect was less than 1%. No significant differences were observed in affective tone of social exchanges during dinnertime as a function of marital status, the number of children, or the gender, age, or ethnicity of the target child. Does this mean emotions are missing from the dinner table? We think this is unlikely. What happens is that during frequently occurring family events, such as dinnertime, family members adopt a fairly neutral affective tone to facilitate the task at hand—namely, eating and exchanging family-related information. Extreme emotions expressed during dinner are likely to require more vigorous response, and sometimes can be disruptive. Furthermore, a matter-of-fact style of interacting often occurs among intimates, who may share many private ways of communicating their feelings. It is also possible that the presence of an observer inhibits expression of emotional extremes. Another possibility is that the emotions family members ascribe to their memories of shared family meals reflect a summative subjective experience that does not have a one-to-one correspondence with observable exchanges.

THE EXPERIENTIAL PERSPECTIVES OF DIVORCED
SINGLE-PARENT AND MARRIED FAMILIES

Perceptions of stress and social support, from in and outside the family, differ in many ways for married and divorced single mothers. First, concerning recent sources of stress, reported on the Family Inventory of Life Events (McCubbin, Patterson, & Wilson, 1981), divorced single mothers report significantly more conflict with their former spouse in the last 12 months than married mothers did with their husbands. For divorced single mothers, 32% report having experienced an increase in conflict with their former spouse during the last year, whereas only 15% of married mothers report comparable increases in conflict with husbands. Parent–child conflict, however, does not differ as a function of maternal status—with less than 2% of married and divorced mothers reporting recent increases in conflict with their children.

On a 5-point scale, with 5 (*very helpful*) and -5 (*not helpful at all*) divorced single mothers reported higher satisfaction with the social support they received both from close friends ($M = 3.23$) and other relatives, excluding grandparents ($M = 2.35$), than did married mothers (close friends: $M = 2.84$; other relatives: $M = 1.46$). The reported frequency of the social support from these sources, however, did not differ for married and divorced mothers. Concerning grandparent social support, both married and divorced, single mothers reported similar levels of satisfaction with the help they received from the target childs grandparents ($M = 2.86$), as well as from the church or temple ($M = 1.99$), from teachers ($M = 2.04$), and from other professionals ($M = 1.60$).

Concerning perceptions of the mother–child relationship, married and divorced single mothers reported high similar and positive levels of satisfaction ($M = 3.74$ for married mothers, $M = 3.73$ for divorced mothers). The children in these families also reported remarkably high levels of satisfaction with maternal social support including emotional, instrumental, informational, and instructional support. Somewhat surprising was the finding that perceptions of social support by mothers and their children did not differ as a function of gender, age, ethnicity, or number of children in the family. For more details about perceived social support, see Reid, Ramey, and Burchinal (1990) and Reid, Landesman, Treder, and Jaccard (1989).

HOW IMPORTANT IS FAMILY STRUCTURE
FOR FAMILY FUNCTIONING?

A primary focus of this study was to evaluate the impact of changes in the demography of middle-class families on the family environment and children's social experiences. Married and divorced single-mother families are undeniably different, even in middle-class, non-distressed homes. In addition to the absence of the father from children's everyday lives, divorce is associated with a significant decrease in household income and an increased likelihood of mothers working fulltime outside the home. This study affirms these well-recognized trends (Teachman & Paasch, 1994; Weiss, 1979) and does so for a large population-based sample of middle-class White/nonHispanic and African-American families with school-age children. More important, the study provides the first findings about the likely impact of divorce on school-age children's typical daily social interactions with parents and siblings.

Key findings concern the dramatic differences in the amount of social interaction for the mother–child dyad for divorced single-mother families. In these families, children initiate social interactions toward their mothers at about double the rate that children in married families do. In reciprocal fashion, divorced, single mothers also initiate about twice as much social behavior toward their children as do married mothers. What does this mean? If only the mother–child dyad had been studied, possible inferences would have included that the mother–child relationship is overly intense or not well-balanced. By observing the entire family as a system, however, it became evident that the marked increase in mother–child interactions in divorced families reflects something like a compensatory or homeostatic mechanism. That is, when one less adult is present, there is a social gap in the dynamics at the family dinner table. Furthermore, single-parent families spend somewhat less time at dinner (by nearly 3 minutes)—perhaps reflecting a combination of factors, such as less time needed to negotiate dinner, a reduced number of social partners at the table, and mothers' fatigue from high rates of interaction.

Support for this hypothesis—that a social gap leads to compensatory processes in the divorced families—comes from contrasting observations of these families with those of the two-parent families. When the behavior of both the married mothers and fathers is added together, almost all of the differences between married and divorced single-parent families disappear. Fathers clearly are not merely indirect influences on children, as is often assumed in the developmental research (e.g., Belsky, 1981). Instead, fathers are observably interactive with their children and wives, at just slightly lower levels than are mothers (at least during dinnertime). In the divorced single-parent setting, both children and mothers appear to compensate for the father's absence (gap) by increasing their interactions with other family members. Evidence for this balance is remarkable in terms of the quantitative precision—namely, that the social engagement of married mothers plus fathers is nearly identical to that of divorced, single mothers. Conversely, children in divorced single-parent homes direct about twice as much behavior toward their mother, matching that of children in married families to both their mother and father.

From a functional perspective, the proportionate distribution of what family members do when they interact with one another (i.e., the content of social exchange), as well as the amount of social interactions during dinnertime, indicate that dinner is predominantly a social experience. In these analyses, differences in absolute rates of social engagement are ignored because the focus is on the relative distribution of social exchanges. Both the rank order of behavioral activities and the percent of social behavior they represent are virtually the same for married and divorced families. These results strongly indicate that the social interactions of children in married and divorced single-mother families are similar, not only in amount of social interactions, but also in respect to the content of social exchanges.

The effect of greater numbers of children in the household on the amount of social interactions during dinner is consistent with the *confluence model* (Zajonc, 1976), which assumes that the social and intellectual resources are reduced for each individual child when there are more children. Although from a structural perspective, such as the confluence model, single-parent families are hypothesized to invest less in children, attributable to the reduction by half in the adults typically available, this study demonstrates that in middle-class, relatively stable families, mothers do double duty in the absence of the father. What is especially remarkable about the double duty role of divorced single mothers is that they achieve this in spite of the increased demands of working outside the home, lowered levels of income, and increased conflict with the child's father (i.e., spouse). Also, divorced, single mothers demonstrated exceptionally positive attitudes about how well single parents can provide for their children, compared to the more skeptical attitudes of married mothers. Married mothers were also significantly more religious than were divorced, single mothers, something that may affect marital stability itself or other attitudes toward the family. Interestingly, divorced, single mothers, when compared to married mothers, reported that they were significantly more satisfied with the social support they received from friends and other relatives, again suggesting active compensatory processes operating to sustain positive parenting and family functioning. Grandparents, however, are perceived as equally and positively supportive for both married and divorced families.

Some caveats are needed to interpret these findings and especially to compare them to the earlier reports about family functioning and social interactions in married and divorced homes. First, this sample was selected to represent a relatively homogeneous subgroup in the general population. This subgroup, however, represents the largest segment of our country's population: families that have not recently experienced major disruption (divorce, death, separation, moving to a new home) or change in family membership (new babies, stepsiblings, or stepparents), families with no major psychopathology or major health conditions affecting any family member, and families above the poverty level. Also, parents have educational and income levels significantly higher than those of the nation as a whole. For example, none of the parents in any family had less than a high school diploma and about 50% earned college degrees; nearly half of the families had incomes above $40,000—nearly 30% more than the average national family income for 1986. Of the divorced, single-mother families, 80% had incomes above $15,000, the national average for single-female households for 1986 (U.S. Bureau of the Census, 1988). The cognitive performance of children, both Whites/non-Hispanic and African Americans, is significantly above national norms by nearly a standard deviation, as are the Peabody Picture Vocabulary Test (PPVT) scores (Dunn & Dunn, 1981) for their parents. Second, this sample differs from the most well-known studies of divorce in three ways: the age of the children, the duration since divorce, and the reliance on a population-based sampling strategy.

Hetherington and colleagues provided valuable and detailed reports on the adjustment of preschool children following parental divorce (Hetherington et al., 1982). Comparison of preschool children of divorced parents and matched children from intact married families indicated a short-term reaction to divorce and a period of adjustment, with almost all differences in the children's social behavior disappearing 2 years following divorce. Hetherington characterized the period following divorce as one of "re-equilibration," emphasizing her main finding that there is a process of adjustment that children undergo following marital transitions.

Differences in social interactions among siblings in married and divorced families (in which the mother has custody), noted by MacKinnon (1989), were also observed in this study. Children in divorced, single-mother families engaged slightly more in negative behavior among themselves than did children in married families. This difference may reflect what occurs when fathers are not present because other studies of married families report that children misbehave more when fathers are absent (Hetherington et al., 1982).

The effect for number of children in the family on amount of social interactions in families affirms a well-established relationship in social research (Terhune, 1974). In the present study, as in many earlier reports, increased number of children in the family is associated with lower child cognitive outcomes. Lewis and Feiring (1982) also found that dyadic social interactions decrease with increased number of children, which may account in part for the children's lower IQs in larger families. Interestingly, our observations indicating compensatory amounts of mother–child social interactions in divorced, single-mother families would predict no negative cognitive outcomes as a consequence of being raised in the divorced, single-mother family per se. In fact, this is what we found.

Lewis and Feiring (1982) observed that mothers talked as much to fathers as they did to the target preschool child and that fathers interacted significantly less with their children. Furthermore, Lewis and Feiring did not find comparable levels of reciprocity in dyadic social interactions at dinner. One likely explanation for these differences is that they only studied families with toddlers, whereas this study focused on families with 6- to 12-year-old children. Also, they only scored verbal exchanges during one dinner session, whereas this study coded a much wider variety of social behaviors and did so during three dinner sessions. Given the pilot research we conducted about the validity of dinnertime observation, it may be that the detected mother–father difference is partially an artifact of mothers' increased self-consciousness and vigilance during a first observation session.

The most important finding of this study—that the absence of the father from the family at dinner does not affect the amount of parent–child social interactions—has not been reported earlier, to our knowledge. The finding is intriguing because it makes an interpretation in a systems perspective appealing. Systems theory (e.g., Belsky, 1981; Landesman, Jaccard, & Gunderson, 1991; Lewis, 1987; Minuchin, 1988) views families as an interdependent network of subsystems, including the mother–father, child–parent, and child–child subsystem. Every subsystem has a function or goal that homeostatic processes in the system seek to maintain. Observed dyadic social behavior in this study between mother and father, parent and child, and among siblings supports the view that these are independent subsystems. Also, family members in these dyads initiate comparable amounts and types of social behavior, affirming active reciprocity. Dyads in both married and divorced families are affected in a similar manner by increased number of children. Systems perspective predicts that changes in the family system, such as the absence of the father (which affects several subsystems), necessitates a new steady state that could fulfill the function of the system. This is exactly what we observed in divorced, single-mother families, where the observed dyadic behavior between the child and parents on one hand, and both parents on the other hand, is statistically indistinguishable. Whether a similar effect occurs in married families during father absence is interesting to study.

In this study, there is also evidence for multiple, positive, mediating mechanisms. These include children's own self-reports about the quality of their relationships with their mothers, as well as their overall satisfaction with the quality of social support they receive from in and outside the family (e.g., Reid, Landesman, Treder, & Jaccard, 1989; Reid, Ramey, & Burchinal, 1990; Wan, Jaccard, & Ramey, 1996). Children in divorced, single-parent homes report high levels of positive social support—equal to that of children in married families. Conversely, the mothers in both married and divorced homes rate the quality of their relationship with their school-age child as equally strong.

We recognize that social interactions among family members at dinner are likely to be situational in character. These findings are important in their own right, however, as the family dinner is a frequent, stable, recurring, and highly valued family activity. Beyond this, social interactions among family members at dinner may reflect well-established patterns of interaction that occur in other contexts. Without empirical data from cross-situational ob-servations, however, this assumption remains unproven in this study.

In summary, some lasting differences were detected in stable, middle-class, married and divorced, single-mother families. Differences related to demo-graphic and attitudinal areas, as well as the dynamics of who interacts with whom and for what amounts of time during family dinners. Remarkably, however, the behavioral differences observed reflect apparent compensatory and reciprocal processes on the part of divorced, single mothers and their 6- to 12-year-old children. The functional result of these differences is a family dinnertime that is almost the same as that experienced by children and mothers in married homes (recognizing that there is social gap attrib-utable to father absence). Because these families experienced divorce for an average of nearly 5 years, with children's mean age when their parents divorced being 5 years old, it is important that generalizations not be made to all divorced families. These findings are highly supportive of a family systems perspective and how it views adjustment of family members over time.

ACKNOWLEDGMENTS

This research was conducted through the support of National Institute of Child Health and Human Development (HD-19348 and HD-24116) and the Civitan International Research Center at the University of Alabama at Bir-mingham. The contributions of Dr. Molly Reid at the University of Wash-ington and Dr. James Jaccard at the State University of New York at Albany in the conceptualization and conduct of the Washington Family Behavior Study are gratefully acknowledged. Thanks go to Dr. Janice Rabkin for organizing data collection, T. V. Kenley for assisting with data coordination and video recording, and the 22 research associates who enthusiastically helped with data collection. Leslie Franklin and Nan Skufca helped im-mensely with tables and the manuscript. Dr. Michael Lewis was a coauthor of the interview about family dinners and contributed in vital ways to the thinking about the importance of combining insider (subjective) and outsider (objective) data about this common and recurring family activity.

REFERENCES

Amato, P. R. (1994). Life-span adjustment of children to their parents' divorce. *The Future of Children, 4,* 143–165.

Amato, P. R., & Keith, B. (1991). Parental divorce and the well-being of children: A meta-analysis. *Psychological Bulletin, 110,* 26–46.

Anastasi, A. (1956). Intelligence and family size. *Psychological Bulletin, 53,* 187–209.

Belsky, J. (1981). Early human experience: A family perspective. *Developmental Psychology, 17,* 3–23.

Bronfenbrenner, U. (1979). *The ecology of human development: Experiments by nature and design.* Cambridge, MA: Harvard University Press.

Chase-Lansdale, P., & Hetherington, E. M. (1990). The impact of divorce on life-span development: Short and long term effects. In P. B. Baltes, D. L. Featherman, & R. M. Lerner (Eds.), *Life-span development and behavior* (Vol. 10, pp. 105–150). New York: Academic Press.

Cirelli, V. G. (1978). The relationship of sibling structure to intellectual abilities and achievement. *Review of Educational Research, 48,* 365–379.

Dornbusch, S. M., & Gray, K. D. (1988). Single-parent families. In S. M. Dornbusch & M. H. Strober (Eds.), *Feminism Children and the New Family* (pp. 274–296). New York: Guilford.

Dreyer, C. A., & Dreyer, A. S. (1973). Family dinner time as a unique behavior habitat. *Family Press, 12,* 291–301.

Dunn, L. M., & Dunn, L. M. (1981). *Peabody Picture Vocabulary Test—Revised.* Circle Pines, MN: American Guidance Service.

Feiring, C., & Lewis, M. (1987). The ecology of some middle class families at dinner. *International Journal of Behavioral Development, 10,* 377–390.

Furstenberg, F. F. (1990). Divorce and the American family. *Annual Review of Sociology, 16,* 379–403.

Hetherington, E. M., & Clingempeel, W. G. (1992). Coping with marital transitions. *Monographs of the Society for Research in Child Development, 57*(2–3).

Hetherington, E. M., Cox, M., & Cox, R. (1982). Effects of divorce on parents and children. In M. E. Lamb (Ed.), *Nontraditional families: Parenting and child development* (pp. 233–288). Hillsdale, NJ: Lawrence Erlbaum Associates.

Landesman, S. (1984). *Observation of Family Functioning (OFF).* Seattle: University of Washington.

Landesman, S. (1987). The changing structure and function of institutions: A search for optimal group care environments. In S. Landesman & P. Vietze (Eds.), *Living environments and mental retardation* (pp. 79–126). Washington, DC: American Association on Mental Retardation.

Landesman, S., Jaccard, J., & Gunderson, V. (1991). The family environment: The combined influence of family behavior, goals, strategies, resources, and individual experiences. In M. Lewis & S. Feinman (Eds.), *Social influences and socialization in infancy* (pp. 63–96). New York: Plenum.

Landesman, S. L., & Lewis, M. (1986). *Families at dinner.* Seattle: University of Washington.

Landesman, S., & Ramey, C. T. (1989). Developmental psychology and mental retardation: Integrating scientific principles with treatment practices. *American Psychologist, 44*(2), 409–415.

Landesman-Dwyer, S., & Berkson, G. (1984). Friendships and social behavior. In J. Wortis (Ed.), *Mental retardation and developmental disabilities: An annual review* (Vol. 13, pp. 129–154). New York: Plenum.

Landesman-Dwyer, S., & Butterfield, E. C. (1983). Mental retardation: Developmental issues in cognitive and social adaptation. In M. Lewis (Ed.), *Origins of intelligence: Infancy and early childhood* (2nd ed., pp. 479–519). New York: Plenum.

Landesman-Dwyer, S., Stein, J. G., & Sackett, G. P. (1978). A behavioral and ecological study of group homes. In G. P. Sackett (Ed.), *Observing behavior: Vol. I: Theory and application in mental retardation* (pp. 349–377). Baltimore: University Park Press.

Lewis, M. (1987). Social development in infancy and early childhood. In J. D. Osofsky (Ed.), *Handbook of Child Development* (2nd ed.). New York: Wiley.

Lewis, M., & Feiring, C. (1982). Some American families at dinner. In L. M. Laosa & I. E. Sigel (Eds.), *Families as learning environments for children*. New York: Plenum.

MacKinnon, C. E. (1989). An observational investigation of sibling interactions in married and divorced families. *Developmental Psychology, 25*, 36–44.

McCubbin, H. I., Patterson, J. M., & Wilson, L. R. (1981). *Family Inventory of Life Events.* St. Paul: University of Minnesota.

Minuchin, S. (1974). *Families and family therapy*. Cambridge, MA: Harvard University Press.

Minuchin, P. (1988). Relationships within the family: A systems perspective on development. In R. A. Hinde & J. Stevenson-Hinde (Eds.), *Relationships within families: Mutual influences* (pp. 7–26). Oxford, England: Clarendon.

Reid, M., Landesman, S., Treder, R., & Jaccard, J. (1989). "My Family and My Friends": Six- to twelve-year-old children's perceptions of social support. *Child Development, 60*, 896–910.

Reid, M., Ramey, S. L., & Burchinal, M. (1990). Dialogues with children about their families. In I. Bretherton & M. W. Watson (Eds.), *Children's perspectives on the family: New directions for child development, 48* (pp. 5–28). San Francisco: Jossey-Bass.

Sackett, G. P., Landesman-Dwyer, S., & Morin, V. N. (1981). Naturalistic observation in design and evaluation of special-education programs. In T. R. Kratochwill (Ed.), *Advances in school psychology* (Vol. 1, pp. 281–306). Hillsdale, NJ: Lawrence Erlbaum Associates.

Shiono, P. H., & Sandham Quinn, L. (1994). Epidemiology of divorce. *The Future of Children, 4*(1), 15–28.

Teachman, J. D., & Paasch, K. M. (1994). Financial impact of divorce on children and their families. *The Future of Children, 4*(1), 63–83.

Terhune, K. W. (1974). *A review of the actual and expected consequences of family size* (NIH Publication No. 75-779). Washington, DC: U.S. Department of Health, Education, and Welfare, Public Health Service.

U.S. Bureau of the Census. (1988). *Current population report: Household after-tax income: 1986* (Series P-23, No. 157). Washington, DC: U.S. Department of Commerce.

Wallerstein, J. S. (1987). Children of divorce: Report of a ten-year follow-up of early latency-age children. *American Journal of Orthopsychiatry, 57*(2), 199–211.

Wan, C. K., Jaccard, J., & Ramey, S. L. (1996, May). The relationship between social support and life satisfaction as a function of family structure: An analysis of four types of support. *Journal of Marriage and the Family, 58*, 502–513.

Weiss, R. S. (1979). Growing up a little faster: The experience of growing up in a single-parent household. *Journal of Social Issues, 35*, 97–111.

Zajonc, R. B. (1976). Family configuration and intelligence. *Science, 192*, 227–236.

Zajonc, R. B., Marcus, G. B., Berbaum, M. L., Bargh, J. A., & Moreland, R. L. (1991). One justified criticism plus three flawed analyses equals two unwarranted conclusions: A reply to Retherford and Sewell. *American Sociological Review, 56*, 159–165.

3

▼▼▼▼▼▼▼

Divergent Family Views
and School Competence
in Early Adolescence

Candice Feiring
Michael Lewis
Robert Wood Johnson Medical School
New Brunswick, NJ

A considerable amount of research has identified the family environment as a potent influence on school performance (Rosenthal & Feldman, 1991; Steinberg, Lamborn, Dornbusch, & Darling, 1992; Stevenson & Lee, 1990). This chapter's main focus is on how the family environment, in particular family members' views of the family's intellectual orientation, is related to school competence in early adolescence. We approach the examination of the family environment in two ways: first, in terms of the extent to which the family is viewed as characterized by intellectual activities; and second, in regard to divergent views among family members about these types of activities. Also, the family environment is thought of as a set of effects, including each individual member's view, particular dyads' views, and the entire family's view of its intellectual environment.

The chapter, therefore, has several objectives. First, we examine whether individuals, dyads, or the entire family provide the better representation of the family environment in regard to the adolescent's school competence. Second, we are interested in whether views of the amount of intellectual orientation, as compared to differences in views, captured different aspects of the family environment. These two objectives were considered in regard to how family views about intellectual orientation were related to the adolescent's school competence. To look at these issues, we first addressed the premise that early adolescence is a time of changing family relationships and increases in parent–adolescent conflict. Having shown the particular importance of early adolescence for examining divergent family views, data from our longitudinal study is presented as it elucidates the relation between the family's intellectual orientation and school competence in adolescence.

DIVERGENT VIEWS OF FAMILY LIFE

Early adolescence is a developmental period during which there are a number of normative changes in parent–child relationships and family functioning (e.g., Steinberg, 1990; Youniss & Smollar, 1985). A central feature of this change is an increase in parent–child disagreements and quarrels as adolescents strive for autonomy. Consequently, early adolescence provides an appropriate window for examining divergent views of family orientation. It is also a time during which there are increased demands for school competence with pressure from parents, as well as school personnel, to reach higher standards of achievement (Entwisle, 1990; Simmons & Blyth, 1987). Family functions associated with school success, such as intellectual and achievement activities, may become one focus of family conflict between parents and adolescents.

In early adolescence, family life typically undergoes a series of disruptions. Parents and young adolescents attempt to maintain some stability in family life while coping with the adolescents' cognitive, social, and pubertal changes that are related to challenges to family rules and efforts to achieve differentiation and autonomy from parents (Gecas & Seff, 1990; Paikoff & Brooks-Gunn, 1991). In early puberty, research indicates that perturbations in the family system occur. In general, pubertal maturation is related to modest decreases in the closeness of parent–adolescent relationships (Paikoff & Brooks-Gunn, 1991). Although a modest distancing effect of puberty on adolescent–parent relationships has been noted in several studies, normative evidence for family life characterized as storm and stress is lacking (Steinberg, 1990).

As a transitional period in children's development, early adolescence is a time of significant change in family relationships. Young adolescents spend less time with their parents and emotionally distance themselves from them (Collins & Russell, 1991; Fuligni & Eccles, 1993; Larson & Richards, 1991). Adolescents have increased unsupervised time with peers, and the importance of peer approval and advice is heightened (Brown, 1990; Simmons & Blyth, 1987). Time spent with peers in early adolescence can frequently surpass that spent with parents and other family members (Csikszentmihalyi & Larson, 1984). It appears that children's increased orientation toward peers is at the expense of closeness to parents. Studies have shown that in addition to an increase in conflict, both parents and young adolescents report less cohesion, engagement, and closeness (Collins, 1990; Steinberg & Silverberg, 1986).

Although major upheavals in family life are not typical, disagreements over family rules and other quotidian matters become more frequent during early adolescence compared to childhood and later adolescence. The frequency of disagreements between offspring and parent increases in early adolescence and remains at a higher level through middle adolescence and then declines, especially when the adolescent leaves the household (Montemayor, 1983). Evidence suggests that young adolescents and their parents fight about twice weekly and more often than do wives and husbands (Larson & Richards, 1994; Montemayor, 1983).

Adolescents perceive relative levels of arguing, quarreling, and getting mad to be greater among family members than among close peers (Furman & Buhrmester, 1992). Whereas conflict with close friends is avoided and minimized because such relationships may be especially susceptible to disruption, the relative permanence of family ties provides greater latitude for disagreement (Collins & Laursen, 1992). In most instances, conflict is not intense nor reflective of a major diminution in the strong emotional relationship between parent and adolescent (Montemayor, 1983; Smetana, 1988a, 1988b). Such conflicts have been described as "mild bickering" and "disagreements over everyday issues." Both parents and adolescents report that school performance, dating, dress code, and personal management issues are areas about which frequent disagreements occur (Smetana, 1988b). Conflicts with fathers center on performance in school and disobedience, whereas those with mothers also include completion of household chores (Youniss & Smollar, 1985). In general, adolescents perceive conflict experiences as dominated by their mothers (Laursen, 1995). Because mothers still predominate as adolescents' socializing agents in the family, their goals and requests for compliance are most likely to be met with opposition simply given the base rate (Montemayor & Hanson, 1985).

A process characteristic of adolescence is individuation. The concept of *individuation* describes how adolescents transform, as opposed to abandon, the centrality of their relationship with parents. Individuation may be viewed as two complementary processes (Grotevant & Cooper, 1985; Youniss & Smollar, 1985). One process involves reconstructing the type of self that was valid during childhood to develop a self that fits with the adolescent's own experiences rather than parental demands or desires. The other process involves remaining connected to parents so that validation of the self-concepts the adolescent has constructed can be received from parents. Individuation entails the ability to use parents as resources (e.g., emotional, informational, material) and the ability to be autonomous, that is, to govern oneself and make important life decisions.

Conflict is an important aspect of the individuation process. Although the topics of parent–adolescent disagreements are often banal, low-level conflict serves an important function in adolescent development. From a sociobiological perspective, it has been suggested that quarreling at puberty is an atavism that promotes leaving the family of origin in order to select a mate outside one's kin (Steinberg, 1989). In most other species, parent–offspring conflict intensifies at puberty, indicating an evolutionary component to this pattern in humans. Some theorists have suggested that arguments with parents facilitate individuation by helping adolescents develop a more realistic and mature view of their parents (Holmbeck & Hill, 1988). Disagreement also functions as a mechanism to provide parents with current feedback about the adolescents' changing expectation of the nature of the parent–adolescent relationship as well as their evolving self-concepts. Employing a cognitive–developmental perspective, Smetana (1988a, 1988b) argued that parent–adolescent conflict is best understood by the different ways each family member defines and comprehends family regulations, rules, and obligations. Adolescents begin to view their parents' rules as reflecting social conventions that they may eschew as they adopt a perspective that emphasizes the importance of personal choices.

Given the numerous fluctuations, hassles, and tensions typical of family life, the early adolescent period is an important time to examine divergent views of family functioning. The beginning of adolescence is the time of greatest tension between individual family members because each member experiences the nature and importance of family life as very different at this time (Larson & Richards, 1994). During adolescence, there are changes taking place in family life that serve to decrease the extent to which family members share similar views of the family environment. Conflict is the highest and family functioning the least satisfying during early adolescence (Montemayor & Hanson, 1985; Olson et al., 1983). In addition, emotional closeness, time spent with parents, and capitulating to parents' decisions all decrease during adolescence (e.g., Buhrmester & Furman, 1987; Steinberg, 1987).

Although parents and adolescents may argue frequently about grades and school work, there often exists agreement among family members about the importance of educational goals. As parents increasingly orient their adolescent's attention toward the importance of school success for future career expectations, conflict is generated. In combination with possible parental pressure, there is evidence that the school environment is one of stress and even alienation for many adolescents. In a study of their emotional lives, young adolescents were asked to describe the biggest problem they encountered on a daily basis (Larson, Kubey, & Colletti, 1989). The most frequent response was school work and school grades. These adolescents also attributed school circumstances as the most common reason for negative emotions (Larson & Asmussen, 1991). The domain of school competence, with its salience and potential for tension in both adolescents and their parents, is thus a good area to examine divergent family views.

PARSING THE FAMILY SYSTEM

Results from studies of mother–father–adolescent triads and siblings have contributed to a greater understanding of families as well as parent–adolescent relationships (e.g., Hauser, Powers, & Noam, 1991). Nevertheless, the study of families with adolescents needs to move from the study of parent–adolescent relationships and interactions to a more systematic study of families. Examining dyadic relationships outside the context of the whole family system limits our understanding of family processes important for family functioning and the development of adolescent competence. Most of the research from a systems perspective assessed the functioning of dyads and triads and has not yet captured the functioning of the family system as a whole.

Most theoretical and methodological approaches to the family tend to focus on characteristics of the adolescent or the dyadic relationship of parent and child as likely to yield important information concerning adolescent competence. In contrast, a family systems approach suggests that the entire family itself needs to be considered for its impact on adolescent competence. A central question this chapter addresses concerns the extent to which the family as a whole, rather than individual or dyadic views of the family, are needed in order to understand how the family influences adolescent competence. For example, is the aggregate of family members' views about the family's intellectual activities more likely to be related to the adolescent's school performance than the adolescent's or parents' view of these activities?

Because we are interested in examining whether an entire family perspective is more informative than an individual's view or a dyadic view, intellectual orientation is conceptualized in several ways. First, there are the individual views of the family reported by the adolescent, the mother, and the father. Each of these family members is considered in terms of the amount of intellectual orientation he or she believes describes the family. Second, there are the dyads of mother–adolescent, father–adolescent, and mother–father and the amount of intellectual orientation pertaining to each of these dyads. At the dyadic level, we also need to consider the extent to which the family subsystems of mother–father, mother–adolescent, and father–adolescent differ in their perceptions of the family's emphasis on intellectual orientations. Many studies demonstrate that the level of family conflict is related to children's adjustment and competence (e.g., Demo & Acock, 1996; Grych & Fincham, 1990). Higher levels of disagreement between family members was expected to be related to poorer school adjustment and performance. Third, there is the aggregate of the adolescents', mothers', and fathers' views of the family. This aggregate is considered both in terms of the total amount of intellectual orientation across all these family members and in terms of the total disagreement between family members about the family's intellectual orientation.

Using data from a longitudinal study of development (e.g., Feiring & Lewis, 1991; Lewis, Feiring, McGuffog, & Jaskir, 1984), we examined how school competence is related to family members' perceptions of the family environment at the individual, dyadic, and aggregate levels for characterizing the family system. The relations between school competence and family environment are considered for both the amount and differences among family members' views of the emphasis and nature of the family's intellectual orientation.

FAMILY CHARACTERISTICS
AND THEIR MEASUREMENT

The functioning of 101 families was examined. All families were participants in a longitudinal study of social and cognitive development from infancy into adolescence. The families consisted of mother, father, and children, and were of European descent. Each family had a 13-year-old target adolescent who was the focus of the study from its inception in infancy. Forty-five families were from the upper-middle socioeconomic group and 56 were from the middle group (as determined by both parents' education and occupation; Feiring & Lewis, 1982). There were 52 girls and 49 boys.

Within a month of the adolescent's 13th birthday, the families participated in an extensive laboratory and home assessment. As part of this assessment, the adolescent completed the family environment scales in the laboratory as did the mother, who did so in a separate room. The father completed this scale at home. Measures of school competence, including grades and achievement scores, were obtained from school records and the adolescent's English teacher provided information on school adjustment by completing the Teacher Report Form.

Families may differ on the extent to which they value and organize family functions around intellectual goals. Parents are the ones who initially define particular family goals, and in regard to educational goals, parental expectations for achievement are one of the strongest predictors of adolescents' achievement levels (e.g., Brown, Mounts, Lamborn, & Steinberg, 1993). During adolescence, the importance of educational goals are often endorsed by both parents and offspring (Bachman, Johnston, & O'Malley, 1987). Family attitudes and behaviors concerning the importance of intellectual activities and achievement goals have been related to school success (Dornbusch, Ritter, Leiderman, Roberts, & Fraleigh, 1987; Entwisle, 1990; Stevenson & Lee, 1990).

Because we wanted to capture the functioning of the family system, we decided to focus on multiple family members' reports of the family's intellectual environment. Each family member is an important source of information about the dynamics of the family system and the family environments in which adolescent competence develops. There are several advantages to using family members as knowledgeable reporters of the family relationships and functions (Cook & Goldstein, 1993). Family members see each other functioning in a variety of situations over an extended period of time. They also observe behaviors that are more likely to be displayed in private, as opposed to public, contexts.

The Family Environment Scale (FES) was used to index the family's intellectual orientation. The FES is a questionnaire designed to tap different aspects of the family environment including family relationships, personal growth, and system maintenance (Moos & Moos, 1976). Intellectual orientation involves the extent to which family members are involved in cultural and intellectual activities such as the pursuit of art, music, and literature, or taking trips to the library and museums. Two sets of measures were constructed, one for amount and one for disagreement. To index amount we obtained the mean level score for each family member; the sum amount in each of the mother–adolescent, father–adolescent, and mother–father dyads as well as a total aggregate amount for the entire family. Because disagreement requires at least two parties, disagreement scores were obtained for the mother–adolescent, father–adolescent, and mother–father dyads as well as for the entire family. Disagreement was calculated by taking the absolute difference of one family member's mean level score and subtracting the other family member's mean score. For example, the intellectual mother–father disagreement score is the absolute difference of the mother's intellectual orientation mean subtracted from the father's intellectual orientation mean. The entire family disagreement score was obtained by summing the mother–adolescent, father–adolescent, and mother–father disagreement scores and dividing by three.

In this chapter, we define school competence in terms of two components: school adjustment and school performance. *School adjustment* refers to the degree of behavior problems expressed in the school setting. Educational attainment requires not only intelligence, but also the capacity to skillfully operate in the school system (Hamilton, 1984). For example, aggressive students are less likely to do well, and have problems following school rules, and being accepted by classmates (e.g., Kupersmidt & Coie, 1990; Parker & Asher, 1987). To measure school adjustment, the adolescent's English teacher completed the Teacher Report Form (TRF; Achenbach, 1991), a standardized rating scale designed to obtain teachers' reports of students' behavioral–emotional problems as observed in the school setting. A total score indicates the extent to which the teacher perceives the student as maladjusted. Standardized achievement scores are necessary to provide a good picture of a student's academic performance (Dornbusch et al., 1987). The adolescents in our study attended many different schools and did not take the same standardized achievement tests. School performance was indexed using the adolescent's National Curve Equivalent for the total achievement score for the particular standardized test that was taken at the end of the eighth-grade year.

Family Functioning and Adolescent School Competence

For amount of intellectual orientation, significant associations with adolescent school competence were expected. Higher amounts of intellectual orientation, whether for individual, dyadic, or entire family measures, should be related to better school performance. We further anticipated that the adolescent's view of the family's intellectual orientation should be more strongly related to adolescent competence. Alternatively, it could be the case that the entire family view yields stronger relations as it represents a more complete picture of the adolescent's experience in the family. Significant relations were predicted for the dyadic and entire family disagreement measures and school adjustment and performance. Higher disagreement was expected to be related to poorer adjustment and performance. The entire family disagreement was expected to show the strongest relations to school outcomes compared to the dyadic disagreement scores. This is because the total score represents the greatest possible difference regarding the family's focus on intellectual activities.

Obviously, school performance is influenced by the adolescent's cognitive ability, and significant associations have been reported between IQ and school success (e.g., Klebanov & Brooks-Gunn, 1992). As in previous research, the association between the adolescent's IQ—as obtained from the Wechsler Intelligence Scale for Children-Revised (WISC-R; Wechsler, 1974)—and the school measures showed moderate correlations ranging from .33 to .59. Consequently, in order to obtain a clearer index of the relation between family measures and school outcomes we partialed out the effects of IQ.

Table 3.1 shows the correlations, with IQ removed, between school adjustment and the amount and disagreement measures for the individual, dyad, and entire family scores. The correlations are presented by sex of adolescent and for the total sample. For the sample as a whole, there were few significant relations between amount or disagreement measures of the family's intellectual orientation and school adjustment. For the mother–adolescent dyad, the greater the amount of intellectual orientation, the better the adolescents' school adjustment. This relation is stronger for girls than boys. For disagreement, as predicted, the greater the mother–adolescent disagreement, the poorer the school adjustment. Again, this relation is stronger for girls than boys.

Table 3.2 shows the correlations between school achievement and the amount and disagreement measures for the individual, dyad, and total scores. For the total sample, mothers', fathers', and adolescents' perception of higher amounts of intellectual orientation is significantly related to higher achievement. The average correlation is .30 for the individual views. The dyadic scores, when compared to individual scores, yield more consistently significant positive relations. The average correlation is .36. The greater the intel-

TABLE 3.1
Correlations Between Measures of Family Intellectual
Orientation and School Behavioral Problems

Individual	Amount			Disagreement		
	Girls	*Boys*	*Total*	*Girls*	*Boys*	*Total*
Adolescent	.25	.13	.19*	—	—	—
Mother	−.19	−.13	−.15	—	—	—
Father	.01	−.14	−.06	—	—	—
Dyads						
Adol-Mother	−.26*	−.15	.20**	.36***	.15	.26***
Adol-Father	−.15	−.17	−.16	−.23	−.26*	−.03
Mother-Father	−.11	−.15	−.13	−.03	−.08	−.02
Family						
Adol-Mother-Father	−.19	.17	.18*	.26*	.12	.11

Note. The IQ scores have been partialed out of these correlations.
* = $p \leq .10$.   ** = $p \leq .05$.   *** = $p \leq .01$.

lectual orientation in the mother–adolescent, father–adolescent, and mother–father dyad, the higher the adolescent's achievement score. The entire family score is also positively related to academic achievement. Although little can be made of the average correlation, it should be noted that the more family members' views included, the higher the relation between intellectual orientation and achievement.

For disagreement about the family's intellectual orientation and academic achievement, there are few significant findings. One interesting result is that

TABLE 3.2
Correlations Between Measures of Family Intellectual
Orientation and NCE Total Achievement

Individual	Amount			Disagreement		
	Girls	*Boys*	*Total*	*Girls*	*Boys*	*Total*
Adolescent	.25	.27	.27**	—	—	—
Mother	.30**	.42***	.35****	—	—	—
Father	.30	.21	.29***	—	—	—
Dyads						
Adol-Mother	.32**	.40***	.36****	−.13	.00	−.04
Adol-Father	.35**	.29*	.35****	−.28*	−.02	−.15
Mother-Father	.37***	.34**	.38****	−.28*	.24	−.02
Family						
Adol-Mother-Father	.37***	.37**	.40****	.32**	.11	.11

Note. The IQ scores have been partialed out of these correlations.
* = $p \leq .10$.   ** = $p \leq .05$.   **** = $p \leq .01$.   **** = $p \leq .001$.

there are more significant findings for girls as compared to boys. In particular, for girls, poorer academic achievement is associated with higher entire family disagreement. There are also trends for mother–father and father–daughter disagreement to be related to daughters' poorer academic achievement.

Gender Differences in Reading and Math Achievement

Gender differences have been noted in particular areas of academic achievement related to language and quantitative skills (Klebanov & Brooks-Gunn, 1992). Such differences emerge most clearly in early adolescence when pressure to adhere to sex-role stereotypes can intensify (Hill & Lynch, 1983; Paikoff & Brooks-Gunn, 1991). Consequently, in addition to the total achievement score, we decided to examine the extent to which the amount of the family's intellectual orientation, as well as the disagreement between family members about these orientations, were related to reading and math achievement.

There are gender differences in the relation between the amount of intellectual orientation in the family and reading achievement. Figure 3.1 presents the correlations, with IQ partialed out, between the individual, dyadic, and entire family amount measures of intellectual orientation and reading achievement by sex of the adolescents. As can be seen in Fig. 3.1, the results for girls are consistent across the individual, dyadic, and entire family amount measures of intellectual orientation. For girls only, higher reading achieve-

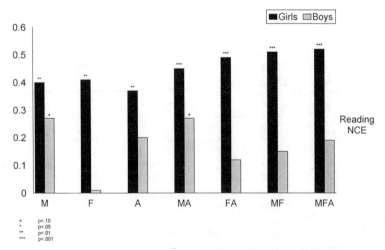

FIG. 3.1. Correlations with IQ partialed out between amount of intellectual orientation and reading achievement. M - mother, F - father, A - adolescent, MA - mother-adolescent, FA - father-adolescent, MFA - mother-father-adolescent.

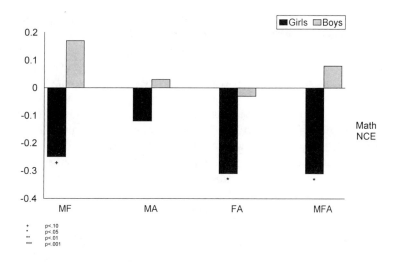

FIG. 3.2. Correlations with IQ partialed out between intellectual orientation disagreement and math achievement. MF - mother-father, MA - mother-adolescent, FA - father-adolescent, MFA - mother-father-adolescent.

ment is significantly related to higher amounts of intellectual orientation in the family. In contrast, none of the amount scores are significantly related to math achievement for girls or boys.

Figure 3.2 presents the correlations, with IQ partialed out, between the dyadic and entire family disagreement measures and math achievement by sex of the adolescents. Although disagreement about the family's intellectual orientation shows no relation to reading achievement, disagreement scores are negatively related to math achievement. Again, the significant findings are for girls, but not boys. In particular, the higher the disagreement between fathers and daughters, and for the entire family disagreement as well, the lower the math achievement. There is also a trend in the same direction for disagreement between mothers and fathers and their daughters' lower math achievement.

Individual, Dyadic, and the Aggregate Views of the Family

Asking family members about their experiences in their families is a way to directly learn about family life. Considering individual family members, dyads, and the entire family's view is an approach likely to yield a complex picture of the family system and its relation to the adolescent's competence. The results of this approach provide little support for the idea that an aggregate, or entire family, measure compared to individual's or dyad's views are more related to the adolescent's behavior. In fact, the entire family's view of intellectual orientation is only marginally more related to school competence than are individual or dyadic measures. Although the aggregate of family views about intellectual orientation does not provide stronger predictive power, it may be the case that in other areas of adolescent competence, family—as compared to individual or dyadic measures—yields significant results. What we hope to demonstrate is the need for, and one way of, considering multiple measures of family functioning in order to obtain a more comprehensive picture of factors related to children's development.

For intellectual orientation and school competence, it appears that dyads yield the most consistently significant results. This is particularly true for adolescent–parent dyads. In contrast to the parent–adolescent dyads, the mother–father dyad yields few findings. This is not to say that disagreement in this dyad is not related to adolescent development. Other research about families has shown mother–father and wife–husband conflict to be negatively related to adolescent outcomes (Grych & Fincham, 1993; Hetherington & Clingempeel, 1992). However, in this sample the amount of disagreement between mothers and fathers was relatively minor, and thus, it was unlikely to contribute to adolescent school competence. In addition, it is more difficult to observe the subtle influences of indirect effects. We found this to be the case, using observation of these families in early childhood (Lewis & Feiring, 1992).

The amount of intellectual activities and differences in family member's views of how characteristic such activities are of family life appear important for the adolescent's school competence. A greater amount of intellectual activity, especially as perceived by parents, seems to foster the adolescent's school competence. Clearly, an intellectual family environment provides the kinds of cognitive stimulation and daily experiences that are compatible with the development of skills necessary for school success. After reviewing the findings, it is clear that mothers play an important role in fostering the intellectual orientation of the family and that this kind of family environment facilitates adolescent achievement. Our previous work on these families showed mothers to be important for facilitating information exchange between family members and for fostering intellectual growth in early childhood (Feiring & Lewis, 1987; Lewis & Feiring, 1982). Fathers' perceptions of the family's intellectual orientation appear to be more strongly related to their daughters', than to their sons', academic achievements. Even when adolescents agree with parents about the importance of school success, parents may be the ones to emphasize and stress the family's intellectual activities at a time when the adolescent's attention may be drawn to other issues, such as popularity with same- and other-sex friends (Brown, 1990). Disagreement among family members concerning the family's intellectual orientation is important for understanding academic achievement. Disagreement, whether between parents and children or among members of the entire family, is related to poorer performance in school, although this is evidently more the case for girls than for boys.

It is not surprising that various family members experience the family in different ways, and different views have varied relations to adolescent competence. That views of the family are inconsistent across family members raises an important issue for understanding the family system. It is assumed that families possess characteristics by which they can be portrayed. The relations between individual, dyadic, and family views of the family's intellectual orientation reveal relatively little consistency. For the amount of intellectual orientation, the association among individual members' views, although significant, accounted for limited variance (mother–adolescent, $r = .53$, $p = .0001$; father–adolescent, $r = .28$, $p = .01$; mother–father, $r = .39$, $p = .001$). Interestingly, the mother–adolescent correlation is stronger than the father–adolescent or mother–father correlations, suggesting that mothers and adolescents share the most similar view of the family's intellectual orientation. The correlations among the disagreement scores also demonstrate the divergent aspect of family member's views. For example, mother–father disagreement is not related to mother–adolescent disagreement ($r = .12$) and is only weakly related to father–adolescent disagreement ($r = .33$, $p = .01$). The association between adolescent–mother and adolescent–father disagreement scores is also quite modest ($r = .40$, $p = .001$). Our findings, as well as those of Larson and Richards (1994) about daily family dynamics, make it clear that the family cannot be portrayed as a single entity, but must be defined by multiple viewpoints. If families cannot be described as possessing a particular characteristic, perceived consistently across family members, then understanding the functioning of the family system and its relation to adolescent competence requires consideration of each member's view.

Our emphasis on the need to characterize the family by multiple viewpoints is directly parallel to the issue in developmental psychopathology regarding the differences that exist among raters of child or adolescent psychopathology (e.g., Feiring & Lewis, 1996; Stanger & Lewis, 1993). There is evidence that different observers base their judgments on different facets of the child's functioning (Routh, 1990). For example, Kazdin, Moser, Colbus, and Bell (1985) showed that parents and children emphasize different aspects of the child's functioning. Children focused on internal feelings and expectancies for the future, whereas parents focused on the child's overt social behavior and observable manifestations of affect. Family members' differing viewpoints of the family also may result from emphasizing different aspects of family functioning and activities. As children enter adolescence, they become more likely to perceive negative events involving parents and siblings, whereas parent's perceptions of negative family events do not change very much (Larson & Ham, 1993). In general, the present approach to examining the family system, taking into account the multiple viewpoints of family members and differences in these viewpoints, revealed a number of interesting relations in the family systems functioning for the domain of intellectual activities and adolescent school competence.

Gender Differences in Family Life

Differing views of the family's intellectual life between parent and adolescent were consistently related to adolescent girl's school competence. Disagreement between parents and their daughters is negatively related to school competence and may constitute one of several factors in and outside the family that accumulate in early adolescence to make girls vulnerable. Reviewing the findings on disagreement and school competence, it is quite striking that for girls, but not for boys, disagreement about the family's intellectual orientation is related to negative outcomes. Although the amount of intellectual orientation is po itively related to school competence for both sexes, girls appear to be particularly vulnerable to disagreement among family members. Disagreement between parents and their daughters is notable for its relation to less success in school. Other researchers found that adolescents who have poor relationships with their parents have lower grades and exhibit more behavior problems (Forehand, Long, Brody, & Fauber, 1986; Simmons & Blyth, 1987).

In the family system, research suggests that adolescent girl's behavior and development is more sensitive to other family members' behavior. For example, based on observed family interactions, the work of Grotevant and Cooper (1985, 1986; Cooper, Grotevant, & Condon, 1983) illustrated how family interactions, related to such processes as self-assertion and mutuality, are related differentially by sex to adolescent development. For boys, it is only the father–son subsystem that is important. For girls, development is related to interactions in father–adolescent, mother–adolescent, mother–father, and adolescent–sibling relationships. Several theorists have suggested that social relations are more central for girls' behavior and competencies than boys (Archer, 1985; Gilligan, 1982).

Early adolescence is a particularly vulnerable time for adolescent girls' susceptibility to differences in family members' points of view about family functioning. Girls become more aware of such differences at this time due to cognitive changes. Selman (1980) suggested that young adolescents become capable of holding the perspective of two individuals in mind simultaneously and of viewing the two perspectives as exerting influence on one another in a reciprocal social relationship. Being more capable of recognizing differences in family members' viewpoints, young adolescent girls also may experience more tension as the result of this awareness. This is because girls feel increased pressure to behave as social leaders in the family and they are encouraged to adopt the feminine role of diminishing conflicts and striving for conciliation and compliance (Gilligan, 1982; Hill & Lynch, 1983). Awareness of differences among family members may be stressful for young adolescent girls and such stress may have negative consequences for their school competence. It also may be the case that such family stress, even if mild, in combination with other life changes that may be perceived as negative at this time (e.g., changes of puberty and school structure) can have a cumulative negative effect on girls' school competence (Simmons & Blyth, 1987).

In summary, characterizing the family system, whether from an individual, dyadic, or aggregate perspective, is an instructive approach for describing multiple views of family functioning. Even during early adolescence, when daily hassles and bickering are more typical, parents and offspring remain invested in the family as a unit with shared values and interests. Our findings indicate that when adolescents and their parents view intellectual activities as an important part of family functioning, adolescents are more likely to be performing well at school. Disagreement about the importance of the family's intellectual orientation can have negative consequences for school functioning, especially for girls. Thus, from multiple perspectives of the family's intellectual functioning, there exist numerous linkages to the adolescent's competence in the school context. Our work, as well as that of Cook and Goldstein (1993), provide further support for the idea that family members are a rich source of information about the family system and that self-report data about the entire family system's functioning, from the perspective of multiple family members, holds particular promise for future research on the development of competence in the family context.

REFERENCES

Achenbach, T. M. (1991). *Manual for the teacher's report form and 1991 TRF profile*. Burlington: University of Vermont.

Archer, S. L. (1985). Identity and choice of social roles. In A. S. Waterman (Ed.), *Identity in adolescence: Processes and contents* (pp. 79–100). San Francisco: Jossey-Bass.

Bachman, J. G., Johnston, L. D., & O'Malley, P. M. (1987). *Monitoring the future: Questionnaire responses from the nation's high school seniors, 1986*. Ann Arbor: University of Michigan, Institute for Social Research.

Brown, B. B. (1990). Peer groups and peer cultures. In S. S. Feldman & G. R. Elliott (Eds.), *At the threshold: The developing adolescent* (pp. 171–196). Cambridge, MA: Harvard University Press.

Brown, B. B., Mounts, N., Lamborn, S. D., & Steinberg, L. (1993). Parenting practices and peer group affiliation in adolescence. *Child Development, 64*, 467–482.

Buhrmester, D., & Furman, W. (1987). The development of companionship and intimacy. *Child Development, 58*, 1101–1113.

Collins, W. A. (1990). Parent–child relationships in the transition to adolescence: Continuity and change in interaction, affect, and cognition. In R. Montemayor, G. R. Adams, &

T. P. Gullota (Eds.), *From childhood to adolescence: A transitional period?* (pp. 85–106). Beverly Hills, CA: Sage.

Collins, W. A., & Laursen, B. (1992). Conflict and the transition to adolescence. In C. U. Shantz & W. W. Hartup (Eds.), *Conflict in child and adolescent development* (pp. 216–241). New York: Cambridge University Press.

Collins, W. A., & Russell, G. (1991). Mother–child and father–child relationships in middle childhood and adolescence: A development analysis. *Development Review, 11*, 99–136.

Cook, W. L., & Goldstein, M. J. (1993). Multiple perspectives on family relationships: A latent variables model. *Child Development, 64*(5), 1377–1388.

Cooper, C. R., Grotevant, H. D., & Condon, S. M. (1983). Individuality and connectedness in the family as a context for adolescent identity formation and role taking skill. In H. D. Grotevant & C. R. Cooper (Eds.), *Adolescent development in the family: New directions for child development* (pp. 43–59). San Francisco: Jossey-Bass.

Csikszentmihalyi, M., & Larson, R. (1984). *Being adolescent: Conflict and growth in the teenage years.* New York: Basic Books.

Demo, D. H., & Acock, A. C. (1996). Family structure, family process, and adolescent well-being. *Journal of Research on Adolescence, 6*(4), 457–488.

Dornbusch, S. M., Ritter, P. L., Leiderman, P. H., Roberts, D. F., & Fraleigh, M. J. (1987). The relation of parenting style to adolescent school performance. *Child Development, 58*, 1244–1257.

Entwisle, D. R. (1990). Schools and the adolescent. In S. S. Feldman & G. R. Elliott (Eds.), *At the threshold: The developing adolescent* (pp. 197–224). Cambridge, MA: Harvard University Press.

Feiring, C., & Lewis, M. (1982). Early mother–child interaction: Families with only and firstborn children. In G. L. Fox (Ed.), *The childbearing decision: Fertility attitudes and behavior* (pp. 179–196). Beverly Hills, CA: Sage.

Feiring, C., & Lewis, M. (1987). The ecology of some middle class families at dinner. *International Journal of Behavioral Development, 10*(3), 377–390.

Feiring, C., & Lewis, M. (1991). The transition from middle childhood to early adolescence: Sex differences in the social network and perceived self-competence. *Sex Roles, 24*(7/8), 489–509.

Feiring, C., & Lewis, M. (1996). Finality in the eye of the beholder: Multiple sources, multiple time points, multiple paths. *Development and Psychopathology, 8*, 721–733.

Forehand, R., Long, N., Brody, G. H., & Fauber, R. (1986). Home predictors of young adolescents' school behavior and academic performance. *Child Development, 57*, 1528–1533.

Fuligni, A. J., & Eccles, J. S. (1993). Perceived parent–child relationships and early adolescents' orientation toward peers. *Developmental Psychology, 29*(4), 622–632.

Furman, W., & Buhrmester, D. (1992). Age and sex differences in perceptions of networks of personal relationships. *Child Development, 63*, 103–115.

Gecas, V., & Seff, M. A. (1990). Families and adolescents: A review of the 1980s. *Journal of Marriage and the Family, 52*, 941–958.

Gilligan, C. (1982). *In a different voice: Psychological theory and women's development.* Cambridge, MA: Harvard University Press.

Grotevant, H. D., & Cooper, C. R. (1985). Patterns of interaction in family relationships and the development of identity exploration in adolescence. *Child Development, 56*, 415–428.

Grotevant, H. D., & Cooper, C. R. (1986). Individuation in family relationships: A perspective on individual differences in the development of identity and role-taking skill in adolescence. *Human Development, 29*, 82–100.

Grych, J. H., & Fincham, F. D. (1990). Marital conflict and children's adjustment: A cognitive-contextual framework. *Psychological Bulletin, 108*(2), 267–290.

Grych, J. H., & Fincham, F. D. (1993). Children's appraisals of marital conflict: Initial investigations of the cognitive-contextual framework. *Child Development, 64*, 215–230.

Hamilton, S. F. (1984). The secondary school in the ecology of adolescent development. In E. W. Gordon (Ed.), *Review of research in education, 11* (pp. 227–258). Washington, DC: American Educational Research Association.

Hauser, S. T., Powers, S. I., & Noam, G. G. (1991). *Adolescents and their families.* New York: The Free Press.

Hetherington, E. M., & Clingempeel, W. G. (1992). Coping with marital transitions: A family systems perspective. *Monographs of the Society for Research in Child Development, 57* (2–3, Serial No. 227).

Hill, J. P., & Lynch, M. E. (1983). The intensification of gender-related role expectations during early adolescence. In J. Brooks-Gunn & A. C. Peterson (Eds.), *Girls at puberty: Biological and psychosocial perspectives* (pp. 201–228). New York: Plenum.

Holmbeck, G., & Hill, J. (1991). Conflictive engagement, positive affect, and menarche in families with seventh-grade girls. *Child Development, 62,* 1030–1048.

Kazdin, A. E., Moser, J., Colbus, D., & Bell, R. (1985). Depressive symptoms among physically abused and psychiatrically disturbed children. *Journal of Abnormal Psychology, 94,* 298–307.

Klebanov, P. K., & Brooks-Gunn, J. (1992). Impact of maternal attitudes, girls' adjustment, and cognitive skills upon academic performance in middle and high school. *Journal of Research on Adolescence, 2*(1), 81–102.

Kupersmidt, J. B., & Coie, J. D. (1990). Preadolescent peer status, aggression, and school adjustment as predictors of externalizing problems in adolescence. *Child Development, 61,* 1350–1362.

Larson, R., & Asmussen, L. (1991). Anger, worry, and hurt in early adolescence: An enlarging world of negative emotions. In M. E. Colten & S. Gore (Eds.), *Adolescent stress, social relationships, and mental health* (pp. 21–41). New York: de Gruyter.

Larson, R. W., & Ham, M. (1993). Stress and "storm and stress" in adolescence: The relationship of negative events with dysphoric affect. *Developmental Psychology, 29,* 130–140.

Larson, R. W., Kubey, R., & Colletti, J. (1989). Changing channels: Early adolescent media choices and shifting investments in family and friends. *Journal of Youth and Adolescence, 18,* 583–600.

Larson, R. W., & Richards, M. H. (1991). Daily companionship in late childhood and early adolescence: Changing developmental contexts. *Child Development, 62,* 284–300.

Larson, R. W., & Richards, M. H. (1994). *Divergent realities: The emotional lives of mothers, fathers, and adolescents.* New York: Basic Books.

Laursen, B. (1995). Conflict and social interaction in adolescent relationships. *Journal of Research on Adolescence, 5*(1), 55–70.

Lewis, M., & Feiring, C. (1982). Some American families at dinner. In L. Laosa & I. Sigel (Eds.), *Families as learning environments for children* (pp. 115–145). New York: Plenum.

Lewis, M., & Feiring, C. (1992). Indirect and direct effects and family interaction at dinner. In S. Feinman (Ed.), *Social referencing and the social construction of reality in infancy* (pp. 111–134). New York: Plenum.

Lewis, M., Feiring, C., McGuffog, C., & Jaskir, J. (1984). Predicting psychopathology in six-year-olds from early social relations. *Child Development, 55,* 123–136.

Montemayor, R. (1983). Parents and adolescents in conflict: All families some of the time and some families most of the time. *Journal of Early Adolescence, 3,* 83–103.

Montemayor, R., & Hanson, E. (1985). A naturalistic view of conflict between adolescents and their parents and siblings. *Journal of Early Adolescence, 5,* 23–30.

Moos, R. H., & Moos, B. S. (1976). A typology of family social environments. *Family Process, 15*(4), 357–371.

Olson, D. H., McCubbin, H. I., Barnes, H. L., Larsen, A., Muxan, M. J., & Wilson, M. (1983). *Families: What makes them work.* Beverly Hills, CA: Sage.

Paikoff, R. L., & Brooks-Gunn, J. (1991). Do parent–child relationships change during puberty? *Psychological Bulletin, 110,* 47–66.

Parker, J. G., & Asher, S. R. (1987). Peer relations and later personal adjustment: Are low accepted children "at risk"? *Psychological Bulletin, 102*, 357–389.

Rosenthal, D. A., & Feldman, S. S. (1991). The influence of perceived family and personal factors on self-reported school performance of Chinese and Western high school students. *Journal of Research on Adolescence, 1*(2), 135–154.

Routh, D. K. (1990). Taxonomy in developmental psychopathology: Consider the source. In M. Lewis & S. M. Miller (Eds.), *Handbook of developmental psychopathology* (pp. 53–62). New York: Plenum.

Selman, R. (1980). *The growth of interpersonal understanding.* New York: Academic Press.

Simmons, R. G., & Blyth, D. A. (1987). *Moving into adolescence: The impact of pubertal change and school context.* Hawthorne, NY: de Gruyter.

Smetana, J. G. (1988a). Adolescents' and parents' conceptions of parental authority. *Child Development, 59*, 321–335.

Smetana, J. G. (1988b). Concepts of self and social convention: Adolescents' and parents' reasoning about hypothetical and actual family conflicts. In M. R. Gunnar & W. A. Collins (Eds.), *21st Minnesota Symposium on Child Psychology: Development during the transition to adolescence* (pp. 79–122). Hillsdale, NJ: Lawrence Erlbaum Associates.

Stanger, C., & Lewis, M. (1993). Agreement among parents, teachers, and children on internalizing and externalizing behavior problems. *Journal of Clinical Child Psychology, 22*, 106–115.

Steinberg, L. (1987). The impact of puberty on family relations: Effects of pubertal status and pubertal timing. *Developmental Psychology, 23*, 451–460.

Steinberg, L. (1989). Pubertal maturation and parent-adolescent distance: An evolutionary perspective. In G. Adams, R. Montemayor, & T. Gullotta (Eds.), *Advances in adolescent development: Vol. 1 (pp. 71–97). Beverly Hills, CA: Sage.*

Steinberg, L. (1990). Autonomy, conflict, and harmony in the family relationship. In S. S. Feldman & G. R. Elliott (Eds.), *At the threshold: The developing adolescent* (pp. 255–276). Cambridge, MA: Harvard University Press.

Steinberg, L., Lamborn, S. D., Dornbusch, S. M., & Darling, N. (1992). Impact of parenting practices on adolescent achievement: Authoritative parenting, school involvement, and encouragement to succeed. *Child Development, 63*, 1266–1281.

Steinberg, L., & Silverberg, S. B. (1986). The vicissitudes of autonomy in early adolescence. *Child Development, 57*, 841–851.

Stevenson, H. W., & Lee, S. (1990). Contexts of achievement. *Monographs of the Society for Research in Child Development, 55* (1–2, Serial No. 221).

Wechsler, D. (1974). *Manual for the Wechsler Intelligence Scale for Children-Revised.* San Antonio, TX: The Psychological Corporation.

Youniss, J., & Smollar, J. (1985). *Adolescent relations with mothers, fathers, and friends.* Chicago: University of Chicago Press.

4

▼▼▼▼▼▼▼

Effective Mothering in a Familial Context: A Nonhuman Primate Perspective

Leonard A. Rosenblum
State University of New York
Health Science Center at Brooklyn

A mother, or any other figure serving as principal caregiver for a developing, relatively helpless infant—the case in both human and nonhuman primates—plays many roles in furthering the survival of her child. Except under relatively atypical circumstances for the primates, the solitary rearing pattern of the orangutan, for example, this primary caregiving role is carried out and is shaped by the larger familial and social context in which it unfolds. The relatively cohesive, quite enduring, and largely consanguineal kinship unit and especially the mother–child relation represents a central feature for virtually all aspects of primate social and affective development. These broadly significant social complements notwithstanding, a considerable range of these diverse functions is expressed in the primates.

THE RELATIONSHIP OF DYADIC FUNCTION TO MATERNAL FITNESS

We consider these activities as parts of an articulated background for the discussion of several summary principles of fitness enhancement that compose the remainder of this chapter. One note of caution: This chapter is not intended to serve as a deconstructionist disquisition of our true understanding of the nature of mother–infant relations and development. I, therefore, forego any attempt to relieve certain words and phrases in common usage of their various connotative references. I hope the reader accepts this mea culpa as an acknowledgment of George Orwell's (1944/1968) admonition that "To write or even speak English is not a science but an art. There are no reliable words. . . ."

One basic, perhaps obvious, point bears mentioning at the outset. The inclusive fitness—the ultimate adaptability and developmental and reproductive success of an infant—depends on the level of effective adaptation at each of many points along the way. Whether in evolutionary or in contemporaneous terms, success of caregivers must be measured not merely by their negotiation of those particular points that have been singularly marked by human observers for various reasons such as birth, school attendance, or puberty. The ultimate success of the developing infant bears the imprint of each step taken by the caregiver, as well as the impact of other close kin, and in most cases, members of the larger social group. If we are to attempt understanding of those putative outcomes of development in which we are interested, we are forced to give consideration to each of these steps.

As the first aspect of her postpubertal contribution, adequate nutrition, avoidance of injury, and the safety afforded by social status in her group are attributes the mother-to-be brings to the critical process of mate selection. In this regard, in most primate groups, the consanguineal kinship group to which the mother belongs plays an important role in affecting her own social status. In general, members of more dominant families each hold more dominant status than they might otherwise obtain in their own right (e.g., Bernstein & Williams, 1983; Cheney, 1977; Rhine, Cox, & Costello, 1989). The female, of course, makes an immeasurably greater investment in the gestation, birth, and development of her baby than can be true of the male (this element is mitigated, but not completely obviated in pair-bonded, monogamous species such as the marmoset, and in some instances, the human). It is now generally recognized that because of this great difference in their respective expenditures in supporting the ontogeny of their offspring, it is generally up to the mother to ensure that the infant receives a blend of her own DNA and that of the most fit male partner. How that choice is made is often as obscure in the nonhuman primates as it is at the human level. Current studies show, for example, although high dominance status of males of group-living species tend to increase reproductive success, high dominance status alone does not necessarily ensure vastly disproportionate breeding outcomes (e.g., Ellis, 1995; Smith, 1994). Nevertheless, for the female, a poor choice means either unduly prolonged postnatal investment in a weakened offspring to the detriment of subsequent breeding success, diminished protection, and thus, endangerment of older offspring, the wasting of a precious pregnancy, or all three.

Maintaining the quality of the prenatal environment is the next major process that is of critical concern in terms of life or death and prosperity of the neonate. This prolonged task requires the mother's continued attention to the conditions she provides for the fetus, whether these entail extensively foraging to find the correctly balanced diet or avoiding excessive plant-containing or street-sold toxins. Delivery, initiation of nursing, achieving the skills needed to move about her environment, and conducting the requirements of the day, while transporting a dependent infant, must all be mastered in short order for this aspect of the passage to progress effectively.

SOCIAL COGNITION AND THE IMPORTANCE OF FAMILY SUPPORT

From the moment of its emergence from the vaginal canal, the infant must be provided with the constant, vigilant protection from the mother that preserves it from the vague threat of a foraging predator or the potential abuse of intensely interested members of the mother's own social group. Here again, the larger familial unit to which the mother belongs—each member of which holds varying degrees of genetic relatedness to the infant and thus varying degrees of fitness investment in it, plays an important role. Mothers are assisted in protection and retrieval of their young infant by sisters and even older prior offspring (Rosenblum, 1968). Moreover, because female nonhuman primates, like their human counterparts, often maintain strong life-long familial bonds, even the presence of grandmothers aid in early rearing success (Fairbanks, 1988, 1990). Similarly, as the infant moves in its first excursions away from her, protection from the pitfalls of an often precarious physical environment—the fall from tree limb to ground or exposure to the elements—are conditions of the physical environment attended to by the successful caregiver and her close kin. Through rapid forms of social learning via observation, in which so-called "prepared" stimuli are identified in the environment, the infant, guided particularly by the mother's own responses (Cook & Mineka, 1990), readily learns the sources of predatory danger. Other, more specific dangers of the immediate surroundings, about which the infant lacks genetic encoding or predisposition, can also be learned, albeit more gradually. This issue of factors affecting more specific learning by the infant, while under the protective cloak of maternal care, is considered later.

As already implied, the social environment for most primates, human and otherwise, is no less laden with potential danger than the physical universe as the youngster moves out into the social world around it. The human admonition, for example, to "never take food from a stranger," holds for the nonhuman primate as well. A naive disregard for the rules of the primate dominance game, when an infant grows past the groups' forebearing tolerance of infant status, might lead to the egregious error of attempting to take food from a dominant group member. Even a slight wound inflicted by an impatient adult can prove debilitating or even fatal to the young infant, thus potentially destroying its own and considerably diminishing it's mother's inclusive fitness. It is the successful mother's unceasing vigilance that allows her to make the swift intervention and departure with her infant that can save the day.

Finally, the caregiver's role involves not merely protection from the physical and social environment, but serves as the facilitating bridge that allows the developing infant to engage an expanding world of its own. During the period of infant carriage and conjoined locomotion, the mother introduces the infant to areas suitable for food, water, and safe sleep as well as the pathways through which they are most efficiently reached. The infant, in short, initially learns the features of its home range while in contact or close proximity with the mother.

Although lacking a means of conducting DNA analyses, or some unrecognized, more natural process of equal reliability in determining genetic relatedness, the infant nonetheless carries the need to differentiate close kin from others in its surroundings. Failure to learn such discriminations means that the infant, as it grows, might dissipate its energies, thus supporting competing genetic lines to the detriment of its own DNA complement and failing to elicit the parallel support of its own kinship group. Either or both of these failures in kin recognition and support may cause diminished representation of the infant's own genetic material, either directly through its own reduced reproduction, that of its close relatives, or both. Organisms that make such behavioral-genetic errors do not play for long in the evolution game because the pressure is to heighten the transmission of one's own hereditary material to subsequent generations, either through one's own reproductive success, or the enhanced reproductive success of one's close family members.

The first and perhaps most critical step in such kin differentiation is, of course, the ability to recognize the mother herself as the infant moves greater and greater distances from her. Although others may not harm, and may even assist at times, it is the mother who can be most reliably counted on to assist the infant in need, even when at risk to herself. It is she who has the most at stake in the baby's welfare and it is she who is most prepared to do, up to a point, whatever is necessary to preserve the infant. This identification process, requiring some months to complete, appears to proceed in union with the infant's developing locomotor capacity and its readiness to move away from the secure maternal base. Interestingly, clear differentiation of mother from nonmother seems to require the infant's repeated opportunity to interact with nonmaternal figures. Infants in our laboratory, for example, raised with their mothers alone, failed to respond selectively to her under controlled conditions even as late as 8 to 12 months of age, whereas infants reared in groups or with one or two other females present demonstrate clear recognition by about 3 months of age (Rosenblum & Alpert, 1977). The mother's vigilance notwithstanding, the ability to distinguish mother from nonmother is critical to the infant's continued safety, as a move in the wrong direction at times of social conflict or other rapidly emerging danger could prove disastrous.

FAMILY FORMATION AND MAINTENANCE

The Important Sex Differences

It is also crucial that the infant be able to distinguish other close kin from nonkin. Because of the nature of the social structure in most primate groups, those close relatives with whom the infant preferentially associates are usually part of the maternal lineage. Although by no means true of all primate groups (i.e., there are some instances in which females may migrate out of their natal group), in most cases, male primates, as they reach puberty, either at their own initiative or as a consequence of the social pressure from the adult males of their group, leave the group in which they were born. Those males who are not severely injured or killed in the process, after some period of further maturation, enter and spend the remainder of their lives in another social group. Males of the most dominant females of the group may remain, but in general the largest cohesive familial units in any given primate group are composed of intergenerational lines of females. Thus, in generating these critical kinship relationships, vital to inclusive fitness, the infant develops selective bonds with those juveniles and adults who stay close to its own mother and who are allowed considerable access to her and the baby. In general, these family members with whom the developing infant most closely associates are its female relatives. In the case of certain subspecies of squirrel monkey, for example, even the adult males in its natal group have little or no contact with the young infant because the males of the group remain quite apart from the female groupings in this sexually segregated species (Coe & Rosenblum, 1974). It seems most likely that sustained propinquity and access, mediated by the mother, serve as a behavioral filter for the developing infant, who distinguishes those close as kin and those further away as of diminishing genetic relatedness. The mother, serving as the hub of a wheel, surrounded by prior offspring and other close relatives, models for the infant the critical kin–nonkin differentiation.

The Father's Role

Pair bonding or *harem* situations (in which a single adult male exclusively mates and associates with a small group of females) in some species means that higher levels of contact with the paternal kinship grouping is seen than are typical of other species of primates. Thus, when paternity is relatively clear or when breeding males are themselves closely related, paternal involvement with the infant may increase. In the bonnet macaque, although the data are not substantial, it appears that under natural conditions, out-migration of males is not prominent, and males in a social group may be closely related family members. Hence, one sees relatively gregarious relationships among adult males, and because any infant of the group carries a substantial genetic relatedness to each of the related males of the group, one sees considerable levels of paternal response to otherwise helpless infants (Rosenblum, 1971a). These variations notwithstanding, these paternal–kin associations may never reach levels that match the infant's emerging relationships in the maternal, largely female, family.

Although as it grows, the infant's social status depends heavily on the social standing of its mother and the remainder of its kinship group and it must attain a place of its own, both in the kinship group and in the larger social assemblage to which they all belong. In large measure, it is from observations of his or her mother's reactions to others in the group and their reactions to her and subsequently, their responses to the infant itself that the infant acquires a sense and experience of its status in the larger social aggregate.

THE MATERNAL DEMAND MATRIX
AND DEVELOPMENT OF INFANT COPING

One can differentiate the primary caregiver's activities into numerous other elements, but from any perspective, the sweep of caregiver responsibility— what we termed the "Maternal Demand Matrix"—is quite extraordinary. One is reminded of the old Yiddish saying that, "God could not be everywhere and so he made mothers." To be sure, the parsing of the matrix of maternal responsibility previously outlined is certainly arbitrary. However, regardless of the level of discourse or the basis of categorization, one essential point is important to remember. Although the adient behaviors of both infant and caregivers gradually decline (and certain behaviors such as nursing or carriage drop out), in general, the supportive, protective role of the mother does not completely disappear, even when subsequent offspring appear. Indeed, as previously described, for those offspring, most generally the females who may remain in the mother's social group as they fully mature, a parental and even grandparental role may be maintained throughout life (Fairbanks, 1988).

Enhancing the initiation and maintenance of the physical well-being of their offspring can thus be seen as a continuous, often quite demanding undertaking for the principal caregiver and any helpers she might have. Yet, for any primate species in which the female, at least, produces relatively few offspring in her lifetime, another equally complex and demanding parental objective must be met: that of ensuring the infant an efficient, flexible capacity to cope psychologically and behaviorally with his or her lifetime environment.

BASIC NEEDS OF THE YOUNG INFANT

The obvious success of the primates (or some of them at least) tells us something. Except for various rodents, we are, after all, the most widely dispersed of the mammals. The considerable time and energy potentially available for investment of parents in their infrequent individual offspring can apparently be put to very good use. These resources can be used by primate caregivers to provide their genetically well-endowed offspring an experiential base through which they can learn the skills necessary for effective coping with the particular environmental demands with which they are increasingly faced. To accomplish this developmental objective, there are several fundamental principles to which the primary caregiver(s), aided by those with relatively high, congruent genetic investment (i.e., other close family members) must adhere.

Principle 1: The Modulation of Arousal

In addition to many other factors that may influence the effectiveness with which the infant employs its early experience as the basis of later coping skills, one principle is paramount. There is a level of central arousal that optimizes an organism's capacity to learn efficiently. Given my purposes in this chapter, I continue to speak here as a behaviorist, not as a zealously reductionist neuroscientist. Therefore, I refer, in this context, to a generalized behavioral state of the organism, rather than to the specific level of motivation in the putatively relevant electrochemical activity in a particular nucleus, or in fact, without particular reference to the CNS (central nervous system) at all. This is not to deny a material universe, of course. Certainly, motivational processes, such as those relating to hunger or sexual arousal, and presumably the activity of particular domains of the CNS, are undoubtedly instrumental in producing the fluctuating central state to which I refer. Regardless of how we categorize the neurochemical and behavioral elements that allow us all to agree on an objective assessment of arousal, following the precepts of the hoary Yerkes–Dodson Law: when these arousal levels are too high, the capacity for learning more complex tasks diminishes. Thus, a monkey may well be stimulated to learn a simple, food-reinforced, black–white discrimination task under conditions of considerable food deprivation. Yet, the same high level of arousal evoked by various paths impedes learning of a more difficult problem—say the differences between the visual appearance of a family member and of some other adult female of the group. By the same token, a satiated animal, or one exhausted from a prolonged journey or difficult encounter, encountering a low incentive reward (external stimuli are an obvious source of arousal) may not be sufficiently interested (aroused) enough to focus in on the problem. In the same fashion, a slightly nervous apprehensive state may allow learning of multiple escape paths (both physical and psychological), whereas a state of absolute terror is likely to interfere with the same critical process.

To the degree that this arousal–learning relationship holds, it is critical that the developing infant, as much as possible, be brought to or maintained in a state of arousal that facilitates the diverse types of complex learning necessary for immediate and long-term success. The mother primate must accomplish this goal in a variety of circumstances. Let me discuss one that is particularly important in some further detail. As infants begin to be able to locomote on their own, they spend increasing periods of time, further and further from the caregiver. How that increase in time away is accomplished, and the state the infant is in as those intervals and distances increase, is critical to the ultimately adaptive—or maladaptive—sequelae of those excursions. Under optimal conditions, the infant leaves the caregiver when it is awake and alert and its emotional state is sufficiently calm to allow discrimination and assessment of salient features of its immediate surround. Certainly, the caregiver herself, in an appropriate affective state to evaluate the current conditions and her offspring's state, encourages this step through her own behavior. Once contact is broken, the arousal state of the infant must rule the day if it is to return from its excursion enriched by a furtherance of its learning about the physical and social environment and its own capacity to interact with it positively. Here again, the role of close family members plays a significant facilitating role. Siblings serve as the earliest companions and play partners of the youngest infants. Family members coalesce in protecting an infant from danger. In the squirrel monkey, for example, sisters or older female offspring of the mother act as aunts to a young infant, actively supplementing the caregiving behavior of the mother, and so, may accompany the early excursions of the infant, retrieving the frightened infant if they are the ones closest at hand, comforting and transporting the infant from danger before it is transferred to the back of the biological mother (Rosenblum, 1968). In the pair-bonded marmoset, the father actually serves as the primary retriever and transporter of the infants (usually there are twins in this species) after the first several weeks of life, transferring the infants to the mother only for nursing (Taub & Mehlman, 1991).

Should the infant grow afraid or should its hunger or thirst increase too much (unless the infant has the opportunity to reduce these tensions through reassertion of soothing contact with a caregiver) the positive shape of the learning curve dramatically shifts. Either nothing of immediate or general value is acquired or even worse, when excessive arousal results in poorly chosen responses, maladaptive patterns, perhaps even those that are sufficient to achieve an immediate goal, but less efficient in the long run, may be enhanced. Particularly with regard to the elusive sense of efficacy or mastery—the sense that positive objectives can be achieved by the infant through its own behavior—may be damaged or may fail to develop at all (Jordan, Coe, Patterson, & Levine, 1989). To optimize the infant's effective coping with the environment that it confronts at present and will confront in the future as well, the vigilant caregiver must provide ready contact and soothing when the infant seeks it and must be ready to initiate contact and soothing herself when the infant is perceived by the caregiver as having shifted to adversely high arousal levels.

Clearly, the caregiver's own perception and judgment of the situation is critical and is one of those conditions in which the more experienced care-giver's assessment may be of particular value. The overreactive caregiver, perhaps as a result of her own anxiety level, may misinterpret both the situation and the infant's response level and may adversely affect both the infant's arousal and learning opportunities, thus perpetuating intergenera-tionally a pattern of inadequate coping. It is clear that in nonhuman, as well as human, primates, the time that an infant spends away from its caregiver in a given situation provides no clear measure of the infant's developing capacity for independent functioning (Rosenblum, 1971b). Any caregiver, given repeated infant-training opportunities, can ensure, through deed or word, that an infant quickly moves from her often. Yet, as we all unfortunately realize, in both human and nonhuman primates, that is no measure of the infant's wish or readiness to be apart from the caregiver, nor is that any indication of how effectively independent the infant will become in the years ahead. I have seen monkey mothers of 1-day-old infants leave them screaming on the ground while they went to feed, and I have seen others of the same species who rarely let their infants out of their grasp 3 or 4 months later. Neither type of infant was in a good position to learn (as early as it might have), what it needed to know about its social group or its environment's little secrets. In a controlled laboratory setting, of course, neither survival nor subsequent breeding success is at stake in these developmental variations, but under more natural conditions, for whichever the primate species with which one is concerned, failures to learn, and to learn on time, can be quite costly.

Principle 2: The Mitigation of Environmental Uncertainty

It is appropriate that this section begins with a confession to a perhaps now-outdated belief. This belief holds that the young infant gains its earliest and strongest sense of the nature of the universe in which it lives and the nature of its own relationship to it from its relationship to its primary caregiver. To be sure, the more exclusive and overwhelming the primariness of the caregiver, the more this early model is potentiated. Complete exclusivity occurs rarely, of course. The more that others, including fathers, grandpar-ents, aunts, siblings, and other family members play critical roles in rearing an infant, the more their patterns of interaction with the infant and between themselves (Lewis & Rosenblum, 1979; Rosenblum, 1974) add to the infant's developing sense of itself and the world around it. The more that subsequent experiences are able to compete with those early interactive patterns that relate to the infant, the more these early expectations may be altered. Primacy certainly gives way to recency. Removing the dominant male from a group rapidly provokes a reassessment of the social realities and allow a previously subordinant group member, perhaps even one born to the role, to assert dominance. Changes in the status of a brother or son may affect the status of the entire family grouping, and this change in a family's status may change an infant's access to incentives and the responses of other group members to it (Rhine et al., 1989). Once again, whether one enters the discourse at a behavioral or more reductionist level, the earlier psychological structures are often difficult to overturn.

Certainly, in the case of the nonhuman primate, it is the mother, through her interactions with the infant, who plays the central role of model. It is my view that if the infant is to develop that sense of efficacy or mastery mentioned earlier, the infant must perceive its mother's reactions to it to be predictive and reliable. The infant's experiences of the predictability of critical environmental events, whether they involve milk from the suckled breast or enclosure of the mother's arms on return from afar, are the elements on which the infant's experience of an at least partially controllable world depend. Certainly, much of life, in and out of the dyad, is, for the infant as well as for the adult, uncertain at best and chaotic at times. Still, I believe that a core of particularly salient survival activities should be generally predictive if that infant is to develop any abiding sense of relative mastery and to undergo the neurodevelopmental progress that mediates effective psychological and affective functioning in the face of future challenges. Given what we know about the resistance to extinction of intermittently reinforced behaviors, a sufficiently reinforced sense of predictability and hence controllability seems likely to survive considerable periods of slackened support. Yet, I contend that if certain of these caregiver responses to pressing infant needs do not reach some critical threshold of perceivable predictability, adverse developmental consequences inevitably ensue. The infant's readiness, in a variety of situations, to carry out behaviors that might enhance its health, well-being, and subsequent adult success, however measured, is diminished. It is my view that primates, no less than organisms more genetically programmed in their repertoires of response, are stuck with Einstein's concern that the eternal mystery of the word is its comprehensibility. Substantial violations of that belief, particularly on the part of the principle caregiver, bodes ill for the developing infant.

We know relatively little about these necessary reinforcement contingencies at either the human or the nonhuman primate level. We may not even be certain what constitutes reinforcement of predictability. Consider the following example in monkeys. Sometime around the end of the first half year of life in the macaques, the mother begins her return to reproductive cyclicity in preparation for the next breeding cycle. The relatively unrestricted access to the breast and ventrum provided by the mother shifts to periods of active weaning, in which the infant's suckling mouth is, at times forcefully, removed from the breast. When surrounding conditions are responded to by mother as being sufficiently calm and safe, the mother may actively push the clinging infant from her ventrum. With a frequency that varies from mother to mother, as well as from situation to situation, the reluctant infant is lightly bitten on the head or arms to encourage it to release its hold and depart. However, regardless of the vigor with which the punitive behavior of the mother is initiated to encourage the infant's departure, immediate acceptance to the safety of her ventrum is provided when that same infant rushes to her in fright a moment later. The acceptance, at least during the early period of infant rejection, must be quite predictable under appropriate circumstances for the infant to avoid uncertainty when rapid return is required. The mother, regardless of her eager rejection under other circumstances, provides it. Incidentally, this relatively uniform response is abruptly changed when the ventrum is occupied by a subsequent offspring, perhaps facilitating the infant's strategy shift when frightened, to something other than a nipple in the mouth.

As mentioned, the mother's investment in the infant does not stop when the next offspring appears, but the prepared older infant must rather suddenly adapt to a rapid change in the mother's ready acceptance and full attention. She still defends her investment and hence her infant's well-being, but in ways that provide significant new challenges for the juvenile—from where and how do you sleep in safety to how to get to that tricky place in the environment when mother does not carry you.

Part of the pathway to these sustained readjustments in the dyadic relationship is paved by the everyday events that disrupt focused dyadic interaction. Whether a mother is foraging for food, engaged with her social partners or older offspring, or mating with a male, she must, at times, shift her attention away from her young offspring. For most mothers, as the infant grows, the duration of these disruptions in the infant's receipt of her undivided attention grow as well. It is evident that how these disruptions are handled by the mother is very important because strong survival responses in the infant, which are at the heart of Trivers' "parent–offspring conflict" (Trivers, 1974), are rapidly triggered by the perceived loss of the mother—whether loss of her body or merely her attention.

MECHANISMS FOR AROUSAL MODULATION, AND MITIGATION OF ENVIRONMENTAL UNCERTAINTY

Based on our studies of primate mothers who are required to forage for their food under laboratory conditions, I suggest that there are three basic behavioral sets in which mothers engage to modulate their infant's affective disturbance at separation and sustain the infant's sense of predictability and controllability (Rosenblum & Andrews, 1995). We labeled these patterns, "Preparation," "Amelioration," and "Compensation." By *preparation*, we mean any form of unusual behavior or discernible change in the characteristics of common forms (e.g., increasing rates of rejection), which precedes periods of imminent departure of the mother. Such behaviors serve to make significant disruptions in the ongoing dyadic relationship more predictable for the infant. *Amelioration*, on the other hand, represents any behaviors in which mothers engage that serve to reduce or modulate a disturbed infant's arousal during periods of dyadic disruption, and perhaps thereby enhance its ability to learn additional separation-coping skills. Finally, and perhaps most important, there is *compensation*. After periods of major disruption in her responsivity to the infant, such as might be involved in the search for food, mothers engage in unusually high levels of close dyadic contact and interaction, primarily in the form of ventral clinging and suckling. Before proceeding with a discussion of these patterns, it is worth noting that notwithstanding the somewhat confusing state of the human departure and separation data regarding what might be termed "preparation," to my knowledge, experimental support for only the third patten exists for nonhuman primates. In spite of the consideration of these mechanisms in the context of this discussion of maternal response to dyadic disturbances in monkeys, I suggest these patterns play a crucial role in the establishment and stabilization of dyadic bonding under a broad range of conditions and in many different species including our own.

Let me outline the type of experimental conditions from which I draw my current perspectives. In addition to various acute studies of foraging, we examined in detail the behavior of mothers and the subsequent development of their offspring under several types of chronic experimental foraging conditions. Food deprivation was not an issue in these studies. In essence, whereas all subjects had enough food available, the amount of time and effort they needed to expend in order to obtain that food was experimentally manipulated. Food was either always easy to find, always difficult to find, or was, in a fashion unpredictable to the animals (though apparent to us), changed repeatedly from easy to difficult and back again. The results of this series of studies have been quite dramatic (Rosenblum & Andrews, 1995). Most significant, the infants raised by mothers facing uncertain foraging conditions during the first half year of their lives, showed remarkably heightened levels of emotional disturbance during this rearing period. In several cases, overt signs of depression, or what some have termed "despair," was shown by young infants when their mothers were preoccupied with their foraging efforts. We never saw these sustained patterns of dropped posture, limp faces, closed eyes, and self-directed orality, other than when mothers were physically removed from the home pen and separation from the infant was complete (Rosenblum, 1984). I might add that we never saw this kind of response in bonnet macaque infants (the primary species used in these experiments) even when they were fully separated from mother. In addition to these early affective disturbances, these variable foraging demand (VFD) infants were more timid and fearful of leaving their mothers when placed with them in a complex novel environment during the second half year (Andrews & Rosenblum, 1994b). These test differences emerged several weeks after all animals were returned to the ad lib, "no demand," feeding conditions typical of nonexperimental lab conditions, in which condition they then remained. Subsequent evidence demonstrated that several years after final removal from the mother, as adolescents 3 years later, VFD infants were still more timid, less easily sociable, and consistently subordinate to their stable-environment counterparts. It was shown, as should be expected, that the early environment demonstrably affected not only behavior, but also underlying neurodevelopment, resulting in considerable differences between the stable- and variable-environment-reared infants in a variety of biochemical measures of brain activity. Both baseline and pharmacologically induced assessments showed striking differences in monoamine and neuropeptide function (Coplan et al., 1996; Rosenblum et al., 1994).

The obvious question emerges regarding the causes of these apparently permanent shifts in development. On the one hand, mothers in VFD conditions do not engage in systematically higher levels of punishment or rejection, at least during the portions of the day in which we are able to observe them. This seemed a likely hypothesis because in previous work, infants tended to react to periods of high maternal rejection with increased dependency rather than the reverse (Rosenblum, 1971b). On the other hand, we now have experimental evidence that suggests that one important difference between stable- and variable-environment mothers may lie in their readiness to engage in compensation behavior after foraging-induced disruptions. Whereas mothers in very easy environments have such brief foraging-related separations from their infants that we saw little overt compensation, mothers of more consistently difficult foraging conditions showed very high levels of dyadic contact after 1 to 2 hours of searching for food (Andrews & Rosenblum, 1994). In the VFD groups, however, the response was different and more variable. Compensation was somewhat lower overall, with some VFD mothers engaging in particularly low levels of this postdisruption pattern. Of course, as suggested at the start of this chapter, when and how this form of maternal compensation response is applied may be even more important than how much total attention the infant receives. Nonetheless, the evidence suggests that even in the VFD group, those whose mothers provided the least compensation behavior were most adversely affected in subsequent challenge tests. We have not as yet determined whether these same animals have particularly aberrant patterns of brain chemistry in comparison to other, less affected animals reared under conditions of uncertainty.

We have not as yet been able to find any consistent preparation differences between treatment groups. It is possible that each mother's signal to her infant, although quite distinguishable and learnable for the infant, might be too idiosyncratic for our ready identification of common patterns across mothers. The same may be said at this time to be true of potential ameliorative patterns.

Lest I leave the implication that mere difficulty for the mother is not a problem for her infant as long as the difficulty is constant, I should make clear that infants raised in consistently difficult foraging environments are also affected, albeit more subtly than seen in the VFD condition. It must be noted that the levels of foraging difficulty that we impose in the laboratory (which are far less than often confronted under natural conditions) are on the order of a few hours a day, and I have no doubt that considerably more severe foraging conditions, no matter how consistent, are likely to wreak havoc on those reared in it. Furthermore, when appropriately challenged, infants reared in difficult foraging conditions show less effective coping than those reared under easier conditions. Thus, when mother is lost, in those reared in consistent difficulty, affective disturbance is considerably greater and lasts considerably longer to the detriment of more normal social and exploratory patterns (Rosenblum & Plimpton, 1981). It is clear from these possibilities that we have a number of paths to follow in exploring these and other possible explanations for the adverse effects of being reared in a setting devoid of other family support and in which one's primary caregiver, and perhaps one's self, face an environment in which fundamental resources are unpredictable in their availability or access.

Principle 3: The Mediation of Kinship Relations

Of the third element of effective mothering, despite its significance, there exists the least systematic experimental confirmation of the ideas that many workers in human and nonhuman primate development share; that is, the role of the mother in mediating the establishment of connections with the infant's kinship group. Appreciation of the evolutionarily adaptive nature of preferential responsivity on the basis of relative kinship is among the most significant contributions of theoretical biology in the last 50 years. Getting as much of your DNA into the next generation as you can is the name of the evolutionary game, whether you are the immediate transmitter of the genetic material or whether some set of close relatives does it instead. As noted earlier, obviously lacking the grand techniques of modern DNA analysis, the infant primate essentially determines the boundaries of its family group via the relations of others with its mother. In a sense, propinquity equals consanguinity. Those juveniles, adolescents, and adults who spend considerable amounts of time in contact with, eating with, grooming, and being protected by (and perhaps protecting) the mother are those most likely to be responded to as kin. When times are tough, it is kin you accept and toward whom you are relatively permissive, and it is nonkin you attempt to repel. When an older member of the family goes up in dominance status, everyone gets a raise in status and the related privileges. When mother is lost or preoccupied, other members of the kinship group, particularly older sisters or aunts, protect or assist the stranded infant of their own family clan while rejecting any appeals for assistance from nonkin infants. Recent evidence shows that members of a large primate troop recognize specific relationships between other mothers and their respective offspring (Cheney & Seyfarth, 1990). When animals (usually males) leave their natal group, they ultimately join another troop that contains a previously emigrated member of their family. That these close, identifiable relationships even subserve a form of incest-avoidance mechanism, limiting the likelihood of matings between siblings and perhaps other close relatives, is another possible product of clear kin recognition.

It is difficult to see how these genetic kinship groups are able to identify the several generations of their membership were it not for the pivotal role of the mother. If selective relationships of offspring with their mother as they grow older were blocked, how might a coherent kinship group form and function? Other mechanisms, involving olfactory imprinting or some similar perceptual labeling processes, have been suggested of course, but alas, to date we have little more to say that can be backed by more than assumption and anecdote (Kaplan, Cubicciotti, & Redican, 1977). Clearly, we currently lack an appreciation of the constituent factors through which associations with the mother appear to permit the construction of functional kinship units. Nonetheless, it is my belief that the infant's relationship with the mother provides the prism through which the remainder of its social world can be refracted into its component kin and nonkin elements.

Although I recognize that the mother–infant dyad is embedded in a social nexus and that the adaptive tasks of the infant ultimately involve others, I remain strongly committed to the view of the special nature of the mother–child relation; it is she who modulates the child's arousal, she who mitigates environmental uncertainty, and she who mediates kinship relations.

REFERENCES

Andrews, M. W., & Rosenblum, L. A. (1994a). The development of affiliative and agonistic social patterns in reared monkeys. *Child Development, 65*, 1398–1404.

Andrews, M. W., & Rosenblum, L. A. (1994b). Developmental consequences of altered dyadic coping patterns in bonnet macaques. In J. J. Roeder, B. Thierry, J. R. Anderson, & N. Herrenschmidt (Eds.), *Current Primatology. Vol. II. Social development, learning and behaviour* (pp. 265–271). Strasbourg, France: Universite Louis Pasteur.

Bernstein, I. S., & Williams, L. S. (1983). Ontogenetic changes and the stability of rhesus monkey dominance relationships. *Behavioural Processes, 8*(4), 379–392.

Cheney, D. L. (1977). The acquisition of rank and the development of reciprocal alliances in free ranging immature baboons. *Behavioral Ecology & Sociobiology, 2*, 303–317.

Cheney, D. L., & Seyfarth, R. M. (1990). The representation of social relations by monkeys. Special Issue: Animal cognition. *Cognition, 37*(1–2), 167–196.

Coe, L. C., & Rosenblum, L. A. (1974). Sexual segregation and its ontogeny in squirrel monkey social structure. *Journal of Human Evolution, 3*, 551–561.

Cook, M., & Mineka, S. (1990). Selective associations in the observational conditioning of fear in rhesus monkeys. *Journal of Experimental Psychology: Animal Behavior Processes, 16*(4), 372–389.

Coplan, J. D., Andrews, M. W., Rosenblum, L. A., Owens, M. J., Friedman, S., Gorman, J. M., & Nemercoff, C. B. (1996). Persistent elevations of cerebrospinal fluid concentrations of corticotropin-releasing factor in adult nonhuman primates exposed to early-life stressors: Implications for the pathophysiology of mood and anxiety disorders. *Proceedings of the National Academy of Science, USA, 93*, 1619–1623.

Ellis, L. (1995). Dominance and reproductive success among nonhuman animals: A cross-species comparison. *Ethology and Sociobiology, 16*, 257–333.

Fairbanks, L. A. (1988). Vervet monkey grandmothers: Interactions with infant grandoffspring. *International Journal of Primatology, 9*(5), 425–441.

Fairbanks, L. A. (1990). Reciprocal benefits of allomothering for female vervet monkeys. *Animal Behaviour, 40*(3), 553–562.

Jordan, T. C., Coe, C. L., Patterson, J., & Levine, S. (1989). Predictability and coping with separation in infant squirrel monkeys. *Behavioral Neuroscience, 98*, 556–560.

Kaplan, J., Cubicciotti, D. D., III, & Redican, W. K. (1977). Olfactory discrimination of squirrel monkey mothers by their infants. *Developmental Psychobiology, 10*, 447–453.

Lewis, M., & Rosenblum, L. A. (Eds.). (1979). *The genesis of behavior: The child and its family*. New York: Plenum.

Orwell, G. (1968). The English people. In S. Orwell & I. Angus (Eds.), *The collected essays, journalism and letters of George Orwell* (Vol. 3). New York: Columbia University Press. (Original work published 1944)

Rhine, R. J., Cox, R. L., & Costello, M. B. (1989). A twenty-year study of long-term and temporary dominance relations among stump tailed macaques (Macaca arctoides). *American Journal of Primatology, 19*(2), 69–82.

Rosenblum, L. A. (1968). Mother–infant relations and early behavioral development in the squirrel monkey. In L. A. Rosenblum & R. W. Cooper (Eds.), *The squirrel monkey* (pp. 207–233). New York: Academic Press.

Rosenblum, L. A. (1971a). Kinship interaction patterns in pigtail and bonnet macaques. *Proceedings of the 3rd Congress of the International Primatological Society*. Basel, Switzerland: Karger.

Rosenblum, L. A. (1971b). The ontogeny of mother–infant relations in macaques. In H. Moltz (Ed.), *Ontogeny of Vertebrate Behavior* (pp.). New York: Academic Press.

Rosenblum, L. A. (1974). In M. Lewis & L. Rosenblum (Eds.), *The effect of the infant on its caregiver: The origins of behavior* (Vol. 1, pp.). New York: Wiley.

Rosenblum, L. A. (1984). Monkeys' responses o separation and loss. In M. Osterweis, F. Solomon, & M. Green (Eds.), *Bereavement: Reactions, consequences and care* (pp. 179–198). Washington, DC: National Academy Press.

Rosenblum, L. A., & Alpert, S. (1974). Fear of strangers and specificity of attachment in monkeys. In M. Lewis & L. A. Rosenblum (Eds.), *Origins of fear* (pp. 165–193). New York: Wiley.

Rosenblum, L. A., & Alpert, S. (1977). Response to mother and stranger: A first step in socialization in primates. In C. Poirier & M. Chevalier-Skolnikof (Eds.), *Socialization in primates* (pp. 463–478). New York: Aldine.

Rosenblum, L. A., & Andrews, M. W. (1995). Primate developmental models of stress. In M. Stein & A. Baum (Eds.), *Chronic Diseases* (pp. 97–113). Hillsdale, NJ: Lawrence Erlbaum Associates.

Rosenblum, L. A., Coplan, J. D., Friedman, S., Bassoff, T., Gorman, J. M., & Andrews, M. W. (1994). Adverse early experiences affect noradrenergic and serotonergic functioning in adult primates. *Biological Psychiatry, 35*, 221–227.

Rosenblum, L. A., & Plimpton, E. H. (1981). The infant's attempts to cope with separation. In M. Lewis & L. A. Rosenblum (Eds.), *The Uncommon Child* (pp. 225–257). New York: Plenum.

Smith, D. G. (1994). Male dominance and reproductive success in a captive group of rhesus macaques (*Macaca mulatta*). *Behaviour, 129*(3–4), 225–242.

Taub, D., & Mehlman, P. (1991). Primate paternalistic investment: A cross-species view. In J. D. Loy & C. B. Peters (Eds.), *Understanding behavior: What primate studies tell us about human behavior* (p. 264). New York: Oxford University Press.

Trivers, R. L. (1974). Parent-offspring conflict. *American Zoologist, 14*, 249–264.

5

▼▼▼▼▼▼▼

Family-Peer Relationships: Cognitive, Emotional, and Ecological Determinants

Ross D. Parke
Robin O'Neil
Susan Isley
Sue Spitzer
Mara Welsh
Shirley Wang
Mary Flyr
Sandi Simpkins
Christine Strand
Michael Morales
University of California, Riverside

Throughout the course of development, children's relationships with others move beyond their initial relationships with parents and other family members and come to include relationships in other social contexts, particularly the peer context. An issue that has intrigued developmental theorists over the last century concerns how children develop the knowledge and skills necessary to manage relationships with others. There is a great deal of research that suggests that children who adjust poorly to their peer groups are at risk for later social and academic problems. In their review, Parker and Asher (1987) noted that children who are socially rejected by their peers are at increased risk for a variety of difficulties including increased risk of school dropout, poorer academic performance, increased delinquency, and mental health problems.

Much research suggests that the family is a particularly salient context in which such knowledge and skills are socialized. Given the important role that experiences in the family context play in the development of social competence and the potential for such skills to generalize to other relationships, there has emerged considerable interest recently in understanding the links between children's relationships in multiple social contexts. Parke and colleagues (Parke, Burks, Carson, Neville, & Boyum, 1994; Parke, Cassidy, Burks, Carson, & Boyum, 1992) proposed a three-tiered model that represents the modes by which parents influence their children's peer relationships. First, parents are viewed as influencing their children's peer relationships through their childrearing practices and interactive styles. This first mode of influence on children's relationships with peers is often indirect because the parent's goal is not explicitly to modify or enhance children's relationships beyond the family. Second, this model suggests that parents directly influence children's peer relationships in their role as instructors or educators. Through such strategies as providing advice about managing peer relationships, supervising and assisting in early child–peer interactions, parents may explicitly set out to educate their children concerning appropriate behavioral strategies for interacting with peers. A third mode of influence is the management of children's social lives. In this role, parents serve as the gatekeepers or providers of opportunities for children to interact with peers and other extrafamilial social partners. Social access to peers is thought to provide essential opportunities to practice and refine the skills that develop in the context of the family.

Whereas the three modes of linkage provide a broad-brush overview of the role of parents as socializing agents, the model also suggests two critical sets of processes that may account for the development and transmission of skills from the family context to extrafamilial social contexts. The development of skills for understanding and regulating emotions and the development of cognitive models or representations of the meaning of social relationships to the individual are hypothesized to be key processes that mediate the direct links that are found between children's experiences in the family and the quality of their relationships with peers.

Over the last several years, considerable progress has been made in each of the three general domains of familial influence and considerable evidence has emerged in support of this model, particularly at the level of modes of influence. Moreover, recent studies are beginning to emerge that are detailing the processes that underlie these influences. In addition, the model has undergone refinement along a number of lines (Parke & O'Neil, 1996). For example, the model was extended to incorporate a systems approach in acknowledgment of the fact that children are exposed to other family subsystems beside the parent–child subsystem, including the parent–parent subsystem and child–sibling subsystems. Also, the model was expanded to incorporate a more ecological framework in recognition of the fact that families are embedded in a variety of external social systems including neighborhoods and communities which, in turn, influence the functioning of the family unit (Bronfenbrenner, 1979, 1989).

The first aim of the chapter is to provide a brief overview of the support for each of the three direct modes of linkage between family and peer systems, which we describe as Phase I research. A second goal is to review recent work that examines the processes that mediate the relations found between family and peer systems. According to our model, this work is defined as Phase II research. A third goal is to take a closer look at ecological factors such as children's neighborhoods and cultural variations in children's experiences that may moderate the links between these two social systems.

A final goal of the chapter is to describe findings from a longitudinal study designed to examine mediating and moderating influences on the familial antecedents of children's peer competence. The UCR Social Development project is a longitudinal study that was initiated in 1990 with the goal of understanding the links between children's experiences in their families during early and middle childhood and their developing social competence with peers, based on the tripartite model described by Parke and colleagues (1992, 1994). The sample in this study was generated using a two-staged procedure. In the first stage, approximately 800 kindergarten children from nine elementary schools in two Southern California communities were interviewed in order to determine children's level of social acceptance by peers. In the second phase of sampling, this sociometric information was used to select children of varying degrees of social acceptance, and the parents of these children were invited to participate in the laboratory assessment phase of the project. The ethnic distribution of the resulting sample of 116 families was approximately 55% Euro-American, 35% Hispanic American, and 10% other ethnicities including Asian and African American. Since 1991, children and their parents have participated in yearly assessments. The assessments in kindergarten through second grade included questionnaires and interviews as well as dyadic interaction tasks between children and their mothers and children and their fathers. In grades 3 through 5, the interaction tasks were augmented to include triadic tasks that involved children, mothers, and fathers, as well as a set of interaction tasks between children and a self-selected friend and an unacquainted peer.

PARENT–CHILD RELATIONSHIP—INTERACTION STYLE, SUPERVISION OF PEER INTERACTION, AND PARENT AS ADVISER: PHASE I RESEARCH FINDINGS

Parent–Child Interaction

A long tradition of research suggests that parents play a primary role in the development of children's competence with peers through their childrearing practices and interactive styles. Consistent with Baumrind's (1973) early classic studies, which found that authoritative parenting was related to positive peer outcomes, more recent studies confirmed that parents who are responsive, warm, and engaging are more likely to have children who are more accepted by their peers (Hinde & Tamplin, 1983; Putallaz, 1987). Further evidence suggests that high levels of positive synchrony and low levels of nonsynchrony in patterns of mother–child interaction are related to school adjustment rated by teachers, peers, and observers (Harrist, Pettit, Dodge, & Bates, 1994). In contrast, parents who are hostile, and overcontrolling have children who experience more difficulty with age-mates (Barth & Parke, 1993; MacDonald & Parke, 1984; Pettit, Dodge, & Brown, 1988).

Not only are differences in interactive style associated with children's social competence, but the nature of the emotional displays during parent–child interaction are important as well. The affective quality of the interactions of popular children and their parents differs from the interactions of rejected children and their parents. Consistently higher levels of positive affect have been found in both parents and children in popular dyads than in the rejected dyads (Burks, Carson, & Parke, 1987; Parke, MacDonald, Beitel, & Bhavnagri, 1988). More recently, Carson and Parke (1996) found that reciprocal, negative-affect exchanges on the part of fathers and pre-school-age children were associated with lower levels of social competence as rated by teachers, including lower levels of sharing, a greater tendency to avoid other children, and higher levels of teacher-rated verbal and physical aggression. It is particularly interesting that the links between reciprocation of negative affect and children's social competence were not evident among mother–child dyads. Taken together, these findings suggest that social interaction such as rough-and-tumble play with fathers may be an important means through which children learn to manage negative emotions in the context of social interactions with other partners. Similar evidence of a relation between peer acceptance and the type of affect expressions between fathers and children comes from a recent study by Boyum and Parke (1995), in which the affect expressions of mothers, fathers, and children during a family dinner were examined. These researchers found that children whose fathers directed more anger toward them were less well-accepted by their peers.

Links Between Affect Expression in the Context
of Parent–Child Play and Children's Social
Competence—Findings From the UCR Social
Development Project

Findings from the UCR Social Development Project add further evidence to a growing body of literature that suggests the affective quality of parents' relationships with their children is an important correlate of children's success in developing relationships with others. Among the kindergarten-aged children in our study, expressions of positive and negative affect by both mothers and fathers during physical play were linked to children's social competence in both kindergarten and 1 year later (Isley, O'Neil, & Parke, 1996).

A major goal of work on our project is to understand the extent to which parental affect has a direct versus an indirect impact on the development of children's level of social competence and acceptance by peers. In the model being examined on our project, variations in the balance of positive and negative affect expressed by parents might be expected to directly influence children's social competence by enhancing or disrupting key developmental processes that lead to competence with peers. In contrast, our model suggests that exposure to varying degrees of positive and negative parental affect might indirectly influence children's social competence by providing a model for the child's own emotional expressions, which over time, might influence the quality of relationships with others outside the family. Results of latent variable path analysis (Isley, O'Neil, Clatfelter, & Parke, 1997) suggest both direct and indirect influences of parental affect on children's affect expression and social competence. Interestingly, the expression of positive affect by parents appears to be linked indirectly to children's social competence and social acceptance through its influence of the expression of positive affect by children. In contrast, although the expression of negative affect by parents is not related to the expression of negative affect by children, it appears to be directly linked to social acceptance and social competence outcomes in kindergarten and first grade. Our data suggest that although young children may not reciprocate negative affect in play interactions with their parents, they may be modeling negative affect in other social contexts or developing patterns of emotional dysregulation that interfere with positive peer relationships.

Parental Instruction, Advice Giving, and Consultation. Learning about relationships through interaction with parents can be viewed as an indirect pathway because the goal is often not explicitly to influence children's social relationships with extrafamilial partners such as peers. In contrast, parents influence children's relationships directly in their roles as direct instructors, educators, or advisers. In this role, parents explicitly set out to educate their children concerning the appropriate manner of initiating and maintaining social relationships. Research that emerged over the last 10 years suggests that young children gain competence with peers when parents supervise and facilitate their experiences, whereas among older children, greater supervision and guidance on the part of parents of children's peer relationships may function more as a remediatory effort.

In a study of parental supervision, Bhavnagri and Parke (1991) found that children exhibited more cooperation and turn taking and had longer play bouts when assisted by an adult than when playing without assistance. Although both fathers and mothers were effective facilitators of their children's play with peers, under natural conditions, mothers are more likely to play this supervisory and facilitory role than are fathers (Bhavnagri & Parke, 1991; Ladd & Golter, 1988).

As children develop, the forms of management shift from direct involvement or supervision of the ongoing activities of children and their peers to a less public form of management, involving advice or consultation concerning appropriate ways of handling peer problems. This form of direct parental management has been termed consultation (Ladd, LeSieur, & Profilet, 1993) or decontextualized discussion (Lollis, Ross, & Tate, 1992). Russell and Finnie (1990) found that the quality of advice that mothers provided their children prior to entry into an ongoing play dyad varied as a function of children's sociometric status. Mothers of well-accepted children were more specific and helpful in the quality of advice that they provided. In contrast, mothers of poorly accepted children provided relatively ineffective kinds of verbal guidance, such as "have fun," or "stay out of trouble." The advice was too general to be of value to the children in their subsequent instructions.

Evidence also suggests that parental style of offering advice may also be an important factor. Pettit and Mize (1993) found that the content of maternal advice, as well as maternal style of interaction during the advice-giving session, made unique contributions to preschoolers' competence with peers, prompting the researchers to conclude that "children appear to benefit both from participation in a positive synchronous relationship and from being recipients of direct guidance and feedback regarding social relationships" (pp. 143–144).

Links Between Content and Style of Parental Advice
Giving and Children's Social Competence—Findings
From the UCR Social Development Project

Findings from the UCR Social Development Project offer further support for the role of both mothers' and fathers' advice giving and the development of children's social acceptance and competence with peers. In one phase of our study (O'Neil, Garcia, Zavala, & Wang, 1995), parents were asked to read to their third-grade child short stories that described common social themes (e.g., group entry, ambiguous provocation, and relational aggression) and to advise the child about the best way to handle each situation. High-quality advice was considered to be advice that promoted a positive, outgoing, social orientation on the part of the child rather than avoidance or aggressive responses. The findings tended to vary as a function of parent–child gender. Among father–son dyads and mother–daughter dyads, parental advice that was more appropriate and more structured was associated with less loneliness and greater social competence among children. Interestingly, when father–daughter dyads and mother–son dyads were the focus of analysis, higher quality advice about how to handle social conflict was associated with poorer teacher-rated social competence. However, in contrast to the gender-specific findings for the content of parental advice, the quality of parent–child interactions during the advice-giving session were positively related to children's social competence. Interestingly, other results from our study, based on a triadic advice-giving session in which mothers, fathers, and their third grader discussed how to handle problems that their child had when interacting with peers indicated that parental style of interaction appeared to be a better predictor of children's social competence than the actual solution quality generated in the advice-giving session (Wang & McDowell, 1996). Specifically, the controlling nature of fathers' style and the warmth and support expressed by mothers during the advice-giving task were significant predictors of both teacher and peer ratings of children's social competence.

The direction of effects in each of these studies, of course, are difficult to determine, and future models that explain links between parental management strategies and children's social development need to incorporate bidirectional processes. Under some circumstances, parents may be making proactive efforts to provide assistance to their children's social efforts, whereas under other circumstances, parents may be providing advice in response to children's social difficulties (see also Ladd & Golter, 1988; Mize, Pettit, & Brown, 1995). Overly involved or extremely specific parents, for example, may simply be responding to their children's poor social abilities. Alternatively, high levels of control may inhibit children's efforts to develop their own strategies for dealing with peer relations (Cohen, 1989).

In summary, a number of studies suggest that direct parental influence in the form of supervision and advice giving can significantly increase the interactive competence of young children and illustrates the utility of examining direct parental strategies as a way of teaching children about social relationships. As work continues to emerge in this area, however, the findings suggest not only that advice content and style of expressing advice or offering guidance are important components, but also that the role that supervision of peer relationships and advice giving play may vary over the course of children's development.

COGNITIVE AND EMOTIONAL MEDIATORS
OF RELATIONS BETWEEN FAMILY AND PEER
SOCIAL CONTEXTS—PHASE II RESEARCH FINDINGS

In a general sense, face-to-face interaction between parents and children, as well as parental supervision and guidance of children's relationships with peers, can be thought to provide the children with the opportunity to learn, rehearse, and refine social skills that are common to successful social interaction with peers. A number of specific processes were hypothesized as mediators between parent–child interaction and peer outcomes. These include emotion encoding and decoding skills, emotional regulatory skills, cognitive representations, attributions and beliefs, and problem-solving skills (Ladd, 1992; Parke et al., 1994). It is assumed that these abilities or beliefs are acquired in the course of parent–child interchanges over the course of development, and in turn, guide the nature of children's behavior with their peers and these styles of interacting with peers may, in turn, determine children's level of acceptance by their peers. In this chapter, we focus on two sets of processes that seem particularly promising candidates for mediator status: affect management skills and cognitive representational processes.

Affect Management Skills

Children learn more than specific affective expressions in the family, such as anger, sadness, or joy. They learn a cluster of processes associated with the understanding and regulation of affective displays that we term "affect management skills" (Parke et al., 1992). It is assumed that these skills are acquired during the course of parent–child interaction, which, in turn, are available to the child for use in other relationships. Moreover, it is assumed that these skills play a mediating role between family and peer relationships. Three aspects of this issue are examined, namely encoding and decoding of emotion, cognitive understanding of causes and consequences of emotion, and emotional regulation.

The Relation Between Emotional Encoding and Decoding Abilities and Sociometric Status. One set of skills that are of relevance to successful peer interaction and may, in part, be acquired in the context of parent–child play, especially arousing physical play, is the ability to clearly encode emotional signals and to decode others' emotional states. Through physically playful interaction with their parents, especially fathers, children may be learning how to use emotional signals to regulate the social behavior of others. In addition, they may learn to accurately decode the social and emotional signals of other social partners.

Several studies (Beitel & Parke, 1985; Field & Walden, 1982; see Hubbard & Coie, 1994 for a review) found positive relations between emotional decoding ability and various measures of children's peer status. It is assumed that this emotional identification skill permits a child to more adequately regulate social interactions with other children; in turn, this ability contributes to greater acceptance by peers.

Evidence suggests that emotional encoding is linked with children's social status as well. Others (Buck, 1975) found positive relations between children's ability to encode emotional expressions and children's popularity with peers. Carson and Parke (1997) extended earlier work by examining how sociometric status is related to emotional production and recognition skills in the family. Children, regardless of their sociometric status and their parents, are able to produce emotional expressions that are recognized by each other. However, some families may utilize idiosyncratic affect cues that are not recognizable in interactions outside the family. Their communications may reflect a "family-centric" bias. In support of this possibility, Carson and Parke found that undergraduates were better able to recognize the facial expressions of popular children than those of rejected children. There were no status differences in the recognition of the facial expressions posed by parents. This suggests that the emotional production skills of popular children are different than those of rejected children because rejected children's facial expressions are not as well recognized outside the family. These studies provide support for the links between children's emotional encoding and decoding skills and children's sociometric status. Our recent work suggests that parent–child play plays a role in the development of emotional encoding and decoding skills that contribute to children's social acceptance.

The Relation of Emotional Understanding to Peer Competence. In order to develop a more comprehensive model of the role of affect in the emergence of peer competence, we recently examined other aspects of this issue. Successful peer interaction requires not only the ability to recognize and produce emotions, but also requires a social understanding of emotion-related experiences, of the meaning of emotions, of the cause of emotions, and of the responses appropriate to others' emotions. Cassidy, Parke, Butkovsky, and Braungart (1992) evaluated this hypothesized role of emotional understanding in a study of 5- and 6-year-old children. Based on interviews with the children about their understanding of emotions, they found that higher levels of peer acceptance were associated with greater ability to identify emotions, acknowledgment of experiencing emotion, ability to describe appropriate causes of emotions, and expectations that they and their parents would appropriately respond to the display of emotions. Other evidence is consistent with this work. Denham, McKinley, Couchoud, and Holt (1990) found that children's understanding of the type of emotion that would be elicited by different situations was positively related to peer likability. These findings confirm the findings of other research that suggests connections between other components of social understanding and peer relations (Dodge, Pettit, McClaskey, & Brown, 1986; Hart, Ladd, & Burleson, 1990). The next step, of course, is to determine how variations in family interaction may, in fact, contribute to individual differences in children's cognitive understanding of emotions (see Cassidy et al., 1992).

Emotional Regulation. An interesting body of research is emerging that suggests parental support and acceptance of children's emotions is related to children's ability to manage emotions in a constructive fashion. Several recent theorists suggest that these emotional competence skills are, in turn, linked to social competence with peers (Denham, 1993; Eisenberg & Fabes, 1992; Parke, 1992; Parke et al., 1992). Parental comforting of children when they experience negative emotion has been linked with constructive anger reactions (Eisenberg & Fabes, 1994). Similarly, several studies suggest that parental willingness to discuss emotions with their children is related to children's awareness and understanding of others' emotions (Denham, Cook, & Zoller, 1992; Dunn & Brown, 1994). Similarly, Eisenberg, Fabes, Schaller, Carlo, and Miller (1991) found that parental emphasis on direct problem solving was associated with sons' sympathy, whereas restrictiveness in regard to expressing one's own negative emotions was associated with sons' physiological and facial indicators of personal distress. This pattern of findings is consistent with recent work by Gottman and his colleagues on parents' emotion philosophy or metaemotion. By *metaemotion* Katz and Gottman (1993) referred to parents' emotions about their own and their children's emotions, and *metacognitive structure* refers to an organized set of thoughts, a philosophy and an approach to one's own emotions and to one's children's emotions. Gottman, Katz, and Hooven (1996) found that fathers' acceptance and assistance with children's sadness and anger at 5 years of age was related to their children's social competence with peers at 8 years of age. Moreover, fathers' assistance with anger predicted academic achievement. Gender of child influenced these relationships. When fathers help daughters with sadness, girls are rated as more competent by their teachers. When fathers help their daughters regulate anger, girls are rated as more socially competent by their teachers, show higher academic achievement, and their dyadic interaction with a best friend is less negative. Fathers who are more accepting of their son's anger and assist their boy's in regulating anger, have sons who are less aggressive. These data are consistent with earlier suggestions that learning to manage moderate levels of negative affect is a skill that is important for management of social relationships (Sroufe, 1979). Moreover, this work highlights the importance of fathers in learning about relationships, especially in learning the emotional regulatory aspects of relationships. Fathers provide a unique opportunity to teach children about emotion in the context of relationships due to the wide range of intensity of affect that fathers display and the unpredictable character of their playful exchanges with their children (Parke, 1996).

Links Between Children's Emotion Regulatory Abilities and Social Competence—Findings From the UCR Social Development Project

Work on our project also suggests that children's skill in regulating emotions may be important to successful development of relationships in the peer context (O'Neil & Parke, 1996). Based on fourth graders' responses to a series of vignettes representing situations that might generate anger, frustration, or excitement, our data indicate that the ability to control the level of emotional arousal and the strategies selected for coping with high levels of emotional arousal are related to a number of indicators of children's social competence with peers. Specifically, children who report better control over their levels of emotional arousal are described by peers as more prosocial and less aggressive. Similarly, teachers view children who report better control over their emotions as better liked by peers, more prosocial, less disruptive of other children's activities, and less verbally aggressive. Children's strategies for handling emotional arousal appear to be linked to their social competence in a similar fashion. Children who report using temper tantrums or other displays of anger to cope with their emotional upset are less well-accepted by peers and described as less prosocial and more disruptive by teachers. In contrast, children who indicate that they would use reasoning to cope with emotional upset are described as more prosocial.

Other work from our project examines the relations between children's use of socially appropriate rules for displaying negative emotions and social competence with peers. We used a procedure developed by Saarni (1992) called the "disappointing gift paradigm," which enables us to assess the ability of children to mask their negative emotions in the face of disappointment. Although Saarni's work suggests that this ability improves with age and may be a critical component of successful emotion regulation, to date, researchers have not examined the links between individual differences in the ability to mask or control negative emotions and children's competence with peers. Our data indicate that among fourth graders, children who display negative affect or behavior during the presentation of a disappointing gift (thus not using display rules) are rated by peers as more withdrawn. In addition, girls who are able to maintain levels of positive affect and boys who express less tension and anxiety after receiving a disappointing gift are better accepted by their peers (McDowell, O'Neil, & Parke, 1996).

Together, these studies suggest that various aspects of emotional development—encoding, decoding, cognitive understanding, and emotional regulation—play an important role in accounting for variations in peer competence. Our argument is that these aspects of emotion may be learned in the context of family interaction and serve as mediators between the parents and peers. Accumulating support for this view suggests that this is a plausible direction for future research.

Cognitive Representational Models: Another Possible Mediator Between Parents and Peers. One of the major challenges in the investigation of links between family and peer relationships is understanding how children transfer the social strategies that they acquire in the family context to their peer relationships. A variety of theories assumes that individuals process internal mental representations that guide their social behavior. Attachment theorists, for example, offer working-model notions (Bowlby, 1969), whereas social and cognitive psychologists provide accounts involving scripts or cognitive maps that serve as a guide for social action (Baldwin, 1992; Bugental, 1991; Nelson, 1986).

Research in a social-interactional tradition reveals links between parents' and children's cognitive representations of social relationships. Burks and Parke (1996) examined the degree of similarity between children and mothers in their goals, attributions and anticipated consequences when they responded to a series of hypothetical social dilemmas. They found evidence that suggests children may learn cognitive representational schemes through their family relationships, which, in turn, serve as guides for their subsequent relationships with peers. Their results suggest the strongest links between parental and child representations of relationships occur when the social context is comparable (e.g., when parents and children are responding to vignettes reflecting parent–child interaction) and become more dissimilar as the social contexts are more dissimilar (e.g., vignettes reflecting social interaction between parent and adult peer and child and same-aged peer). Specifically, when responding to vignettes that reflected ambiguous provocation or conflict resolution in the context of a parent–child interaction, mothers and children were similar in attributions, anticipated consequences, and goals. However, such similarities in mothers' and children's representations did not emerge when social contexts were dissimilar. Although this study points to links between mothers' and children's cognitive representational schemes that may develop over the course of children's experiences with family members, this study provides no links between adults' and children's representations and their social competence.

Further Evidence of Links Between Parents' and Children's Representations of Social Relationships— Findings From the UCR Social Development Project

Recently, we also explored the links between parent and child cognitive representations of social relationships (Spitzer & Parke, 1994). In our study, parents and their children responded to a series of vignettes reflecting interpersonal dilemmas by indicating how they might react in each situation, and these open-ended responses were coded for goals, causes, strategies, and advice. Paralleling earlier work, we find that the cognitive representations of social behavior of both fathers and mothers are related to their children's representations. This confirms earlier work that showed maternal and child representations are linked (Burks & Parke, 1991, 1996) and provided the first evidence that fathers' representational models are linked to children's models of social relationships. Although our study and the work of Burks and Parke (1996) pointed to links between mothers' and children's cognitive representational schemes that develop over the course of children's experiences with family members, the precise mechanisms through which these schema are acquired is not yet specified.

Links Between Parents' Cognitive Models of Relationships and Children's Social Competence. Recent evidence also supports the general hypothesis that children of varying sociometric statuses differ in their cognitive models of social relationships. Similarly, parents' cognitive models of social relationships also tend to be predictive of variations in children's sociometric status and social competence. Several aspects of cognitive models including attributions, perceptions, values, goals, and strategies have been explored (see Grusec, Hastings, & Mammone, 1994; Mills & Rubin, 1993, for recent reviews). Several recent studies illustrate this line of research. Pettit, Dodge, and Brown (1988) found that mothers' attributional biases concerning their children's behavior (e.g., the extent to which they view an ambiguous provocation as hostile or benign) and the endorsement of aggression as a solution to interpersonal problems were related to children's interpersonal problem-solving skill that, in turn, was related to their social competence. Other evidence suggests that parents hold different patterns of beliefs about problematic social behaviors, such as aggression and withdrawal, and that these patterns are associated with their children's membership in various sociometric status groups (Rubin & Mills, 1990). This work is important because it suggests that parents do, in fact, have sets of beliefs concerning children's social behavior that may, in part, govern their behavior (Goodnow & Collins, 1991; Parke, 1978).

Links Between Parents' and Children's Social
Cognitions and Children's Social Competence—Findings
From the UCR Social Development Project

Recently, in an extension of the work described earlier (Spitzer & Parke, 1994) based on parents' and children's open-end responses to social dilemmas, we found that in addition to the existence of links between parents' and children's cognitive models of relationships, the quality of both mothers' and fathers' goals and strategies for handling social conflict are linked to children's social acceptance. Mothers who are low in their use of relational and prosocial strategies have children with high levels of peer-nominated aggression. Similarly, mothers who provide specific and socially skilled advice have more popular children. Fathers' strategies that are rated high on confrontation and instrumental qualities are associated with low teacher ratings of children's prosocial behavior and high teacher ratings of physical and verbal aggression, avoidance, and being disliked. Fathers with relational goals have children who are less often nominated as aggressive by their peers and are rated by teachers as more liked and less disliked. This work suggests that cognitive models of relationships may be transmitted across generations and these models, in turn, serve as mediators between family contexts and children's relationships with others outside of the family.

BEYOND PARENT–CHILD INTERACTION: PARENTS AS MANAGERS OF CHILDREN'S SOCIAL RELATIONSHIPS

Parents influence their children's social relationships not only through their direct interactions with their children. Parents function as managers of their children's social lives (Hartup, 1979; Parke, 1978) and serve as regulators of opportunities for social contact with extrafamilial social partners.

Parental Monitoring, Limit Setting, and Rule Provision

One way in which parents can affect their children's social relationships is through monitoring their children's social activities. Monitoring refers to a range of activities, including the supervision of children's choice of social settings, activities, and friends. This form of management is particularly evident as children move into preadolescence and adolescence, which is associated with the relative shift in importance of family and peers as sources of influence on social relationships. Studies indicate that parents of delinquent and antisocial children engage in less monitoring and supervision of their children's activities, especially with regard to children's use of evening time, than do parents of nondelinquent children (Dishion, 1992; Patterson & Stouthamer-Loeber, 1984).

Links Between Objective and Subjective Characteristics of Children's Neighborhoods, Parents' Management of Children's Activities, and Children's Social Competence—Findings From the UCR Social Development Project

Work on the UCR Social Development Project has also been devoted to assessing links between characteristics of children's neighborhoods and children's social competence with peers (O'Neil & Parke, 1997). The communities selected for our study comprised neighborhoods reflecting a range of rural, suburban, and urban features, and we derived both objective assessments of neighborhood quality as well as parental perceptions of the neighborhood environment for neighborhoods in which our sample families reside. Additionally, parents' supervisory strategies and rules regarding access to the neighborhood were based on a series of telephone interviews and questionnaires. Our findings suggested that parents', particularly mothers', perceptions of poorer neighborhood quality were related to children's social competence. In a number of instances, these relations appeared to be mediated by greater use of regulatory strategies such as adult supervision and limitation of children's activities in the neighborhood.

Parental Participation in Children's Organized Activities. Parents influence their children's social behavior by functioning as an interface between children and institutional settings, such as child-oriented clubs and organizations (e.g., Brownies, Cub Scouts, etc.). This role is important because it permits the child access to a wider range of social activities and opportunities to practice developing social skills that may, in turn, contribute to their social development. Bryant (1985) found that participation in formally sponsored organizations with unstructured activities was associated with greater social perspective-taking skill among 10-year-old children, but had little effect on 7 year olds. In light of the importance of this skill for successful peer interaction (Hartup, 1983), this finding assumes particular significance. Moreover, Bryant (1985) suggested that activities that "allow the child to experience autonomy, control and mastery of the content of the activity are related to expressions of enhanced social–emotional functioning on the part of the child" (p. 65). In support of this argument, Ladd and Price (1987) found that children who were exposed to a higher number of unstructured peer activities (e.g., church, school, or going to the swimming pool or library) were less anxious and had fewer absences at the beginning of kindergarten.

Although we have limited understanding of how these activities vary as a function of children's age, it appears that there is an increase with age in participation in sponsored organizations with structured activities (e.g., clubs, Brownies, and organized sports), with participation most prevalent among preadolescent children (Bryant, 1985). Finally, more attention to the ways in which fathers participate in these types of activities is needed, especially in light of their shifting parental roles (Parke, 1996).

Parent as Social Initiator and Arranger. Parents also play an important role in the facilitation of their children's peer relationships by initiating informal contact between their own children and potential play partners, especially among younger children (Bhavnagri & Parke, 1991). Ladd and his colleagues suggest that the parent's role as arranger may play a facilitory part in the development of his or her children's friendships. Ladd and Golter (1988) found that children of parents who tended to arrange peer contacts had a larger range of playmates and more frequent play companions outside school than children of parents who were less active in initiating peer contacts. When children entered kindergarten, boys, but not girls, with parents who initiated peer contacts were better liked and less rejected by their classmates than were boys with noninitiating parents.

Children's own initiation activity was linked with measures of social competence. Children who initiated a larger number of peer contacts outside school tended to be better liked by their peers in preschool settings (Ladd & Hart, 1991). Such work serves as a corrective to the view that initiation activity is only a parental activity and reminds us that variations in how active a role children play in organizing their own social contacts is an important correlate of their social competence.

Together, these studies provide evidence of the possible facilitory role of parents in the development of social competence with peers. Little is known, however, about the possible determinants of parental utilization of neighborhood social resources, including other children as playmates. More work is needed on the determinants of parental initiating and arranging activities.

Social Networks as a Source of Potential Peer Contacts for Children. In addition to the role played by parents in arranging children's access to other children, parents' own social networks of other adults, as well as the child members of parental social networks, provide a source of possible play partners for children. Cochran and Brassard (1979) suggested several ways in which these two sets of relationships may be related. First, the child is exposed to a wider or narrower band of possible social interactive partners by exposure to the members of the parent's social network. Second, the extent to which the child has access to the social interactions of his or her parents and members of their social network may determine how well the child may acquire particular styles of social interaction. Third, in view of the social support function of social networks, parents in supportive social networks may be more likely to have positive relationships with their children, which, in turn, may positively affect children's social adjustment both in and outside the family.

Cochran and Davila (1992) provided support for the first issue, namely that there is overlap between parental and child social networks. Specifically, these investigators found that 30% to 44% of 6-year-old children's social networks were also included in the mothers' networks. In other words, children often listed other children as play partners who were children of their mothers' friends. Finally, the overlap was higher in the case of relatives than nonrelatives, but both kin and nonkin adult networks provided sources of peer play partners for young children.

Several other studies suggest that the quality of adult social networks do, in fact, relate to children's social behavior. In an Australian study, Homel, Burns, and Goodnow (1987) found positive relations between the number of dependable friends that parents report, and 11-year-old children's self-rated happiness, the number of regular playmates, and maternal ratings of children's social skills. Second, parent's affiliation with various types of formal community organizations were related to children's happiness, school adjustment, and social skills. Unfortunately, reliance on self-reports limits the value of these findings, but they do support the importance of parental, or at least maternal, social networks as a factor in potentially affecting children's social relationships.

Oliveri and Reiss (1987) found distinctive patterns between maternal and paternal networks and the networks of adolescent children as well. The structural aspects (size or density) of networks were more closely related to maternal network qualities, which is consistent with prior work that suggests that mothers function as social arrangers and "kin keepers" more than fathers (Tinsley & Parke, 1984). In contrast, the relationship aspects of adolescent social networks (positive sentiment between individuals and help received from network members) more closely resembled these aspects of fathers' social network characteristics. This is consistent with the view that fathers may, in fact, play an important role in the regulation of emotion—a central ingredient in the maintenance of close personal relationships (Parke et al., 1992). A variety of mechanisms are probably involved in accounting for these patterns, including the increased availability of social initiation and maintenance strategies.

Links Between Parents' and Children's Social Networks
and Children's Social Competence—Findings
From the UCR Social Development Project

Recently, in a study in our lab, Lee and Welsh (1995) extended this work by showing a relation between parents' enjoyment of friends in their network and independent peer ratings. The more parents enjoyed their friends, the less the child was disliked and perceived as aggressive. Moreover, the more contact parents had with relatives, the less disliked children were by their peers. Finally, these investigators found that maternal and paternal social networks have distinctive links to children's social relationships. Fathers who rated their networks as less enjoyable had children who were more aggressive and more disliked by peers, whereas the less contact that mothers had with their friends, the higher teachers rated their children on avoidance of inter-action with other children.

AN EXAMINATION OF ECOLOGICAL FACTORS
THAT MODERATE THE LINKS BETWEEN FAMILY
AND PEER SYSTEMS

Evidence is beginning to emerge that suggests a number of ecological factors outside the immediate context of the family, such as family structure, the socioeconomic circumstances of the family, the quality of children's neigh-borhoods, and cultural variations in children's experiences that may directly influence or moderate the links between family and peer social systems (Patterson, Griesler, Vaden, & Kupersmidt, 1992).

The neighborhood environment has increasingly come to be viewed as an important context for children's development and the management of children's activities in the neighborhood has come to be viewed as an important avenue of influence on the development of children's social competence. Recent concerns regarding the impact of impoverished urban neighborhoods on children's development prompted vigorous investigation of neighborhood effects on parenting practices and developmental outcomes of young children and adolescents. However, the associations between neighborhood quality and children's social development outcomes do not appear to be direct or uncomplicated. Kupersmidt, Griesler, DeRosier, Patterson, and Davis (1995), for example, examined second- through fifth-grade children's behavioral adjustment as a function of the combined influence of neighborhood context and family context using federal census tract information to characterize each neighborhood (e.g., age distribution, ethnicity, household composition, and occupational characteristics). A number of neighborhood context by family context interactions emerged, suggesting that better quality neighborhoods protect some children who are at risk because of problematic family lives (in their particular sample, African-American children from low-income, single-parent families). In other cases, the difficulties of children who are at risk on the basis of family characteristics appear to be exacerbated by living in a middle-socioeconomic status (SES) neighborhood (in this sample, Euro-American, low-income children from single-parent families). In general, the results of much of the recent work examining neighborhood effects suggest that place of residence, in and of itself, is not a robust predictor of children's successful development. According to Furstenberg, Eccles, Elder, Cook, and Sameroff (in press), "family variations in neighborhoods are expressed by different socialization styles, featuring particular management strategies and child outcomes" and a number of recent studies suggest that the management of children's social experiences in the context of the neighborhood environment appears to be a critical process that varies even in relatively impoverished neighborhoods (Klebanov, Brooks-Gunn, & Duncan, 1994; Steinberg, Darling, & Fletcher, 1995). However, because the focus of these studies has typically been on neighborhoods in large, urban cities, less is known about the contribution that neighborhood characteristics make to the social development of children who reside in a wider range of neighborhoods.

REMAINING ISSUES

Several issues need to be addressed in future research. First, it is important to underscore that parental strategies outlined in this chapter operate together rather than independently in naturalistic socialization. As Parke (1992) noted earlier, "this array of socialization strategies that is available to parents can be viewed as a 'cafeteria model' in which various combinations of items can be chosen or ignored in various sized portions" (p. 426).

Second, a lingering problem in this area of research concerns the issue of direct effects. While it is assumed that parents play a causative role in modifying children's peer relationships, in view of the bidirectionality of parent–child relationships, it is likely that peers influence parents as well. Recent evidence (Repetti, 1996), for example, suggested that children who experience difficulties with peers at school may change their patterns of interaction with family members, at least in the short run. Third, the issue of intracultural variation needs more attention. Our research program is beginning to address this issue, but our understanding of this complex issue, to date, is relatively meager. Not only are there issues of ethnic identity, per se, that need to be addressed, but also issues of the relation between ethnicity and the larger social context of the classroom and neighborhood need to be examined. The impact on social relationships of being a member of an ethnic minority group varies with the ethnic mix of these other contexts. An Hispanic-American child in a neighborhood or classroom of largely other Hispanic-American children has different social challenges than an Hispanic-American child who is one of only a few Hispanic-American children in a predominantly Anglo setting. Fourth, the need to better understand developmental issues remains paramount because the ways in which these three pathways change across time are not well-articulated. Two aspects of this issue can be distinguished: (a) do the three pathways differ in importance across age? (b) do the forms that these three pathways assume differ as a function of developmental status of the child? Regarding the first issue, it is likely that parent–child interaction is more important in the early year of development while the managerial aspects of the model assume more importance as the child matures. In regard to the second issue, it is likely that the form of enactment of these strategies shift across development. Advice giving, for example, may become less direct and assume the form of consultation as the child develops. Similarly, arranging activities on behalf of the child probably gives way to indirect monitoring of children's social activities.

Fifth, there are implications of the work reviewed in this chapter for intervention and prevention programs. Although much of the work devoted to the amelioration of peer-related difficulties has focused on modifying children's behavior with peers, our research suggests that family-based intervention paradigms need more attention. These approaches are not mutually exclusive and a combination of family-based and peer-oriented interventions may be most effective. Process-based interventions are not only likely to be most successful, but these field experiments provide an opportunity to evaluate the assumed role of theoretically derived hypotheses in modifying children's social behavior with peers. Our work clearly suggests that a focus on emotional regulatory and cognitive representational processes represents a reasonable starting point for a family- and peer-based intervention program. By moving forward in this way, we may be better able to modify, or prevent, the emergence of social and cognitive problems that have been linked with early at-risk social relationships with peers. In the final analysis, reducing the long-term problems of at-risk children is our goal.

ACKNOWLEDGMENTS

Preparation of this chapter and the research reported here were supported by grants to Ross Parke from the National Science Foundation (BNS 8919391), the National Institute of Child Health and Human Development (HT 32391), and the MacArthur Foundation (Network on Early Childhood Transitions). We also thank the staffs of the Fontana Unified School District and the Jurupa Unified School District for their generous and continued support of the UCR Social Development Project.

REFERENCES

Baldwin, M. J. (1992). Relational schema and the processing of information. *Psychological Review, 112*, 461–484.

Barth, J. M., & Parke, R. D. (1993). Parent–child relationship influences on children's transition to school. *Merrill-Palmer Quarterly, 39*, 173–195.

Baumrind, D. (1973). The development of instrumental competence through socialization. In A. D. Pick (Ed.), *Minnesota Symposium on Child Psychology* (Vol. 7, pp. 3–46). Minneapolis: University of Minnesota Press.

Beitel, A., & Parke, R. D. (1985). *Relationships between preschoolers' sociometric factors and emotional decoding ability.* Unpublished manuscript, University of Illinois, Urbana.

Bhavnagri, N., & Parke, R. D. (1991). Parents as direct facilitators of children's peer relationships: Effects of age of child and sex of parent. *Journal of Personal and Social Relationships, 8*, 423–440.

Bowlby, J. (1969). *Attachment and loss* (Vol. 1). New York: Basic Books.

Boyum, L., & Parke, R. D. (1995). Family emotional expressiveness and children's social competence. *Journal of Marriage and Family, 57*, 593–608.

Bronfenbrenner, U. (1979). *The ecology of human development.* Cambridge, MA: Harvard University Press.

Bronfenbrenner, U. (1989) Ecological systems theory. In R. Vasta (Ed.), *Annals of child development* (Vol. 6, pp. 187–250). Greenwich, CT: JAI.

Bryant, B. (1985). The neighborhood walk: Sources of support in middle childhood. *Monographs of the Society for Research in Child Development, 50*(3, Serial No. 210).

Buck, R. (1975). Nonverbal communication of affect in children. *Journal of Personality and Social Psychology, 31*, 644–653.

Bugental, D. (1991). Affective and cognitive processes within threat-oriented family systems. In I. E. Sigel, A. V. McGillicuddy-DeLis, & J. J. Goodnow (Eds.), *Parental belief systems: The psychological consequences for children* (2nd ed.). Hillsdale, NJ: Lawrence Erlbaum Associates.

Burks, V. M., Carson, J. L., & Parke, R. D. (1987). *Parent–child interactional styles of popular and rejected children.* Unpublished manuscript, University of Illinois, Urbana, IL.

Burks, V. M., & Parke, R. D. (1991). *Parent and child representations of social relationships: Mediators of children's social adjustment.* Paper presented at the meeting of the International Society for the Study of Behavioral Development, Minneapolis, MN.

Burks, J. S., & Parke, R. D. (1996). Parental and child representations of social relationships: Linkages between families and peers. *Merrill-Palmer Quarterly, 42,* 358–378.

Carson, J. L., & Parke, R. D. (1996). Reciprocal negative affect in parent–child interactions and children's peer competency. *Child Development, 67,* 2217–2226

Carson, J., & Parke, R. D. (1997). *Parent and child encoding and decoding and sociometric status.* Manuscript submitted for publication.

Cassidy, J., Parke, R. D., Butkovsky, L., & Braungart, J. (1992). Family–peer connections: The roles of emotional expressiveness within the family and children's understanding of emotions. *Child Development, 63,* 603–618.

Cochran, M., & Brassard, J. A. (1979). Child Development and personal social networks. *Child Development, 50,* 601–616.

Cochran, M., & Davila, V. (1992). Societal influences on children's peer relationships. In R. D. Parke & G. W. Ladd (Eds.), *Family-peer relationships: Modes of linkage* (pp. 191–212). Hillsdale, NJ: Lawrence Erlbaum Associates.

Cohen, J. S. (1989). *Maternal involvement in children's peer relationships during middle childhood.* Unpublished doctoral dissertation, University of Waterloo, Waterloo, Canada.

Denham, S., McKinley, M., Couchoud, E. A., & Holt, R. (1990). Emotional and behavioral predictors of preschool peer ratings. *Child Development, 61,* 1145–1152.

Denham, S. A. (1993). Maternal emotional responsiveness to toddlers' social–emotional functioning. *Journal of Child Psychology and Psychiatry, 34,* 715–728.

Denham, S. A., Cook, M., & Zoller, D. (1992). Baby looks very sad: Implications of conversations about feelings between mother and preschooler. *British Journal of Developmental Psychology, 10,* 301–315.

Dishion, T. J. (1992). The peer context of troublesome child and adolescent behavior. In P. E. Leone (Ed.), *Understanding troubled and troubling youth: A multidisciplinary perspective.* Newbury Park, CA: Sage.

Dodge, K. A., Pettit, G. S., McClaskey, C. L., & Brown, M. (1986). Social competence in children. *Monographs of the Society for Research in Child Development, 51*(2, Serial No. 213).

Dunn, J., & Brown, J. (1994). Affect expression in the family, children's understanding of emotions and their interactions with others. *Merrill-Palmer Quarterly, 40,* 120–137.

Eisenberg, N., & Fabes, R. A. (1992). Young children's coping with interpersonal anger. *Child Development, 63,* 116–128.

Eisenberg, N., & Fabes, R. A. (1994). Emotion, regulation and the development of social competence. In M. Clark (Ed.), *Review of personality and social psychology.* Newbury Park, CA: Sage.

Eisenberg, N., Fabes, R. A., Schaller, M., Carlo, G., & Miller, P. (1991). The relations of parental characteristics and practices to children's vicarious emotional responding. *Child Development, 62,* 1393–1408.

Field, T. M., & Walden, T. A. (1982). Production and discrimination of facial expressions by preschool children. *Child Development, 53,* 1299–1311.

Furstenberg, F. F., Eccles, J., Elder, G. H., Cook, T. D., & Sameroff, A. (In press). *Urban families and adolescent success.* Chicago: University of Chicago Press.

Goodnow, J., & Collins, A. (1991). *Ideas according to parents.* Hillsdale, NJ: Lawrence Erlbaum Associates.

Gottman, J. M., Katz, L. F., & Hooven, C. (1996). Parental meta-emotional philosophy and the emotional life of families: Theoretical models and preliminary data. *Journal of Family Psychology, 10,* 243–268.

Grusec, J. E., Hastings, P., & Mammone, N. (1994). Parenting cognitions and relationship schemas. In J. G. Smetana (Ed.), *Beliefs about parenting: Origins and developmental implications* (pp. 5–19). San Francisco: Jossey-Bass.

Harrist, A. W., Pettit, G. S., Dodge, K. A., & Bates, J. E. (1994). Dyadic synchrony in mother–child interaction-relation with children's subsequent kindergarten adjustment. *Family Relations, 43*, 417–424.

Hart, C. H., Ladd, G. W., & Burleson, B. R. (1990). Children's expectations of the outcomes of social strategies: Relations with sociometric status and maternal disciplinary styles. *Child Development, 61*, 127–137.

Hartup, W. W. (1979). The social worlds of childhood. *American Psychologist, 34*, 944–950.

Hartup, W. W. (1983). Peer relations. In P. Mussen & E. M. Hetherington (Eds.), *Manual of child psychology* (4th ed.). New York: Wiley.

Hinde, R., & Tamplin, A. (1983). Relations between mother–child interaction and behavior in preschool. *British Journal of Developmental Psychology, 1*, 231–257.

Homel, R., Burns, A., & Goodnow, J. (1987). Parental social networks and child development. *Journal of Social and Personal Relationships, 4*, 159–177.

Hubbard, J. A., & Coie, J. D. (1994). Emotional correlates of social competence in children's peer relationships. *Merrill-Palmer Quarterly, 40*, 1–20.

Isley, S., O'Neil, R., Clatfelter, D., & Parke, R. D. (1997). *Parent and child expressed affect and children's social acceptance and competence: Modeling direct and indirect pathways.* Unpublished manuscript.

Isley, S., O'Neil, R., & Parke, R. D. (1996). The relation of parental affect and control behaviors to children's classroom acceptance: A concurrent and predictive analysis. *Early Education and Development, 7*, 7–23.

Katz, L. F., & Gottman, J. M. (1993). Patterns of marital conflict predict children's internalizing and externalizing behaviors. *Developmental Psychology, 29*, 940–950.

Klebanov, P. K., Brooks-Gunn, J., & Duncan, G. J. (1994). Does neighborhood and family poverty affect mothers' parenting, mental health, and social support? *Journal of Marriage and the Family, 56*, 441–455.

Kupersmidt, J. B., Griesler, P. C., DeRosier, M. E., Patterson, C. J., & Davis, P. W. (1995). Childhood aggression and peer relations in the context of family and neighborhood factors. *Child Development, 66*, 360–375.

Ladd, G. W. (1992). Themes and theories: Perspective on processes in family–peer relationships. In R. Parke & G. Ladd (Eds.), *Family–peer relationships: Modes of linkage* (pp. 3–34). Hillsdale, NJ: Lawrence Erlbaum Associates.

Ladd, G. W., & Golter, B. S. (1988). Parents' management of preschoolers' peer relations: Is it related to children's social competence? *Developmental Psychology, 24*, 109–117.

Ladd, G. W., & Hart, C. H. (1991). *Parents' management of children's peer relations: Patterns associated with social competence.* Paper presented at the 11th meeting of the International Society for Behavioral Development, Minneapolis, MN.

Ladd, G. W., LeSieur, K., & Profilet, S. M. (1993). Direct parental influences on young children's peer relations. In S. Duck (Ed.), *Learning about relationships* (Vol. 2, pp. 152–183). London: Sage.

Ladd, G. W., & Price, J. M. (1987). Predicting children's social and school adjustment following the transition from preschool to kindergarten. *Child Development, 58*, 1168–1189.

Lee, J., & Welsh, M, (1995). *The relation of parents' and children's social networks to children's social acceptance and behavior.* Paper presented at the biennial meeting of the Society for Research in Child Development, Indianapolis, IN.

Lollis, S. P., Ross, H. S., & Tate, E. (1992). Parents regulation of children's peer interactions: Direct influences. In R. Parke & G. Ladd (Eds.), *Family–peer relationships: Modes of linkage* (pp. 255–281). Hillsdale, NJ: Lawrence Erlbaum Associates.

MacDonald, K., & Parke, R. D. (1984). Bridging the gap: Parent–child play interaction and peer interactive competence. *Child Development, 55,* 1265–1277.

McDowell, D. J., O'Neil, R., & Parke, R. D. (1996). *Children's ability to mask negative emotions: Links to social competence with peers.* Unpublished manuscript, University of California, Riverside.

Mills, R. S. L., & Rubin, K. H. (1993). Parental ideas as influences on children's social competence. In S. Duck (Ed.), *Learning about relationships* (pp. 117–148). Newbury Park, CA: Sage.

Mize, J., Pettit, G. S., & Brown, E. G. (1995). Mothers' supervision of their children's peer play—Relations with beliefs, perceptions, and knowledge. *Developmental Psychology, 31,* 311–321.

Nelson, K. (1986). Event knowledge and cognitive development. In K. Nelson (Ed.), *Event knowledge: Structure and function in development.* Hillsdale, NJ: Lawrence Erlbaum Associates.

Oliveri, M. E., & Reiss, D. (1987). Social networks of family members: Distinctive roles of mothers and fathers. *Sex Roles, 17,* 719–736.

O'Neil, R., Garcia, J., Zavala, A., & Wang, S. (1995). *Parental advice giving and children's competence with peers: A content and stylistic analysis.* Paper presented at the biennial meeting of the Society for Research in Child Development, Indianapolis, IN.

O'Neil, R., & Parke, R. D. (1996). *Parental antecedents of emotion regulation in middle childhood: Links to children's social competence.* Poster session presented at the 3rd annual Family Research Consortium Summer Institute, San Diego, CA.

O'Neil, R., & Parke, R. D. (1997). *Objective and subjective features of children's neighborhoods: Relations to parental regulatory strategies and children's social competence.* Unpublished manuscript.

Parke, R. D. (1978). Children's home environments: Social and cognitive effects. In I. Altman & J. F. Wohlwill (Eds.), *Children and the environment* (pp. 33–81). New York: Plenum.

Parke, R. D. (1992). Epilogue: Remaining issues and future trends in the study of family–peer relationships. In R. D. Parke & G. Ladd (Eds.), *Family–peer relationships: Modes of linkage.* Hillsdale, NJ: Lawrence Erlbaum Associates.

Parke, R. D. (1996). *Fatherhood.* Cambridge, MA: Harvard University Press.

Parke, R. D., Burks, V. M., Carson, J. L., Neville, B., & Boyum, L. A. (1994). Family–peer relationships: A tripartite model. In R. D. Parke & S. G. Kellam (Eds.), *Exploring family relationships with other contexts* (pp. 115–145). Hillsdale, NJ: Lawrence Erlbaum Associates.

Parke, R. D., Cassidy, J., Burks, V. M., Carson, J. L., & Boyum, L. (1992). Familial contributions to peer competence among young children: The role of interactive and affective processes. In R. D. Parke & G. W. Ladd (Eds.), *Family–peer relationships: Modes of linkage* (pp. 107–134). Hillsdale, NJ: Lawrence Erlbaum Associates.

Parke, R. D., MacDonald, K., Beitel, A., & Bhavnagri, N. (1988). The role of the family in the development of peer relationships. In R. DeV. Peters & R. J. McMahon (Eds.), *Social learning and systems approaches to marriage and the family* (pp. 17–44). New York: Brunner/Mazel.

Parke, R. D., & O'Neil, R. (1996). The influence of significant others on learning about relationships. In S. W. Duck (Ed.), *Handbook of personal relationships* (2nd ed., pp. 29–59). New York: Wiley.

Parker, J. G., & Asher, S. R. (1987). Peer relations and later personal adjustment: Are low accepted children at risk? *Psychological Bulletin, 102,* 357–389.

Patterson, C. J., Griesler, P. C., Vaden, N. A., & Kupersmidt, J. B. (1992). Family economic circumstances, life transitions, and children's peer relations. In R. D. Parke & G. Ladd (Eds.), *Family–peer relationships: Modes of linkage* (pp. 385–424). Hillsdale, NJ: Lawrence Erlbaum Associates.

Patterson, C. J., & Stouthamer-Loeber, M. (1984). The correlation of family management practices and delinquency. *Child Development, 55,* 1299–1306.

Pettit, G. S., Dodge, K. A., & Brown, M. M. (1988). Early family experience, social problem solving patterns, and children' social competence. *Child Development, 59,* 107–120.

Pettit, G. S., & Mize, J. (1993). Substance and style: Understanding the ways in which parents teach children about social relationships. In S. Duck (Ed.), *Learning about relationships* (Vol. 2, pp. 118–151). London: Sage.

Putallaz, M. (1987). Maternal behavior and sociometric status. *Child Development, 58,* 324–340.

Repetti, R. L. (1996). The effects of perceived daily social and academic failure experiences on school-age children's subsequent interactions with parents. *Child Development, 12,* 125–131.

Rubin, K. H., & Mills, R. S. L. (1990). Maternal beliefs about adaptive and maladaptive social behaviors in normal, aggressive and withdrawn preschoolers. *Journal of Abnormal Child Psychology, 18,* 419–435.

Russell, A., & Finnie, V. (1990). Preschool children's social status and maternal instructions to assist group entry. *Developmental Psychology, 26*(4), 603–611.

Saarni, C. (1992). Children's emotional-expressive behavior as regulators of others' happy and sad states. *New Directions for Child Development, 55,* 91–106.

Spitzer, S., & Parke, R. D. (1994). *Family cognitive representations of social behavior and children's social competence.* Paper presented at the meeting of the American Psychological Society, Washington, DC.

Sroufe, L. A. (1979). The coherence of individual development. *American Psychologist, 34,* 834–841.

Steinberg, L., Darling, N. E., & Fletcher, A. C. (1995). Authoritative parenting and adolescent development: An ecological journey. In P. Moen, G. H. Elder, & K. Luscher (Eds.), *Examining lives in context* (pp. 423–466). Washington, DC: American Psychological Association.

Tinsley, B. R., & Parke, R. D. (1984). The person–environment relationship: Lessons from families with preterm infants. In D. Magnusson & V. Allen (Eds.), *Human development: An interactional perspective* (pp. 93–110). New York: Academic Press.

Wang, S. J., & McDowell, D. J. (1996). *Parental advice-giving: Relations to child social competence and psychosocial functioning.* Poster session presented at the annual meeting of the Western Psychological Association, San Jose, CA.

6

▼▼▼▼▼▼▼

Everyday Experiences of Infants in Euro-American and Central American Immigrant Families

Michael E. Lamb
Birgit Leyendecker
Axel Schölmerich
Maria P. Fracasso
National Institute of Child Health and Human Development
Bethesda, Maryland

Infants are raised in an array of developmental niches that vary along psychosocial, geographic, and demographic dimensions (Lamb & Sternberg, 1992; Super & Harkness, 1986). Unfortunately, developmental psychologists have been somewhat inattentive to these variations, treating them as curiosities or irritations rather than crucial considerations in the search for an inclusive understanding of developmental processes. Descriptive research about divergent early experiences is especially important in light of the many unquestioned presumptions about the universality of developmental norms and principles. Research in various cultures and subcultures not only provides valuable data about basic developmental processes in different contexts, but also affords opportunities for obtaining a more comprehensive and representative picture of biobehavioral development. The long-term goal of the research described here is to explore developmental processes across developmental niches in order to identify transcultural principles of human development. The first step toward this goal required that we describe infant experiences in different rearing ecologies. Only by carefully studying children in diverse circumstances can we determine whether and how developmental trajectories and processes differ across cultures and thus, whether contemporary professional constructions of human development deserve to be widely generalized. Likewise, it is crucial to assess the extent to which behavior and interaction vary from one setting or observation session to another, in order for researchers to adequately and reliably sample the patterns in which they are interested (see Lewis, 1978; Lewis & Feiring, 1979, 1982).

113

In the 1960s and 1970s, most researchers and theorists focused on the quality of infant–mother interactions (Ainsworth, Blehar, Waters, & Wall, 1978; Lamb, Thompson, Gardner, & Charnov, 1985). More recently, they emphasized that relationships with fathers, siblings, careproviders, and peers are also formatively significant (e.g., Dunn, 1993; Howes, 1988; Lamb, 1997, 1998; Lamb & Nash, 1989). Thus, the focus shifted to the study of social networks rather than individual relationships (e.g., Lamb, Ketterlinus, & Fracasso, 1993; Lewis, 1987; Parke & Kellam, 1994). In addition, cross-cultural researchers have begun to document varying parenting roles in different socioecological niches (e.g., Hewlett, 1992; Leiderman, Tulkin, & Rosenfeld, 1977; Tronick, Morelli, & Ivey, 1992; West, 1988).

Infants adapt to a variety of social environments that shape their socioemotional and cognitive capacities, emergent self-representations, social competencies, and relationships with others. Detailed knowledge of the extent and breadth of infants' social worlds may thus be very helpful in understanding individual differences in early developmental trajectories. Unfortunately, our existing developmental theories are primarily informed by research about middle-class samples from Euro-American backgrounds, although they represent a minute proportion of the world's population. By studying infants whose circumstances differ from these, researchers identify limits to the generalization of research findings as well as culture-specific childrearing practices (Cole, 1992; Rogoff & Morelli, 1989).

Many researchers have reported that early interactions vary as a function of maternal age, ethnicity, cultural background, education, and income. Mothers around the world vocalize to, hold, and have eye contact with their infants quite frequently, whereas play is less common (Bornstein, Tamis-LeMonda, Pecheux, & Rahn, 1991; Leiderman et al., 1977; Lewis & Ban, 1977; Richman, LeVine, New, Howrigan, Welles-Nyström, & LeVine, 1988; Richman, Miller, & LeVine, 1992). Subcultural and SES differences exist as well. Euro-American mothers, especially upper-middle-class mothers, talk to and look at their infants more frequently than do mothers of other ethnic backgrounds (Feiring & Lewis, 1981; Field & Widmayer, 1981; Lewis & Freedle, 1977; Lewis & Wilson, 1972; Richman et al., 1988). Most of these findings were based on brief observations in semistructured contexts, however. Prolonged observations like those reported here are necessary to analyze the patterns of behavior and interaction more inclusively and to assess the distribution of time spent in various social or functional contexts (e.g., feeding, caretaking, and play). In addition, the description of unstructured interaction may help to establish the frequency with which social interactions occur in different contexts and with visual and verbal interactions more or less common, depending on the type of activities in which mothers and infants are involved (see Lewis, 1978; Lewis & Feiring, 1979).

In this chapter, we describe the social worlds of infants in two rearing environments that are likely to provide contrasting early experiences: Central

American immigrant families and affluent Euro-American families. Central Americans are a rapidly growing ethnic minority group in the United States; frequently they migrate, at great risk, to the United States because of war and poverty in their native lands. When they arrive in the United States, they usually face difficulties speaking the language, finding employment and accommodations, and developing social support networks. Some live in poverty and fear of deportation. These problems combine to have harmful effects on family relationships and on interactions between infants and their parents. By contrast, the Euro-American families we studied live much more comfortable lives; they speak the local language, have steady employment, live in large homes, and enjoy advantaged lifestyles. Although they also experience stressful life events, the stresses they experience do not stem from threats to their basic survival (food or shelter) and thus, do not profoundly affect their family relationships.

Whereas the middle-class Euro-Americans, who have dominated previous research efforts, tend to emphasize individualism and nuclear rather than extended family relationships (e.g., Lewis, Feiring, & Kotsonis, 1984; Sampson, 1985, 1988; Spence, 1985), immigrants from Central America, like the members of many other cultures, highly value the extended family and make extensive efforts to maintain relationships with relatives (e.g., Harrison, Wilson, Pine, Chan, & Buriel, 1990; Sabogal, Marin, Otero-Sabogal, Marin, & Perez-Stable, 1987). Such familialism represents a core feature of Central-American and Hispanic cultures (Triandis, Marin, Betancourt, Lisansky, & Chang, 1982; Vega, 1990) and has two important implications for the social experiences of young infants fostering multiple significant relationships in the extended family (not only in the nuclear family) and assuring a supportive social network for, by, and with adult family members. Mindel (1980) further speculated that Hispanics are more likely to migrate toward family networks, whereas Euro-Americans are more likely to migrate away from their families, maintaining more diffuse long-distance relationships. For various interrelated reasons, therefore, Euro-American families in urban areas tend to live as isolated nuclear families and are less likely to rely on members of the extended family for emotional support or childcare than are Hispanic Americans (e.g., Sampson, 1985, 1988; Spence, 1985). We assumed that these values would affect the social experiences of their infants and thus, that infants growing up in families from Central America would be cared for by an extensive network of relatives and would enjoy frequent opportunities for interaction with a variety of different people.

Differences between the two groups of families we studied could, of course, be attributed to a host of factors (including ethnic origins, socioeconomic and educational status, stress, etc.). Our research was designed primarily to describe the experiences of infants in Central-American and Euro-American families, not to account for differences between them. Because of the obvious confound between culture and social class, we focused on describing the infants' experiences in each sociocultural niche, rather than on group comparisons.

On the basis of extended observations, we attempted to identify and describe the typical experiences of 3-month-old children and the proportion of time infants and adults spent in discrete activities such as feeding, playing, and care provision. Detailed diaries were used to gather comparable information about these children and their families when the children were 8 and 12 months of age (Leyendecker, Lamb, Schölmerich, & Fracasso, 1995). Data derived from parental reports have been criticized on the grounds that parents' reports may be biased, but the many potential advantages of using parents as observers and reporters have been recognized as well (e.g., Lewis, 1987; Maccoby & Martin, 1983; Parke & Tinsley, 1987). Parents seem to provide accurate descriptions of the amount of time spent in general activities (feeding, playing, nonsocial activities, etc.), as well as in the presence of other people. Recall data concerning the past 24 hours appear to be as reliable as data obtained from diaries kept by the respondents themselves (Michelson, 1987; Robinson, 1985). Furthermore, data gathering by parental report is nonintrusive and allows us to obtain information about experiences in the early mornings, evenings, and nights, which are seldom observed. Because recall data seem most reliable when restricted to a 24-hour period (Juster, 1985), we limited ourselves to this time frame. We also limited our focus to broad descriptions of ongoing activities and social contexts. More detailed information on the infants' interactions with each potential partner would have been valuable, but the reliability of these data would have been questionable. Using both observational and diary data, we thus sought to determine who spent time with the infants, the proportion of time spent in discrete contexts with different adults present, and the levels and quality of mother–infant interaction in these different social and functional contexts.

Over the years, researchers occasionally attempted to observe infants for extended periods of time. With few exceptions (e.g., Clarke-Stewart, 1973), however, these studies focused primarily on the development of sleep–wake cycles (Dittrichova & Lapackova, 1964; Whitney & Thoman, 1994), smiling (Wolff, 1963), or aspects of proximal stimulation and interaction (e.g., Greenbaum & Landau, 1977; Wachs, 1984; Yarrow, Rubenstein, & Pedersen, 1975) rather than on the overall quality of mother–infant interaction. In the best-known study involving repeated and extensive observations, Ainsworth and her colleagues (1978) reported that mothers who were sensitively responsive to their infants' signals, interpreted these correctly, and reacted appropriately, consistently, and promptly had securely attached infants. Some researchers have since conducted short but highly structured observations in the laboratory in attempts to focus on specific behaviors and situations (e.g., Izard, Haynes, Chisholm, & Baak, 1991; Malatesta, Culver, Tesman, & Shepard,

1989), but most have continued to study the antecedents of attachment in the home. The length of these observations and the range of functional contexts sampled varied, however. Whereas some researchers examined shorter episodes of feeding or free play (e.g., Cox, Owen, Henderson, & Margand, 1992; Mangelsdorf, Gunnar, Kestenbaum, Lang, & Andreas, 1990), most have relied on unstructured home observations lasting 1 hour or less at each point in time (e.g., Isabella, 1993; Isabella & Belsky, 1991; Lamb & Elster, 1985; Lyons-Ruth, Connell, Zoll, & Stahl, 1987) and rarely 2 hours and more at each point in time (e.g., Bates, Maslin, & Frankel, 1985; Lamb, 1977; Lewis & Feiring, 1982, 1989). Inconsistencies in the results of these studies may thus be due to cross-contextual variations or measurement differences.

It is widely assumed that maternal sensitivity influences both the security of infant–mother attachment as well as many aspects of later development (Lamb & Easterbrooks, 1981; Lamb, Thompson, Gardner, & Charnov, 1985). Maternal sensitivity embraces such notions as warmth, attunement, appropriate responsiveness, attentiveness, cooperation, parental affect, and appropriate stimulation; although individual differences in sensitivity should be consistent across time and situations, the immediate context surely affects dyadic interactions (Lamb, 1979; O'Brien, Johnson, & Anderson-Goetz, 1989; Seifer, Sameroff, Anagnostopolou, & Elias, 1992). Most researchers treated unstructured home observations ("follow your normal routine and ignore the presence of the observer") as the most natural setting in which to study the development of infant–mother interaction, but the length of these observations, as well as the extent to which they sample diverse everyday contexts, may be crucial. Brief observations, in which the functional contexts sampled vary, are likely to yield noisy and unreliable measures, whereas longer observations are more likely to average across various contexts and thus, to yield more valid and generalizable measures of individuals (Epstein, 1980; Maccoby & Martin, 1983). Variations in sociocultural background may also be significant; little is known of the extent to which observations in such contexts as play, feeding, or caretaking yield accurate, valid, and comparable information in different subcultural samples. One purpose of our study was to examine the impact of the functional and social contexts on the quality of infant–adult interaction and the effects such variations had on the expected associations between the security of infant–mother attachment and the observed quality of earlier mother–infant interaction in diverse, naturally occurring contexts.

THE CENTRAL AND EURO-AMERICAN FAMILIES

The data reported in this chapter are based on two samples of children and families, first observed when the infants averaged 13 weeks of age. The first sample consisted of 40 firstborn children (18 girls and 22 boys) whose parents migrated from Central America to the Washington, DC, area within 5 years of the infants' births. The second sample was comprised of 42 firstborn infants (22 girls and 20 boys) and their well-educated, affluent parents from Euro-American backgrounds. The parents in these two samples represented contrasting socioeconomic circumstances. The immigrants relied predominantly on temporary jobs and thus, their employment status, work schedules, and work hours fluctuated over the course of the infants' first year. The mean reported household income was around $11,000. When interviewed about their sociocultural backgrounds, most of the immigrant mothers recalled that they had frequent contact with extended family members when growing up. Half of the mothers had other relatives living in their households in addition to nuclear family members, three fourths of them had relatives who helped care for their infants, and two thirds recalled that their own mothers received similar help. Only four homes contained both parents and the infant living alone, as a family unit.

In Euro-American families, by contrast, all of the mothers were married and reported a mean annual household income of over $82,000 per year. Half of the mothers and fathers completed college educations and the others obtained at least some postgraduate education. Only two of the Euro-American parents shared their homes with anyone other than their infants.

DESCRIBING THE NICHES

Observations

Data were gathered by observation when the infants were approximately 3 months old, and by interview when they averaged 8 and 12 months of age. The four home observations had the same general format, with the emphasis on unstructured, infant-focused, time-sampled interactions. Each visit lasted for approximately 4 hours, with the start and end of each visit scheduled to ensure that the 12-hour period between 8 am and 8 pm was sampled in each family. During the visits, observers recorded the behavior of the infants and their social partners using the coding scheme originally developed by Belsky (Isabella & Belsky, 1991; Isabella, Belsky, & von Eye, 1989) in a 20-second observe followed by a 10-second record format. This procedure was designed to allow relatively easy, rapid, and reliable data collection without using an electronic recording device.

The coding system sampled relevant mother and infant behaviors in six domains. *Visual orientation* included behaviors such as face-to-face, mutual visual attention, an infant looking at his or her mother, and mother watching or checking her infant. *Vocalization* included sounds and speech of infant and adult (mother, father, or other). *Adult activities* included soothing affect, playing, caring, feeding. *Infant activities* included playing, and *infant location* provided information about the room and the infant's location in the room.

For purposes of analysis, we identified five mutually exclusive and exhaustive contexts (feeding, caretaking, object play, social interaction, and no interaction). Feeding and caretaking were indicated as such by the coders, dyadic object play was coded when both infant and caretaker were involved in object play, and social interaction was coded when the dyads were engaged in visual–verbal interactions such as physical expressions of affection (kissing, hugging, etc.) and nonphysical expressions of affection (such as verbal terms of endearment) and soothing outside of the other contexts. No interaction was defined by the absence of mutually directed behavior (e.g., the infant looks at mother while mother does not look at the infant and vice versa; infant plays with object while mother is at leisure, etc.).

When the infants were 8 and 12 months old, trained interviewers visited the families in their homes and helped the mothers to reconstruct the previous day in as much detail as possible. Events lasting less than 5 minutes were ignored (Michelson, 1987). The interviewers recorded any reported changes in the infants' or the caregivers' activities, their location, and the presence of other people. Other adults (e.g., care providers) were interviewed about the times that the mothers were not with the infants.

PORTRAITS OF EVERYDAY LIFE

Adult Presence When Infant Is Awake

In both groups of families, mothers spent more time with their 3-month-old infants (87% and 73% of waking time in the Euro-American and Central-American families, respectively) while they were awake than did any other adults; both fathers (18% and 16%, respectively) and other adults (19% and 26%, respectively) spent little time with the infants, usually while the mothers were also present. In the Central-American families, the total amount of time with others was equally divided between relatives who shared the home and visited friends. Central-American mothers left the infants alone about 18% of the time they were awake, compared with 9% of the time in Euro-American families. Further details are provided by Fracasso, Lamb, Schölmerich, and Leyendecker (1997).

Much the same pattern was evident when the infants were 8 and 12 months old: The Central-American infants spent 76% and the Euro-American infants spent 69% of their waking time with their mothers present (see Leyendecker, Lamb, Schölmerich, & Fracasso, 1995, for further details). At 8 months old, the Central-American infants spent much more time in the presence of their fathers (35%) than did the Euro-American infants (23%), but only a small percentage of this time was spent with fathers alone (2% and 1%, respectively).

On average, the Central-American infants spent about half of their time with just one person, and they also encountered more people (four on average) during the average day than the Euro-American infants did (two). The people encountered by Central-American infants were predominantly relatives who were present for 30% of the infants' waking time. By contrast, the Euro-American infants spent most of their waking time (69%) in the presence of just one person, and the two parents were simultaneously present very rarely. With few exceptions, babysitters (16%) were the only persons other than the parents who spent time alone with these infants. Most of the people other than parents whom the Euro-American infants met were either babysitters or friends of their parents. These infants were most likely to meet other people when they were with their mothers.

Circadian Distribution of Activities

Differences in the infants' social worlds had interesting implications for the organization of their days. Figures 6.1 and 6.2 show how many infants in the Central-American sample were reportedly asleep, playing with an adult, feeding, or in the presence or their fathers during their waking time at any given moment. Most children were awake in the late afternoon or early

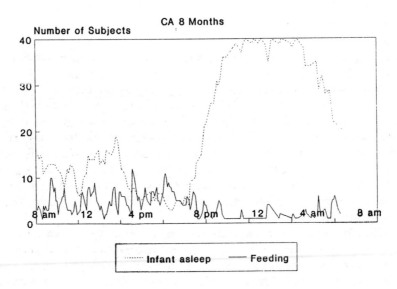

FIG. 6.1. Infants' cycles: Wake-sleep and feeding.

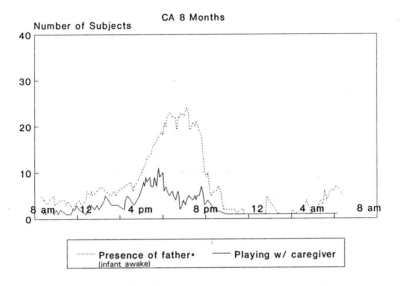

FIG. 6.2. Infants' cycles: Presence of father and play.

evening hours, yet many Central-American infants started their night sleep quite late or woke up quite early in the mornings, making up for this with extensive daytime naps. The Central-American fathers were often present during the day, and the peak hours for dyadic play stretched out between 4 pm and 8 pm. Furthermore, feeding in the Central-American group did not follow a tripartite morning–noon–evening pattern. Feeding was less common between 11 pm and 4 am, but otherwise, feeding took place throughout the day. Even between 11 pm and 5 am, most of the Central-American infants were fed at least once, whereas very few of the Euro-American infants were fed at this time.

Figures 6.3 and 6.4 reveal a somewhat different structure to the daily routines of infants in Euro-American families. The figures show that many of these infants slept until around noon and, like the Central-American infants, were awake in the late afternoon or early evening hours. Feeding had three distinct peaks (morning, noon, and evening), however, and dyadic play was most likely to occur between 5:30 pm and 7:30 pm. Other activities such as nonsocial play and care provision were evenly distributed across the infants' waking hours. The Euro-American infants went to bed earlier and awakened in the morning later than the Central-American infants. Figure 6.4 indicates that the presence of fathers not only coincided with the early morning and early evening hours when most infants were awake, but also co-occurred with a high proportion of feeding and dyadic play, both of which constituted major social activities at that age.

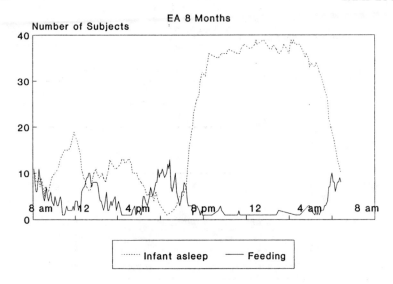

FIG. 6.3.   Infants' cycles: Wake-sleep and feeding.

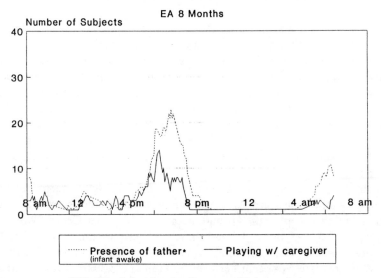

FIG. 6.4.   Infants' cycles: Presence of father and play.

Despite group differences in the number of nighttime feedings, the mean number of feedings per day and the average length of the feedings did not differ between the two groups, and there were likewise no differences in the percentage of time the infants were awake and engaged in any of the activities previously mentioned. In both groups, nonsocial play was the predominant activity, followed by feeding, dyadic play, and caregiving.

Effects of Adults' Presence on the Amount
of Time Spent in Different Contexts

The social context also affected the infants' social experiences. When only
the mothers were with their 3 month olds, for example, social interactions
were the most prominent context in both groups, followed by feeding and
caretaking. When other adults were also present, however, the amount of
caretaking and social interaction with the infants decreased. Identical trends
were evident in data drawn from the diaries completed by the mothers when
their infants were 8 and 12 months old. According to the mothers' reports,
fathers were also more likely to play with their infants when alone with them
than when other adults were present.

IMPLICATIONS FOR THE UNDERSTANDING
OF CULTURAL VARIATIONS

Despite cultural and economic differences, the everyday experiences of infants from affluent, middle-class, Euro-American families and from impoverished immigrant families appeared very similar in many respects. Specifically,
mothers and infants in the two groups spent similarly limited amounts of
time in the various discrete contexts. We found no differences in the amounts
of time the infants engaged in various activities, suggesting that participation
in these activities was independent of SES or subcultural differences, and
was perhaps driven by the infants' needs and demands. In this respect, the
findings were consistent with previous reports indicating that, even when
there are large differences between cultures, there are many similarities in
mother–infant interaction (Lewis & Ban, 1977). Fathers and other adults in
the two groups spent similar amounts of time with their infants and their
presence had similar effects on the infants' activities. In both groups, nonsocial activities decreased and dyadic play increased when the fathers were
present, as had also been reported in middle-class populations (Lamb,
1979).

Just as the presence of other people changed the patterns of interaction,
so too did the functional context. In both Central-American and Euro-American families, mothers and infants vocalized more and paid more mutual
attention during caretaking, play, and social interaction than during bouts
of feeding. The existence of powerful context-related effects makes it crucial
to consider social contexts when comparing either sociocultural groups or
the results of different studies and when assessing individual differences
among dyads.

Using similar recording techniques for much shorter periods (2 hours),
Lewis and Ban (1977) found few differences among Dutch, Senegalese,

American, and Yugoslavian mothers. In these cultures, play was relatively infrequent, whereas mothers vocalized to and frequently held their infants. Similarly, Richman et al. (1992) reported that holding and vocalization were the most frequently observed behaviors of Gusii and Bostonian mothers. Others reported that Euro-American mothers, especially upper-middle-class mothers, talk to and look at their infants more frequently than do mothers of other ethnic backgrounds (Feiring & Lewis, 1981; Richman et al., 1988). Our findings, like these, underscore the emphasis that Euro-American mothers place on verbal and visual interaction and on the ability of their infants to communicate at an early age. In addition, our findings accent the significance of verbal and visual interaction for the Central-American mothers as well. Although the Central-American mothers engaged in less visual and verbal interaction with their infants than the Euro-American mothers did (see also Richman et al., 1988), such interactions were still common in both groups.

Beside these similarities, group differences were evident in the organization and breadth of the infants' social ecology and in the circadian distribution of activities. Perhaps most compelling were group differences in the number of persons simultaneously present and in the parents' relationships with these persons. The Central-American infants spent little time with just one person and much time in the company of several people, including relatives and coresident adults. Accordingly, the social worlds of the Central-American children were broad, and they often had the opportunity to interact with several social partners simultaneously. Nonparental care was mainly provided by relatives and family friends, ensuring the flexibility necessary to accommodate unpredictable changes in jobs and work schedules. Thus, broad social networks and extended family arrangements not only represent adaptive strategies for sharing the available resources (Harrison, Wilson, Pine, Chan, & Buriel, 1990), but also shape the family ecology experienced by infants from early in life. By contrast, the Euro-American children had fewer social partners overall, more opportunities for one-on-one interactions, and few opportunities to interact with babysitters and parents together. Thus, individualism affected some of the earliest childhood experiences.

Several other findings illustrate the differing everyday experiences of infants in these two subcultural groups. Daily life was quite structured and predictable for the Euro-American infants, whereas the daily lives of the Central-American infants' families were less routinized. In part, this may be because the Euro-American parents had similar, regular work hours, whereas the Central-American parents worked on less traditional schedules. In addition, family-to-family variations in bedtimes and mealtimes might result from the living conditions of the Central-American families (crowded apartments or infants sleeping with their parents) as well as from different attitudes toward the infants. For whatever reason, the Central-American parents included the infants in their own lives and routines and did not seek to establish special schedules and environments for their infants in the way that the Euro-American parents did.

The notion that Central-American parents are less eager to establish special schedules for their infants is also suggested by variations in the influence of others' presence on the infants' activities. Whereas the presence of other people did not affect the feeding of the Euro-American infants, feeding appeared to be a social activity in the Central-American families, more likely to occur when others were present than when the infants were alone with either parent. This might also explain why feeding occurred around the clock depending on when the family was together, rather than on a regular schedule like that sought by Euro-American parents. The flexibility of the Central-American immigrants is probably more internationally common than the Western practice of living by the clock.

Overall, the social ecology of the two groups differed substantially, suggesting that familism and individualism are appropriate descriptions not only for different adult lifestyles; but also for the infants' social worlds. It is likely that the different early social experiences of infants growing up in these two rearing environments also affect their later lives, perhaps shaping their tolerance for intense social interaction, their need to be with others or to be alone, and their dependence on and preference for time-structured lifestyles.

INTERACTIONAL HARMONY, FUNCTIONAL CONTEXT, AND ATTACHMENT

More fine-grained analyses of the observational data also revealed important variations across functional context in the quality of mother–infant interaction. For purposes of these analyses, the observational codes just mentioned were also used to quantify the levels of well-attuned and disharmonious states over a 12-hour day and thus across a variety of naturally occurring contexts (Leyendecker, Lamb, & Schölmerich, 1997). Isabella and Belsky (1991; Isabella et al., 1989) showed that the variables describing infant and maternal behaviors can be combined to create temporally related indices of well-attuned or synchronous (e.g., infant fusses or cries–mother soothes) and disharmonious or asynchronous (e.g., infant fusses or cries–mother stimulates or arouses) dyadic states, and a similar strategy was adopted in this study. Isabella et al. (1989) showed that these synchrony scores were predictive of later attachment status, as assessed in the Strange Situation (Ainsworth et al., 1978), whereas Schölmerich, Fracasso, Lamb, and Broberg (1995) found a systematic relation between similarly constructed measures of interactional harmony and attachment security as assessed using Waters and Deane's (1985) Q-set. In our study, attachment was assessed in the Strange Situation when the infants were 12 months old, 9 months after the home observations.

In both groups, about one fourth of the infants' waking time was spent in well-attuned states, whereas the Euro-American dyads spent significantly more time (31%) in disharmonious states than the Central American dyads (22%) did. The proportions of time spent in well-attuned and disharmonious states substantially varied across contexts, however. In both groups, well-attuned interactions occurred proportionately most often during object play, followed by social interaction, caretaking, and feeding, although the Central American dyads engaged in significantly more well-attuned interactions while feeding. The percentages of disharmonious interactions were more evenly distributed across contexts, with the highest amount occurring, as expected, during periods involving no interaction.

Despite these variations across context, overall harmony and disharmony scores were related to attachment security in both groups. The securely attached dyads were significantly more likely than the insecurely attached dyads to engage in harmonious interactions. Comparable analyses of the disharmony scores revealed that insecurely attached Central-American dyads had lower harmony and disharmony scores, whereas the insecurely attached Euro-American dyads spent a higher proportion of time engaged in disharmonious interaction than did secure Euro-American dyads. Securely attached dyads spent significantly less time without interaction and more time engaged in object play and in social interaction than did insecure dyads. A significant interaction between security and the subcultural group indicated that the securely attached Central-American dyads spent more, and the securely attached Euro-American dyads less, time in caretaking.

DIRECTIONS FOR CROSS-CULTURAL RESEARCH ON ATTACHMENT

Our examination of interactions in different functional contexts yielded two findings of special importance. First, different contexts involve reliably different levels of attuned and disharmonious states. The highest levels of attunement were observed during nongoal-directed, playful interactions (object play and social interactions), whereas disharmony was most common during periods without interaction or during caretaking. Second, although this rank ordering was the same in both cultural groups, the levels of both attunement and disharmony differed in all contexts but social interaction, suggesting that the 3-month-old infants in the two groups might have quite different experiences while in similar functional contexts. The higher attunement scores of the Central-American dyads during feeding are probably attributable to the fact that the Euro-American mothers were more likely to breastfeed, which reduced the amount of (observable) interaction. Meanwhile, the low levels of disharmony during times spent by the Central-American dyads without interaction reflect the higher proportion of time Central-American mothers were not in the same room during these periods (42% vs. 23%). The disharmony scores include instances of both nonresponsiveness, as well as intrusiveness, and mothers who are not present obviously cannot be intrusive. By contrast, the disharmony scores of the Central-American dyads were higher during object play, a finding that is consistent with an earlier report that Hispanic mothers tend to be more directive and overstimulating during play episodes than do Euro-American mothers (Garcia Coll et al., 1992). Analyses of the overall disharmony scores put these findings into perspective, however, showing that the quality of mother–infant interaction varies across contexts and that inferences about cross-contextual and cross-time individual differences based on a single context may lack validity. Thus, our findings show how different functional contexts disclose different levels of attuned and disharmonious interactions in diverse cultural groups.

IMPLICATIONS FOR FUTURE RESEARCH

Overall, these findings have substantial implications for the design of future studies. Limiting the focus to interaction in any one context ensures that the levels of attuned and disharmonious interactions are more comparable than when interactions in varying contexts are sampled for brief periods of time. When studying diverse groups, the choice of the context can serve to maximize or minimize apparent group differences, and it is thus important to determine whether any observed group differences are unique to specific contexts.

Developmental changes must obviously be viewed in both functional and cultural contexts. The degree of dyadic involvement observed in any context is likely to change over time as the developmental repertoire changes, as well as in response to differing cultural practices. Middle-class, Euro-American families, for example, put special emphasis on early self-feeding, which is believed to reflect and promote autonomy and independence. Thus, maternal involvement increases in the second part of the first year when infants learn how to self-feed and decreases again as they master this task. In other cultures, self-feeding might occur later; as a result, maternal involvement during feeding may increase and decrease later as well. In addition, the dynamics of cultural changes have to be kept in mind. Most of the Central-American families we studied migrated to the United States fairly recently, but it is likely that the process of adaptation to life in the United States eventually changes parental attitudes and beliefs (e.g., Sabogal et al., 1987). Research involving individuals from differing cultural and subcultural groups must attend to the different yet complementary goals of identifying broad, generalizable principles of human development and recognizing the complexity of human lives and the interactions among individual differences, culture, and social class.

Research designed to assess cultural variations in childrearing practices can also provide insight into the heterogeneity and homogeneity of experiences in and across various societies. Such descriptive information is very important to both practitioners and theorists, particularly because most developmental theories were developed by and tested on middle-class caucasian North Americans, who are seldom aware of the ethnocentric biases built in their accounts of universal or normative developmental processes.

REFERENCES

Ainsworth, M. D. S., Blehar, M. C., Waters, E., & Wall, S. (1978). *Patterns of attachment: A psychological study of the Strange Situation*. Hillsdale, NJ: Lawrence Erlbaum Associates.

Bates, J. E., Maslin, L. A., & Frankel, K. A. (1985). Attachment security, mother–child interaction, and temperament as predictors of behavior problem ratings at age three years. In I. Bretherton & E. Waters (Eds.), *Growing points in attachment theory and research: Monographs of the Society for Research in Child Development* (Vol. 50, Serial No. 209, 167–193).

Bornstein, M. H., Tamis-LeMonda, C. S., Pecheux, M., & Rahn, C. W. (1991). Mother and infant activity and interaction in France and the United States: A comparative study. *International Journal of Behavioural Development, 14,* 21–43.

Clarke-Stewart, K. A. (1973). Interactions between mothers and their young children: Characteristics and consequences. *Monographs of the Society for Research in Child Development, 38* (6–7, Serial No. 153).

Cole, M. (1992). Culture in development. In M. H. Bornstein & M. E. Lamb (Eds.), *Developmental psychology: An advanced textbook* (3rd ed., pp. 731–789). Hillsdale, NJ: Lawrence Erlbaum Associates.

Cox, M. J., Owen, M. T., Henderson, V. K., & Margand, N. A. (1992). Prediction of infant–father and infant–mother attachment. *Developmental Psychology, 28,* 474–483.

Dittrichova, J., & Lapackova, V. (1964). Development of waking states in young infants. *Child Development, 35,* 365–370.

Dunn, J. (1993). *Young children's close relationships: Beyond attachment*. Newbury Park, CA: Sage.

Epstein, S. (1980). The stability of behavior II. Implications for psychological research. *American Psychologist, 35,* 790–806.

Feiring, C., & Lewis, M. (1981). Middle class differences in mother–child interaction and the child's cognitive development. In T. M. Field, A. M. Sostek, P. Vietze, & P. H. Leiderman (Eds.), *Culture and infancy: Variations in the human experience* (pp. 63–94). Hillsdale, NJ: Lawrence Erlbaum Associates.

Field, T. M., & Widmayer, S. M. (1981). Mother–infant interactions among lower SES Black, Cuban, Puerto Rican and South American immigrants. In T. M. Field, A. M. Sostek, P. Vietze, & P. H. Leiderman (Eds.), *Culture and infancy: Variations in the human experience* (pp. 41–62). Hillsdale, NJ: Lawrence Erlbaum Associates.

Fracasso, M. P., Lamb, M. E., Schölmerich, A., & Leyendecker, B. (1997). The ecology of mother–infant interaction in Euro-American and immigrant Central American families living in the United States. *International Journal of Behavioral Development, 20*, 207–217.

Garcia Coll, C., Perez-Febles, A., Halpern, L., Nevarez, M., Andreozzi, L., & Valcarcel, M. (1992, May). *Maternal–infant interactions in Puerto Rico*. Paper presented at the International Conference on Infant Studies, Miami, FL.

Greenbaum, C. W., & Landau, R. (1977). Mothers' speech and early development of vocal behavior: Findings from a cross-cultural observation study in Israel. In P. H. Leiderman, S. R. Tulkin, & A. Rosenfeld (Eds.), *Culture and infancy: Variations in the human experience* (pp. 245–270). New York: Academic Press.

Harrison, A. O., Wilson, M. N., Pine, C. J., Chan, S. Q., & Buriel, R. (1990). Family ecologies of minority children. *Child Development, 61*, 347–362.

Hewlett, B. S. (1992). (Ed.). *Father–child relations: Cultural and biosocial contexts*. New York: de Gruyter.

Howes, C. (1988). Peer interaction of young children. *Monographs of the Society for Research in Child Development, 53* (1, Serial No. 217).

Isabella, R. A. (1993). Origins of attachment: Maternal interactive behavior across the first year. *Child Development, 64*, 605–621.

Isabella, R. A., & Belsky, J. (1991). Interactional synchrony and the origins of infant–mother attachment: A replication study. *Child Development, 62*, 373–384.

Isabella, R. A., Belsky, J., & von Eye, A. (1989). The origins of infant–mother attachment: A replication study. *Developmental Psychology, 25*, 12–21.

Izard, C. E., Haynes, O. M., Chisholm, G., & Baak, K. (1991). Emotional determinants of infant–mother attachment. *Child Development, 62*, 906–917.

Juster, F. T. (1985). The validity and quality of time use estimates obtained from recall diaries. In F. T. Juster & F. P. Stafford (Eds.), *Time, goods, and well-being* (pp. 63–91). Ann Arbor: University of Michigan Press.

Lamb, M. E. (1977). Father–infant and mother–infant interaction in the first year of life. *Child Development, 48*, 167–181.

Lamb, M. E. (1979). The effects of the social context on dyadic social interaction. In M. E. Lamb, S. J. Suomi, & G. R. Stephenson (Eds.), *Social interaction analysis: Methodological issues* (pp. 253–268). Madison: University of Wisconsin Press.

Lamb, M. E. (Ed.). (1997). *The role of the father in child development* (3rd ed.). New York: Wiley.

Lamb, M. E. (1998). Nonparental child care: Context, quality, correlates, and consequences. In W. Damon (Series Ed.), & I. Sigel & K. A. Renninger (Vol. Eds.), *Handbook of child psychology: Child psychology in practice* (5th ed. Volume 4; pp. 73–133). New York: Wiley.

Lamb, M. E., & Easterbrooks, M. A. (1981). Individual differences in parental sensitivity: Origins, components, and consequences. In M. E. Lamb & L. R. Sherrod (Eds.), *Infant social cognition* (pp. 127–153). Hillsdale, NJ: Lawrence Erlbaum Associates.

Lamb, M. E., & Elster, A. B. (1985). Adolescent mother–infant–father relationships. *Developmental Psychology, 21*, 768–773.

Lamb, M. E., Ketterlinus, R., & Fracasso, M. (1993). Parent–child relationships. In M. H. Bornstein & M. E. Lamb (Eds.), *Developmental psychology: An advanced textbook* (3rd ed., pp. 465–518). Hillsdale, NJ: Lawrence Erlbaum Associates.

Lamb, M. E., & Nash, A. (1989). Infant–mother attachment, sociability, and peer competence. In T. J. Berndt & G. W. Ladd (Eds.), *Peer relationships in child development* (pp. 219–245). New York: Wiley.

Lamb, M. E., & Sternberg, K. J. (1992). Sociocultural perspectives on nonparental child care. In M. E. Lamb, K. J. Sternberg, C-P. Hwang, & A. G. Broberg (Eds.), *Child care in context* (pp. 1–23). Hillsdale, NJ: Lawrence Erlbaum Associates.

Lamb, M. E., Thompson, R. A., Gardner, W., & Charnov, E. L. (1985). *Infant–mother attachment*. Hillsdale, NJ: Lawrence Erlbaum Associates.

Leiderman, P. H., Tulkin, S. R., & Rosenfeld, A. (Eds.). (1977). *Culture and infancy: Variations in the human experience*. New York: Academic Press.

Lewis, M. (1978). Situational analysis and the study of behavioral development. In L. A. Pervin & M. Lewis (Eds.), *Situational analysis and the study of behavioral development* (pp. 49–66). New York: Plenum.

Lewis, M. (1987). Social development in infancy and early childhood. In J. D. Osofsky (Ed.), *Handbook of infant development* (pp. 419–493). New York: Wiley.

Lewis, M., & Ban, P. (1977). Variance and invariance in the mother–infant interaction: A cross-cultural study. In P. H. Leiderman, S. R. Tulkin, & A. Rosenfeld (Eds.), *Culture and infancy: Variations in the human experience* (pp. 329–355). New York: Academic Press.

Lewis, M., & Feiring, C. (1979). The child's social network: Social object, social functions, and their relationships. In M. Lewis & L. A. Rosenblum (Eds.), *The child and its family* (pp. 9–27). New York: Plenum.

Lewis, M., & Feiring, C. (1982). Some American families at dinner. In L. M. Laosa & I. E. Sigel (Eds.), *Families as learning environments for children* (pp. 115–145). New York: Plenum.

Lewis, M., & Feiring, C. (1989). Infant, mother, and mother–infant interaction behavior and subsequent attachment. *Child Development, 60,* 831–837.

Lewis, M., Feiring, C., & Kotsonis, M. (1984). The social network of the young child: A developmental perspective. In M. Lewis (Ed.), *Beyond the dyad: The genesis of behavior* (pp. 129–160). New York: Plenum.

Lewis, M., & Freedle, R. (1977). The mother and infant communication system: The effects of poverty. In H. McGurk (Ed.), *Ecological factors in human development* (pp. 205–215). Amsterdam, The Netherlands: North-Holland.

Lewis, M., & Wilson, C. D. (1972). Infant development in lower class American families. *Human Development, 15,* 112–127.

Leyendecker, B., Lamb, M. E., & Schölmerich, A. (1997). Studying mother–infant interaction: The effects of context and length of observation in two subcultural groups. *Infant Behavior and Development, 20,* 325–337.

Leyendecker, B., Lamb, M. E., Schölmerich, A., & Fracasso, M. P. (1995). The social worlds of 8- and 12-month-old infants: Early experiences in two subcultural contexts. *Social Development, 4,* 194–208.

Lyons-Ruth, K., Connell, D. B., Zoll, D., & Stahl, J. (1987). Infants at social risk: Relations among infant maltreatment, maternal behavior, and infant attachment behavior. *Developmental Psychology, 23,* 223–232.

Maccoby, E. E., & Martin, J. A. (1983). Socialization in the context of the family: Parent–child interaction. In E. M. Hetherington (Ed.), *Handbook of child psychology* (Vol. 4, pp. 1–101). New York: Wiley.

Malatesta, C. Z., Culver, C., Tesman, J. R., & Shepard, B. (1989). The development of emotion expression during the first two years of life. *Monographs of the Society for Research in Child Development, 219* (54, Serial Nos. 1–2, 1–104).

Mangelsdorf, S., Gunnar, M., Kestenbaum, R., Lang, S., & Andreas, D. (1990). Infant proneness-to-distress temperament, maternal personality, and mother–infant attachment: Associations and goodness of fit. *Child Development, 61,* 820–831.

Michelson, W. (1987). Measuring macroenvironment and behavior: The time budget and time geography. In R. B. Bechtel, R. W. Marans, & W. Michelson (Eds.), *Methods in environmental and behavioral research* (pp. 216–243). New York: Van Nostrand Reinhold.

Mindel, C. H. (1980). Extended familism among urban Mexican Americans, Anglos, and Blacks. *Hispanic Journal of Behavioral Sciences, 2,* 21–34.

O'Brien, M., Johnson, J. M., & Anderson-Goetz, D. (1989). Evaluating quality in mother–infant interaction: Situational effects. *Infant Behavior and Development, 12,* 451–464.

Parke, R. D., & Kellam, S. G. (Eds.). (1994). *Exploring family relationships with other social contexts.* Hillsdale, NJ: Lawrence Erlbaum Associates.

Parke, R. D., & Tinsley, B. J. (1987). Family interaction in infancy. In J. D. Osofsky (Ed.), *Handbook of infant development* (2nd ed., pp. 579–641). New York: Wiley.

Richman, A. L., LeVine, R. A., New, R., Howrigan, G. A., Welles-Nyström, B., & LeVine, S. C. (1988). Maternal behavior to infants in five cultures. In R. A. LeVine, P. M. Muller, & M. M. West (Eds.), *Parental behavior in diverse societies* (pp. 81–96). San Francisco: Jossey-Bass.

Richman, A. L., Muller, P. M., & LeVine, R. A. (1992). Cultural and educational variations in maternal responsiveness. *Developmental Psychology, 28,* 614–621.

Robinson, J. P. (1985). The validity and reliability of diaries versus alternative time use measures. In F. T. Juster & F. P. Stafford (Eds.), *Time, goods, and well-being* (pp. 33–62). Ann Arbor: University of Michigan Press.

Rogoff, B., & Morelli, G. (1989). Perspectives on children's development from cultural psychology. *American Psychologist, 44,* 343–348.

Sabogal, F., Marin, G., Otero-Sabogal, R., Marin, B. V., & Perez-Stable, E. (1987). Hispanic familism and acculturation: What changes and what doesn't? *Hispanic Journal of Behavioral Sciences, 9,* 379–412.

Sampson, E. E. (1985). The decentralization of identity. *American Psychologist, 40,* 1203–1211.

Sampson, E. E. (1988). The debate on individualism. *American Psychologist, 43,* 15–22.

Schölmerich, A., Fracasso, M. P., Lamb, M. E., & Broberg, A. G. (1995). Interactional harmony at 7 and 10 months of age predicts security of attachment as measured by Q-sort ratings. *Social Development, 4,* 62–74.

Seifer, R., Sameroff, A. J., Anagnostopolou, R., & Elias, P. K. (1992). Mother–infant interaction during the first year: Effects of situation, maternal mental illness, and demographic factors. *Infant Behavior and Development, 15,* 405–426.

Spence, J. T. (1985). Achievement American style: The rewards and costs of individualism. *American Psychologist, 40,* 1285–1295.

Super, C. M., & Harkness, S. (1986). The developmental niche: A conceptualization at the interface of child and culture. *International Journal of Behavioral Development, 9,* 545–569.

Triandis, H. C., Marin, G., Betancourt, H., Lisansky, J., & Chang, B. H. (1982). *Dimensions of familism among Hispanic and mainstream Navy recruits.* (Technical Report No. 14). Champaign: University of Illinois, Department of Psychology.

Tronick, E. Z., Morelli, G. A., & Ivey, P. K. (1992). The Efe forager infant and toddler's pattern of social relationships: Multiple and simultaneous. *Developmental Psychology, 28,* 568–577.

Vega, W. A. (1990). Hispanic families in the 1980s: A decade of research. *Journal of Marriage and the Family, 52,* 1015–1024.

Wachs, T. D. (1984). Proximal experience and early cognitive development: The social environment. In A. Gottfried (Ed.), *Home environment and early cognitive development* (pp. 273–328). New York: Academic Press.

Waters, E., & Deane, K. E. (1985). Defining and assessing individual differences in attachment relationships: Q- methodology and the organization of behavior in infancy & early childhood. In I. Bretherton & E. Waters (Eds.), *Growing points of attachment theory and research. Monographs of the Society for Research in Child Development, 50* (Serial No. 209).

West, M. M. (1988). Parental values and behavior in the outer Fiji Islands. In R. A. LeVine, P. M. Miller, & M. M. West (Eds.), *Parental behavior in diverse societies* (pp. 13–25). San Francisco: Jossey-Bass.

Whitney, M. P., & Thoman, E. B. (1994). Sleep of premature and full-term infants from 24-hour home recordings. *Infant Behavior and Development, 17,* 223–234.

Wolff, P. H. (1963). Observations on the early development of smiling. In B. M. Foss (Ed.), *Determinants of infant behavior* (Vol. 11, pp. 113–133). London: Methuen.

Yarrow, L. J., Rubenstein, J. L., & Pedersen, F. A. (1975). *Infant and environment: Early cognitive and motivational development.* New York: Wiley.

7

▼▼▼▼▼▼▼

Home Environment and Children's Development: Age and Demographic Differences

Robert H. Bradley
Leanne Whiteside-Mansell
University of Arkansas at Little Rock

For over 20 years, our professional lives centered around studies of families. Our investigations of family life led us to develop a number of measures of parenting, the most well-known being the Home Observation for Measurement of the Environment (HOME) inventory (Bradley, 1994; Caldwell & Bradley, 1984). More recently, we designed Parental Investment in Children (Bradley, Whiteside-Mansell, Caldwell, & Brisby, 1997), a measure of parents' attachment to their children. We visited hundreds of homes, and were bombarded with questions regarding measurement of the home environment. Two lasting impressions emerged from this experience: the diversity of family life and corresponding challenge of trying to understand its role in children's development.

It seems useful to think of the environment for parenting as including all of the social and physical phenomena in the home place (Wachs, 1992; Wapner, 1987). However, it is probably counterproductive to confine the concept of the parenting environment to a particular place. In a child's mind, or in a parent's mind, what constitutes home probably does not exclusively refer to those events, objects, and actions in the four walls of a particular residence. A walk around the block with Dad, a visit to the local library with Mom, or an argument between Mom and Dad in the car on the way to MacDonald's may all be strongly associated with the network of acts and events that comprise a child's family life. By the same token, the concept of home environment as fully divorced from any place of residence is probably not useful either. For both parent and child, many of the ideas connected with home have their roots in scenes and scripts that emanate from particular concrete places where family activities occur (Abelson, 1981).

A capacious definition of home is consistent with the position of social anthropologists who contend that the social boundaries of household units do not necessarily coincide with the physical boundaries of their dwellings (Altman, 1977). An expansive definition seems appropriate given the living conditions for some children (e.g., families living in cars or makeshift shelters). The concept of the parenting environment as not fully confined to a specific place becomes useful because the role of parent tends to shift from that of direct provider and teacher (most of which may well take place with the family residence) to that of mentor, guide, and arranger of experiences, some of which almost certainly occur outside the four walls of the residence (Fagot & Kavanaugh, 1993; Maccoby & Martin, 1983). For individual parents, there is a sense of boundary to the spaces where parenting takes place, but what actually constitutes the boundary varies across parents and time (Belsky, 1984). In effect, what is appropriated to the idea of the home environment is the meaning of the acts, objects, and places connected to parental caregiving. Different families utilize different geographic settings to be part of the parenting environment (e.g., the street beside the house, the backyard, a neighborhood park).

THE HOME INVENTORY—A "MARKER" MEASURE

The purpose of this chapter is to help clarify the relation between the home environment and children's development and particularly to look at age and demographic differences. To aid in organizing our thoughts on the topic, we use the HOME as a marker measure—not that the inventory fully captures all the myriad aspects of home life, but HOME is widely known and its properties are well understood. The HOME inventory is different from some other measures of the home environment in that the data are collected from the perspective of a particular child. Such an approach to measuring the environment seems in keeping with current ecological–developmental theories that portray humans as phylogenetically advanced, self-constructing organisms (Ford & Lerner, 1992) and the environment as a regulator (actually, coregulator) of complex developmental processes (Sameroff & Fiese, 1990).

There are four versions of this inventory: the infant–toddler version (birth to 3 years old), the early childhood version (3 to 6 years old), the middle childhood version (6 to 10 years old), and the early adolescent version (10 to 14 years old). The information needed to score the inventories is obtained through a combination of observations and semistructured interviews done at home when both the child and the child's primary caregiver were present. Other family members were often present during the 45 to 90 minute visit as well.

What have we learned from our long history with HOME? The first thing is that HOME seems to work in the sense that it provides a reasonably accurate picture of a child's home environment. Even in the bleak conditions present in the mountains of Chile, where children have almost no toys to play with, HOME accurately portrayed this lack of material resources, along with the gentle nurturance that Chilean families tend to provide to young children. However, the inventory contains only a limited census of objects, events, and caregiver actions. Thus, the actual level of stimulation and support present in the environment may not be fully portrayed—in a way that is phenomenologically more truthful (see Bradley, Corwyn, & Whiteside-Mansell, 1997 for a discussion of cross-cultural uses of the HOME).

The second thing we learned from our experience with HOME is that life is incredibly diverse in any particular social class or cultural group. One of the most memorable home visits made using HOME involved a large Mexican-American family in Los Angeles. During the visit, there were 14 people present at one time or another, a large tightly knit, extended family group. The home was rich with language and personal exchanges among family members—it was also rich with joy. The family offered a strong contrast to the family situation of a young Mexican-American mother in San Diego, separated from the father of her only child and living with her father, who was separated from her mother. The young mother's discomfort with her living arrangement was readily apparent. So keen was this discomfort that she did not even bring her child's toys to her father's home. One of the most notable differences in family life is the increased number of fathers who function as primary (or coequal) caregivers (Casper, Hawkins, & O'Connell, 1994). One Denver stay-at-home dad converted part of the living room into a play area complete with pitched tent for indoor camping and pretend games.

Visits to homes, using HOME, make it abundantly clear how different life is for children. In the context of 1 hour's visit, we saw children held, touched, patted, or caressed dozens of times; however, we also saw children whose parents never made contact with them. We saw homes filled with toys and books and homes where there were no toys present and the family was living out of cardboard boxes. We made visits where 1 hour was full of spontaneous teaching exchanges between mother and child and visits where the only exchanges involved control of the child's behavior, and requests for information were rebuffed. The list goes on. None of the commonly used measures of the home environment, including HOME, captures these differences fully and completely.

The third thing we learned from using HOME is that scores on the inventory are correlated with nearly everything: race, family structure, neighborhood, parental personality and competence, and parental history. Many HOME items index objects and parenting practices more common to better educated, wealthier families. Most investigators found low to moderate correlations between HOME and social status variables (see Bradley, 1994 for a review). However, the strength of association can sometimes be quite modest (.24), as a study of working mothers from Italy attested (Fein, Gariboldi, & Boni, 1993). Results indicate that in cultures with a highly defined class structure, such as India, the link between social status and parenting practice is likely to be tight. By comparison, in societies with more mobility across classes and more nearly universal access to education (but not employment), the association may be weaker. HOME also reflects parental personality, parental substance abuse, parental IQ, parental knowledge about child development, parental attitudes toward childrearing, social support, psychosocial climate of the home, presence of traumatic events, and a variety of other community and cultural factors (Bradley, 1994). Ragozin, Landesman-Dwyer, and Streissguth (1980) even observed birth-order effects.

HOME scores also varied with maternal age. Coll and her colleagues (Coll, Vohr, Hoffman, & Oh, 1986; Coll, Hoffman, & Oh, 1987) found that even with total child-care support and stress controlled, older mothers scored higher on HOME. However, parenting practices of young mothers are not uniformly lower than those of older mothers. We conducted a study of 193 mothers ranging in age from 15 to 24 years old (Whiteside-Mansell, Pope, & Bradley, 1996). Each mother was assessed when her infant was 12 months old and again when her child was 36 months old. A cluster analysis was performed on the HOME subscale scores for both ages. Results showed that the majority of young mothers had HOME score profiles similar to those of older mothers. However, four of the five clusters had at least some HOME scores that had at least one standard deviation lower than those of older mothers. These profiles were related to maternal competence and family context as well as to children's development.

A little over 10 years ago, we looked at the relation of HOME and an array of demographic factors in a racially diverse sample (Bradley & Caldwell, 1984). We found two things: no one demographic factor accounted for much of the variance in HOME scores, and all the demographic factors we used (put together) only accounted for about 50% of the variance. Recently, we repeated this study with a much larger and even more diverse sample (Bradley, Mundfrom, Whiteside, Caldwell, et al., 1994). In our analysis, using data from the Infant Health and Development Program (1990) study, we essentially reproduced the findings from the earlier study: no one factor accounted for more than about 20% of the variance and a substantial amount of variance was left unaccounted for (see Table 7.1).

Measurement Equivalence Across Groups

Although HOME has been used with many deomographic groups, little work has been done to verify the measure's equivalence across these groups. Formal testing of measurement invariance across groups is critical to determine whether an instrument such as HOME yields information about the same

TABLE 7.1
Correlations Between HOME Scores and Demographic Factors

Demographic Variable	Variance Accounted for	
	12 Month HOME	36 Month HOME
African American versus Caucasian	8%	9%
African American versus Mexican American	1%	1%
Income	5%	4%
Maternal education	2%	6%
Gestatational age	1%	4%
Marital status	2%	3%
Maternal age	1%	1%
Parity	1%	4%
R^2	.38	.53

Note. Same data used as were used in Bradley, Mundfrom, Whiteside, Caldwell, Casey, Kirby, and Hansen (1994).

attributes in all groups. There are multiple ways to provide evidence of measurement invariance, some more exacting than others. *Factorial invariance* requires that the structure of a measure is similar at the item level for the groups being compared (Horn & McArdle, 1992). Bradley, Mundfrom, Whiteside, Barrett, and Casey (1994) examined the factor structure of both the infant–toddler HOME and the early childhood HOME for Euro-Americans, African Americans, and Hispanics using data from the Infant Health and Development Program. They determined that the factor structures for Whites and Blacks were similar on the infant–toddler and early childhood HOME. However, the factor structures for Hispanics were different in several small respects.

Although it is useful to examine the factorial invariance of home environment measures before comparing groups, the use of exploratory factor analysis with such measures involves some difficulty. Bollen (1989) made the distinction between measures composed of cause indicators and measures composed of effect indicators. Most measures of the environment (such as HOME) appear to be composed largely of cause indicators (e.g., toys produce stimulation for the child; coming to a child to provide comfort in times of distress and answering a child's questions create a responsive environment for the child). Unlike indicators that result from a common cause (e.g., the many indicators of depression), indicators that produce a common effect may themselves be uncorrelated. For example, a wide variety of different objects, events, persons, and settings may produce stimulation, but there may be little connection among these disparate elements other than the fact that they are all stimulating. Thus, the underlying structure of environmental measures are difficult to define and factor analysis results vary from one population to another.

Because different cultures and communities are characterized by different resources, values, and styles, the combination of persons, objects, events, and settings common to one group are quite uncommon in a second. Co-variations among environmental elements that produce stimulation, respon-siveness, and nurturance may likewise vary considerably across groups (e.g., see Bornstein et al., 1992 for an illustration of the differences in how mothers from the United States, France, and Japan show responsiveness to their infants). Not surprisingly, applying exploratory factor analysis to items in home environment measures may result in a quite diffuse factor structure for a given group, as well as structures that markedly vary across groups. Bollen and Lennox (1991) offered strong arguments in favor of using different analytic approaches when evaluating measures composed of cause indicators and measures composed of effect indicators, including the careful application of confirmatory factor analysis and structural equation modeling. The bot-tom line is, factorial invariance is extraordinarily difficult to establish across demographic groups. This does not mean that a measure is not equally valid for use with each group, but comparing scores is tricky.

A somewhat less restrictive form of measurement comparability is func-tional equivalence. HOME can be said to have functional, or scale level, equivalence for two groups if scores on HOME have similar precursors (e.g., parental characteristics), similar consequents (e.g., child outcomes), and simi-lar correlates (e.g., family contextual factors) across two groups. Whether establishing functional equivalence is sufficient to allow comparisons of scores across groups is a matter of debate. Labouvie and Ruetsch (1995) and others (Knight & Hill, in press) support its use; however, the concept was attacked as a method that gives misleading impressions about group differences (Meredith, 1995). Also, it is sometimes difficult to know whether observed differences in patterns of correlations between the measure of interest and theoretically related measures represent nonequivalence of measures or sim-ply a true difference in how the variables (constructs) themselves are related in the groups being compared.

Despite the fact that research has not established measurement equiva-lence for HOME (or any other home environment measure for that matter) across age groups or demographic groups, reviewing results of the studies that focused on these issues is still helpful. Current theory helps in deciding whether observed age and demographic differences reflect expected variations in underlying processes or measurement artifacts. Also, observed differences help in the refinement of theory. In this regard, it is unfortunate that tradi-tions in measuring home environments followed the more general psychomet-ric traditions in scale construction. Measurement developers generally tried to construct very efficient measures; that is, they tried to measure constructs using the fewest items possible while still retaining reliability. This approach makes good sense for measures composed of effect indicators because each indicator supposedly reflects the same underlying construct. However, because home environment measures are composed chiefly of cause indicators (numerous different things that have the same presumed effect), the use of factor analysis or coefficient *alpha* to reduce items with the goal of measurement efficiency may well have been misguided. In effect, we may have left out or discarded just those indicators that most often produce a particular effect in a given age or demographic group.

Ethnic and Social Class Differences

Ethnic and social class differences in the home environment were the subject of many investigations in child development (Bloom, 1964; Bradley, Caldwell, et al., 1989; Coll, 1990; Gottfried & Gottfried, 1984, 1988; McLoyd, Jayaratne, Ceballo, & Borquez, 1994). We present data from our studies and from studies done by others using HOME to illustrate what is known about ethnic group and social class differences.

Children from the Infant Health and Development Program (1990) were used to examine differences in relations between HOME scores and children's growth and development for Euro-American, African American, and Hispanic families. The study was a multisite clinical trial of a multifaceted intervention involving 985 low-birthweight children. Children were given a battery of developmental measures at 3 years old: the Child Behavior Checklist, the expressiveness scale from the Adaptive Social Behavior inventory (Hogan, Scott, & Bauer, 1994), and the Stanford–Binet Intelligence Test. For each child, a body mass index was also calculated. Although correlations between HOME scores and these four child measures tend to vary somewhat across these three groups, there is considerable similarity, especially for Euro-Americans and African Americans (see Table 7.2). These findings suggest a reasonable level of functional equivalence in the home environment for Blacks and Whites. The situation with respect to Hispanics is more difficult to interpret. It may be that HOME does not contain as relevant a set of environmental indicators for Hispanic families. However, the results may reflect the fact that the child measures were also not developed on Hispanic children or the fact that the native language of some of the respondents was Spanish rather than English.

Part of the difficulty in interpreting differences in patterns of correlations for various sociocultural groups is that group status tends to be confounded with SES and there are mean differences on key variables. To help deal with these problems families from three sociocultural groups (Euro-American, African American, and Hispanic) were matched on 12-month HOME scores prior to correlating HOME scores with child developmental measures. There were 131 children from each group. Data were obtained from six sites in

TABLE 7.2

Correlations Between HOME Scores and 3-Year Child Measures by Sociocultural Group

Child Measures	IT-HOME (1 year)			EA-HOME (3 years)		
	Euro-American	African American	Hispanic	Euro-American	African American	Hispanic
CBCL - Externalizing	-.31	-.17	-.24	-.48	-.24	-.20
ASBI - Expressiveness	.39	.23	.20	.42	.42	.01
IQ	.41	.29	.11	.60	.45	.35
Body Mass Index	-.10	.01	.03	.09	-.03	.06

Note. Data used were obtained from The Infant Health and Development Program (1990).

North America (see Bradley, Caldwell, et al., 1989 for a description of the combined sample). HOME scores obtained at 12, 24, and 36 months were correlated with 12-month Bayley MDI, 24-month Bayley MDI, and 36-month IQ. Correlations between HOME scores and child measures were generally higher for Euro-Americans than for the two minority groups, albeit there were some important exceptions such as the correlation for HOME and 3-year IQ for African Americans shown in Table 7.3. Again, the lowest correlations were for Hispanics.

Correlations were also computed between HOME scores and two demographic measures (maternal education and occupation of head of household). There was no relation between occupational status and HOME for African Americans or Hispanics, nor was maternal education correlated with HOME scores for Hispanics. The patterns of correlations between HOME and maternal education for Euro-Americans and for African Americans make clear that the relation is not constant across time. The correlations for African Americans became stronger as children aged, the correlations for Euro-Americans fluctuated some across time, and by 3 years old they were no different from that of African Americans.

The reasons for the sociocultural group differences in correlations between HOME, maternal education, and occupation of head of household are multiple. The results probably reflect differential access to educational and

TABLE 7.3
Correlations Between HOME Scores, Socioeconomic Status, and
Mental Test Scores for Samples Matched by Sociocultural Group

	Maternal Education	Occupation of Head of Household	Bayley MDI (12 mo.)	Bayley MDI (24 mo.)	IQ (36 mo.)
12 Month HOME					
Euro-American	.46	.53	.23	.52	.47
African American	.16	−.06	.17	.19	.41
Hispanic	−.07	−.01	.03	.41	.22
24 Month HOME					
Euro-American	.62	.46	.22	.62	.57
African American	.28	.11	.13	.28	.49
Hispanic	.11	.07	−.08	.24	.14
36 Month HOME					
Euro-American	.39	.41	.09	.46	.42
African American	.30	−.03	.25	.33	.50
Hispanic	−.07	−.18	.17	.05	.10

Note. Sample Size: Euro-American (N = 131), African American (N = 131), Hispanic (N = 131), cross-matched on 12 month HOME total score. The same data were analyzed as from Bradley, Caldwell, et al. (1989).

employment opportunities. Both epidemiologists (Liberatos, Link, & Kelsey, 1988) and psychologists (Citro & Michael, 1995) commented on the limitations of standard demographic indices as applied to minority groups. Recency of immigration (i.e., degree of acculturation) further compounds the difficulties for Hispanics. In effect, part of the difference in patterns of correlations across groups likely devolve from the fact that the parenting practices of Euro-Americans lines up reasonably consistently with the total array of resources, opportunities, and constraints present in the larger ecology. The situation for minorities is more complex, however. For example, a bright, young, recently immigrated Hispanic mother has little formal education, and the family has quite a limited income. Nonetheless, the family is well-connected to a larger group of kith and kin and the mother is well-disposed and well-tutored, regarding how to provide good care for her children. The HOME score reflects these personal and familial factors more closely than the socioeconomic ones. The sociocultural differences in patterns of correlations between HOME scores and child outcomes may say less about the differential salience of HOME items across groups, than about the fact that the capacity of the home environment to effect children's development depends on the broader ecological context in which the family operates.

Complicating the interpretation of sociocultural differences in patterns of relations between HOME and child measures is a variation on the long-standing nature versus nurture debate: Do observed correlations between home environment and children's development represent the environmental contribution to development or do they at least partially mask actual genetic influence (Longstreth, 1979; Wilson & Matheny, 1983)? To examine this issue, Plomin and his colleagues (Plomin & Bergeman, 1991; Plomin, Loehlin, & DeFries, 1985) compared 185 adoptees and a matched set of nonadopted children. For both behavioral problems and temperament, the mean correlation with environmental measures was higher in nonadoptive than adoptive families. Braungart, Fulker, and Plomin (1992) found that about 40% of the variance in HOME scores was attributable to genetic effects. In this regard, it is interesting to note that the correlation between HOME scores and maternal IQ is different for the three sociocultural groups that participated in the IHDP study. It is also interesting to note that when only mothers with low education are examined, the correlations are almost identical.

In general, the studies using HOME suggest that the measure is essentially assessing the same environmental dimensions in most cultural groups. However, this does not mean that the measure contains the ideal set of indicators of the dimensions being assessed in every group or that all the items work equally well in every group. Figure 7.1 shows the upper and lower bound mean scores for six ethnic subsamples based on a review of literature using the infant–toddler version of HOME. These findings show that mean scores

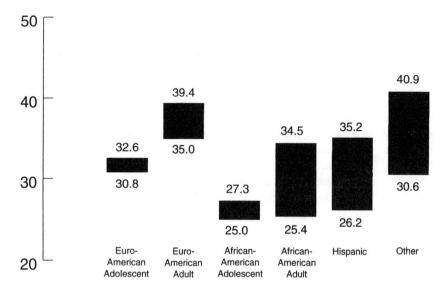

FIG. 7.1.   Range of mean scores on infant/toddler HOME.

for Euro-American mothers are generally higher than scores of either African-American or Hispanic mothers, with scores for the latter being perhaps slightly higher than for African Americans. Scores from other ethnic subgroups varied enormously, with Asian-American groups generally scoring in the same range as Euro-Americans. For both African-American and Euro-American mothers, adolescent mothers generally scored lower than adult mothers.

Although most researchers observed higher scores on HOME for Euro-American families than for African-American or Hispanic families, there were some interesting exceptions (see Bradley, 1994 for a review), such as the study of low SES Spanish-speaking mothers by Finello and Baron (1992). In a recent study, Field, Widmayer, Adler, and DeCubas (1990) also found that Cuban Americans scored higher than African Americans even though most participants from each group were from a lower class. The problem is that ethnicity tends to be confounded with both social status and family configuration, preventing any clear-cut determination of the precise reason for any observed differences between groups. A review of 54 studies done outside the United States reveals even greater complexity (Bradley, Corwyn, & Whiteside-Mansell, 1997). Scores on HOME are similar to those obtained in the United States to the extent that the average economic level of a country is comparable to that of the United States and to the extent that the country has an individualistic versus a collectivistic value orientation.

In sum, the available evidence suggests that there are mean differences in the home environments of families from different sociocultural groups, both across major racial or ethnic groups and in such groups. There is also evidence that the pattern of relations between home-environment and children's development varies somewhat across cultural groups and that the factor structures of home-environment measures (using HOME as a proxy) vary across groups, especially the pattern for Hispanics. There are two basic problems with the currently available research. First, the total amount of research remains quite limited on these issues (especially in cultural group comparisons). Second, the meaning of findings is complicated due to: (a) uncertainties about the comparability of all measures across groups; (b) the numerous confounds between sociocultural group status, family configuration, and contextual factors; (c) uncertainties regarding the use of factor analysis with home environment measures; (d) lack of compelling evidence for factorial invariance for Hispanics; and (e) a restricted range for variables in many analyses.

Age Differences and the Issue of Continuity

There is no evidence that, at a deep level, adolescents need anything different from their environments than do infants—actually, there is no evidence that it changes at any time in the lifespan (Bradley & Caldwell, 1995). However, the patterns and amounts of particular ingredients salient for well-being certainly change. The younger the child, the more life is lived in the moment. What counts is what is happening here and now. There is an immediacy and an intimacy to life's experiences. As children age, the meaning of life (its phenomenology) stretches in time and space—such is the advantage of growing memory and competence.

When constructing the four versions of HOME, we faced two central substantive concerns: What environmental dimensions or constructs are most salient to measure at each developmental period? How does one most accurately capture the salient dimensions or constructs? That is, what set of indicators are most informative? Some of the dimensions measured for the various age periods are the same (e.g., parental responsivity, the amount and variety of materials for learning, whether harsh child-management techniques are used, and whether a variety of enriching experiences are made available to the child). However, at each developmental period, we also include items that seem particularly relevant for that age period. For example, during infancy, we assess whether parents encourage the development of particular developmental competencies (e.g., walking or talking). During early childhood the focus shifts to an assessment of whether parents teach preacademic skills, such as learning colors and shapes, and whether parents provide conditions that facilitate the development of the kind of social skills required to function well outside the home. During middle childhood, there is, for the first time, an assessment of the overall emotional climate in the home and an assessment of whether the family does things as a unit. During early adolescence, there is a particular concern with the kinds of rules and policies established for the adolescent and the types of monitoring practices used. Clearly, as children age, the role of parent shifts gradually from that of direct provider of experiences and conditions (caretaker) to that of guide, broker, and facilitator of experiences. Things are often done at a greater distance and over a longer period of time—monitoring the whereabouts of a baby and monitoring the life and times of an adolescent require quite different actions. For parents of adolescents, things are more often done in league with other adults and other institutions (church, school, youth organization, etc.).

How one views the issue of age differences in the parenting environment depends on one's level of analysis. As we stated earlier, we measure some dimensions (e.g. parental responsivity) at every developmental age, but the particular indicators we use to reveal those dimensions may change (respond-ing to an infant's vocalization vs. encouraging a 10 year old to contribute to a conversation, giving an infant a rattle vs. giving an 8 year old a guitar, taking a 4 year old to the park vs. arranging for an adolescent to go to a dance camp). Two things are clear: First, the particular needs that children express from moment to moment change with age and what children require from their home environments in order to do well changes accordingly; second, children become more competent (self-sufficient) as they grow older—they are able to fashion their environments more to meet their own desires. Scarr and McCartney (1983) argued that when children are young, their influence on the environment is mostly passive; by their actions, they elicit different responses from others. However, as they become more competent, children seek out or construct environments that more fully meet their needs.

Cognitive Development.   What have we learned about changes in the relation between home environment and children's cognitive development across childhood from studies involving HOME? Correlations between the infant–toddler HOME and measures of infant developmental status (usually the Bayley Scales) rarely exceed .40 during the first year of life (see Bradley, 1994 for a review). However, the strength of the relation increases during the second year of life, with correlations generally ranging from .20 to .50. Although the upward trend in correlations partially reflects the fact that infant tests contain a larger proportion of language-oriented items by 2 years old, research by Belsky and his colleagues (1984) suggested that the higher correlations are not mere artifacts of the changing content of infant tests. They obtained correlations between HOME scores and children's perform-ance (.64 to .73), competence (.51 to .63), and executive capacity (.27 to .46) during play at 12, 15, and 18 months. Exceptions to the generally upward trend for correlations during the second year of life included poor Hispanics and poor African Americans (Adams, Campbell, & Ramey, 1984; Johnson, Breckenridge, & McGowan, 1984). Although these two exceptions may reflect a lack of measurement equivalence, they may instead reflect a more restricted range of scores on HOME for Hispanics. They may also reflect chronic conditions of poverty that are prevalent in these minority groups (McLoyd, 1990).

Most studies showed low to moderate correlations (.20 to .60) between HOME scores during the first 2 years of life and later tests of intelligence and achievement (Bradley, 1994). However, in a study of Hispanic children (Johnson & Breckenridge, 1981), correlations were negligible; for lower middle-class Costa Ricans, they were somewhat lower than correlations observed in most other groups, but were still significant. The results from these two studies indicate that different relations obtain for Hispanic populations, but the differences are difficult to interpret given that neither HOME nor the measures of intellectual competence were originally constructed using Hispanics (Super & Harkness, 1986). Had measures normed and standardized on Hispanics been used, the correlations observed for Hispanics may have resembled those observed for Whites. The contributions of culture, social status, and recency of immigration to the observed disparate results remain unclear. The increasing magnitude of correlations from birth to 3 years old probably results from a number of factors: early biological protection, the changing content of mental tests, and the timing of measurements for particular children.

HOME scores obtained when children were between 3 and 5 years old showed moderate correlations (.30 to .60) with contemporaneous measures of children's intellectual and academic performance (Bradley, 1994). The more restricted the SES range, the more attenuated the correlations. However, no difference was found between farm and nonfarm children who otherwise had a similar diversity in SES (Jacobson et al., 1987).

Transactional and general systems theories of development (Lerner, 1986; Sameroff, 1983) portray development as a joint function of what the environment affords a person by way of experiences and what the person brings to the environment by way of capabilities and behavioral tendencies. As an example, Bradley, Caldwell, Rock, Casey, and Nelson (1987) found that for low birthweight infants, home environment in combination with child medical status predicted 18-month Bayley scores better than either did alone. A study of language-delayed Down syndrome and normally developing children by Wulbert and her colleagues (1975) offered yet another view of the transactional process. A high correlation (.76) was obtained in the combined sample. The results are ambiguous with respect to direction of causality. It could result as well from effects of the children's low capabilities on the richness of the environment these children are afforded, as from effects on the children's capabilities by an environment in which stimulation and support for development are far below average.

Correlations between Early Childhood HOME scores and later academic achievement were generally low to moderate (Bradley, 1994). In one study involving 55 African American and 30 Caucasian children, HOME scores were correlated about .5 with SRA Achievement Test scores obtained when the children were 6 to 10 years old (Bradley & Caldwell, 1979). Moderate correlations were obtained for both African-American males and females; but significant residual correlations remained for males only when socioeconomic status and 3-year IQs were partialed out (Bradley & Caldwell, 1980). Gottfrieds and their colleagues (Gottfried, Gottfried, Bathurst, & Guerin, 1994), found that high achieving 7 and 8 year olds experienced more enriched home environments than classmates who had lower levels of achievement.

Only a few studies included use of HOME during middle childhood. Low to moderate correlations were obtained between HOME and school performance for 11 year olds (Bradley, Caldwell, Rock, Hamrick, & Harris, 1988). Responsivity, learning materials, active stimulation, and physical environment showed the strongest relations. A separate analysis of 8- to 10-year-old African American students (Bradley, Rock, Caldwell, Harris, & Hamrick, 1987) revealed that responsivity and emotional climate had the most consistent relations. High-achieving students from the Fullerton longitudinal study (Gottfried et al., 1994) were living in homes characterized by more learning materials, more active stimulation, greater family participation in enriching activities, and a higher level of parental responsivity.

Information on the HOME-achievement relation, though scanty, indicates that children's achievement during middle childhood is related to the home environment. Results from studies by Gottfried and Gottfried (1988) and Gottfried et al. (1994), by Bradley and Caldwell (1981), and Jordan (1976) indicate that the relation is strong for both Euro-Americans and African Americans. Kurtz, Borkowski, and Deshmukh (1988) also found a significant relation between HOME scores and school achievement for children in Nagpur, India. However, the sex, race, and social class differences obtained in those investigations suggest a complex relation.

We recently completed the first study of the relation between scores on the early adolescent (EA) version of HOME and children's achievement. We found that EA-HOME scores were correlated with scores on the Wide Range Achievement Test III for Euro-American ($r = .28$), African-American ($r = .35$), Hispanic American ($r = .50$), and Asian American adolescents ($r = .19$; Bradley, Corwyn, & Whiteside-Mansell, 1997).

Socioemotional Development.   Because of the limited number of studies, it is more difficult to describe age-related differences in the relation between HOME and social development. A major component of social competence is the ability to enter into and sustain social relations. Bakeman and Brown (1980) followed 21 preterm and 22 full-term African-American low-income children from 9 months to 3 years old. The child's social participation was assessed using videotapes at camp sessions at 3 years old. Children's social competence was also rated. The combination of infant's birth status and the responsivity subscale from HOME best predicted social participation. As for social competence, the best prediction (35.7% of the variance) was provided by a combination of responsivity and infant's early behavioral responsiveness. Other studies also indicate that the quality of the home environment in general, and responsivity in particular, are related to adaptive social competence during early and middle childhood (Jordan, 1979; Tedesco, 1981). A good example is a study of behavior problems in very low birthweight Dutch children (Weisglas-Kuperus, Koot, Baerts, Fetter, & Sauer 1993). They found that HOME scores at ages 1 and 3½ years old were correlated with clinician ratings of behavior problems. Scores on HOME at 3½ years old were also correlated with the total problems score on the Child Behavior Checklist.

Lamb et al. (1988) found that early development of a socially competent personality was a complex function of both child and family characteristics, as well as the general level of social support available to parents. Specifically, they found that a composite measure of child personality, consisting of scores on field independence, ego resiliency, and ego control, was best predicted by a combination of early child temperament, HOME, family SES, and support from maternal grandparents.

One of the most intensive investigations of the relation between HOME and children's social and behavioral competence was a prospective longitudinal study involving 267 high-risk mothers from Minnesota (Erickson, Sroufe, & Egeland, 1985). Among securely attached children who later showed behavior problems, mothers provided less support and encouragement during problem solving and families had lower scores on the learning materials and involvement subscales from HOME. Among anxiously attached infants who later showed no behavior problems, mothers were more supportive, provided clearer structure and better instruction during instructional tasks, had better social support and better relationships, and had families who scored higher on the learning materials and involvement subscales. Families of the children were administered the middle childhood version of HOME when children were 6 years old; the children were rated on peer competence and emotional health by their teachers through third grade (Sroufe, Egeland, & Kreutzer, 1990). Teacher ratings were regressed on 6-year HOME, 2½-year HOME, kindergarten rank, child functioning or preschool, and infant attachment classification. All variables in the model, except attachment classification, made significant contributions to the model. In general, the findings tended to support Bowlby's (1982) general model of development in which both the total developmental history and current circumstances were given important roles.

We analyzed data from a multisite study of 549 low-birthweight children, which illustrates some of the potential complexity of the relation between home environment and adaptive social behavior during the first 3 years of life (Bradley et al., 1995). This study, involving HOME at 1 and 3 years old, plus three measures of adaptive social behavior at 2½ to 3 years old, showed that: (a) correlations between 3-year HOME and social competence tended to be higher than correlations with 1-year HOME, though not uniformly so; (b) different HOME subscales were related to different aspects of adaptive social functioning; (c) there was little evidence that parental nurturance (e.g., acceptance and responsivity) during infancy was more strongly associated with 3-year adaptive social behavior than was parental nurturance around 3 years old, but apparently cognitive stimulation (e.g. learning materials and variety) at 3 years old was more important than at 1 year old; and (d) social behavior was predicted better by a combination of support and stimulation factors than with either alone.

We also examined the relation of both infant–toddler HOME and middle childhood HOME to classroom behavior at 10 to 11 years old (Bradley, Rock, Caldwell, & Brisby, 1989). A few significant correlations emerged between infant–toddler HOME and the three dimensions tapped by the Classroom behavior inventory. Many more emerged between the middle childhood HOME and classroom behavior. Both active involvement and family participation were moderately correlated with consideration, task orientation, and school adjustment. Responsivity was also correlated with consideration and adjustment. The researchers also used the data to examine three models of environmental action: Model I (primacy of early experience), Model II (predominance of contemporary environment), and Model III (cumulative effects in stable environments). Though all three models received some support, the strongest support was for Model II. The importance of the early environment was supported in terms of significant partial correlations between responsivity and considerate classroom behavior, even with the intervening environment controlled. Similar results were obtained for variety. The salience of the contemporary environment received greatest support in the case of the family participation and active involvement subscales and classroom behavior (i.e., task orientation, consideration, adjustment). The relation of involvement to considerate behavior seems largely a function of the cumulative effects of parental involvement.

Findings by Bakeman and Brown (1980), Lamb et al. (1988), Erickson, Sroufe, and Egeland (1985), Mink and Nihira (1987), and Bradley, Rock, et al. (1989) suggested that particular parenting practices interact with both particular child characteristics (e.g., quality of attachment, difficult temperament, and level of disability) and broader ecological factors (e.g., marital quality, support from extended family, and overall family style) to affect the course of social development. Moreover, the study by Plomin, Loehlin, and DeFries (1985) showed little relation between HOME and behavior problems in adopted children, but a significant—yet small (.23)—relation for nonadopted children suggests that genetic factors may play a role.

Continuity in the Home Environment.   Clearly, at the surface of life (i.e., what goes on from moment to moment, the conditions present in a place at a given time), the home environment differs from age to age—and needs to. Yet, at a deeper level, these surface differences seem only to camouflage what is constantly required by children in order to do well. Children of all ages seem to require an environment that not only meets their needs in a timely and responsive way, but also one that promotes their self-sustaining capacities as well.

Even if one accepts our premise that sustenance, stimulation, support, structure, and surveillance are required ingredients of a facilitative home environment from infancy through adolescence (Bradley & Caldwell, 1995), making meaningful statements about age differences and making useful statements about continuity in the parenting process is not a simple matter. How is a dimension like support (or a construct included in that dimension, such as parental responsiveness) most often manifested in infancy, and how does that compare to how it is most often manifested in adolescence? How does such a process reorganize itself across time? Does it become connected or integrated with other processes in characteristic ways? What is the relation between keeping track of a crawling infant and keeping track of the activities of an adolescent? Clearly, both involve surveillance, but does knowing who an adolescent hangs with have its roots in keeping an eye on a crawling infant? What little evidence we have about these issues seems to suggest that the most obvious connections (e.g., more hugging during infancy is related to more hugging during adolescence) may not always be the most meaningful. Beckwith, Roding, and Cohen (1992), for example, found that the manner in which responsiveness expressed itself changed from infancy through early adolescence. Understanding better continuities in the parenting process and how such continuities relate to children's development enables us to better inter- pret age-related differences in the home environment and their significance.

RESILIENCY—THE HOME ENVIRONMENT AS PROTECTION FOR CHILDREN AT RISK

For those interested in the practical application of research on home envi- ronments for children at risk, the issue of whether stimulating and supportive home environments offer protection from risks posed by the larger environ- ment has substantial currency. As federal, state, and local governments grap- ple with how to reform the welfare system, the health-care system, the criminal justice system, and even the early education system (e.g., new Head Start initiatives), how to effectively involve the family in the lives of children remains at the center of most debates. The fact that children living in good home environments manifest better health and well-being than children living in poor home environments is not disputed (Bradley & Whiteside-Mansell,

1997). The extent to which a good home environment can afford protection to children at biological or environmental risk is not as clear, however. Recently, we examined the issue using children from the Infant Health and Development Program (IHDP; Bradley, Whiteside, et al., 1994b). All the children in IHDP were born prematurely and with low birthweights; that is, they were at increased biological risk for poor development (Bradley & Casey, 1992). From the total IHDP sample of 985 children, we selected 243 who lived in chronic poverty and had not participated in the IHDP intervention. In effect, these children were at dual risk and were not receiving any formal (nonfamilial) support for their development, other than those that would normally be available through governmental assistance programs (such as WIC). Our purpose was to determine whether the availability of protective factors in the home environment at 1 year old and at 3 years old increased the probability of resiliency. *Resiliency* was operationalized as being in good to excellent health, being in the normal range for growth, not being below clinically designated cutoffs for maladaptive behavior on the Child Behavior Checklist, and having an IQ of 85 or higher. Six home environment factors were considered potentially protective: low household density, the availability of a safe play area, parental acceptance or lack of punitiveness, the availability of learning materials, parental responsivity, and variety of experiences. Fifteen percent of the children, with three or more protective factors present in the home at 1 year old, were classified as resilient. By contrast, only 2% of children with two or fewer protective factors were classified as resilient. Similarly, 20% of children, with three or more protective factors present in the home at 3 years old, were classified as resilient, whereas only 6% of children with two or fewer protective factors were resilient.

We conducted a second study in which the potential joint contribution of the IHDP intervention and a protective home environment to resilience was examined (Bradley, Whiteside, et al., 1994a). For this second study, four groups of children were identified: children living in homes low in protection who did not experience the intervention, children living in home high in protection who did not experience the intervention, children living in homes low in protection who experienced the intervention, and children living in homes high in protection who experienced the intervention. Figure 7.2 displays the results. The children living in protective home environments (who also received the IHDP intervention) were about 10 times as likely to be resilient at 3 years old as those children without either.

POSTSCRIPT

Over the last 50 years, particularly the past 30 years, a fair amount of attention has been devoted to constructing measures of the home environment and using them in studies of child development. These studies make

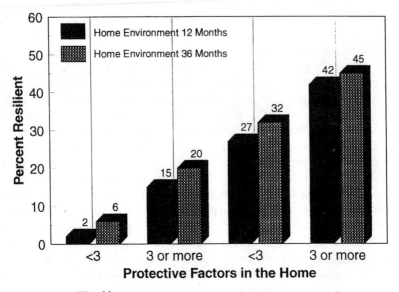

FIG. 7.2.

clear that the conditions present in the home environment change throughout childhood and that conditions vary across demographic groups. Yet, at best, we are at a point of commencement—where a whole new generation of research is needed (Wachs, 1992). Much remains unclear about age and demographic differences and their meaning for child behavior and development. Further delineation of the relations requires determining the degree of measurement equivalence across groups. It is important to bear in mind that home environment measures are mostly inventories of causal indicators and that something close to a census of all relevant indicators for particular environmental dimensions is probably required to map relations between characteristics of the environment and children's development. Refinements in theory and research design are also needed. Too often in the past, research concentrated on looking at the home environment writ large (e.g., a total score from a measure that contains a broad array of indicators) or on one environmental dimension at a time (e.g., parental responsiveness, the availability of toys and learning materials, and the type of punishment used). Yet, children do not experience particular dimensions of the environment in isolation from other dimensions. However significant parental responsiveness may be for the development of attachment or cooperativeness, its impact on those child characteristics is likely to hinge on other conditions present in the environment during the same time periods and even the overall climate present (Darling & Steinberg, 1993). At different ages and in different cultures, certain aspects of the environment are likely to covary with other aspects; we need to know more about how these various aspects interrelate for different groups and how they jointly function to shape the course of development. Finally, we need to learn much more about continuities and discontinuities in environmental processes. A better understanding of these processes should aid in doing research on the kinds of dynamic patterns of influence stipulated in ecological and developmental models (Ford & Lerner, 1992).

REFERENCES

Abelson, R. (1981). Psychological status of the script concept. *American Psychologist, 36,* 715–729.

Adams, J. L., Campbell, F. A., & Ramey, C. T (1984). Infants' home environments: A study of screening efficiency. *American Journal of Mental Deficiency, 89,* 133–139.

Altman, I. (1977). Privacy regulation: Culturally universal or culturally specific? *Journal of Social Issues, 33,* 66–84.

Bakeman, R., & Brown, J. V. (1980). Early interaction: Consequences for social and mental development at three years. *Child Development, 51,* 437–447.

Beckwith, L., Roding, C., & Cohen, S. (1992). Preterm children at early adolescence and continuity and discontinuity in maternal responsiveness from infancy. *Child Development, 63,* 1198–1208.

Belsky, J. (1984). The determinants of parenting: A process model. *Child Development, 55,* 83–96.

Bloom, B. S. (1964). *Stability and change in human characteristics.* New York: Wiley.

Bollen, K. A. (1989). *Structural equations with latent variables.* New York: Wiley.

Bollen, K. A., & Lennox, R. (1991). Conventional wisdom on measurement: A structural equation perspective. *Psychological Bulletin, 110*(2), 305–314.

Bornstein, M., Tamis-LeMonda, C., Tal, M., Ludeman, P., Toda, S., Rahn, C., Pecheux, M., Azuma, H. N., & Vardi, D. (1992). Maternal responsiveness to infants in three societies: The United States, France, and Japan. *Child Development, 63,* 808–821.

Bowlby, J. (1982). *Attachment and loss: Vol. 1. Attachment* (2nd rev. ed.). New York: Basic Books.

Bradley, R. H. (1994). The HOME Inventory: Review and reflections. In H. Reese (Ed.), *Advances in child development and behavior* (pp. 241–288). San Diego, CA: Academic Press.

Bradley, R. H., & Caldwell, B. M. (1979). Home Observation for Measurement of the Environment: A revision of the preschool scale. *American Journal of Mental Deficiency, 84,* 235–244.

Bradley, R. H., & Caldwell, B. M. (1980). Home environment, cognitive competence and IQ among males and females. *Child Development, 51,* 1140–1148.

Bradley, R. H., & Caldwell, B. M. (1981). The HOME Inventory: A validation of the preschool scale for black children. *Child Development, 52,* 708–710.

Bradley, R. H., & Caldwell, B. M. (1984). The HOME inventory and family demographics. *Developmental Psychology, 20,* 315–320.

Bradley, R. H., & Caldwell, B. M. (1995). Caregiving and the regulation of child growth and development: Describing proximal aspects of caregiving systems. *Developmental Review, 15,* 38–85.

Bradley, R. H., & Casey, P. H. (1992). Family environment and behavioral development in low birthweight children: Annotation. *Developmental Medicine and Child Neurology, 34,* 822–826.

Bradley, R. H., Caldwell, B. M., Rock, S. L., Barnard, K. E., Gray, C., Hammond, M. A., Mitchell, S., Siegel, L., Ramey, C. T., Gottfried, A. W., & Johnson, D. L. (1989). Home environment and cognitive development in the first 3 years of life: A collaborative study involving six sites and three ethnic groups in North America. *Developmental Psychology, 28*, 217–235.

Bradley, R. H., Caldwell, B. M., Rock, S. L., Casey, P. H., & Nelson, J. (1987). The early development of low-birthweight infants: Relationship to health, family status, family context, family processes, and parenting. *International Journal of Behavioral Development, 10*, 301–318.

Bradley, R. H., Corwyn, R., & Whiteside-Mansell, L. (1997). Life at home: Same time, different places, An examination of the HOME Inventory in different cultures. *Early Education and Parenting, 5*, 251–269.

Bradley, R. H., Mundfrom, D. J., Whiteside, L., Barrett, K., & Casey, P. H. (1994). A factor analytic study of the infant/toddler and early childhood versions of the HOME Inventory for White, Black, and Hispanic Americans with low birthweight children. *Child Development, 65*, 880–888.

Bradley, R. H., Mundfrom, D. J., Whiteside, L. Caldwell, B. M., Casey, P. H., Kirby, R. S., & Hansen, S. (1994). The demography of parenting: A re-examination of the association between HOME scores and income. *Nursing Research, 43*, 260–266.

Bradley, R. H., Rock, S. L., Caldwell, B. M., & Brisby, J. A. (1989). Uses of the HOME inventory for families with handicapped children. *American Journal of Mental Retardation, 94*, 313–330.

Bradley, R. H., Rock, S. L., Caldwell, B. M., Harris, P. T., & Hamrick, H. M. (1987). Home environment and school performance among Black elementary school children. *Journal of Negro Education, 56*, 499–509.

Bradley, R. H., Whiteside, L., Mundfrom, D. J., Blevins-Knabe, B., Casey, P. H., Caldwell, B. M., Pope, S., & Barrett, K. (1995). Home environment and adaptive social behavior among premature, low birthweight children. Alternative models of environmental action. *Journal of Pediatirc Psychology, 20*, 347–362.

Bradley, R. H., Whiteside, L., Mundfrom, D. J., Casey, P. H., Kelleher, K. J., & Pope, S. K. (1994a). The contribution of early intervention and early caregiving experiences to resilience in low birthweight, premature children living in poverty. *Journal of Clinical Child Psychology, 23*, 425–434.

Bradley, R. H., Whiteside, L., Mundfrom, D. J., Casey, P. H., Kelleher, K. J., & Pope, S. K. (1994b). Early indications of resilience and their relation to experiences in the home environments of low birthweight, premature children living in poverty. *Child Development, 65*, 346–360.

Bradley, R. H., & Whiteside-Mansell, L. (1997). Children in poverty. In R. T. Ammerman & M. Hersen (Eds.), *Handbook of prevention and treatment with children and adolescents* (pp. 13–58). New York: Wiley.

Bradley, R. H., Whiteside-Mansell, L., Caldwell, B. M., & Brisby, J. (1997). Parents' socioemotional investment in children. *Journal of Marriage and the Family, 59*, 77–90.

Braungart, J. M., Fulker, D. W., & Plomin, R. (1992). Genetic mediation of the home environment during infancy: A sibling adoption study of the HOME. *Developmental Psychology, 28*, 1048–1055.

Caldwell, B. M., & Bradley, R. H. (1984). *Home Observation for Measurement of the Environment.* Little Rock: University of Arkansas at Little Rock.

Casper, L. M., Hawkins, M., & O'Connell, M. (1994). *Who's minding the kids? Child care arrangements*, Fall, 1991. Washington, DC: U.S. Bureau of the Census.

Citro, C. F., & Michael, R. T. (1995). *Measuring poverty, A new approach.* Washington, DC: National Academy Press.

Coll, C. G. (1990). Developmental outcome of minority infants: A process oriented look into our beginnings. *Child Development, 61,* 270–289.

Coll, C. G., Hoffman, J., & Oh, W. (1987). The social ecology and early parenting of Caucasian adolescent mothers. *Child Development, 58,* 955–963.

Coll, C. G., Vohr, O., Hoffman, J., & Oh, W. (1986). Maternal and environmental factors affecting developmental outcomes of infants of adolescent mothers. *Developmental and Behavioral Pediatrics, 7,* 230–236.

Darling, N., & Steinberg, L. (1993). Parenting style as context. An integrative model. *Psychological Bulletin, 113,* 487–496.

Erickson, M. F., Sroufe, L. A., & Egeland, B. (1985). The relationship between quality of attachment and behavior problems in a high risk sample. In I. Bretherton & E. Waters (Eds.), Growing points of attachment theory and research. *Monographs of the Society for Research in Child Development, 50* (Serial No. 209, pp. 147–166).

Fagot, B. I., & Kavanaugh, K. (1993). Parenting during the second year: Effects of children's age, sex, and attachment classification. *Child Development, 64,* 258–271.

Fein, G. G., Gariboldi, A., & Boni, R. (1993). Antecedents of maternal separation anxiety. *Merrill-Palmer Quarterly, 39,* 481–495.

Field, T. M., Widmayer, S. M., Adler, S., & DeCubas, M. (1990). Teenage parenting in different cultures, family constellations, and caregiving environments: Effects on infant development. *Infant Mental Health Journal, 11,* 158–174.

Finello, K., & Baron, J. (May, 1992). *Use of the HOME inventory in a very low SES Spanish speaking sample.* Paper presented at the International Conference on Infancy Studies, Miami, FL.

Ford, D. H., & Lerner, R. M. (1992). *Developmental systems theory, an integrative approach.* Newbury Park, CA: Sage.

Gottfried, A. W., & Gottfried, A. E. (1984). Home environment and cognitive development in young children of middle-socioeconomic status families. In A. W. Gottfried (Ed.), *Home environment and early cognitive development* (pp. 329–342). Orlando, FL: Academic Press.

Gottfried, A. E., & Gottfried, A. W. (1988). *Maternal employment and children's development: Longitudinal research.* New York: Plenum.

Gottfried, A. W., Gottfried, A. E., Bathurst, K., & Guerin, D. W. (1994). *Gifted IQ, early developmental aspects.* New York: Plenum.

Hogan, A., Scott, K., & Bauer, C. (1994). The Adaptive Social Behavior Directory (ASBI): A new assessment of social competence in high risk three year olds. *Journal of Psychoeducational Assessment, 10,* 230–239.

Horn, J. L., & McArdle, J. J. (1992). A practical and theoretical guide to measurement invariance in aging research. *Experimental Aging Research, 18,* 117–144.

Infant Health and Development Program. (1990). Enhancing outcomes of low-birth-weight, premature infants. *Journal of the American Medical Association, 263,* 3035–3070.

Jacobson, S. W., Jacobson, J. L., Brumitt, G. A., & Jones, P. D. (1987, April). *Predictability of cognitive development in farm and non-farm children.* Paper presented at the meeting of the Society for Research in Child Development, Baltimore.

Johnson, D., & Breckenridge, J. (1981, April). *The impact of a parent education program on the home environment and cognitive development of Mexican-American children.* Paper presented at the biennial meeting of the Society for Research in Child Development, Boston.

Johnson, D. L., Breckenridge, J. N., & McGowan, R. (1984). Home environment and early cognitive development in Mexican-American children. In A. Gottfried (Ed.), *Home environment and early cognitive development* (pp. 151–196). Orlando, FL: Academic Press.

Jordan, T. E. (April, 1976). *Measurement of the environment for learning and its effects on educational and cognitive attainment.* Paper presented at the meeting of the American Educational Research Association, San Francisco.

Jordan, T. E. (1979). *Old man river's children.* New York: Academic Press.

Knight, G. P., & Hill, N. E. (in press). Measurement equivalence in research involving minority adolescents. In V. McLoyd and L. Steinberg (Ed.), *Reseach on minority adolescents: Conceptual, methodological and theoretical issues.*

Kurtz, B. C., Borkowski, J. G., & Deshmukh, K. (1988). Metamemory and learning in Maharashtrian children: Influences from home and school. *Journal of Genetic Psychology, 149,* 363–376.

Labouvie, E., & Ruetsch, C. (1995). Testing for equivalence of measurement scales: Simple structure and metric invariance reconsidered. *Multivariate Behavioral Research, 30,* 63–76.

Lamb, M. E., Hwang, C., Bookstein, F. L., Broberg, A., Hult, G., & Frodi, M. (1988). Determinants of social competence in Swedish preschoolers. *Developmental Psychology, 24,* 58–70.

Liberatos, P., Link, B. G., & Kelsey, J. L. (1988). The measurement of social class in epidemiology. *Epidemiology Reviews, 10,* 87–121.

Longstreth, L. (1979). A comment of "race, IQ, and the middle class" by Trotman: Rampant false conclusion. *Journal of Educational Psychology, 70,* 469–472.

Maccoby, E. E., & Martin, J. A. (1983). Socialization in the context of the family: Parent–child interaction. In P. H. Mussen (Series Ed.), & E. M. Hetherington (Vol. Ed.), *Handbook of child psychology, Vol. 4: Socialization, personality, and social development* (4th ed., pp. 1–102). New York: Wiley.

McLoyd, V. C. (1990). The impact of economic hardship on Black families and children: Psychological distress, parenting, and socioemotional development. *Child Development, 61,* 311–346.

McLoyd, V. C., Jayaratne, T. E., Ceballo, R., & Borquez, J. (1994). Unemployment and work interruption among African American single mothers: Effects on parenting and adolescent socioemotional functioning. *Child Development, 65,* 562–589.

Meredith, W. (1995). Two wrongs may not make a right. *Multivariate Behavioral Research, 30,* 89–94.

Mink, I. T., & Nihira, K. (1987). Direction of effects: Family life styles and behavior of TMR children. *American Journal of Mental Deficiency, 92,* 57–64.

Plomin, R., & Bergeman, C. (1991). The nature of nurture: Genetic influence on "environmental" measures. *Behavior and Brain Sciences, 14,* 373–427.

Plomin, R., Loehlin, J., & DeFries, J. (1985). Genetic and environmental components of "environmental" influences. *Developmental Psychology, 21,* 391–402.

Ragozin, A., Landesman-Dwyer, S., & Streissguth, A. (1980). *The relationship between mothers' drinking habits and children's home environments* (Report no. 77-10). Seattle: University of Washington, Alcoholism and Drug Abuse Institute.

Sameroff, A. J., & Fiese, B. H. (1990). Transactional regulation and early intervention. In S. J. Meisels & J. P. Shonkoff (Eds.), *Handbook of early intervention* (pp. 119–149).

Scarr, S., & McCartney, K. (1983). How people make their own environments: A theory of genotype environment effects. *Child Development, 54,* 424–435.

Sroufe, L. A., Egeland, B., & Kreutzer, T. (1990). The fate of early experience following developmental change: Longitudinal approaches to individual adaptation in childhood. *Child Development, 61,* 1363–1373.

Super, C. M., & Harkness, S. (1986). The developmental niche: A conceptualization at the interface of child and culture. *International Journal of Behavioral Development, 9,* 545–569.

Tedesco, L. (1981). *Early home experience, classroom social competence, and academic achievement.* Unpublished doctoral dissertation, State University of New York, Buffalo.

Wachs, T. D. (1992). *The nature of nurture.* Newbury Park, CA: Sage.

Wapner, S. (1987). A holistic, developmental, systems-oriented environmental psychology: Some beginnings. In D. Stokols & I. Altman (Eds.), *Handbook of environmental psychology* (Vol. 2, pp. 1433–1465). New York: Wiley.

Weisglas-Kuperus, N., Koot, H. M., Baerts, W., Fetter, W. P., & Sauer, P. J. (1993). Behavior problems of very low-birthweight children. *Developmental Medicine and Child Neurology, 35,* 406–416.

Whiteside-Mansell, L., Pope, S., & Bradley, R. H. (1996). Patterns of parenting behavior in young mothers. *Family Relations, 45,* 1–9.

Wilson, R. S., & Matheny, A. P. (1983). Mental development: Family environment and genetic influences. *Intelligence, 7,* 195–215.

Wulbert, M., Inglis, S., Kriegsman, E., & Mills, B. (1975). Language delay and associated mother/child interactions. *Developmental Psychology, 2,* 61–70.

FAMILIES AT RISK

The study of families at risk provides, at one and the same time, the opportunity to see how family systems and dynamics change over different contexts and also how the characteristics of the child or the family affect these dynamics. In this section, two major categories of risk are considered. In the first, risk is defined by the socioeconomic status of the family, whereas in the second, the characteristics of the child, in particular, retardation and developmental delay, operate as a risk factor with which the family must cope. Finally, although not a risk factor in the common sense, the gifted child presents a significant challenge to the family system.

Sameroff, Bartko, Baldwin, Baldwin, and Seifer (chap. 8) examine multiple sources of risk as additive contributors to a positive or negative trajectory for the development of competence. Using data from preschool children and adolescents, they explore the impact of risk factors from a variety of ecological levels, including family process, parent characteristics, family management of the community, and family structure. As the number of risk factors increases, there is a precipitous drop in child competence, and at the highest accumulation of risk, personal protective factors appear to have no effect. The results have important implications for intervention, suggesting that changing environments should be more effective than relying on individual children's resilience under conditions of accumulated risk.

A six-type topology for understanding the nature of families with pre-school children living in poverty is the focus of Ramey, Landesman-Ramey, and Lanzi (chap. 9). From a national sample of former Head Start families, the topology includes traditional, single unemployed mothers, single working mothers, non-English-speaking traditional, chronic maternal health problems, and homeless families. Analyses reveal differences in children's language, social development, and special education placement as a function of family type. Such a topology can be useful in designing two generation intervention programs to improve child and family development outcomes.

To what extent is children's development adversely affected when parent–child relationships are inadequate or hostile and when the relationship between the parents is conflictual or violent? Dawud-Noursi, Lamb, and Sternberg (chap. 10) examine this issue in families from Israel. Of particular interest is how children's school competence varies as a function of whether children were victims, witnesses, or both of violence in the family. In the initial phase of the study, there were few differences between the group that experienced some form of domestic violence and the comparison group. However, as the children entered adolescence, violence in the home was related to problems in school with teachers and peers.

In their chapter, Brody, Flor, and Neubaum (chap. 11) examine cocaregiving in poor, rural, African-American families. They offer an expanded view of family processes that places transactions in the extended family context. Although different factors emerge as significant for promoting cocaregiving in married and single-parent families, the importance of mutual support by caregivers for the development of child competence is evident. Religiosity and no-nonsense parenting are noted as facilitating factors.

Wachs (chap. 12) is interested in processes through which variability in family environment is related to variability in children's development. Of central concern is how the family environment influences development in undernourished children from Egypt and Kenya. Exploring the consequences of undernourishment, he demonstrates the complexity of effects, such as changes in the impact and nature of salient environmental influences over time, environmental specificity, and both covariance and interaction between individual and environment. As in other chapters about risk, he argues for multifocal rather than monofocal interventions that take into account nutritional, as well as family environment, parameters.

The adjustments and adaptations of families and children with disabilities is the focus of Keogh, Bernheimer, Gallimore, and Weisner (chap. 13). Following children with nonspecific delays from infancy through childhood, they employ an ecocultural model for understanding how families proactively accommodate the needs of their members, including, but not limited to, a child with disabilities. They identify and describe the daily activities in five types of families—multiply troubled, vulnerable but struggling, improving resilient, active but less satisfied, and satisfied or stable. These family types vary in the degree to which they are able to provide a sustainable family routine that promotes a sense of family well-being.

According to Sigel (chap. 14), the child's cognitive development and representational thinking skills evolve in the family context. In his chapter, he examines how parental beliefs and behaviors that foster distancing in children are related to cognitive competence and school achievement. Comparing families with and without a child who has a communication handicap, issues concerning the complexity of relations between parenting beliefs and strategies and developing competence, depending on children's language proficiency, are explored. The importance of parental beliefs in designing intervention for children with learning disabilities is discussed.

Families with gifted children are not usually considered to be at risk. Nevertheless, such families may share similarities with other marginalized groups in the ways they are regarded and treated. Robinson (chap. 15) considers the types of family characteristics and environments that foster the potential of gifted children, such as parental involvement in education, setting high goals for achievement, and the fostering of independence and individuation. The nature of sibling relationships in families with gifted children is also of interest.

Overall, these chapters recognize the complexity of family processes and influences that affect the developing child in positive and negative ways. The need to consider differences in family functioning, circumstances, and goals in designing interventions is a recurring theme as is a recognition of the mutual influences and feedback between children, their families, and communities.

8

▼▼▼▼▼▼▼

Family and Social Influences on the Development of Child Competence

Arnold J. Sameroff
W. Todd Bartko
University of Michigan, Ann Arbor

Alfred Baldwin
Clare Baldwin
University of Rochester

Ronald Seifer
Brown University

The American family has been given various degrees of credit for the fate of children in our society. Ever since the issue of family values became central in the presidential electoral campaign of 1992, the debate about family influences has been in the forefront of our political rhetoric, but as is usually the case, rhetoric has little relation to the scientific evidence that either supports or negates this factor as an influence in children's lives.

In this chapter, we enumerate a variety of factors that impact child competence. Using an ecological model (Bronfenbrenner, 1979), we examine a range of social influences, from the parent practices that have direct influence on the child to community and economic factors that only impinge on the child through the action of others. Depending on disciplinary background, different variables were proposed to explain the problems of society. Economists focused on poverty and deprivation as the roots of social maladjustment, sociologists implicated problems in the community and family structure as the variables that promote deviancy, educators blame the school system, and psychologists focused on processes in the family and its members as the environmental influences that most profoundly affect successful development. We accepted all of these proposals, but rather than viewing them as competing, we saw them as additive contributors to a positive or negative trajectory through life. It is not any one of these factors that is damaging to or facilitating for children, but their accumulation in the life of any one child. Children reared in families with a large number of negative influences do worse than children in families with few risk factors. Such a view militates against any simplistic proposal that by changing one thing in society, we change the fate of our children. Competence is the result of a complex interplay of children, with a range of personalities, in different kinds of families, and in communities with varying economic and social resources. Only by attending to such complexity is the development of competence understood and perhaps altered for the better.

The pursuit of happiness is a fundamental right in our society, yet the goal of achieving a sense of satisfaction with one's abilities and achievements is becoming increasingly elusive for large groups of children. For example, over half of today's 10 to 17 year olds engage in two or more behaviors that we regard as indicating a lack of competence in today's society. These include unsafe sex, teenage pregnancy, drug or alcohol abuse, school failure, delinquency, and crime. Moreover, 10% of these youth engage in all of these risks (Dryfoos, 1991). Clearly, there is a need to understand why so many youth are unsuccessful by society's standards.

As children age, the range of outcomes that are indicators of successful child development change. During early childhood, good cognitive skills and social–emotional adjustment are the two primary indicators of such success. In adolescence, in addition to doing well in school and feeling good about oneself, we add elements of positive engagement with the community. These include activities such as extracurricular clubs, scouts, church, and sports. Such participation stands as a marker for a trajectory that eventually leads to successful employment and a happy family life. What we examine are the ecological correlates of the progression of child competence from early childhood through adolescence. In the process, we explore the relative contributions of not only different social factors to child competence, but also the child's own capacity for adaptation in the face of adverse environmental circumstance.

ROCHESTER LONGITUDINAL STUDY

Despite the nominal interest of developmentalists in the effects of the environment, the analysis and assessment of context has fallen more in the domain of sociology than of developmental psychology (Clausen, 1968; Elder, 1974; Kohn & Schooler, 1983; Mayer & Jencks, 1989). The magnitude of a social ecological analysis involving multiple settings and multiple systems (Bronfenbrenner, 1979) daunted researchers primarily trained to focus on individual behavioral processes. A further daunting factor was the increasing necessity to use multicausal models to explain developmental phenomena (Sameroff, 1983).

To examine the effects of the social environment on child competence, we began an investigation of the development of a group of children from the prenatal period through adolescence—the Rochester Longitudinal Study (RLS). They lived in a socially heterogeneous set of family circumstances and about half of their mothers had a mental illness. During the early childhood phase of the RLS (Sameroff, Seifer, & Zax, 1982), we assessed children and their families at birth and then at 4, 12, 30, and 48 months of age both in the home and in the laboratory. At each age, we evaluated two major indicators of competence—the child's cognitive behavior and social–emotional behavior.

In our search for family risk factors that adversely affect children's growth, we considered three major hypotheses: that problem behavior is related to a specific parental psychiatric diagnosis (e.g., schizophrenia); that problem behavior is attributable to variables associated with parental mental illness in general, especially severity and chronicity of disorder, but no diagnosis in particular; and that problem behavior in children is associated with other aspects of the family's condition, especially SES. Because many of the families had single parents, we focused our assessments on characteristics of the mother. This approach was taken not because we believed that fathers were unimportant, but because there were too few available for participation in our study.

When we examined the data, we found little support for the first hypothesis. There was no specific effect of parents' psychiatric diagnosis on the behavior of their offspring during early childhood. The second hypothesis—that mental illness in general produces substantial effects—was supported more strongly. Global effects of the severity and chronicity of parental psychopathology were ubiquitous throughout the study. Our third hypothesis—that differences in family socioeconomic circumstance produce differences in child behavior—was also strongly supported. The social status effects were apparent throughout the first 4 years of life. Children from the poorest families in our sample exhibited the poorest development. They had poorer obstetrical status, more difficult temperaments at 4 months old, less responsivity during the home and laboratory observations at 12 months old, and less adaptive social and emotional behavior in the home and laboratory at 30 and 48 months old (Sameroff, Seifer, & Barocas, 1983; Sameroff, Seifer, & Zax, 1982). When the number of differences in child behavior was compared for the diagnostic, mental illness, and SES comparisons, social status differences were the most frequent.

At that point in our study, we discovered, on the one hand, that if the only developmental risk for a child was a mother with a mental illness, the child was doing fine. On the other hand, if the child had a mother who was mentally ill, who was also poor, uneducated, without social supports, and with many stressful life events, the child was doing poorly. Yet, we also found that children whose mothers were poor, uneducated, without social supports, and with many stressful life events had worse outcomes, even if the mother did not have a psychiatric diagnosis. In the RLS, social circumstance was a more powerful risk factor than any of the parental mental illness measures. What we learned was the overriding importance of attending to the context of the children in the study in order to understand their development. However, to better understand the role of SES, more differentiated views of environmental influences needed to be taken. We needed to transform measures of parent's educational and occupational achievement that constituted SES scores into variables that would have a conceptually more direct influence on the child. We had to discover what was different about the experience of children raised in different socioeconomic environments.

Environmental Conditions as Developmental Risks

Although SES was our best single variable for predicting children's cognitive competence, it was also an important, if less powerful, predictor of social–emotional functioning. The circumstances of families in the same social class differ quite markedly. We decided to add more psychological content to this primarily economic variable because SES affects many levels of the ecology of children. It impacts parenting, parental attitudes and beliefs, family interactions, and many institutions in the surrounding community. From the data available in the RLS, we searched for a set of variables that were related to economic circumstance, but were not the same as SES. The factors we chose homed in from distal variables, such as the financial resources of the family, to intermediate variables, such as the mother's mental health, to proximal variables, such as the mother's behavioral interactions with the child.

From the 4-year assessment of the children in the RLS, we selected a set of 10 environmental variables that were correlates of SES, but were not equivalents (Sameroff, Seifer, Barocas, Zax, & Greenspan, 1987). We then tested whether poor cognitive and social–emotional development in our preschool children was a function of the compounding of environmental risk factors found in low-SES groups. The definitions of the 10 environmental risk variables can be seen in Table 8.1: (1) a history of maternal mental illness, (2) high maternal anxiety, (3) parental perspectives that reflected rigidity in the attitudes, beliefs, and values that mothers had in regard to their children's development, (4) few positive maternal interactions with the child observed during infancy, (5) heads of household in unskilled occupations, (6) minimal maternal education, (7) disadvantaged minority status, (8) single parenthood, (9) stressful life events, and (10) large family size. We found, indeed, that each of these variables was a risk factor. We compared the high-risk and low-risk group for each variable separately. For both the cognitive and mental health outcomes, the low-risk group had higher scores than the high-risk group. Most of the differences were of medium-effect size,

TABLE 8.1
Risk Variables in Rochester Longitudinal Study

Risk Variables	Low Risk	High Risk
Mental illness	0–1 psychiatric contact	More than 1 contact
Anxiety	75% least	25% most
Parental perspectives	75% highest	25% lowest
Spontaneous interaction	75% most	25% least
Education	High school	No high school
Occupation	Skilled	Semi- or unskilled
Minority status	No	Yes
Family support	Father present	Father absent
Stressful life events	75% fewest	25% most
Family size	1–3 children	4 or more children

enough to demonstrate the differences in group comparisons, but certainly not enough to detect which specific individuals with the risk factor would have an adverse outcome.

Other investigators found statistically significant differences in outcomes associated with single environmental risk factors that rarely explain large proportions of outcome variance. As a way of improving predictive power, Rutter (1979) argued that it was not any particular risk factor, but the number of risk factors in a child's background, that led to psychiatric disorder. Psychiatric risk for a sample of 10 year olds he studied rose from 2% in families with zero or one risk factors to 20% in families with four or more risk factors. The six risk factors considered included severe marital distress, low SES, large family size or overcrowding, paternal criminality, maternal psychiatric disorder, and admission of the child to foster care. In another study, Williams, Anderson, McGee, and Silva (1990) related behavioral disorders in 11 year olds to a cumulative disadvantage score based on number of residence and school changes, single parenthood, low SES, marital separation, young motherhood, low maternal cognitive ability, poor family relations, seeking marriage guidance, and maternal mental health symptoms. For the children with less than two disadvantages, only 7% had behavior problems, whereas for the children with eight or more disadvantages the rate was 40%.

Accumulating Risk Factors

In the RLS, there were significant effects for the single risk factors, but it was clear that most children with only a single risk factor would not end up with a major developmental problem. Yet, what would be the result if a comparison was made between children growing in environments with many risk factors compared to children with very few? We created a multiple risk score that was the total number of risks for each individual family. In the RLS, the range was well distributed between scores of 0 and 8, with one family having as many as 9 risks. When these risk factors were related to the child's intelligence and mental health, major differences were found between those children with few risks and those with many. On an intelligence test, children with no environmental risks scored more than 30 points higher than children with 8 or 9 risk factors. On average, each risk factor reduced the child's IQ score by four points.

A similar relation was found between the multiple risk scores and the social–emotional outcome. The more risk factors, the higher prevalence of clinical symptoms. It is clear that the effect of combining the 10 risk variables was to strongly accentuate the differences noted for the individual factors previously described. As the number of risk factors increased, competence decreased for preschool children (Sameroff, Seifer, Zax, & Barocas, 1987).

These analyses of the RLS data were attempts to elaborate environmental risk factors by reducing global measures, such as SES, to component social and behavioral variables. We were able to identify a set of risk factors that were predominantly found in lower SES groups, but affected child outcomes in all social classes. Moreover, no single variable was determinant of outcome. Only in families with multiple risk factors was the child's competence placed in jeopardy.

The multiple pressures of environmental context, in terms of amount of stress from the environment, the family's resources for coping with that stress, the number of children who must share those resources, and the parents' flexibility in understanding and dealing with their children, all play a role in the contemporary development of child intelligence test performance and mental health. However, the RLS sample was biased toward families in which a parent had a psychiatric diagnosis. Would we find the same effects of multiple risks in a sample more representative of the general community?

THE PHILADELPHIA STUDY

Another opportunity to examine the effects of multiple environmental risks on child development was provided by data emerging from a study of adolescents in a large sample of Philadelphia families we were following under the auspices of the MacArthur Foundation (Furstenberg, Cook, Eccles, Elder, & Sameroff, 1998). We interviewed mothers, fathers, and children in nearly 500 families in which there was a youth between the ages of 11 and 14 years old. The sample varied widely in SES and racial composition. There were 64% African Americans, 30% non-Hispanic Whites, and 6% other groups, primarily Puerto Rican families.

Other studies of multiple risk factors, like the RLS, were important in demonstrating the power of such analyses, but did not explicitly use an ecological model to identify domains of risk. Typically, there was a selection process in which the risks were chosen from the available measures already in the data set of the study. In the Philadelphia project, we took a more conceptual approach in designing the project so that we had environmental measures at a series of ecological levels.

For our analyses of environmental risk, we examined variables in systems that affected the adolescent, from those microsystems (Bronfenbrenner, 1979) in which the child was an active participant to those systems more distal to the child in which any effect had to be mediated by more proximal variables. We made a distinction between the characteristics of systems that were theoretically independent of the child and those in which the child was an active participant. For example, the family system was subdivided into management processes in which it is difficult to determine if the behavior is influenced more by the parent or by the child (e.g., behavioral control), and structural variables (e.g., marital status and household density) that were relatively independent of the child.

The risk factors were from six groupings reflecting different ecological relations to the adolescent (see Table 8.2). We selected 20 variables to serve as risk factors, twice as many as in the Rochester study. Our intention was to be able to have multiple factors in each of our six ecological levels. *Family process* was the first grouping and included variables in the family micro-system that were directly experienced by the child. These included support for autonomy, behavior control, parental involvement, and family climate. The second grouping was *parent characteristics*, which included the mother's mental health, sense of efficacy, resourcefulness, and level of education. This group included variables that influenced the child but, generally speaking, were less influenced by the child. The third grouping was *family structure*, which included the parents' marital status, and socioeconomic indicators of household crowding and receiving welfare payments. The fourth grouping was *family management of the community* and was comprised of variables that characterized the family's management of its relation to the larger community as reflected in institutional involvement, informal networks, so-cial resources, and adjustments to economic pressure. The fifth grouping, *peers*, included indicators of another microsystem of the child, the extent to which the youth was associated with prosocial and antisocial peers. *Community* was the sixth grouping, representing the ecological level most distal to the youth and the family. It included a census tract variable reflecting the average income and educational level of the neighborhood in which the

TABLE 8.2
Risk Variables in Philadelphia Study

Domain	Variable
Family process	Support for autonomy
	Discipline effectiveness
	Parental investment
	Family climate
Parent characteristics	Education
	Efficacy
	Resourcefulness
	Mental health
Family structure	Marital status
	Household crowding
	Welfare receipt
Management of community	Institutional involvement
	Informal networks
	Social resources
	Economic adjustment
Peers	Prosocial
	Antisocial
Community	Neighborhood SES
	Neighborhood problems
	School climate

family lived, a parental report of the number of problems in the neighborhood, and the climate of the adolescent's school.

In addition to the larger number of ecological variables in the Philadelphia study, we had a wider array of assessments available for interpreting developmental competence. The five outcomes that we thought would characterize successful adolescence were parent reports of adolescent *psychological adjustment* on a number of mental health scales; youth reports of *self-competence* measures and *problem behavior* with drugs, delinquency, and sexual behavior; and combined youth and parent reports of *activity involvement* in sports, religious, extracurricular, and community projects; and *academic performance* as reflected in grade reports reported by the parent and the adolescent.

Identifying Risks

As in the RLS, once we determined a representative list of potential risk factors at different levels of the child's ecology, we needed to assess whether or not each of these variables was indeed a risk factor. We used two criteria for identifying each risk factor. The first was that the raw variable was correlated with one of our five outcome variables, and the second was that adolescents in families that had the risk factor did significantly worse on at least one of the outcomes than adolescents in families without that environmental risk. For those variables that met the correlational criteria, we chose a cutoff score to optimize the difference between the outcomes for adolescents with the risk factor and those without. In general, the cutoff separated about 25% of the sample as a high-risk group from the remaining 75% who were defined as low risk.

The first important conclusion was that, indeed, we were successful in identifying risk factors. We found that there were risks at every ecological level associated with child outcomes. It was not only the parent or the family who had an influence on child competence, but also the peer group, neighborhood, and community together with their interactions with the family. Some of the variables were risks for each of our five outcomes. These included lack of support for autonomy, a negative family climate, and few prosocial peers. At the other extreme were variables that affected only a few outcomes such as having parents who lacked education and resourcefulness, single marital status and much economic adjustment, a lack of informal networks, and low census tract SES.

Many risk factors were identified in previous research that used only a single adolescent outcome such as delinquency (Stouthamer-Loeber et al., 1993). Examination of the generality of risk factors requires that there be multiple outcomes in the study. In the Philadelphia study, we found that the pattern of relations between ecological variables chosen as our risk factors and adolescent behavior was different for each outcome. On the one hand, academic performance, psychological adjustment, and problem behavior were related to risks at every ecological level. On the other hand, the correlates of self-competence and activity involvement presented two more limited and contrasting pictures. Activity involvement was strongly related to family management of the community and community characteristics, whereas self-competence was unrelated to either. In contrast, family structure played a significant role in adolescent self-competence but not in activity involvement.

As in the RLS, when the differences between high- and low-risk groups were examined for each individual risk factor, the effect sizes were small or moderate, rarely exceeding two thirds of a standard deviation. Yet, as in the RLS, we could ask the question: "What would be the consequence on adolescent competence if the youth experienced a number of these risk factors?" Moreover, what would be the increase in predictive efficiency if we used a cumulative risk score as our predictor for adolescent success?

Multiple-Risk Scores

Multiple environmental risk scores were calculated for each adolescent. The resulting range was from a minimum of 0 to a maximum of 13, with a mode of 5 out of a possible 20 risk factors. Only one family had no risk factors. For the multiple risk analysis, we wanted to have adequate sample size in

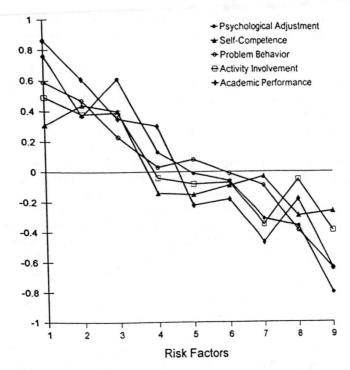

FIG. 8.1. Relation of five youth outcomes to multiple risk score in Philadelphia study.

each group so we combined the single family with no risk factors with the one-risk factor group and at the other extreme combined the 65 families with 9 or more risk factors into a single group. When the five normalized adolescent outcome scores were plotted against the number of risk factors, a very large decline in outcome was found with increasing risk.

As can be seen in Fig. 8.1, the maximum effect of cumulative risk was on psychological adjustment and academic performance, with a difference of more than one and one-half standard deviations between adolescents with only one risk factor compared to those with nine or more. The smallest effects were for the youth's report of self-competence and activity involvement where the difference was less than one standard deviation.

Odds-Ratio Analysis

Whether or not our cumulative risk score meaningfully increases our predictive efficiency was demonstrated by an odds-ratio analysis. We compared the odds of having a bad outcome in a high-risk versus a low-risk environment. For the typical analysis of relative and attributable risk, the outcome variable is usually discrete, succumbing to a disease or disorder. For our sample of young adolescents, there were few discrete negative outcomes. The adolescents were generally too young to have many pregnancies or arrests, and the rate of academic failure was not particularly high. We had to artificially create bad outcomes by making cut scores in our outcome measures. We dichotomized each of the five outcomes by making a cut at the 25th percentile for worse performance. These were the 25% of adolescents who were doing the most poorly in terms of mental health, self-competence, problem behavior, activity involvement, or academic performance. To simplify the report, we examined the relation between these bad outcomes and adolescent environmental risk scores, subdivided into four multiple risk groups: a *low-risk group* was defined as 3 or less, two *moderate-risk groups* of 4 to 5 and 6 to 7 risks, and a *high-risk group* with 8 or more risks (see Fig. 8.2).

The relative risk in the high-risk group for each of the bad outcomes was substantially higher than in the low-risk group. The strongest effects were for academic performance, in which the relative risk for a bad outcome increased from 7% in the low-risk group to 45% in the high-risk group, an odds ratio of 6.7 to 1. The weakest effect was for activity involvement, in which the relative risk only increased from 12% to 33%, an odds ratio of 2.7 to 1. In some sense, this is not unexpected because whereas everyone agrees that academic failure and poor mental health are bad outcomes, there might be some dispute as to whether an adolescent's desire not to participate

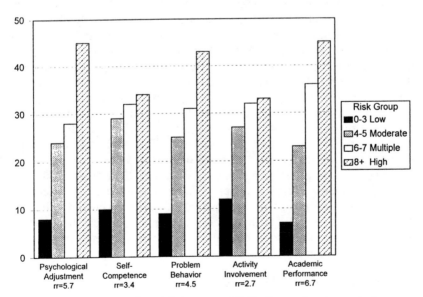

FIG. 8.2.   Percent of youth in lowest quartile for five youth outcomes in the Philadelphia study separated into four multiple risk groups. Relative risk is calculated as the ratio between percent of youth in the lowest quartile in the high-risk and low-risk groups.

in the scouts, religious activities, or sports reflects a lack of competence. In any case, for the important cognitive and social–emotional outcomes of youth, there seem to be powerful negative effects of the accumulation of environmental risk factors.

Promotive Factors

The concern with preventing developmental failures often clouds the fact that the majority of children in every social class and ethnic group are not failures. They get jobs, have successful social relationships, and raise a new generation of children. The concern with the source of such success fostered an increasing concern with the development of competence and the identification of protective factors (Garmezy, Masten, & Tellegen, 1984). However, the differentiation between risk and protective factors is far from clear (Seifer & Sameroff, 1987), and there continues to be many theoretical and methodological limitations in their identification (Luthar & Zigler, 1991).

Although some argued that protective factors only have meaning in the face of adversity (Rutter, 1987), in most cases, protective factors appear to be simply the positive pole of risk factors (Stouthamer-Loeber et al., 1993). In this sense, a better term for the positive end of the risk dimension is *promotive*, rather than protective, *factors*. To test this simplification, we created a set of promotive factors by cutting each of our risk dimensions at the top quartile (Sameroff, Bartko, & Eccles, 1997). So, for example, whereas a negative family climate was a risk factor, a positive family climate now became a promotive factor or whereas a parent's poor mental health was a risk factor, her good mental health became promotive. We then summed these promotive factors and examined their relation to our five outcomes. The results mirrored our analysis of the effects of multiple risks. There was a similar range of promotive factors (from families with none to families with 15 out of a possible 20) and a similar relation to outcomes; families with many promotive factors doing substantially better than families from contexts with few promotive factors. For the youth in the Philadelphia sample, there does not seem to be much difference between the influence of risk and promotive variables. The more risk factors, the worse the outcomes; the more promotive factors, the better the outcomes. In short, when taken as part of a constellation of environmental influences on child development, most contextual variables in the parents, the family, the neighborhood, and the culture at large seem to be dimensional, aiding child development at one end and inhibiting it at the other.

Seeking Vulnerability and Resilience

Although most of the family and social factors we studied seem to have linear effects on child competence, we thought it worthwhile to determine if there were some factors that showed an interactive effect. One approach is to determine if some environmental factor buffered the effects of multiple risk. Another is to search for factors in the child that serve such functions.

On the environmental side, we examined the effect of two single risk factors that economists and sociologists were very concerned about: income level and marital status. Although one would think these factors should have powerful effects on the fate of children, we did not find such differences when these single variables were put into a broader ecological framework. Differences in effects on child competence disappeared when we controlled the number of other environmental risk factors in each family. To test the effects of different amounts of financial resources, we split our sample of families into those with high-, middle-, and low-income levels. For the family structure comparison, we split the sample into groups of children living in two-parent versus single-parent families. To simplify the analysis further, we combined the five youth outcomes into one overall adolescent competence score, which reflected general adaptation across personal, academic, and social domains. In each case, there were no differences in the relation to child competence when we compared groups of children with the same number of risk factors raised in rich or poor families, or families with one or two parents (see Figs. 8.3 and 8.4).

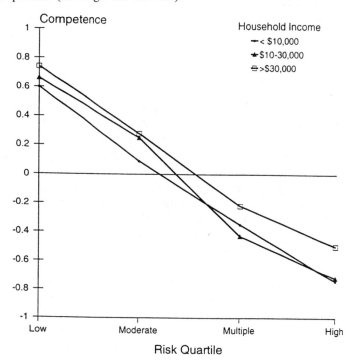

FIG. 8.3.   Relation of risk scores to a composite measure of adolescent competence in groups with different amounts of total household income.

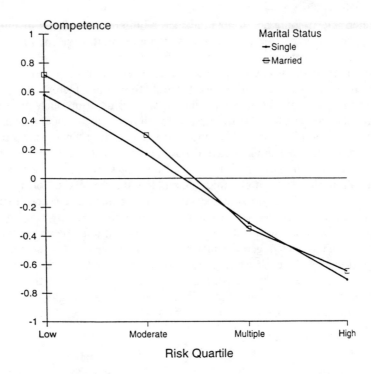

FIG. 8.4. Relation of risk scores to a composite measure of adolescent competence in single vs. two parent families.

Our analyses of the data reveal that it is not single environmental factors that make a difference, but the constellation of risks in each family's life. The reason that income and marital status seem to make major differences in child development is not because they are overarching variables in themselves, but because they are strongly associated with a combination of other risk factors. For example, one can see in the last row of Table 8.3 that where 39% of poor children lived in high-risk families with more than 7 risk factors, only 7% of affluent children did. Similarly, where 29% of single-parent families live in high-risk social conditions, only 15% of two-parent families do.

In our sample, income or marital status taken alone may have statistically significant effects on adolescent behavior, but these differences are small or nonexistent in comparison with the effects of the accumulation of multiple negative influences that characterize our high-risk groups. The overlap in outcomes for youth in high- and low-income families, and in single- and two-parent families is substantial for any and all psychological outcomes. There are many successful adults who were raised in poverty and unsuccessful ones who were raised in affluence. There are many healthy and happy adults

TABLE 8.3

Percent of Philadelphia Study Families in Different Risk Groups
With Household Incomes Less Than $10,000, Between
$10,000 and $30,000, and Greater Than $30,000 and in
Single-Parent Versus Two-Parent Homes

	Income Level			Family Structure	
Risk Group	$10,000 (n = 113)	$10–30,000 (n = 208)	>$30,000 (n = 142)	Single Parent (n = 250)	Two Parent (n = 235)
Low	13%	35%	60%	34%	54%
Moderate	17%	22%	23%	25%	22%
Multiple	26%	28%	11%	19%	17%
High	44%	15%	6%	22%	7%

who come from broken homes, and there are many unhappy ones who were raised by two parents.

Personal Factors

To search for effects of personal factors, we started with two basic variables of gender and race. We found the same correlations between risk scores and outcomes for boys and girls and for Blacks and Whites. When the relation between our summary competence measure and risk factors was compared for gender and racial groups, the curves were essentially overlapping.

Like the SES variable on the environmental side, race and gender are not behavioral variables. Therefore, it is of greater interest to investigate the influence of variables with psychological content. A personality variable that is given great importance in discussions of successful development is resourcefulness. Is it possible that despite social adversity, those children with high levels of "human capital" (Coleman, 1988) are able to overcome minimal resources at home and in the community to reach levels of achievement comparable to children from more highly advantaged social strata?

In the Philadelphia study, we were able to measure this construct of resourcefulness with a set of questions asked of the parent and child about the youth's capacity to solve problems, overcome difficulties, and bounce back from setbacks. We divided the sample into high and low efficacy groups and looked at their adolescent outcomes. Indeed, highly efficacious youth were more competent than those with low efficacy on our measures of adolescent competence. A sense of personal resourcefulness seemed to pay off.

Yet, what happens to this effect when we take environmental adversity into account? When we matched high and low efficacy children for the number of environmental risk factors, the difference in general competence between youth in the high and low environmental risk conditions was far greater than that between high-resourceful and low-resourceful groups (see

Fig. 8.5). Highly efficacious adolescents in high-risk conditions did worse than low efficacious youth in low-risk conditions. It may not be a surprise to learn that the ineffective offspring of advantaged families have a much easier ride than resourceful multirisk children.

We did the same analysis using academic achievement as an indicator of competence and examined whether good work at school was related to better mental health, more engagement in positive community activities, and less involvement in delinquent problem behavior. Again, for every outcome, high academic-achieving adolescents in high-risk conditions did worse than youth with low school grades in low-risk conditions.

One of the major weaknesses in the Philadelphia study is that it is cross-sectional. Causal modeling is impossible unless one has longitudinal developmental data, and this is difficult even then. The RLS had a series of developmental assessments that permitted a longitudinal view of the contribution of individual factors to developmental success.

From the RLS data collected during the first year of life, we created a multiple competence score for each child during infancy that included 12 factors. These were neonatal behavioral test scores, easy temperament scores,

FIG. 8.5.   Relation of multiple risk to outcome for Philadelphia youth in high- and low-resourcefulness groups.

and developmental quotients. We then divided the sample into low-, me-
dium-, and high-competence groups of infants and examined as outcomes
their 4-year IQ and social–emotional functioning scores. We found no relation between infant scores and 4-year IQ, especially when compared to the
effects of contemporaneous infant environmental multirisk scores. Similarly,
there was no relation between infant multirisk scores and the global rating
of 4-year social competence. However, there is a general feeling that infant
developmental scales are weak predictors because they assess different developmental functions than are captured by later cognitive and personality
assessments. Perhaps if we move up the age scale, we would find that
characteristics of these children at 4 years old contribute to adolescent
achievements at our 18-year assessment.

We did not have a specific measure of resourcefulness at 4 years, but we
had our global measures of child social competence and IQ. We divided the
4 year olds into high- and low-social competence groups and high- and
low-IQ groups. We then compared these groups to how they did at 18 years
on mental health assessments and measures of school achievement (see Fig.
8.6). More resourceful children did better on average than less resourceful
children, but as in the Philadelphia data, when we controlled for environ-

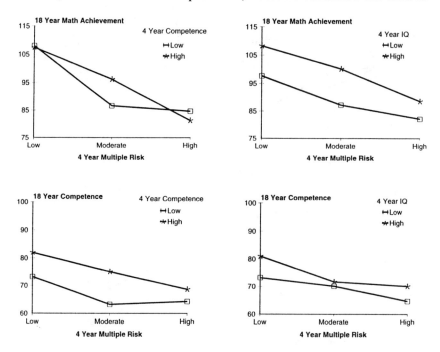

FIG. 8.6.   Relation of 4-year multiple risk to 18-year math achievement or
social–emotional competence for groups of children who were high and low
on 4-year social–emotional competence or IQ.

mental risk, the differences between children with high and low levels of human capital paled when compared to the differences in performance between children in high- and low-risk social environments. In each case, high competent children in high-risk environments did worse than low competent children in low-risk environments.

Perhaps 4-year competence is still too ephemeral to resist the negative consequences of adverse social circumstance. Would competent children at 13 years old succeed where competent children at 4 years old failed? How would they stack up at our 18-year assessments of mental health and school achievement? At 13 years old, we did an index of resourcefulness in scores on an internal sense of locus of control. We divided the sample of children into a high- and low-internal-locus-of-control group and a high- and low-intelligence group and examined their 18-year behavior.

Again, in each case, when we controlled for environmental risk, we found that the highly competent children in personality or intelligence did far less well than expected. Those groups of children with high levels of human capital living in conditions of high environmental risk did worse than similar groups in low-risk conditions, but more to the point, did worse than low competent children in low-risk environments (see Fig. 8.7). The negative

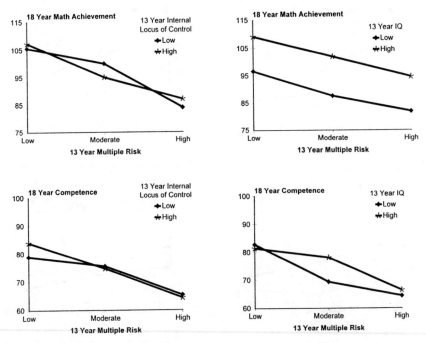

FIG. 8.7. Relation of 13-year multiple risk to 18-year math achievement or social emotional competence for groups of children who were high and low on 13-year internal locus of control or IQ.

effects of a disadvantaged environment seem to be more powerful contributors to child achievement at every age than the personality characteristics of the child.

These analyses tell us that income level and marital status (on the family side) and gender, race, and efficacy and achievement (on the personal side) taken alone may have statistically significant effects on adolescent behavior, but these differences pale in comparison to the accumulation of multiple negative influences that characterize our high-risk groups. The overlap in outcomes for low-income versus high-income families, families with one or two parents, boys versus girls, Blacks versus Whites, and high-resourceful and low-resourceful youth is substantial for most psychological outcomes, but the overlap is far less in comparisons of groups of children reared in conditions of high- versus low-multiple risk, where gender, race, resourcefulness, income, and number of parents in the home are only single factors. The important implication is that a focus on individual characteristics of individuals of families, such as whether their skin color is different, can never explain more than a tiny proportion of variance in behavioral development. To truly appreciate the determinants of competency requires attention to a broad constellation of ecological factors in which these individuals and families are embedded.

CONTINUITY OF ENVIRONMENTAL RISK

The Rochester and Philadelphia studies revealed major consequences for children living in multiproblem families. What are the long-term consequences of these early adverse circumstances? Will later conditions alter the course for such children or will early experiences lock children into pathways of deviance? To answer this question, we must return to a consideration of data from the adolescent phase of the RLS.

In the RLS, our attention was devoted to the source of continuities and discontinuities in child performance. We completed a new assessment of the sample when the children were 13 and 18 years old (Baldwin et al., 1993; Sameroff, Seifer, Baldwin, & Baldwin, 1993). Because of the potent effects of our multiple-risk index at 4 years old, we calculated new multiple environmental risk scores for each family based on their situation 9 and 14 years later. To our surprise, there were very few families that showed major shifts in the number of risk factors across the intervening periods. Between 4 and 13 years old, the factor that showed the most improvement was maternal education, in which the number of mothers without a high-school diploma or equivalent decreased from 33% to 22% of the sample. The risk factor that increased the most was single parenthood, with the number of children being raised by their mothers alone increasing from 24% to 41%. In the main, however, there was little change in the environments of the children in our sample.

The typical statistic reported in longitudinal research is the correlation between early and later performance of the children. We too found such correlations. Intelligence at 4 years old correlated .72 with intelligence at 13 years old. The usual interpretation of such a number is that there is a continuity of competence or incompetence in the child. Such a conclusion cannot be challenged if the only assessments in the study are of the children. In the RLS, we examined and were able to correlate both environmental and child characteristics across time. We found a high correlation of .77 between environmental risk scores at the two ages that was as great, or greater than, any continuity in the child. Whatever the child's ability for achieving higher levels of competence, it was severely undermined by the continuing paucity of environmental support in high-risk contexts and was fostered in low-risk contexts. Whatever the capabilities provided to the child by individual factors, the environment acted to limit or further expand opportunities for development.

Because of the very high stability in the number of risks experienced by these families, it was impossible to determine if the effects of early adversity or contemporary risk were having the greater effect on the later behavior of the children. Those children who were living in high-risk environments at 4 years old were still living in them at 13 years old. Moreover, these contemporary high-risk contexts were producing the same negative effects on behavior as the earlier ones had done. In Fig. 8.8, one can see the relation between the IQ outcome and low-, medium-, and high-risk scores at the three assessment ages. The curves substantially overlap with similar ranges of outcomes at each age. We found the same relationship between the number of risk factors and the child's intellectual competence; those children from families with no risk factors scored more than 30 points higher on intelligence tests and had significantly better mental health than those with the most risk factors.

PROTECTIVE FACTORS AND THE SEARCH
FOR RESILIENCY

When studies are successful in identifying truly protective factors (i.e., promotive only under conditions of risk), the issue is raised of identification on an individual basis of resilient (or protected) individuals. Ideally, one would like to find a substantial subset of children who, by any measure of competence, were doing better than average, despite the adversity they faced in daily life. In the RLS, we examined the high-risk subsample of children who had four or more environmental risks to determine the characteristics of

**Longitudinal Associations Between
Cumulative Risk and Children's IQ**

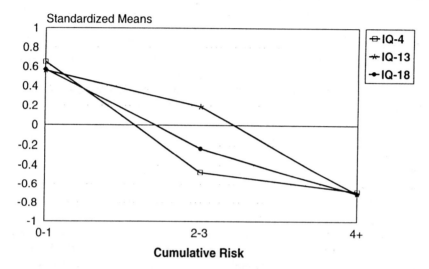

FIG. 8.8.   Relation of contemporary multiple risk scores to child IQ at 4, 13, and 18 years of age.

those who were doing better than expected. Only 3 of the 50 children in this group were above the total sample mean on our 13-year-old child outcome measures of cognitive competence and mental health, but all 3 also improved in their risk status. They were in the highest risk category at 4 years old, but by 13 years old, were doing better. Thus, it is unclear whether the more favorable outcomes in these children were due to protective factors or to a lessening of risk.

When we examined the whole RLS sample to see what the consequences of moving from the high (4 or more) to the low (0 or 1) environmental risk group or from the low to the high risk group were for children in the study, we found striking effects. Those who changed from high risk at 4 years old to low risk at 13 years old improved in IQ by 13 points. In contrast, those who changed from low risk at 4 years old to high risk at 13 years old dropped in IQ by 15 points. These findings make a strong case for the powerful effects of environmental risks on the children, except for the fact that only one child in the sample went from high to low risk and only one child went from low to high risk. Decreases or increases of three risk factors were rare because of the strong continuity of advantage or adversity from early childhood to adolescence just described. Stability rather than change appeared to be the rule.

SECULAR TRENDS

The thrust of a contextual analysis of developmental regulation is not that individual factors in the child are nonexistent or irrelevant, but that they must be studied in a context larger than the single child. The risk analyses discussed so far implicated parent characteristics and the immediate social conditions of family support and life-event stress as important moderators of healthy psychological growth in the child. To this list of risks must be added changes in the historical supports for families in a given society. The importance of this added level of complexity was emphasized when we examined secular trends in the economic well-being of families in the United States.

At 4 years old, we divided the sample into high-, medium-, and low-risk groups based on the number of cumulative risks: 0 or 1 in the low-risk group, 2 or 3 in the medium-risk group, and 4 or more in the high-risk group. We found that 22% of the high-risk group had IQs below 85, whereas none of the low-risk sample did. Conversely, 59% of the low-risk group had IQs above 115, but only 4% of the high-risk sample did.

After the 13-year assessment we made the same breakdown into high-, medium-, and low-risk groups and examined the distribution of IQs in risk groups. Again, we found a preponderance of low IQ scores in the high-risk group and a preponderance of high IQ scores in the low-risk group, indicating the continuing negative effects of an unfavorable environment. However, strikingly, the number of children in the high-risk group with IQs below 85 had increased from 22% to 46%, more than doubling. If our analysis was restricted to the level of the child and family, we hypothesize that high-risk environments operate synergistically to further worsen the intellectual standing of these children during the period from preschool to adolescence, placing them in a downward spiral of increasing incompetence.

An alternative hypothesis was that society was changing during the 9 years between the RLS assessments. In a study completed by the House of Representatives' Ways and Means Committee (Passel, 1989), it was found that between the years 1973 and 1987, while we were doing this study, the average household income of the poorest one fifth of Americans fell 12%, whereas the income of the richest one fifth increased 24%. Elder (1994) made a strong case for attending to major changes in society as determinants of the life course for growing children. His work centered on the Great Depression of the 1930s. Similar effects seem to be apparent in our own times.

SOCIAL AND POLITICAL AGENDAS

What we just described are the results of an academic agenda for understanding the effects of poverty on children. In two studies of children and adolescents, we found large relations between the number of ecological risk factors in the family and community environment and cognitive and social competence. Because of the high stability of environmental advantage or adversity and of personal competence of the child, it is not clear from these data whether the environmental influences act early to change the child or continue to have effects at each stage of development.

There are many who argue that children do poorly in conditions of poverty because they do not have individual characteristics that promote resilience, overcome challenge, and eventuate in productive work and family life. By identifying characteristics of children who achieve despite adverse circumstances, some hope that we could instill those characteristics in other children to help them overcome environmental adversity. In contrast is the position that environmental risks are so pervasive that opportunities do not exist for positive development, even if the child has excellent coping skills.

In our analyses we found that individual personality characteristics of mental health, efficacy, and resourcefulness or achievement characteristics of high intelligence or high academic grades contribute to developmental competence. However, the effects of such individual competencies do not overcome the effects of high environmental risk. In analyses of both the Rochester and Philadelphia data we found that groups of high-resilient children in high-risk environments always did worse than groups of low-resilient children in low-risk environments (Sameroff, 1996). When we matched high- and low-efficacy children for the number of environmental risk factors, the difference in competence between youth in the high- and low-environmental risk conditions is far greater than that between high-resourceful and low-resourceful groups of children.

In discussions about the consequences of environmental risk and methods for amelioration, a focus on resiliency takes the form of blaming the victims. If children show poor outcomes, it is because they were not resilient. Clearly, if one believes it is the resiliency of the individual child that is the determining factor in their outcomes, then the intervention agenda is different than if one believes it is social and familial risk factors that are more important.

The Holocaust was a major environmental event from which there were few survivors. If one were a scientist seeking methods to survive the Holocaust, a resilience strategy would be to determine the characteristics of those who survived and then instill those characteristics in the rest of the affected population. The stories of how these survivors overcame adversity is remarkable. If they were not remarkable, there would not have been survival. Do such survival stories provide lessons that could be used to save a larger proportion of the victims of the Holocaust? A more fruitful strategy would have been to have prevented or eliminated the Holocaust. In terms of what we are discussing now, the best preventive strategy would be to reduce environmental risk rather than trust in individual personality to overcome such risks.

REFERENCES

Baldwin, A. L., Baldwin, C. P., Kasser, T., Zax, M., Sameroff, A., & Seifer, R. (1993). Contextual risk and resiliency during late adolescence. *Development and Psychopathology, 5*, 741–761.

Bronfenbrenner, U. (1979). *The ecology of human development.* Cambridge, MA: Harvard University Press.

Clausen, J. A. (1968). *Socialization and society.* Boston: Little, Brown.

Coleman, J. (1988). Social capital in the creation of human capital. *American Journal of Sociology, 94*, S95–S120.

Dryfoos, J. G. (1991). Adolescents at risk: A summation of work in the field: Programs and policies. *Journal of Adolescent Health, 12*, 630–637.

Elder, G. H., Jr. (1974). *Children of the great depression.* Chicago: University of Chicago Press.

Elder, G. H., Jr. (1984). Families, kin and the life course: A sociological perspective. In R. D. Parke (Ed.), *Review of child development research: The family* (Vol. 7, pp. 80–136). Chicago: University of Chicago Press.

Furstenberg, F. F., Jr., Cook, T. D., Eccles, J., Elder, G. H., Jr., & Sameroff, A. (1998). *Managing to make it: Urban families and adolescent success.* Chicago: University of Chicago Press.

Garmezy, N., Masten, A. S., & Tellegen, A. (1984). The study of stress and competence in children: A building block of developmental psychopathology. *Child Development, 55*, 97–111.

Kohn, M., & Schooler, C. (1983). *Work and personality: An inquiry into the impact of social stratification.* Norwood, NJ: Ablex.

Luthar, S. S., & Zigler, E. (1991). Vulnerability and competence: A review of research on resilience in childhood. *American Journal of Orthopsychiatry, 61*, 6–22.

Mayer, S. E., & Jencks, C. (1989). Growing up in poor neighborhoods: How much does it matter? *Science, 243*, 1441–1445.

Passell, P. Forces In Society And Reaganism, Helped By Deep Hole For Poor. (1989, July 16). *The New York Times*, pp. 1–20.

Rutter, M. (1979). Protective factors in children's responses to stress and disadvantage. In M. W. Kent & J. E. Rolf (Eds.), *Primary prevention of psychopathology: Vol. 3. Social competence in children* (pp. 49–74). Hanover, NH: University Press of New England.

Rutter, M. (1987). Psychosocial resilience and protective mechanisms. *American Journal of Orthopsychiatry, 57*, 316–331.

Sameroff, A. (1996, Fall). Democratic and Republican models of development: Paradigms or perspectives. *Developmental Psychology Newsletter*, 1–9.

Sameroff, A. J. (1983). Developmental systems: Contexts and evolution. In P. H. Mussen (Series Ed.) & W. Kessen (Vol. Ed.), *Handbook of child psychology: Vol. 1. History, theories, and methods* (pp. 237–294). New York: Wiley.

Sameroff, A. J., Bartko, W. T., & Eccles, J. (1997). *Effects of accumulated ecological risk on successful adolescent development.* Unpublished manuscript.

Sameroff, A. J., Seifer, R., Baldwin, A., & Baldwin, C. (1993). Stability of intelligence from preschool to adolescence: The influence of social and family risk factors. *Child Development, 64*, 80–97.

Sameroff, A. J., Seifer, R., & Barocas, R. (1983). Developmental impact of parental psychopathology: Diagnosis, severity or social status effects? *Infant Mental Health Journal, 4*, 236–249.

Sameroff, A. J., Seifer, R., & Zax, M. (1982). Early development of children at risk for emotional disorder. *Monographs of the Society for Research in Child Development, 47* (Serial No. 199).

Sameroff, A. J., Seifer, R., Barocas, R., Zax, M., & Greenspan, S. (1987). Intelligence quotient scores of 4-year-old children: Social environmental risk factors. *Pediatrics, 79*, 343–350.

Sameroff, A. J., Seifer, R., Zax, M., & Barocas, R. (1987). Early indicators of developmental risk: The Rochester longitudinal study. *Schizophrenia Bulletin, 13*, 383–393.

Seifer, R., & Sameroff, A. J. (1987). Multiple determinants of risk and vulnerability. In E. J. Anthony & B. J. Cohler (Eds.), *The invulnerable child* (pp. 51–69). New York: Guilford.

Stouthamer-Loeber, M., Loeber, R., Farrington, D. P., Zhang, Q., van Kammen, W., & Maguin, E. (1993). The double edge of protective and risk factors for delinquency: Interrelations and developmental patterns. *Development and Psychopathology, 5*, 683–701.

Williams, S., Anderson, J., McGee, R., & Silva, P. A. (1990). Risk factors for behavioral and emotional disorder in preadolescent children. *Journal of the American Academy of Child and Adolescent Psychiatry, 29*, 413–419.

9

▼▼▼▼▼▼▼

Differentiating Developmental Risk Levels for Families in Poverty: Creating a Family Typology

Craig T. Ramey
Sharon Landesman Ramey
Robin Gaines Lanzi
Civitan International Research Center
University of Alabama at Birmingham

The family is central to children's economic and social resources and provides a primary framework for children's cognitive and social development. In the family context, children engage in activities that foster intelligence and academic skills, learn how to think critically and creatively, understand how to evaluate their own thought processes, develop positive interaction skills to initiate and maintain relationships, and acquire the ability to avoid or resolve social conflict. Lack of adequate economic and social resources, however, can negatively affect children's growth and development, particularly in the areas of cognitive and social development (Ramey & Ramey, 1994).

A link between familial economic poverty and delayed cognitive development in children has been well-established (Ramey & Ramey, 1992). Slower rates of cognitive development during the preschool years were correlated with reduced rates of school readiness and higher rates of poor academic performance, grade retention, and special education (Campbell & Ramey, 1995). Although these correlations are strong, understanding the significance of the family context and poverty for the ontogeny of the child's cognitive and social development has not been well-established.

CONCEPTUAL FRAMEWORK

Recently, we advanced a conceptual framework for understanding how intervention programs (specifically, two-generation intervention programs) can alter the well-being of children and families from economically impoverished environments (Ramey, Ramey, Gaines, & Blair, 1995). This framework was helpful, over the past 10 years, in developing a family typology to better understand variations in risk for poor school readiness among families below the economic poverty line. This conceptual framework was also used to guide the development of early intervention programs designed to improve readiness for school by children, readiness for improved parenting, and economic and social well-being of the families. Figure 9.1 depicts the key sources of influence on the well-being of both generations: children and adult family members. Initially, it is recognized that the current biological and behavioral status of children and adults reflects the cumulative effects of their personal histories and environments.

At the start of a two-generation, early intervention program, gathering information in a culturally appropriate manner and appreciating the family's place in the larger ecology is important. For example, are parents longtime members of the community? What characteristics (e.g., beliefs or resources) do they feel they share with their neighbors or that set them apart? How do they regard local institutions as potential sources of support?

Next, this model illustrates a potential range of resources and activities that are used to produce changes in adults, children, and the family's environment. These span those targeted primarily to: (a) the family as a unit, such as those related to income, housing, utilities, food, clothing, safety, health care, transportation, cultural and recreational activities, and healthy lifestyles; (b) the adults, including adult education, job training, employment, social and emotional supports, parenting and family management skills; and (c) the children, such as educational supports, child care, and social and emotional supports. These resources and supports are provided via many routes, including direct provision by the two-generation program, the program's referral of families to existing services and agencies, and other means (such as friends and natural helpers, pre-existing supports like community churches and schools, family initiated activities or self-referrals, and the media).

For an individual family, the decisions about allocating programmatic resources and activities in two-generation programs are frequently made after a comprehensive needs assessment or intake process. Ideally, this individualized family assessment considers the full range of a family's needs, including needs that may not be readily apparent (such as needs related to recurring depression or substance abuse). Almost all two-generation programs developed some form of *case management*—that is, a way to establish a trusting and continuous relationship between program staff and the family, so that as additional relevant information is gathered about the family's life circumstances and progress, appropriate changes in the family's service plan can be made. To the extent that resources permit and to the extent that family members and the program mutually endorse similar goals, then comprehensive interventions are planned.

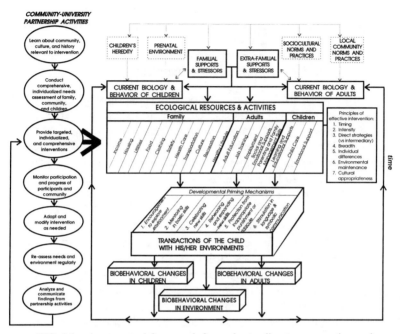

FIG. 9.1. A conceptual framework for understanding two generation early intervention programs.

In this conceptual framework, changes in individual and family status are mediated by developmental priming mechanisms. That is, the supports and services have their effects by producing changes in the experience and behavior of individual family members, who then engage in altered transactions with other family members and with their environments. It is through these transactions that long-term, sustainable benefits are thought to be realized.

In Fig. 9.1, the provision of two-generation program activities includes monitoring the participation and progress of both generations and adapting and modifying interventions as needed. These programmatic activities serve to increase positive outcomes by ensuring that those supports that are highly valued and used are continued, those that are not are discontinued or modified, and new supports in response to developmental changes in the family or family members are obtained in a timely manner. Given the breadth of most two-generation programs and the initial differences in families when they are enrolled, few (if any) of the program's activities are timed specifically in advance (such as when a mother completes her education or job training and is ready for competitive employment, when health care that is not routine is needed, or when a child is ready for more advanced books and learning activities). Last, by regularly reassessing needs, with active involvement of program participants in this reassessment, and then adapting and modifying supports, two-generation programs become engaged in a formative evaluation process.

Transactions of Family Members
With One Another and Their Environments:
The Role of Developmental Priming Mechanisms

We discern at least six likely psychosocial mechanisms that account for changes in the developmental status of children and adults that are especially pertinent to intellectual and social outcomes (Ramey & Ramey, 1992). We labeled these developmental priming mechanisms to emphasize both their potential role in altering the course of human development and the fact that they help individuals to be primed or to get ready for subsequent opportunities. Admittedly, maturational and developmental processes are complex and far from completely delineated. What is established is that what an individual does (behavioral activities) influences the development of the central nervous system (in turn, setting the stage for changes in future learning and social opportunities) just as biological maturation itself influences behavior. This fundamental interdependence of people with their environments (especially social environments) is why the success of two-generation programs relies on their ability to alter both the individuals (including their skills, health, and positive self-esteem) and their environments (reducing major stressors and sources of harm).

The six developmental priming mechanisms, identified in Fig. 9.1, are:

1. Opportunities to explore and gather information.
2. Being mentored in new skills.
3. Celebration of developmental achievements.
4. Review and rehearsal of new skills and knowledge.
5. Avoidance of inappropriate punishment and ridicule.
6. Language as a mechanism for learning.

Exploration.   The first developmental priming mechanism concerns opportunities to explore and gather information about the environment. Infants and very young children need to be encouraged to explore their immediate surroundings. Through this exploration, they acquire confidence in their own sensory and perceptual abilities and acquire vitally needed information. To the extent that care-giving adults foster young children's natural curiosity, this active orientation to one's environment is likely to become a positive and useful attribute. At the same time caregivers encourage exploration, they also provide critical cues about times and places when exploration or information seeking is potentially dangerous. This developmental priming mechanism is one that is logically extended to older children and adults as well.

In a two-generation program, adults are helped to explore employment and career options that fit their aptitudes and interests, new ways of spending spare time (such as a newly awakened interest in reading), and alternative means of learning, getting along with others, and pursuing personal goals. The general orientation to situations and people that such exploration supports contributes to better coping and problem-solving skills across many domains, including work and parenting.

Mentoring.   Being mentored in basic skills is identified as another important developmental priming mechanism. Mentoring is used to connote a form of teaching or guidance that occurs in a caring and responsive relationship. Much of the mentoring of young children occurs as part of the everyday activities in a family, rather than as a discrete educational activity unto itself. The types of basic skills young children need to acquire via mentoring include labeling of objects and events, sorting, sequencing, comparing, noting means–ends (or cause–effect) relations, basic number concepts, and symbol recognition. Ideally, learning opportunities for adults in two-generation programs include opportunities to receive mentoring, in addition to more traditional forms of education and training. It seems likely that adults who experience learning as part of a caring relationship internalize a supportive learning style and use it in interactions with their children.

Celebration.   A third hypothesized mechanism is that of celebrating developmental advances. Young children show remarkable and frequent gains in their skills and understanding of how the world works. When these developmental achievements are responded to in a positive and vigorous manner, children feel valued, important, and successful. Young children's responses to such celebrations of their developmental accomplishments are frequently of great delight. Such celebrations serve to strengthen the overall adult–child relationship as well as to encourage children to continue to practice and display their new skills and knowledge. In two-generation programs, the case manager or family advocate is often someone who helps celebrate the adult's developmental accomplishments. Designing programs that allow for early accomplishments and celebration of these events may be key to speeding the progress that adult participants make in their self-sufficiency activities. For example, a program that recognizes a week of excellent attendance as an important accomplishment provides this type of support, in contrast to a program that does not count anything as a significant accomplishment until a difficult-to-reach milestone, such as GED completion, is reached.

Rehearsal.   After a child or adult has explored, learned new skills, and had new behavior celebrated, it is helpful to have opportunities to review, rehearse, and extend these new skills. This phase of guided rehearsal serves to strengthen and refine the new behavior and facilitate its appropriate application in diverse settings or situations. Often, children's developmental advances occur in bursts, and sometimes children appear to forget new things they learned. With encouragement from caring adults, children more readily resume and improve their repertoires. Adults also need such encouragement and practice. It is questionable whether some of the two-generation interventions give parents enough time for this rehearsal. Unfortunately, it is often expected that once adults acquire a new skill, they are ready to quickly move on to new challenges. Thus, for adults, as for children, it is important to design the celebration of accomplishments in ways that allow for the practice and extension of recently acquired skills and an acceptance of temporary or apparent setbacks.

Inappropriate Punishment. One of the most important developmental priming mechanisms concerns the avoidance of inappropriate disapproval, teasing, or punishment. This mechanism recognizes that when adults are inappropriately and repeatedly negative, punitive, or ridiculing of children's normative behavior, they cause children to withdraw from trying new activities or expressing their desire to become more skilled. Unavoidably, young children make many mistakes, show unevenness in their day-to-day behavior, and often have unintended (usually minor) consequences associated with their developmental exploration and trial-and-error learning. Parenting education often helps parents to appreciate what is normative for a given age or stage of development. We note, however, that this priming mechanism does not mean that parents cannot use constructive criticism and negative consequences for unacceptable negative behaviors that children can understand and control. Finding ways to give corrective feedback about adult behavior (such as failure to attempt an important accomplishment; e.g., getting a GED certificate) while protecting the adult participant from overly harsh criticism is a major challenge for two-generation interventions.

Language. Above all, young children become acculturated and capable through their acquisition of language in its many forms. The significance of language is particularly elevated in societies that rely on spoken, printed, and other symbolic means of communication. Evidence is accruing (e.g., Kuhl, Williams, Lacerda, Stevens, & Lindblom, 1992) that young children are ready to receive linguistic input and learn about language many months before they actually speak. All cultures have special forms of orally communicating with infants and toddlers, often referred to as *motherese.* Studies indicate that such adaptations in language serve to make certain sounds and meanings more salient to young children. It is hypothesized that central nervous system development in this area depends on exposure to language and symbols from an early age on. Unfortunately, many infants and toddlers experience deprivation in their language transactions with caregivers, who may not realize the importance of these exchanges early in life or who may not take the time to provide the amount of direct language experience that very young children need. Simply exposing an infant or toddler to distal conversations, music, or television is not adequate for very early learning; in fact, excessive exposure to meaningless sounds encourages young children to ignore important linguistic information from the audible environment.

For adults, of course, language is also a primary vehicle for learning. Exposure to increasingly complex language, presented in many forms, including newspapers, instructional materials, and computers, is especially critical to parents who are building skills that can be used in the workplace. Consistent with the goals of a two-generation intervention, it is also hoped that this exposure to language primes not only parents' acquisition of work-related competencies, but also their ability to support their children's emerging language and literacy skills.

We proposed the presence of these developmental priming mechanisms based on a review of the early child development literature, including cross-cultural research (e.g., Barnard, Bee, & Hammond, 1984; Belsky, 1980; Bradley et al., 1989; Hetherington & Parke, 1993; Lewis, 1983). We hypothesize that all of these mechanisms must be present in children's everyday lives (on a frequent and predictable basis) to support normal development. Even when children have disabilities or detected developmental delays, these mechanisms are relevant to their further advances.

FAMILIAL VARIATIONS IN POVERTY

Relatively few studies compared familial variations in poverty to children's outcome, yet there is a wide spectrum of children's developmental outcomes among poor families. Thus, although familial poverty predicts high rates of school failure relative to families who are not in poverty, not all poor children fail in school. This lack of predictive precision suggests that, in the highest risk economic strata, other variables or factors are playing active roles in determining success or failure in school. One such factor is systematic variations in noneconomic resources or in family dynamics. Examination of systematic variations in family configurations, resources, and dynamics in poverty may distinguish which children in which poverty families are at highest risk for poor academic and social outcomes.

A long-standing area of deliberation and scientific concern was how to adequately capture important dimensions of risk and how it relates to children's developmental outcomes. Sameroff (e.g., Sameroff, Seifer, Baldwin, & Baldwin, 1993) suggested using a cumulative risk measure that aggregates 10 risk factors. This line of research showed that it is the number of risk factors, not the kind of risk factor, that is the major influence. Lewis and colleagues (e.g., Bendersky & Lewis, 1994) argued that combining proximal variables (e.g., social support and maternal responsivity) and distal variables (e.g., socioeconomic status) in an individual score conceals their independent effects. However, a useful classification of families, in terms of their demographic and functional characteristics that fall under the heading of "poverty" has not yet been addressed.

CLUSTER ANALYSIS: PREVIOUS RESEARCH

To increase understanding of variations among poverty families, we began a line of research that uses cluster analysis to develop and refine a "typology of poverty families." Preliminary work on the typology of poverty families was begun by Ramey, Yeates, and MacPhee (1984). We used a sample that combined 175 children from two early intervention programs (Ramey & Campbell, 1992; Wasik, Ramey, Bryant, & Sparling, 1990).

Even though most research considers children and families in poverty as relatively homogenous, the data indicated that in fact, all children in poverty are not at equal disadvantage or risk for later dysfunctional development. Children from families with young mothers, who lack formal education and have low intelligence, were shown to be at even greater risk for social and cognitive problems than the remaining family types. Conversely, children from families with older mothers, who are more educated and have higher IQs, as well as provide a more supportive home environment for the child, were shown to be at lesser risk for poor academic and social development.

There were, however, at least two important limitations to this work. First, information obtained was gathered at a single site in the United States. The lack of a multisite sample impedes adequate representation of diverse social, economic, and political influences, as well as varying life circumstances. Second, the relatively small sample size ($N = 175$) hinders the ability to perform certain complex, interdependent analyses that require high amounts of statistical power.

CLUSTER ANALYSIS: PRESENT RESEARCH

This investigation examines a longitudinal, national, multisite, randomized trial of over 5,000 former Head Start children and their families—the National Head Start–Public Early Childhood Transition Demonstration project. Established over 30 years ago, the Head Start program was designed to provide services to low-income children and families to help ensure that these children do not start public school at a disadvantage because of limited early learning experiences. Inclusion in Head Start is based on the family's income level—below the federal poverty level. Head Start is mandated to serve at least 10% of children with special needs. From its onset, Head Start provided and secured services in the areas of education, health, social services, and parent involvement for millions of children and families across the country (Zigler & Muenchow, 1992).

The National Transition Demonstration project (NTDP) builds on a partnership model at the local level among three key partners: Head Start programs, public schools, and universities or nonprofit research organizations. Data were collected on all participants in this project during their kindergarten year. The NTDP collected data on two cohorts of children: Cohort 1 in the Fall of 1992 and Cohort 2 in the Fall of 1993. A final data set consisting of the baseline measures on each of the cohorts was assembled for analysis. This data set contained 5,406 children and families.

A series of data analyses were conducted to develop a typology of former Head Start families at entry to school. The NTDP recognized (from the beginning) the importance of taking into account differences in families and children when they are enrolled in the program. These differences influence who benefits more (or less) from participating in the NTDP and who is more (or less) likely to have a positive transition to school experiences. The general strategy used for developing a typology was as follows. First, 13 widely used variables known to describe aspects of family characteristics were selected. These variables were maternal education, presence of father in the home, maternal age at the time of child's entry to kindergarten, number of children in the home, number of adults in the home, mean household annual income, mother's employment status, maternal U.S. citizenship, whether the family was homeless in the last year, whether the mother reported parenting assistance in the home, whether the mother reported chronic health problems, whether mothers received Aid to Families With Dependent Children (AFDC) benefits, and whether mothers reported English as the language spoken in the home.

To perform our cluster analysis, we used the correlation coefficient as the measure of similarity and Ward's method as the clustering criterion. As noted, this approach was used with previous studies (Ramey et al., 1984). The validity of the cluster analysis solution is an important concern because random data gives rise to seemingly appropriate cluster solutions (Dubes & Jain, 1979). Thus, consideration was given to whether groupings of families were an artifact of the cluster analysis. Because of the size of our data set, we elected to apply replication and significance tests on the independent variables. Hence, we randomly divided our data set into two equal groups. We then applied the previously mentioned cluster procedure to each data set using the 13 variables previously listed to determine if similar solutions were obtained.

Another critical issue in conducting a cluster analysis is determining the appropriate number of clusters or groups supported by the data (Milligan &

Cooper, 1985). Milligan and Cooper listed 30 techniques proposed for this problem. We selected the clustering criterion available in the statistical analysis software program (SAS). Somewhat surprisingly, in applying the SAS criterion in our cluster analysis, we found six clusters for both data sets. Furthermore, there was a one-to-one correspondence between the two sets of clusters. A MANOVA was performed to compare the two sets of clusters and was found to be nonsignificant. The results obtained from this replication procedure clearly indicated the existence of six groupings of families.

Thus, to determine a final cluster solution, we applied the clustering procedure to the original full data set. Again, the clustering criterion indicated six groups and these groups corresponded to those previously observed. The findings from these analyses in this NTDP reveal that there are remarkably clear major distinctions in the low-income population that Head Start serves. A clear identification of six major family types emerged. Table 9.1 presents the means for each of the variables for each family type. A brief characterization of these six family types follows. A central finding is that all of these family types occur in all major ethnic or cultural groups studied: Caucasian, African American, Hispanic, and Native American.

Family Type A: Traditional Family. This family type represents 30% of the former Head Start families. Fathers are present in almost 90% of these homes. In nearly 95% of these homes, mothers report that someone else helps regularly in caring for their child or family. The average educational level of these mothers is above high school (12.4 years) and they were typically 24 or 25 years old when the child in the study was born. This family type also has the highest average income. (Note: In describing each family type, it is important to recognize that there are some families that vary in terms of some characteristics; e.g., for Family Type A, about 10% do not have fathers present in the homes and some mothers have less than a high school education.)

Family Type B: Single Unemployed Mother, Larger Family. This group represents the next largest family type (29%). Typically, the father is not present in these families (the father absence rate is 72%) and the mother is not employed (95% unemployment rate). Overwhelmingly, the mothers received AFDC (92%). Virtually all of these families have mothers born in the United States, who speak English at home, and who do not report having chronic health problems themselves. The mothers' average educational level is less than high school (11.3 years) and these families have the largest number of children (an average of 3.1) of any family type.

Family Type C: Working Mother, Usually Single, Smaller Family. The third major family type represents 24% of the families and may be primarily distinguished by high rates of maternal employment (72%) and by corre-

TABLE 9.1
Family Typology Cluster Analysis: National Transition Demonstration Research Project ($N = 5,406$)

Variables	Type A Traditional n = 1629	Type B Single, Unemployed Mother, Larger Family n = 1585	Type C Working Mother, Usually Single, Smaller Family n = 1295	Type D Traditional, Foreign Born, NonEnglish Speaking at Home n = 555	Type E Chronic Maternal Health Problems, Older Mothers n = 172	Type F Homeless in last year, Unemployed n = 170	Total Sample N = 5406
Average maternal education years (M,SD)	12.4 (1.5)	11.3 (1.8)	12.3 (1.3)	10.0 (3.5)	11.6 (2.1)	11.5 (1.7)	11.7 (2.0)
Percentage of families having father present	89%	28%	24%	70%	39%	37%	51%
Average age of the mother upon child's entrance into kindergarten (M,SD)	29.5 (5.3)	28.2 (5.1)	29.5 (5.3)	30.3 (6.1)	31.1 (6.3)	27.8 (4.5)	29.4 (5.6)
Average number of children in the home (M,SD)	2.7 (1.2)	3.1 (1.5)	2.5 (1.2)	3.0 (1.4)	2.9 (1.6)	3.1 (1.4)	2.9 (1.4)
Average monthly income category[a] (M,SD)	2.0 (1.1)	1.1 (0.4)	1.4 (0.6)	1.5 (0.7)	1.3 (0.6)	1.2 (0.5)	1.5 (0.8)

(Continued)

TABLE 9.1
(Continued)

Variables	Type A Traditional n = 1629	Type B Single, Unemployed Mother, Larger Family n = 1585	Type C Working Mother, Usually Single, Smaller Family n = 1295	Type D Traditional, Foreign Born, NonEnglish Speaking at Home n = 555	Type E Chronic Maternal Health Problems, Older Mothers n = 172	Type F Homeless in last year, Unemployed n = 170	Total Sample N = 5406
Average number of adults in the home (M,SD)	2.3	1.7	1.5	2.2	1.8	2.0	1.9
	(1.0)	(0.8)	(0.6)	(0.9)	(1.0)	(1.0)	(0.9)
Percentage of families mother is employed	62%	5%	72%	44%	21%	26%	43%
Percentage of mothers born in United States	89%	99%	100%	20%	90%	91%	86%
Percentage of families homeless at some point during past 12 months	0%	0%	0%	0%	6%	100%	4%
Percentage of mothers reporting parenting assistance in the home	94%	58%	51%	57%	69%	57%	67%
Percentage of mothers reporting chronic health problems	0%	0%	0%	0%	100%	0%	3%
Percentage of mothers receiving AFDC	4%	92%	18%	25%	51%	60%	39%
Percentage reporting English as the language spoken in the home	99%	100%	100%	<1%	92%	92%	87%

Note. The numbers in parentheses are standard deviations for the means listed above them.
[a]Monthly income categories are as follows: 1: less than or equal to $1000/month 2: less than or equal to $2000/month 3: less than or equal to $3000/month

sponding much lower rates of receiving AFDC (18%). All of the mothers were born in the United States, and the fathers are present in 24% of these families. The average number of children is 2.5 per family, smaller than any other family type. All of these families speak English at home, and the mothers have no chronic maternal health problems.

Family Type D: Traditional, Foreign Born, Non-English-Speaking at Home. The most important feature that differentiates this family type is that more than 99% do not speak English as their primary language at home, and 80% of the mothers were not born in the United States. Fathers are present in 70% of these families, although only 57% of the mothers report that they have someone who helps them in major parenting duties. These mothers report having the least amount of formal schooling (average years of schooling = 10). This group represents 10% of the sample participating in the NTDP.

Family Type E: Chronic Maternal Health Problems, Older Mothers. This family type represents only 3% of the study families. In all of these families, the mother has chronic major health problems. These mothers are, on the average, 2 to 4 years older than are mothers in the other family types, and their family incomes are very low. Fathers are present in 39% of these homes, although 69% of the mothers report that someone else in their home helps them with childrearing. The mothers in this group have an average educational level of 11.6 years.

Family Type F: Homeless in Last Year, Unemployed. This family type represents 3% of the study sample. All of these families were homeless at least some time in the past 12 months. On the average, they have more than three children, and most mothers are not employed (unemployment rate is 74%). AFDC is received by 60% of these families. Only 8% do not speak English as their first language at home. These mothers have less than a high-school education, on the average (11.5 years).

Using the six-family typology determined from the cluster analysis, additional descriptive analyses were conducted to determine whether these family types systematically relate to other aspects of children's receptive language, special education placement, and social development.

Receptive Language. Children's receptive language in kindergarten was assessed by the Peabody Picture Vocabulary Tests–Revised (PPVT-R; Dunn & Dunn, 1981). A one-way analysis of variance indicated that children's receptive vocabularies varied as a function of family typology (F (5, 4552) = 101.59, $p < .001$). These results are displayed in Fig. 9.2.

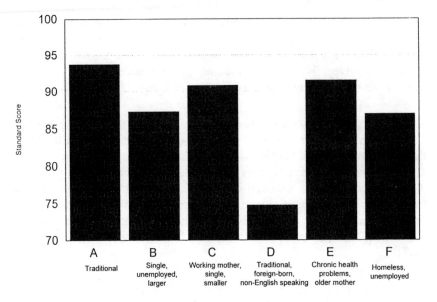

FIG. 9.2. Peabody Picture Vocabulary Tests scores by family type.

Post hoc multiple comparisons were performed ($\alpha = .05$) using Duncan's Multiple Range Test. These analyses indicated that, understandably, Family Type D children from traditional, foreign-born, non-English-speaking families significantly had the lowest receptive language scores. Family Type F children from homeless, unemployed families and Family Type B children from single, unemployed, larger families significantly scored the next lowest. The families that significantly scored the highest were those from Family Type A traditional families (i.e., both parents present in the home and not on welfare).

Special Education Placement.   Overall, 9% of the children were placed in special education, with 70% having speech or language impairments. Chi-square analyses indicate that special education placement differed by family typology ($\chi^2 (5) = 18.31, p < .01$). Figure 9.3 shows the percentages of special education placement by family types.

Between 8% and 9% of the children were placed in special education from the following three family types: traditional (Family Type A), working mother, single, smaller family (Family Type C), and chronic health problems, older mother families (Family Type E). Over 10% of the children from two family types were placed in special education: single, unemployed, larger families (Family Type B); and homeless, unemployed families (Family Type F). Interestingly, only 4% of the children from traditional, foreign-born, non-English-speaking families (Family Type D) were placed in special edu-

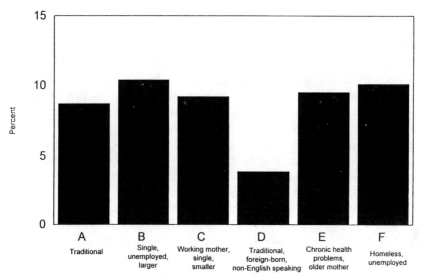

FIG. 9.3. Special education placement by family type.

cation. This finding illuminates at least two interesting points. As these children are only in their first year of formal schooling, there may be a greater reluctance on the part of the school system to label children from non-English-speaking families as requiring special education. Alternatively, the study child may actually be an English-speaking person in a non-English-speaking home. This may be the case because the variable—the percent of families reporting English as the language spoken in the home—was obtained by asking the child's primary caregiver, "When talking with (child's name) in the home, what language is used most often?" Thus, the child may potentially be bilingual—speak Spanish in the home and English in the school.

Social Skills. Children's social skills were assessed by the Social Skills Rating System developed by Gresham and Elliott (1990) for use by teachers and parents. The teacher questionnaire focuses on social skills and behaviors observed in the classroom, behavior problems, and academic performance and motivation. Similarly, the parent questionnaire focuses on the parent's ratings of social skills and behaviors observed in the family and community and problem behaviors. Also included is an item about parental encouragement for the child to succeed academically. This 38-item questionnaire scale measures how often each positive behavior occurs on a 3-point Likert scale (0 for *never* to 3 for *very often*).

A one-way analysis of variance indicated that teacher and parental ratings of children's social skills varied as a function of family typology (F (5, 4433)

= 10.64, $p < .0001$, and $F (5, 4394) = 9.31$, $p < .0001$, respectively). These results are displayed in Fig. 9.4.

Post hoc multiple comparisons were performed ($\alpha = .05$) using Duncan's Multiple Range Test separately for teacher and parental ratings. For teacher ratings, these analyses indicated that children from both of the traditional families (both parents in the home, not on welfare), Family Types A and D, were rated as having significantly more positive social skills than were the other children. Children's social skills from three family types: homeless families (Family Type F), older mothers with chronic health problems families (Family Type E), and single, unemployed, larger families (Family Type B) were rated by their teachers as having significantly lower positive social skills than were the other children.

For parent ratings, parents from traditional, foreign-born, non-English-speaking families (Family Type D) rated their children's social skills significantly higher than did parents from the other family typologies. Conversely, older mothers with chronic health problems (Family Type E) rated their children's social skills as significantly lower than did parents from the other family typologies. According to the Duncan groupings, parents from the remaining family typologies overlapped somewhat in their appraisals of their children's social skills. Yet, remarkably, the same general pattern of ratings was revealed for teachers as for parents, with children from traditional-type families rated the highest and children from homeless families or families with chronic maternal health problems rated the lowest.

Although teachers' patterns of ratings were similar, their ratings were consistently 10 to 12 points lower for children than were parent ratings. This is attributable to children having large differences in their social skills and

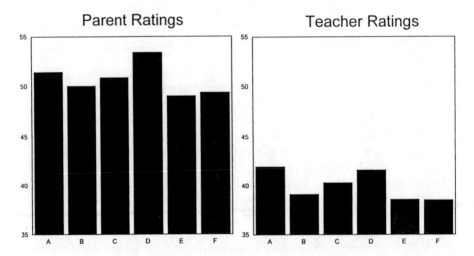

FIG. 9.4. Social Skills Rating System by family type.

behavioral adjustment at school versus home. Children may actually have better social skills at home than at school or children may be acting out more at school than at home. On the other hand, teachers may be stricter in their evaluations of children's behavior than are parents or parents may qualitatively view their children in a more positive light than do teachers. This is a finding that deserves more empirical attention.

CONCLUSIONS

Overall, these findings indicate that there are systematic and practically important differences among poverty families with respect to their children's levels of academic and social risk. This finding is a necessary prelude to the more intriguing question: "What kinds of interventions work best for whom?"

Two-generation intervention programs are very promising for addressing the specific needs of the various family types of poverty families as well as for enhancing and promoting the growth and development of their children. There are several ways to utilize the family typology findings in the two-generation intervention conceptual framework.

First, this family typology analysis identified six distinct family types. These qualitatively different family types affirm the diversity and natural clustering that exists among poverty families. They also serve to counter some of the negative stereotypes about the uniformity of Head Start participants and other low-income families, such as being uniformly unemployed and dependent on AFDC and having fathers absent from the home and not active in their parenting role. For example, about 40% of former Head Start families are traditional families, with both parents present in the home and not on welfare (Family Types A and D). In extreme contrast, the two most challenged family types—those who have been homeless in the past year and those with parents who have chronic health problems—together represent only 6% of the study sample.

Second, these analyses indicate that a single model of service delivery or early intervention is unlikely to work equally well for all types of low-income families. Programs for families and children in poverty need to have a basis for more precise planning of the provision of services that meet the actual needs of participating families. When conducting an initial comprehensive needs assessment, a balanced view of the family that recognizes the presence of both supports (or strengths) and stressors (or problem areas) is vital to avoid negative stereotypes, to build on the family's natural support systems, and to allocate limited program resources wisely. These interventions are usually targeted (rather than universal) to maximize positive developmental changes in children (such as improved social, emotional, and intellectual functioning), changes in the environment (such as increased home safety and stimulation for the children, provision of a center-based, high-quality, early childhood education program, transportation to adult education, and a more nutritious diet), and changes in adults (such as increased reading and language skills, ability to obtain a better-paying job, and improvement in or stabilization of preexisting health conditions).

To the degree that two-generation programs systematically document and reassess children's and families' needs on a regular basis, along with the observed and reported changes in the biological and behavioral status of children and adults, a cumulative knowledge base about a program's operation and impact on families accrues. This knowledge base can help guide the program's future activities and resource allocation process as well as inform other programs and professionals working with similar types of families in comparable community contexts.

Third, a well-established finding is that children and families vary in their responses to intervention programs (Ramey & Ramey, 1992). What has been unclear is the degree to which differential levels of program participation and differential responses to various aspects of the program are affected by the known family characteristics (i.e., recognized differences at the time of entry in a program). This family typology permits conducting data analyses that yield new insights to who benefits the most from which aspects of a two-generation intervention program.

Thus, the family typology is further examined to determine whether these family types relate systematically to other aspects of family functioning and to children's developmental competencies as they progress in school. We examine whether cluster type predicts response to treatment. These analyses, which only cover baseline or entry into school status, strongly suggest that this typology approach is providing meaningful differentiation of important child outcomes at an important developmental marker—the entry to school. Due to the longitudinal nature of the present research, we eagerly look forward to a closer examination of the developmental trajectories of these children and their families.

REFERENCES

Barnard, K. E., Bee, H. L., & Hammond, M. A. (1984). Home environment and cognitive development in a healthy, low-risk sample: The Seattle study. In A. W. Gottfried (Ed.), *Home environment and early cognitive development* (pp. 117–149). Orlando, FL: Academic Press.

Belsky, J. (1980). A family analysis of parental influence on infant exploratory competence. In F. A. Pedersen (Ed.), *The father–infant relationship: Observational studies in a family setting.* New York: Praeger.

Bendersky, M., & Lewis, M. (1994). Environmental risk, biological risk, and developmental outcome. *Developmental Psychology, 30,* 484–494.

Bradley, R. H., Caldwell, B. M., Rock, S. L., Ramey, C. T., Barnard, K. E., Gray, A., Hammond, M. A., Gottfried, A. W., Siegel, L. S., & Johnson, D. L. (1989). Home environment and cognitive development in the first three years of life: A collaborative studying involving six sites and three ethnic groups in North America. *Developmental Psychology, 25*, 217–235.

Campbell, F. A., & Ramey, C. T. (1995). Cognitive and school outcomes for high risk students at middle adolescence: Positive effects of early intervention. *American Educational Research Journal, 32*(4), 743–772.

Dubes, R., & Jain, A. K. (1979). Validity studies in clustering methodologies. *Pattern Recognition, 11*, 247–260.

Dunn, L. M., & Dunn, L. M. (1981). *Peabody Picture Vocabulary Tests–Revised.* Circle Pines, MN: American Guidance Service.

Gresham, F. M., & Elliott, S. N. (1990). *Social Skills Rating System.* Circle Pines, MN: American Guidance Service.

Hetherington, E. M., & Parke, R. D. (1993). *Child psychology: A contemporary viewpoint* (4th ed.). New York: McGraw-Hill.

Kuhl, P. K., Williams, K. A., Lacerda, F., Stevens, K. N., & Lindblom, B. (1992). Linguistic experience alters phonetic perception in infants by 6 months of age. *Science, 255*(5044), 606–608.

Lewis, M. (1983). *Origins of intelligence: Infancy and early childhood* (2nd ed.). New York: Plenum.

Maccoby, E., & Martin, J. A. (1983). Socialization in the context of the family: Parent–child interaction. In P. H. Mussen (Series Ed.) & E. M. Hetherington (Vol. Ed.), *Handbook of child psychology: Vol. 4. Socialization, personality, and social development* (4th ed., pp. 1–102). New York: Wiley.

Milligan, G. W., & Cooper, M. C. (1985). An examination of procedures for determining the number of clusters in a data set. *Psychometrika, 50*, 159–179.

Ramey, C. T., & Campbell, F. A. (1992). Poverty, early childhood education, and academic competence. The Abecedarian experiment. In A. Huston (Ed.), *Children in poverty* (pp. 190–221). New York: Cambridge University Press.

Ramey, C. T., & Ramey, S. L. (1992). Effective early intervention. *Mental Retardation, 30*(5), 337–345.

Ramey, C. T., & Ramey, S. L. (1994). Which children benefit the most from early intervention? *Pediatrics, 94*, 1064–1066.

Ramey, C. T., Ramey, S. L., Gaines, K. R., & Blair, C. (1995). Two generation early interventions: A child development perspective. In I. Siegel (Series Ed.) & S. Smith (Vol. Ed.), *Advances in applied developmental psychology: Vol. 9. Two generation programs: A new intervention strategy* (pp. 199–228). Norwood, NJ: Ablex.

Ramey, C. T., Yeates, K. O., & MacPhee, D. (1984). Risk for retarded development among disadvantaged families: A systems theory approach to preventive intervention. In B. Keogh (Ed.), *Advances in special education* (pp. 249–272). Greenwich, CT: JAI.

Sameroff, A. J., Seifer, R., Baldwin, A., & Baldwin, C. (1993). Stability of intelligence from preschool to adolescence: The influence of social and family risk factors. *Child Development, 64*, 80–97.

Wasik, B. H., Ramey, C. T., Bryant, D. M., & Sparling, J. J. (1990). A longitudinal study of two early intervention strategies. Project CARE. *Child Development, 61*, 1682–1696.

Zigler, E., & Muenchow, S. (1992). *Head Start: The inside story of America's most successful educational experiment.* New York: Basic Books.

10

▼▼▼▼▼▼▼

The Relations Among Domestic Violence, Peer Relationships, and Academic Performance

Samia Dawud-Noursi
Michael E. Lamb
Kathleen J. Sternberg
National Institute of Child Health and Human Development
Bethesda, Maryland

For many decades, developmentalists focused on the ways in which early experiences shape children's personalities, emergent social skills, and cognitive development. In these endeavors, experiences in the family were viewed as especially influential, with effects on individual characteristics and relationships in the family initially given greatest attention, especially when early development was of interest. Over time, the focus shifted to embrace the effects of family relationships on extrafamilial behavior and performance. In this context, the effects of family experiences on both peer relationships and academic performance have come to elicit a substantial amount of attention (Parke & Kellam, 1994; Parke & Ladd, 1992). The goal of this chapter is to review the ways in which certain family experiences and relationships affect social and academic performance at school. We are especially concerned with the effects of family violence, and our analysis is informed primarily by data recently obtained in an ongoing longitudinal study in Israel.

To help place the results of this study in context, we begin the chapter with a summary of recent scholarship concerned with the effects of variations in family relationships on children's peer relationships and academic performance. We especially focus on domestic violence and its apparent effects, and then describe our research study, discuss some recent findings, and consider the directions in which this research program is likely to proceed in the future.

THE EFFECTS OF FAMILY RELATIONSHIPS
ON BEHAVIOR OUTSIDE THE FAMILY

Many psychologists believe that the development of social understanding, the establishment of effective peer relationships, and school adjustment are among the most salient developmental issues that children need to master in the early and middle years of childhood (e.g., Bornstein & Lamb, 1992; Sroufe & Rutter, 1984). Successful mastery of these issues is thought to lay the foundation for successful adaptations in subsequent developmental periods. In general, the relationships children form in their peer groups play a very important role in the development of social skills, and because social competence is both attained and maintained through interactions with other children, peers serve as models for each other, punishing or ignoring nonnormative behaviors and reinforcing culturally appropriate activities (Hartup, 1983; Rubin & Coplan, 1992). In addition, peer acceptance appears to be positively associated with the development of prosocial, cooperative, mature, and friendly behaviors in later life (Hartup, 1983; Hymel & Rubin, 1985), whereas peer rejection is associated with many negative characteristics, including the display of agonistic, immature, and nonnormative behaviors (Hymel & Rubin, 1985), academic difficulties, truancy and early withdrawal from high school (Ulman, 1957), anxiety, sadness, and social withdrawal (Coie, Dodge, & Kupersmidt, 1990), feelings of loneliness and social dissatisfaction (Asher, Hymel, & Renshaw, 1984), lower perceived social competence (Harter, 1982), depression (Vosk, Forehand, Parker, & Rickard, 1982), and poor group entry skills (Volling, MacKinnon-Lewis, Rabiner, & Baradaran, 1993). Positive or negative interactions in childhood reflect the quality of adjustment and contribute to individual differences in social and emotional competence in later life (Hartup, 1983; Kohlberg, LaCrosse, & Ricks, 1972). Indeed, peer relationships in childhood are increasingly recognized as among the most powerful predictors of concurrent and future mental health status (Rubin & Coplan, 1992). Difficult relationships with peers in middle school indicate a heightened risk of schizophrenia, general mental health problems, and school-related problems (Kupersmidt, Coie, & Dodge, 1990; Parker & Asher, 1987), whereas sociometric ratings by third graders are better predictors of adult psychiatric disturbances than a diversified battery of measures derived from school records and self-reports (Berndt & Ladd, 1989; Cowen, Pederson, Babigian, Izzo, & Trost, 1973).

Because peer relations appear to be so central to psychosocial adaptation, the possible links between family relations and peer relations are of great importance to developmentalists and students of socialization. Many scholars sought to identify and describe the ways in which family experiences—especially patterns of parent–child interaction—influence the development of social competence with peers (e.g., Finnie & Russell, 1988; Parke & Ladd,

1992; Parke, MacDonald, Beitel, & Bhavnagri, 1988; Rubin & Coplan, 1992), motivated, in part, by Bronfenbrenner's (1979, 1986) efforts to highlight the interrelations among the different contexts in which children develop, and by Parke's (1994) amplified emphases on bidirectional patterns of influence.

Parents influence extrafamilial behavior styles both directly (by way of explicit instruction) and indirectly, by way of the quality of their relationships with their children. Parents directly influence their children's peer relationships by providing advice, support, and suggestions about activities and strategies to pursue when attempting to initiate or maintain interactions and relationships (Lollis, Ross, & Tate, 1992). Through interactions with family members, especially parents, children have opportunities to learn, rehearse, and improve their social skills—including skills that are directly relevant to interactions with peers. Family members who model and reward friendly social behaviors assist their children's development by helping them acquire such interpersonal styles (Cole, Baldwin, Baldwin, & Fisher, 1982). Parents also manage their children's social lives, especially when they are younger, and thus determine how much and what kinds of opportunities children have for interactions with other social partners (Parke, Neville, Burks, Boyum, & Carson, 1994). Despite the apparent significance of these practices, however, little is known about their effectiveness or importance. Similarly, little is known about the effects of parental behavior—especially didactic behavior—on children's academic performance.

By contrast, the indirect effects of parent–child relationships on peer relationships were studied quite extensively, with attachment theorists taking the lead in recent efforts to explain the mechanisms involved. These theorists argued that variations in the quality of parent–child attachment generate an orientation to the social world that generalizes over time and contexts.

According to attachment theory, children form and maintain secure attachment relationships to parents who respond sensitively and appropriately to their children's signals and needs. Such consistent and predictable responses foster a sense of effectiveness and self-control in children (Lamb, 1981; Matas, Arend & Sroufe, 1978), which may in turn foster socially appropriate interpersonal styles (Sroufe, 1983). In addition, securely attached infants develop effective internal representational models of relationships that they draw on and generalize from when they interact with other people, including peers. Through secure parent–child attachments, therefore, children learn that relationships can be reciprocal, complementary, and rewarding, and they bring these expectations to interactions and relationships with peers. As a result, children who have warm relationships with their parents tend to learn friendly, assertive, social behaviors (Cole et al., 1982). Such friendly assertiveness is considered to be an essential component of social competence, affecting the degree to which children can effectively engage others in interactions and develop networks of friends. Thus, securely attached infants interact with their peers more extensively and successfully than insecurely attached infants (Easterbrooks & Lamb, 1979; Pastor, 1981) and appear to adapt to peer groups more easily (Parke & Beitel, 1988). Children who are friendly and outgoing create friendly, supportive environments for themselves by fostering positive social interactions with others. Inductive forms of discipline and affectively positive interactions between parents and their children predict children's prosocial orientations toward peers (Bryant & Crockenberg, 1980) and are associated with socially competent functioning in children (Baumrind, 1971). In addition, children whose parents are accepting, firm, and democratic perform better in academic contexts (Dornbusch, Ritter, Leiderman, Roberts, & Fraleigh, 1987; Eckenrode, Laird, & Doris, 1993; Kendall-Tackett & Eckenrode, 1996; Melby & Conger, 1996). Presumably, this is because such children developed a sense of personal efficacy through repeated experiences of successfully shaping their parents' behavior (Lamb, 1981).

When parental qualities, such as predictability, are lacking (i.e., when parent–child interactions are characterized by abruptness or intrusiveness, high rates of ignoring, the inconsistent use of rewards and punishments, or frank abuse), children view their social worlds as threatening and uncontrollable, developing maladaptive personal styles as a result (Brown & Siegel, 1988; Egeland, 1985). Abused children are less likely to develop secure attachments to their parents (Crittenden, 1985; Crittenden & Ainsworth, 1989; Lamb, Gaensbauer, Malkin, & Schultz, 1985) and can generalize their distorted expectations to relationships with peers (Rienken, Egeland, Marvinney, Mangelsdorf, & Sroufe, 1989). In addition, parents who are inattentive, inconsistent, and noncontingently responsive teach their children that they terminate or avoid parental demands and constraints by behaving in a sufficiently aversive manner (Patterson & Reid, 1984). In the absence of effective parental behavior, therefore, interactions are increasingly marked by aversive interchanges, in which both parents and children use hostile control techniques (Patterson, 1986). Such aversive interactions between parents and children foster negative attributions and expectations, which in turn, promote further hostile interactions (MacKinnon, Lamb, Belsky, & Baum, 1990; MacKinnon-Lewis, Lamb, Arbuckle, Baradaran, & Volling, 1992; MacKinnon-Lewis, Lamb, Hattie, & Baradaran, 1996). Children who have hostile interactions with their parents tend to generalize these styles; furthermore, they are viewed as more hostile and aggressive in the peer group (Lamb, Ketterlinus, & Fracasso, 1992; MacKinnon-Lewis, Volling, Lamb, Dechman, Rabiner, & Curtner, 1994). In addition, physically abused children have more behavioral problems and internalizing symptoms than do children who have never been abused (Aber, Allen, Carlson, & Cicchetti, 1989; Dodge, Bates, & Pettit, 1990; Sternberg, Lamb, Greenbaum, Cichetti, Dawud,

Cortes, Krispin, & Lorey, 1993; Toth, Manly, & Cicchetti, 1992) and are more likely to engage in delinquent, antisocial, and violent behavior than are their nonabused peers (Hoffman-Plotkin & Twentyman, 1984; Widom, 1989).

Children's development is adversely affected not only when parent–child relationships are inadequate or hostile, but also when the relationships between the parents are conflictive or violent. A substantial body of evidence confirms a strong association between marital hostility and filial maladjustment (e.g., Cummings & Davies, 1994; Cummings & O'Reilly, 1997) and especially marked effects are evident, not surprisingly, when the family is characterized by spouse abuse. Children of abused mothers are at risk for adverse mental health outcomes such as symptoms of anxiety, depression, and lowered self-esteem (Christopoulos et al., 1987; Fantuzzo et al., 1990; Holden & Ritchie, 1991; Hughes, 1988; Jaffe, Wolfe, Wilson, & Zak, 1986; Wolfe, Jaffe, Wilson, & Zak, 1985). These symptoms are accompanied by aggression and deficient social problem-solving skills (George & Main, 1979; Hoffman-Plotkin & Twentyman, 1984; Jaffe et al., 1986; Price & Van Slyke, 1991; Reidy, 1977; Rosenberg, 1987) that might be expected to influence peer relationships. According to Dodge et al. (1990), family dysfunction is widely associated with disturbed and coercive relationships with peers. In addition, abused children have poorer levels of cognitive functioning, are more likely to repeat grades at school, and are more likely to misbehave at school (Eckenrode et al., 1993; Hoffman-Plotkin & Twentyman, 1984).

Most studies on the effects of domestic violence involve children who experienced a variety of stressful life events in addition to domestic violence (Fantuzzo & Lindquist, 1989; Wolfe et al., 1985). Several social scientists suggested that factors associated with abuse, such as single parenthood, divorce, poverty, foster care, substance abuse, and shelter placement, are at least partially responsible for the adverse effects of maltreatment (Elmer, 1977; Emery, 1989; Starr, 1979). Thus, although some researchers found that abused and nonabused children from disadvantaged socioeconomic circumstances differed on important dimensions, the relative impact of family violence, poor socioeconomic conditions, and other negative life events still need to be disentangled. By focusing on children who lived at home with both biological parents, we hoped to better understand the effects of violence independent of these other factors. We also specified the types of domestic violence to which children were exposed, expecting that different types of violence (spouse abuse, child abuse) are associated with different effects. Unfortunately, most researchers have not distinguished among types of maltreatment, leaving this issue poorly understood. In our study, we attempted to determine whether each child was a victim of child abuse, a witness to spouse abuse, both a victim and a witness, or neither a victim nor a witness.

The available research on the effects of domestic violence is further flawed by the nearly exclusive reliance on single informants (often mothers) as sources of information about domestic violence and child adjustment. As we noted elsewhere (Sternberg et al., 1993; Sternberg, Lamb, & Dawud-Noursi, 1997, 1998), the reliance on a single informant is extremely problematic, providing, at best, a narrow and potentially biased understanding of the phenomena. To better understand how domestic violence affects the various aspects of children's lives, it is important to gather information about behavior in diverse contexts from multiple informants. By collecting information from the target children, their peers, teachers, and parents in our longitudinal study, we hoped to better understand the effects of child and spouse abuse. We chose a wide range of psychosocial measures to evaluate children's social and academic competencies and their relationships with peers and compared the children in our study with those in standardization samples, as well as with those in our own comparison group. We also sought to tease apart the effects of child and spouse abuse, and to determine whether children who experienced multiple types of violence were at greater risk than children who were either victims of child abuse or were witnesses of spouse abuse.

In this chapter, we describe our attempt to evaluate children's social, cognitive, and emotional adjustment in the school context using teachers, classmates, and counselors as informants. Based on available literature, we predicted that children who experienced any violence in the familial context would have more behavioral and interpersonal problems than their counterparts. We expected to find that those children who were exposed to violence would be rated as less social, more aggressive, and more isolated from their peers, and that they would perform more poorly at school than children in the nonviolent comparison group. We also expected that abused witnesses would evince the poorest performance on these dimensions, followed by abused children, witnesses, and children in the comparison group, and that some of the effects would persist over time.

THE ISRAELI DOMESTIC VIOLENCE STUDY

The Israeli Domestic Violence study, launched in 1988, is an intensive longitudinal evaluation of a cohort of Israeli children who were either victims of physical abuse, witnesses of spouse abuse, both victims and witnesses, or neither victims nor witnesses. Children were evaluated three times. In Phase I, when the children averaged 10½ years of age, mothers, fathers, the target children, their classmates, and their homeroom teachers were asked to evaluate the children's peer relationships. In Phase II, approximately 12 to 18 months later, homeroom teachers, school counselors, and truancy officers were asked to provide information about the target children's school adjustment and academic performance. In Phase III, when the participants averaged 14½ years of age, mothers, fathers, and the adolescents themselves were interviewed about various aspects of their development. The current report focuses on children's adjustment in school, as reflected by data collected in Phases I and II.

Phase I

The sample comprised 110 8- to 12-year-old children (61 boys) and their parents, recruited with the assistance of social workers from the Department of Family Services in Jerusalem and Tel Aviv, Israel. In order to control for risk factors that hampered the interpretation of earlier findings, we only selected children who were living at home with both biological parents. Mentally retarded children, children who were victims of sexual abuse, and only children who were victims of psychological maltreatment were excluded from the study. Also excluded from the sample were children whose parents were diagnosed with psychiatric disorders.

Social workers were asked to identify children in their caseloads who were believed to be victims or witnesses of domestic violence and to provide detailed descriptions of at least one incident of child or spouse abuse in the past 6 months. If the child was identified as an abused witness, the caseworker was asked to describe one incident of physical abuse and one incident of spouse abuse. Although the social workers were our primary informants, the information they provided was supplemented by interviews with parents and children. Specifically, husbands' and wives' responses to questions on the Area of Change Questionnaire (ACQ; Margolin, Talovic, & Weinstein, 1983) about hitting one another, as well as mothers' and children's responses in semistructured interviews were used to corroborate the social workers' reports. For purposes of our initial analysis, a report of child or spouse abuse by any informant was sufficient to place the child in one of four groups—child abuse ($n = 33$; 18 boys and 15 girls), spouse abuse ($n = 16$; 8 boys and 8 girls), abused witnesses ($n = 30$; 21 boys and 9 girls), and comparison ($n = 31$; 14 boys and 17 girls).

The sample only included lower-class, two-parent families of Jewish origin, and children in the four groups were matched with respect to birth order, birth complications, chronic or serious health problems, family size, ethnicity, religious practices, SES, and unemployment. On the average, mothers and fathers completed 9.4 years of formal education and had four children. The families included in this study were representative of the Jewish social welfare population with respect to ethnic origin (75% had parents born in Middle Eastern or North African countries) and background characteristics.

Communication with the families began when the project coordinator contacted the families by phone and asked them to participate in a study examining the effects of stressful life events on children's development. After obtaining the parents' permission, an appointment was made for two females, who were unaware of the family's history, to visit the home and interview the child and his or her parents. The mother and father were individually interviewed by one female interviewer while another interviewed the child.

Data Collection in the Home.   The children's and parents' reports of the children's behavior problems, depressive symptomatology, and perceptions of the parents were analyzed and described in earlier reports (Sternberg et al., 1993; Sternberg, Lamb, Greenbaum, Dawud, Cortes, & Lorey, 1994). Briefly, we found that, although there were differences among children in the four groups with respect to behavior problems, these differences depended on the informant. For example, women who were abused by their husbands reported the highest level of behavior problems in their children, whereas women who were not abused reported similar levels of behavior problems whether or not the child was abused. In contrast, when children were the informants, those children who themselves were abused (child abuse and abused witness) reported the highest levels of behavioral problems. Interestingly, although children reported fewer problems than mothers did, group differences were evident on the internalizing subscales of the Youth Self-Report (Achenbach & Edelbrock, 1987), whereas analyses of parental reports revealed no group differences in internalized behavior problems. Differences among informants underscore the fact that different reporters are sensitive to different types of information (Sternberg et al., 1997), and highlight the importance of obtaining information from more than one informant.

An analysis of children's perceptions of their parents using the Family Relations Test (Bene & Anthony, 1957) revealed that children who were abused by their parents assigned more negative attributes to abusive parents (Sternberg et al., 1994). When only one parent was abusive, however, children's perceptions of their nonabusive parents resembled those of children in the comparison group. These findings show how important it is to collect information about both perpetrating and nonperpetrating parents in violent families.

Data Collection in the Schools.   Unfortunately, we were able to interview only a subset of the children's teachers and peers, 63 teachers and 55 classmates. Fifteen schools refused to allow teachers and peers to participate in the study (10 of them for religious reasons).

Three female research assistants visited the children's classrooms and administered several questionnaires to the teachers and their pupils. The administration occurred at least 2 months after school began in order to ensure that children and teachers had enough time to become familiar with each other. To ensure confidentiality and anonymity, the target children were not identified to either research assistants or teachers. Instead, the teachers were asked to complete several questionnaires concerning the target children and two additional randomly selected classmates of the same gender, and to describe the social skills of all children in their classrooms. While homeroom teachers completed the questionnaires in the teachers' lounge, classmates of the target children completed the *Revised Class Play* (RCP; Masten, Morison, & Pellegrini, 1985), a sociometric technique that involved nominating classmates for a hypothetical school play. Children's responses were scored on four factors (sociability, sensitivity, good behavior, and aggression) that were created after conducting a factor analysis of data obtained from 1,445 Israeli children (Krispin, Sternberg, & Lamb, 1992).

Homeroom teachers evaluated the target children's school adjustment on a variety of social, cognitive, and emotional dimensions. The *Teacher Rating Scales of Peer Relations* (TRSPR; Morison, 1982), a measure designed to complement the RCP, was used to assess teachers' perceptions of the target child's relationships with classmates. Teachers rated the children's leadership-sociability, aggressiveness, and isolation on TRSPR using 7-point Likert scales with options ranging from *Does Not Apply At All* to *Applies Very Well*. The Child Behavior Checklist–Teacher Report Form (TRF; Achenbach & Edelbrock, 1986) was used to quantify teachers' perceptions of the target children's behavior problems, academic performance, and overall adjustment relative to peers. Teachers also completed the Harter Teacher Scale–Child's Actual Behavior (Harter, 1982), with 15 items tapping 5 subscales (scholastic competence, social acceptance, athletic competence, physical appearance, and behavioral conduct) and the Harter Teacher Scale–Child's Classroom Orientation (Harter, 1982) with 10 items tapping 5 subscales (preference for challenge, independent judgment, interest or curiosity, independent mastery, and internal–external criteria for success).

Because the cell sizes were so small, there were very few differences among children in the four groups, so for purposes of the analyses reported here, we combined children in the three violent groups (child abuse, witnesses, abused witnesses) into a single group of children who experienced any form of violence.

Phase I Results.   Contrary to our predictions, teachers perceived few differences between children who were exposed to family violence and their counterparts in the comparison group. On the TRF, teachers reported no differences between children in the violence group and children in the comparison group, although it is noteworthy that the majority of children in this sample were reported to have many behavior problems. On the average, teachers assigned the children scores ranging from 1 to 1.5 standard deviations above the mean scores in Achenbach's standardization sample, and two thirds of the children in this sample were viewed by their teachers as in need of clinical intervention.

Children who experienced some violence differed from those in the comparison group on the Adaptive Functioning Dimension on the TRF, however, with children in the violence group deemed less competent than children in the comparison group. It was again interesting to note that most of the children in this sample were assigned scores below the average in Achenbach's standardization sample. Whereas the average scores in Achenbach's sample ranged between 17 and 19 (depending on gender), the average scores in our sample ranged from 10 to 15, with children in the violence groups obtaining lower scores than children in the comparison group (see Table 10.1). Interestingly, there were no group differences on the academic functioning dimension; most of the children were considered by their teachers to be performing quite poorly, regardless of their exposure to family violence (see Table 10.1).

We next examined peers' and teachers' perceptions of children's peer relationships on the RCP and the TRSPR, respectively. A review of the RCP ratings suggests that classmates did not view target children in the violent and nonviolent groups differently (see Table 10.2). Likewise, teachers did not report group differences on the TRSPR, although children in the study (whether in the violence or comparison groups) were considered more aggressive, more isolated, and less effective as leaders than their classmates. These findings suggest that the children in the sample had less competent peer styles than randomly selected classmates, but that their social competence was not affected by violent experiences in the home.

Finally, we examined teachers' responses on the two questionnaires developed by Harter (1982). Teachers reported that children who were not exposed to any type of domestic violence had more athletic and behavioral competencies than children in the three clinical groups (combined), although they did not appear to have more social, physical, and scholastic competencies than the maltreated children. Similarly, teachers believed that children in the comparison group displayed more independent judgment and independent mastery than children in the violence group. There were no group differences in preferences for challenge, interest or curiosity, and reliance on internalizing versus externalizing criteria when evaluating personal success in the classroom, however.

TABLE 10.1
Group Differences in Adaptive Functioning Score—Phase I

Dimension	Child Abuse (n = 16)	Witnesses (n = 9)	Abused Witnesses (n = 13)	Combined Violence (n = 38)	Comparison (n = 19)
Total adaptive	11.20*	11.22*	10.85*	11.08*	15.17*
functioning	(4.07)	(5.38)	(3.53)	(4.13)	(5.29)
Academic	2.56	2.00	2.20	2.29	2.18
functioning	(1.23)	(1.29)	(.77)	(1.09)	(.81)

Note. Standard deviations appear in parentheses, *p < .05.

TABLE 10.2
Peer and Teacher Ratings of the Children's Social Styles With Peers

Social Style	Child Abuse	Witnesses	Abused Witnesses	Combined Violence	Comparison
Revised classroom play (peer rating)	(n = 16)	(n = 10)	(n = 13)	(n = 39)	(n = 16)
Sociability	2.64	1.90	1.79	2.17	2.06
	(1.48)	(1.56)	(1.05)	(1.40)	(1.53)
Sensitivity	1.80	1.56	1.51	1.64	1.53
	(1.01)	(1.02)	(1.09)	(1.02)	(1.19)
Well-behaving	1.35	1.45	1.30	1.37	1.14
	(1.03)	(1.01)	(1.08)	(1.04)	(1.10)
Aggression	2.07	1.76	1.62	1.84	1.47
	(.74)	(1.16)	(.86)	(.90)	(1.23)
Teacher rating scales	(n = 18)	(n = 11)	(n = 13)	(n = 42)	(n = 21)
Leadership	2.72	2.09	3.70	2.86	3.19
	(1.3)	(2.1)	(1.8)	(1.7)	(1.5)
Aggression	3.55	3.90	3.00	3.48	2.20
	(2.3)	(2.1)	(1.8)	(2.1)	(1.6)
Isolation	3.94	5.20	2.80	4.10	3.35
	(2.36)	(2.1)	(1.8)	(2.3)	(2.3)

Note. There were no significant group differences; standard deviations appear in parentheses.

In summary, although there were few differences between children who had and had not been exposed to domestic violence, most of the children in this sample were rated by their teachers as having more behavioral symptoms than average, poorer than average social skills, and poorer academic skills than average. This suggests that the other disadvantages faced by these relatively impoverished children overwhelmed any effects of exposure to domestic violence. If true, this would underscore the importance of evaluating other possible influences on child adjustment when exploring the effects of domestic violence or other traumategenic events.

Phase II

Approximately 2 years after the initial assessment, we began contacting the teachers and school counselors of the 110 children who participated in Phase I of the study. By this time, the adolescents were studying in 61 different schools across Israel, and 9 adolescents were no longer at schools. Eighteen principals refused to participate, six of them for religious reasons. We were able to obtain information from 83 of the teachers, however. The participants averaged 14.7 years of age when their teachers were interviewed about their adjustment.

In order to examine the long-term effects of family violence, we attempted to re-assess the presence and extent of family violence by asking social workers to describe violent incidents reported to them since Phase I. Unfortunately, we were able to obtain detailed information from social workers concerning only 48% of the families. Many of the families were no longer under the supervision of the original caseworkers, and no new information was available, so for purposes of the analyses reported here, we classified the adolescents into violence groups based on the information obtained in Phase I.

All information was collected a few months after the school year started to ensure that the informants had sufficient knowledge of the target children. The teachers were asked to evaluate the social competence of the target child using a revision of the Taxonomy of Problematic Situations Questionnaire (TOPS; Dodge, McClaskey, & Feldman, 1985). This measure was designed to assess the extent to which the adolescents had problems in specific situations and the degree to which they appropriately responded. Teachers rated the adolescents on eight factor-analytically derived dimensions: peer group entry, response to peer provocation, response to failure, response to success, social expectations, teacher expectations, reactive aggression, and proactive aggression. Answers to this 60-item questionnaire reflected teachers' perceptions of how much of a problem each of these situations posed for the target adolescents. Scores ranged from 1 (*never has problems*) to 5 (*almost always has problems*).

As in Phase I, teachers were also asked to assess the children's behavioral problems using the Teacher Report Form of the Child Behavioral Checklist (TRF; Achenbach & Edelbrock, 1986), which included assessments of the children's behavior problems as well as ratings of their academic and adaptive functioning. School counselors completed questionnaires asking them to identify any behavioral and family problems known to them, and information about academic performance and truancy was obtained from official school records.

Phase II Results. In Phase II, teachers' responses on the TRF revealed significant differences between children in the violence and comparison groups on the externalizing and total behavior problems (see Table 10.3). Children who experienced violence were perceived by their teachers as having more problems and poorer overall adjustment in school than the children who did not experience violence. In addition, most of the children in this sample (77%), including two thirds of the adolescents in the comparison group, were believed by their teachers to have behavior problems severe enough to warrant clinical intervention.

Furthermore, based on the norms developed by Achenbach, most of the adolescents in this sample were assigned below average adjustment scores.

TABLE 10.3
Teachers' Evaluations of Adolescents' Behavior Problems in Phase II

Behavior Problem	Child Abuse (n = 20)	Witnesses (n = 14)	Abused Witnesses (n = 25)	Combined Violence (n = 59)	Comparison (n = 24)
Narrow-Band Scales:					
Withdrawal	59.05	59.21	60.80	59.85	60.21
	(7.76)	(5.58)	(9.99)	(8.29)	(8.57)
Somatic	54.32	59.00	58.20	57.12	53.33
	(6.69)	(10.66)	(10.00)	(9.29)	(6.69)
Anxiety/depression	63.52	60.64	63.88	62.98*	58.92*
	(7.27)	(7.84)	(7.57)	(7.52)	(7.59)
Thoughts problems	63.05	59.93	60.12	61.03*	55.83*
	(12.20)	(10.97)	(9.09)	(10.55)	(8.97)
Attention	58.32	59.79	59.12	59.02*	55.92*
	(6.56)	(6.92)	(6.62)	(6.58)	(5.68)
Delinquency	59.16	63.14	62.48	61.55	58.17
	(7.09)	(10.03)	(8.01)	(8.29)	(8.67)
Aggression	60.53	60.14	63.44*	61.69*	55.83*
	(8.49)	(7.08)	(8.39)	(8.14)	(6.70)
Social	62.53	61.43	64.32*	63.03*	58.08*
	(6.49)	(6.61)	(9.44)	(7.89)	(6.84)
Broad-Band Scales:					
Total problems	61.26	61.57	63.92*	62.48*	56.13*
	(8.69)	(10.14)	(8.30)	(8.83)	(10.19)
Internalizing problems	61.21	59.64	63.24	61.71	57.92
	(7.7)	(10.75)	(9.17)	(9.09)	(10.85)
Externalizing problems	59.84	60.86	62.84*	61.38*	54.63*
	(8.26)	(8.37)	(9.05)	(8.59)	(9.24)
Total adaptive functioning	14.25	11.77	14.59	13.80	15.65
	(6.80)	(4.69)	(4.72)	(5.59)	(5.99)
Academic functioning	2.55	2.53	2.57	2.55	2.36
	(1.07)	(.75)	(1.00)	(.97)	(1.01)

Note. Standard deviations appear in parentheses; sample sizes vary slightly depending on the extent of the teachers' responsiveness.

*$p < .05$.

Children in violence groups were perceived by their teachers as performing well below average, whereas adolescents in the comparison group were perceived as somewhat less than average in their performance. Viewed together, these findings suggest that most of the adolescents in this sample were having substantial problems in the school context. These results also suggest that violence in the family posed an additional risk to a group of children already vulnerable to behavioral and academic problems.

After examining teachers' reports of the adolescents' behavior problems, we explored their perceptions of the adolescents' social competence on the revised TOPS questionnaire. Children in the violence group were rated more negatively by teachers in six of the eight domains covered: peer group entry, response to failure, response to peer provocation, teacher expectations, reactive aggression, and proactive aggression (see Table 10.4). The mean scores of children in the violence group are similar in magnitude to those obtained in Dodge et al.'s (1985) sample of rejected children and MacKinnon-Lewis et al. (1994) sample of children selected because they were unusually aggressive (C. E. MacKinnon-Lewis, personal communication, January 12, 1997).

An examination of the counselors' and truancy officers' reports revealed no group differences in school grades and in the extent and types of school performance difficulties, truancy, and psychosocial problems. There was a tendency for children in the violence group to be truant more often, however; 10 of the 50 children (17%) in the clinical groups, compared with 2 of the 25 in the comparison group (8%), skipped school.

In summary, the data collected from teachers in Phase II suggested that domestic violence had clear effects on these adolescents' peer skills. They had more difficulties with their peers than children in the comparison group, as well as more difficulties than children in general. Most of the adolescents in this study, including those in the comparison group, appeared to have substantial academic and social problems, making the apparent effects of domestic violence especially noteworthy.

TABLE 10.4
Teacher Ratings on the Revised Taxonomy of
Problematic Situations Questionnaire in Phase II

Problematic Situation	Child Abuse (n = 19)	Witnesses (n = 14)	Abused Witnesses (n = 25)	Combined Violence (n = 58)	Comparison (n = 25)
Peer group entry	14.95*	12.86	14.28*	14.16*	9.32*
	(5.05)	(5.75)	(3.86)	(4.74)	(5.66)
Response to success	4.11	3.86	4.08	4.03	3.72
	(1.41)	(2.14)	(2.14)	(1.90)	(2.07)
Response to peer provocation	28.42*	29.57*	30.32*	29.52*	20.32*
	(9.70)	(9.44)	(8.99)	(9.21)	(8.92)
Teacher expectations	12.79	13.29	14.36	13.59*	10.52*
	(4.99)	(6.51)	(5.98)	(5.75)	(4.75)
Response to failure	21.74	22.50	24.20*	22.98*	17.08*
	(8.21)	(9.80)	(9.16)	(8.91)	(6.66)
Social expectations	18.26	23.00	23.96	21.86	19.48
	(6.15)	(7.91)	(7.66)	(7.58)	(8.19)
Reactive aggression	19.78	18.64	21.64*	20.29*	14.48*
	(8.69)	(9.00)	(8.86)	(8.77)	(7.50)
Proactive aggression	13.47	15.64	17.64	15.79*	11.88*
	(5.91)	(9.19)	(9.20)	(8.32)	(8.33)

Note.   Standard deviations appear in parentheses, $*p < .05$.

DISCUSSION

In this chapter, we summarized the results of a longitudinal study concerned with the effects of domestic violence on children's peer relationships. In Phase I of the study, we found that neither teachers nor peers were able to discern many differences between children who had and had not experienced domestic violence. We were somewhat surprised by the small number of group differences, especially because other researchers showed domestic violence to have harmful effects on children's adjustment and school performance (Eckenrode et al., 1993; Salzinger, Kaplan, Pelcovitz, Samit, & Krieger, 1984). What might account for the differences between these reports and our own findings?

The absence of group differences on the measures of school performance and motivation indicate that children in all four groups performed equivalently, not that the children exposed to family violence performed particularly well. In fact, the range of scores obtained by children in Phase I suggests that most of the children in this study were deemed at risk for behavioral and academic problems by their teachers and were perceived as less competent socially than classmates. Although sociometric ratings by classmates did not distinguish between target children in the violent and nonviolent groups, for example, classmates assigned more negative and fewer positive roles to the children in our sample than to other classmates. The absence of differences between our violence and comparison groups is attributable to the care with which we recruited our comparison group. All of the families in our study were recruited from among those Israeli families who faced multiple economic and social hardships. The disadvantaged environments in which these children live may help explain the relatively high levels of behavior problems reported by teachers and other informants. In this multiproblem context, the net effects of exposure to family violence are less dramatic than when the effects of family violence are unknowingly confounded with effects of various other stresses and strains. Interestingly, Eckenrode et al. (1993) also reported that SES influenced children's academic performance independent of their maltreatment status.

The magnitude of the group differences reported by other researchers is also exaggerated because the children exposed to family violence often experienced additional traumatic events such as parental divorce and separation, residential moves, foster placement, and shelter living, and the effects of these stressful and disruptive experiences may be misattributed to the domestic violence itself. This observation speaks to a continuing need for researchers to be sure that their comparison groups are carefully matched on all relevant characteristics, something that has not always been achieved in the research about domestic violence. Additional research is needed to better explore the relative impact of child and spousal abuse on children in families facing many social and economic challenges.

In Phase II, the findings were more congruent with our predictions. As in Phase I, most of the adolescents (including those in the comparison group) were perceived as having substantial behavioral and academic problems. In addition, however, children who experienced violence in the home were viewed by their teachers as displaying more behavior problems and more problematic relationships with their peers than adolescents from nonviolent families. As in Eckenrode et al.'s study (1993), children in our sample behaved in ways that were likely to get them in trouble with others. Information provided by the teachers in Phase II suggested that children in this sample, particularly those exposed to violence, lack important social and academic skills, and are thus, not likely to manifest social and emotional problems as they enter adulthood (Achenbach & Edelbrock, 1986; Kupersmidt et al., 1990; Parker & Asher, 1987).

Contrary to our predictions, however, few differences among the three violence groups (child abuse, witnesses, and abused witnesses) were discerned by teachers in either phase of the study.

There are several possible explanations for our inability to distinguish among the groups of children who experienced different types of violence. First, children in the child abuse, child witnesses or abused witnesses groups presumably experienced quite different experiences, and differences in the types of events, as well as their frequency, chronicity, and severity are expected to influence children's responses. Unfortunately, these parameters are difficult to measure reliably and continue to bedevil the interpretation of research on family violence.

Second, children surely respond differently, even to the same experiences. Although most children are adversely affected by being victims or witnesses of violence, their responses are too diverse to constitute any kind of syndrome, and the relatively small cell sizes in this study precluded efforts to explore individual differences more thoroughly.

Finally, differences among the perceptions of different informants deserve explicit reiteration. In the eyes of the mothers and children, children exposed to both spouse and child abuse had the most behavior problems in Phase 1, whereas the children, but not their mothers, reported that the abused children were more disturbed than the children exposed only to spousal abuse (Sternberg et al., 1993). The absence of similar differences in the eyes of the teachers and peers underscores both the importance of divergent informant perspectives and the dynamic nature of family violence (Sternberg et al., 1997, 1998).

REFERENCES

Aber, L. J., Allen, J. P., Carlson, V., & Cicchetti, D. (1989). The effects of maltreatment on development during early childhood: Recent studies and their theoretical, clinical, and policy implications. In D. Cicchetti & V. Carlson (Eds.), *Child maltreatment: Theory and research on the causes and consequences of child abuse and neglect* (pp. 579–619). New York: Cambridge University Press.

Achenbach, T. M., & Edelbrock, C. (1986). *Manual for the Teacher's Report Form and teacher's version of the child behavior profile.* Burlington: University of Vermont.

Achenbach, T. M., & Edelbrock, C. (1987). *Manual for the Youth Self-Report and profile.* Burlington: University of Vermont.

Asher, S. R., Hymel, S., & Renshaw, P. D. (1984). Loneliness in children. *Child Development, 55,* 1456–1464.

Baumrind, D. (1971). Current patterns of parental authority. *Developmental Psychology Monographs, 4,* (1,2), 1–103.

Bene, E., & Anthony, E. J. (1957). *Manual for the Family Relations Test.* London, England: National Foundation for Education Research.

Berndt, T. J., & Ladd, G. W. (Eds.). (1989). *Peer relationships in child development.* New York: Wiley.

Bornstein, M. H., & Lamb, M. E. (Eds.). (1992). *Developmental psychology: An advanced textbook.* Hillsdale, NJ: Lawrence Erlbaum Associates.

Bronfenbrenner, U. (1979). *The ecology of human development.* Cambridge, MA: Harvard University Press.

Bronfenbrenner, U. (1986). Ecology of the family as a context for human development: Research perspectives. *Developmental Psychology, 22,* 723–742.

Brown, J. D., & Siegel, J. M. (1988). Attribution of negative life events and depression: The role of perceived control. *Journal of Personality and Social Psychology, 54,* 316–322.

Bryant, B. K., & Crockenberg, S. B. (1980). Correlates and dimensions of prosocial behavior: A study of female siblings and their mothers. *Child Development, 51,* 529–544.

Christopoulos, C., Cohn, D. A., Shaw, D. S., Joyce, S., Sullivan-Hanson, J., Kraft, S. P., & Emery, R. E. (1987). Children of abused women: Adjustment at time of shelter residence. *Journal of Marriage and the Family, 49,* 611–619.

Coie, J. D., Dodge, K. A., & Kupersmidt, J. B. (1990). Peer group behavior and social status. In S. R. Asher & J. D. Coie (Eds.), *Peer rejection in childhood* (pp. 17–59). New York: Cambridge University Press.

Cole, R. E., Baldwin, A., Baldwin, C., & Fisher, L. (1982). Family interaction in free play and children's social competence. *Monographs of the Society for Research in Child Development, 47,* (5, Serial No. 197).

Cowen, E., Pederson, A., Babigian, H., Izzo, L., & Trost, M. A. (1973). Long term follow-up of early detected vulnerable children. *Journal of Consulting and Clinical Psychology, 41,* 438–446.

Crittenden, P. M. (1985). Maltreated infants: Vulnerability and resilience. *Journal of Child Psychology and Psychiatry, 26,* 85–96.

Crittenden, P. M., & Ainsworth, M. D. S. (1989). Child maltreatment and attachment theory. In D. Cicchetti & V. Carlson (Eds.), *Child maltreatment: Theory and research on the causes and consequences of child abuse and neglect* (pp. 432–463). New York: Cambridge University Press.

Cummings, E. M., & Davies, P. (1994). *Children and marital conflict: The impact of family dispute and resolution.* New York: Guilford.

Cummings, E. M., & O'Reilly, A. W. (1997). Fathers in family context: Effects of marital quality on child adjustment. In M. E. Lamb (Ed.), *The role of the father in child development* (3rd ed., pp. 49–65). New York: Wiley.

Dodge, K. A., Bates, J. E., & Pettit, G. S. (1990). Mechanisms in the cycle of violence. *Science, 250,* 1678–1683.

Dodge, K. A., McClaskey, C., & Feldman, E. (1985). Situational approach to the assessment of social competence in children. *Journal of Consulting and Clinical Psychology, 53,* 344–353.

Dornbusch, S. M., Ritter, P. L., Leiderman, P. H., Roberts, D. F., & Fraleigh, M. J. (1987). The relation of parenting style to adolescent school performance. *Child Development, 58,* 1244–1257.

Easterbrooks. M. A., & Lamb, M. E. (1979). The relationship between the quality of mother–infant attachment and infant competence in initial encounters with peers. *Child Development, 50*, 380–387.

Eckenrode, J., Laird, M., & Doris, J. (1993). School performance and disciplinary problems among abused and neglected children. *Developmental Psychology, 29*, 53–62.

Egeland, B. (1985, April). *The impact of an interfering style of parenting behavior on the later development of the child.* Paper presented at the meeting of the Society for Research in Child Development, Toronto, Canada.

Elmer, E. (1977). A follow-up study of traumatized children. *Pediatrics, 59*, 273–279.

Emery, R. E. (1989). Family violence. *American Psychologist, 44*, 321–328.

Fantuzzo, J. W., DePaola, L. M., Lambert, L., Martino, T., Anderson, G., & Sutton, S. (1990). Effects of interparental violence on the psychological adjustment and competencies of young children. *Journal of Consulting and Clinical Psychology, 59*, 258–265.

Fantuzzo, J. W., & Lindquist, C. U. (1989). The effects of observing conjugal violence on children: A review of research methodology. *Journal of Family Violence, 4*, 77–94.

Finnie, V., & Russell, A. (1988). Preschool children's social status and their mothers' behavior and knowledge in the supervisory role. *Developmental Psychology, 24*, 789–801.

George, C., & Main, M. (1979). Social interactions of young abused children: Approach, avoidance, and aggression. *Child Development, 50*, 306–318.

Harter, S. (1982). The perceived competence scale for children. *Child Development, 53*, 87–97.

Hartup, W. W. (1983). Peer interaction and social organization. In P. Mussen (Ed.), *Carmichael's manual of child psychology* (Fourth Edition, Vol. 2, pp. 361–456). New York: Wiley.

Hoffman-Plotkin, D., & Twentyman, C. T. (1984). A multimodel assessment of behavioral and cognitive deficits in abused and neglected preschoolers. *Child Development, 55*, 794–802.

Holden, G. W., & Ritchie, K. L. (1991). Linking extreme marital discord, child rearing and child behavior problems: Evidence from battered women. *Child Development, 6*, 311–327.

Hughes, H. M. (1988). Psychological and behavioral correlates of family violence in child witnesses and victims. *American Journal of Orthopsychiatry, 55*, 260–266.

Hymel, S., & Rubin, K. H. (1985). Children with peer relationship and social skills problems: Conceptual, methodological, and developmental issues. *Annals of Child Development, 2*, 251–297.

Jaffe, P. G., Wolfe, D. A., Wilson, S. K., & Zak, L. (1986). Similarities in behavioral and social adjustment among child victims and witnesses to family violence. *American Journal of Orthopsychiatry, 57*, 186–192.

Kendall-Tackett, K. A., & Eckenrode, J. (1996). The effects of neglect on academic achievement and disciplinary problems: A developmental perspective. *Child Abuse and Neglect, 29*, 161–169.

Kohlberg, L., LaCrosse, J., & Ricks, D. (1972). The predictability of adult mental health from childhood behavior. In B. Wolman (Ed.), *Manual of child psychopathology* (pp. 1217–1284). New York: McGraw-Hill.

Krispin, O., Sternberg, K. J., & Lamb, M. E. (1992). The dimensions of peer evaluation in Israel: A cross-cultural perspective. *International Journal of Behavioral Development, 15*, 299–314.

Kupersmidt, J., Coie, J. D., & Dodge, K. A. (1990). The role of poor peer relationships in the development of disorder. In S. R. Asher & J. D. Coie (Eds.), *Peer rejection in childhood* (pp. 274–305). New York: Cambridge University Press.

Lamb, M. E. (1981). The development of social expectations in the first year of life. In M. E. Lamb & L. R. Sherrod (Eds.), *Infant social cognition* (pp. 155–175). Hillsdale, NJ: Lawrence Erlbaum Associates.

Lamb, M. E., Gaensbauer, T. J., Malkin, C. M., & Schultz, L. (1985). The effects of abuse and neglect on security on infant–adult attachment. *Infant Behavior and Development, 8*, 35–45.

Lamb, M. E., Ketterlinus, R. D., & Fracasso, M. P. (1992). Parent–child relationships. In M. H. Bornstein & M. E. Lamb (Eds.), *Developmental psychology: An advanced textbook* (3rd ed., pp. 465–518). Hillsdale, NJ: Lawrence Erlbaum Associates.

Lollis, S. P., Ross, H. S., & Tate, E. (1992). Parents' regulation of children's peer interactions: Direct influences. In R. Parke & G. Ladd (Eds.), *Family–peer relationships: Modes of linkage* (pp. 255–281). Hillsdale, NJ: Lawrence Erlbaum Associates.

MacKinnon, C. E., Lamb, M. E., Belsky, J., & Baum, C. (1990). An affective-cognitive model of mother–child aggression. *Development and Psychopathology, 2*, 1–13.

MacKinnon-Lewis, C. E., Lamb, M. E., Arbuckle, B., Baradaran, L. P., & Volling, B. L. (1992). The relationship between biased maternal and filial attributions and the aggressiveness of their interactions. *Development and Psychopathology, 4*, 403–415.

MacKinnon-Lewis, C. E., Lamb, M. E., Hattie, J., & Baradaran, L. P. (1996). *A longitudinal examination of the associations between mothers' and children's attributions and their aggression.* Unpublished manuscript, University of North Carolina at Greensboro.

MacKinnon-Lewis, C. E., Volling, B. L., Lamb, M. E., Dechman, K., Rabiner, D., & Curtner, M. E. (1994). A cross-contextual analysis of boys' social competence: From family to school. *Developmental Psychology, 30*, 325–333.

Margolin, G., Talovic, S., & Weinstein, C. D. (1983). Areas of Change Questionnaire: A practical approach to marital assessment. *Journal of Consulting and Clinical Psychology, 51*, 944–955.

Masten, A., Morison, P., & Pellegrini, D. (1985). A revised class play method of peer assessment. *Developmental Psychology, 21*, 523–533.

Matas, L., Arend, R. A., & Sroufe, L. A. (1978). Continuity of adaptation in the second year: The relationship between quality of attachment and later competence. *Child Development, 49*, 547–556.

Melby, J. N., & Conger, R. D. (1996). Parental behaviors and adolescent academic performance: A longitudinal analysis. *Journal of Research on Adolescence, 6*, 113–137.

Morison, P. (1982). *Teacher rating scales of peer relations.* Minneapolis: University of Minnesota.

Parke, R. D. (1994). Epilogue: Unresolved issues and future trends in family relationships with other contexts. In R. D. Parke & S. G. Kellam (Eds.), *Exploring family relationships with other social contexts* (pp. 215–229). Hillsdale, NJ: Lawrence Erlbaum Associates.

Parke, R. D., & Beitel, A. (1988). Disappointment: When things go wrong in the transition to parenthood. *Marriage and Family, 12*, 221–265.

Parke, R. D., & Kellam, S. G. (Eds.). (1994). *Exploring family relationships with other social contexts.* Hillsdale, NJ: Lawrence Erlbaum Associates.

Parke, R. D., & Ladd, G. W. (1992). *Family–peer relationships: Modes of linkage.* Hillsdale, NJ: Lawrence Erlbaum Associates.

Parke, R. D., MacDonald, K. B., Beitel, A., & Bhavanagri, N. (1988). The role of the family in the development of peer relationships. In R. Peters & R. J. McMahon (Eds.), *Social learning systems approaches to marriage and the family* (pp. 17–44). New York: Brunner/Mazel.

Parke, R. D., Neville, B., Burks, V. M., Boyum, L. A., & Carson, J. L. (1994). Family–peer relationships: A tripartite model. In R. D. Parke & S. G. Kellam (Eds.), *Exploring family relationships with other social contexts* (pp. 115–145). Hillsdale, NJ: Lawrence Erlbaum Associates.

Parker, J. G., & Asher, S. R. (1987). Peer relations and later personal adjustment: Are low-accepted children at risk? *Psychological Bulletin, 102*, 357–389.

Pastor, D. L. (1981). The quality of mother–infant attachment and its relationship to toddlers' initial sociability with peers. *Developmental Psychology, 17*, 326–335.

Patterson, G. R. (1986). The contribution of siblings to training for fighting: A microsocial analysis. In D. Olweus, J. Block, & M. Radke-Yarrow (Eds.), *Development of antisocial and prosocial behavior: Research, theories, and issues* (pp. 235–261). New York: Academic Press.

Patterson, G. R., & Reid, J. B. (1984). Social interactional processes within the family: The study of moment-by-moment family transaction in which human social development is embedded. *Journal of Applied Developmental Psychology, 5*, 237–262.

Price, J. M., & Van Slyke, D. (1991, April). *Social information processing patterns and social adjustment of maltreated children.* Paper presented at the meeting of the Society for Research in Child Development, Seattle.

Reidy, T. J. (1977). The aggressive characteristics of abused and neglected children. *Journal of Personality, 57*, 257–281.

Rienken, B., Egeland, B., Marvinney, D., Mangelsdorf, S., & Sroufe, L. A. (1989). Early antecedents of aggression and passive-withdrawal in early elementary schools. *Journal of Personality, 57*, 257–281.

Rosenberg, M. S. (1987). New directions for research on the psychological maltreatment of children. *American Psychologist, 42*, 166–171.

Rubin, K. H., & Coplan, R. J. (1992). Peer relationships in childhood. In M. H. Bornstein & M. E. Lamb (Eds.), *Developmental psychology: An advanced textbook* (3rd ed., pp. 519–578). Hillsdale, NJ: Lawrence Erlbaum Associates.

Salzinger, S., Kaplan, S., Pelcovitz, D., Samit, C., & Krieger, R. (1984). Parent and teacher assessment of children's behavior in child maltreating families. *Journal of the American Academy of Child Psychiatry, 23*, 458–464.

Sroufe, L. A. (1983). Infant–caregiver attachment and patterns of adaptation in preschool: The roots of maladaptation and competence. In M. Perlmutter (Ed.), *Minnesota symposia on child psychology* (Vol. 16, pp. 41–84). Hillsdale, NJ: Lawrence Erlbaum Associates.

Sroufe, L. A., & Rutter, M. (1984). The domain of developmental psychopathology. *Child Development, 55*, 17–29.

Starr, R. H., Jr. (1979). Child abuse. *American Psychologist, 34*, 872–878.

Sternberg, K. J., Lamb, M. E., & Dawud-Noursi, S. (1997). Using multiple informants and cross-cultural research to study the effects of domestic violence on developmental psychopathology: Illustrations from research in Israel. In S. S. Luthar, J. A. Burack, D. Cicchetti, & J. Weisz (Eds.), *Developmental psychopathology: Perspectives on risk and disorder, Essays in Honor of Edward F. Zigler* (pp. 417–436). New York: Cambridge University Press.

Sternberg, K. J., Lamb, M. E., & Dawud-Noursi, S. (1998). Understanding domestic violence and its effects: Making sense of divergent reports and perspectives. In G. W. Holden, R. Geffner, & E. N. Jouriles (Eds.), *Children exposed to family violence.* Washington, DC: American Psychological Association.

Sternberg, K. J., Lamb, M. E., Greenbaum, C., Cicchetti, D., Dawud, S., Cortes, R. M., Krispin, O., & Lorey, F. (1993). Effects of domestic violence on children's behavior problems and depression. *Developmental Psychology, 29*, 44–52.

Sternberg, K. J., Lamb, M. E., Greenbaum, C., Dawud, S., Cortes, R. M., & Lorey, F. (1994). The effects of domestic violence on children's perceptions of their perpetrating and nonperpetrating parents. *International Journal of Behavioral Development, 17*, 779–795.

Toth, S. L., Manly, J. T., & Cicchetti, D. (1992). Child maltreatment and vulnerability to depression. *Development and Psychopathology, 4*, 97–112.

Ulman, C. A. (1957). Teachers, peers, and tests as predictors of adjustment. *Journal of Educational Psychology, 48*, 257–267.

Volling, B. L., MacKinnon-Lewis, C., Rabiner, D., & Baradaran, L. P. (1993). Children's social competence and sociometric status: Further exploration of aggression, social withdrawal, and peer rejection. *Development and Psychopathology, 5*, 459–483.

Vosk, B., Forehand, R., Parker, J., & Rickard, K. (1982). A multimethod comparison of popular and unpopular children. *Developmental Psychology, 18*, 795–805.

Widom, C. (1989). Does violence beget violence? A critical examination of the literature. *Psychological Bulletin, 106*, 3–28.

Wolfe, D. A., Jaffe, P., Wilson, S. K., & Zak, L. (1985). Children of battered women: The relation of child behavior to family violence and maternal stress. *Journal of Consulting and Clinical Psychology, 53*, 657–655.

11

▼▼▼▼▼▼▼

Coparenting Processes and Child Competence Among Rural African-American Families

Gene H. Brody
Douglas L. Flor
Eileen Neubaum
University of Georgia

McHale (1995) defined coparenting as "the extent to which partners share leadership and support one another in their mutual roles as architects and heads of the family" (p. 985). McHale further said that, "Well-functioning coparenting systems are those in which partners find ways to accommodate their individual styles and preferences. The essence of coparenting thus involves mutual support and commitment to parenting the child" (p. 985). The kinds of coparenting relationships that parents form impact children's development and adjustment. Given the importance of the coparenting relationship to child development, it is important to study it in a variety of family settings.

The coparental relationship was primarily studied in divorced families (Belsky, Crnic, & Gable, 1995), as parents find ways of relating to one another in their continuing responsibility for childrearing after their marriage ends. Coparenting in intact families was not studied as extensively, so comparatively little information was gained about it (Belsky et al., 1995; McHale, 1995). In this chapter, we briefly review the extant literature concerning coparenting, in both divorced and nondivorced families. Following this, we present information concerning our own studies in which we examined cocaregiving among a particularly underresearched population, rural African-American families. We studied coparenting between married African-American parents, but went a step further in the exploration of adults' caregiving relationships by examining caregiving alliances between African-American single mothers and members of their extended families.

COPARENTING RELATIONSHIPS
IN DIVORCED FAMILIES

In the literature about coparenting following divorce, attention is given to the types of coparental relationships that parents form to meet the ongoing need that their children have for care. Some parents are able to cooperate and establish a well-functioning coparental relationship with their former spouses (Camara & Resnick, 1989), whereas others are less able to do so.

The type of coparental relationship that former spouses establish was found to be associated with several family variables. Maccoby, Depner, and Mnookin (1990) found that parents who were more satisfied with their custody arrangements were less discordant. Parents who experienced more hostility toward each other at the beginning of the divorce process were lower in cooperative communication and higher in discord an average of 15 months after filing for divorce. Dozier, Sollie, Stack, and Smith (1993) found that a continuation of friendly attachment between the former husband and wife was associated with more supportive coparenting relationships, more sharing of parental responsibilities, and less conflict.

Camara and Resnick (1989) found that interparental cooperation between divorced parents was associated with better relationship quality between the child and the noncustodial parent, and with more contact between the noncustodial parent and the child. They also found that, for both divorced and nondivorced families, the use of avoidance, verbal attacks, or physical attacks as means of dealing with conflict was associated with less interparental cooperation, more conflict, and escalation of conflict in the coparental relationship. More compromise was associated with less conflict and more cooperation and led to an increase in closeness between the parents. Furthermore, the degree of conflict between parents was not related to child adjustment, but the style of conflict resolution was. The children of parents who negotiated and compromised, rather than avoiding or using physical or verbal attacks, were more socially competent. Greater parental cooperation was also associated with less aggression among children. The degree of conflict was not associated with parent–child relationship quality either, but again, the style of conflict resolution was associated with it, with more compromise associated with better parent–child relationship quality.

Buchanan, Maccoby, and Dornbusch (1991) studied adolescents' feelings of being caught between their divorced parents. They hypothesized that the potential for these feelings to arise could vary with parents' coparenting styles as defined by Maccoby et al. (1990), who classified a sample of divorced parents into four groups according to the levels of cooperative communication and discord they were experiencing. *Cooperative parents* had high levels of cooperative communication and low levels of discord, whereas *conflicted parents* experienced low levels of cooperative communication and high levels of discord. *Disengaged parents* were low on both dimensions, and *mixed parents* were high on both. The authors suggested that conflicted parents might be more likely to triangulate with their children and to allow intergenerational boundary diffusion to occur. Disengaged parents, for their part, might use their children as their means of communicating with one another when it is necessary to do so. Cooperative parents, on the other hand, might communicate better with each other and avoid pulling the children into their relationship.

Buchanan et al. (1991) found that, when parental discord was higher and cooperative communication was lower, adolescents were more likely to feel caught between their parents. Adolescents in cooperative families were least likely to feel caught, those in disengaged families were next most likely, and those in conflicted families were most likely. Mixed-style families were not included in these analyses. Coparenting style was indirectly associated with adolescents' depression, anxiety, and deviant behavior, through feelings of being caught, and the coparenting relationship was the strongest predictor of these feelings.

Levels of conflict and communication, however, were not the only predictors of adolescents' feelings of being caught. This was evident because some adolescents from low-conflict families felt caught anyway, and some adolescents from high-conflict families did not feel caught. Buchanan et al. (1991) suggested that specific parenting behaviors that lead adolescents to feel caught, such as asking the child questions about the other parent or using the child as a go between, can occur independently from conflict levels.

COPARENTING RELATIONSHIPS
BETWEEN MARRIED PARENTS

Much of the literature about coparenting relationships between married parents deals with the description of coparenting behavior and the correlates among various features of this behavior. Gable, Belsky, and Crnic (1995) observed naturalistic coparenting behavior in the home in order to describe the various ways in which parents supported or did not support one another during interactions with their sons at age 15 months and again at age 21 months. The study focused on *coparenting events,* which involved both parents and the child in an interaction in which one parent "advance[d] a parenting goal for the child (e.g., praise, comfort, command/direct)" (p. 611), and the other parent responded to the first parent's action. They found that supportive coparenting occurred more often than nonsupportive or mixed coparenting. In mixed coparenting, the responding parent's response was partly supportive and partly unsupportive. Among unsupportive exchanges, matter-of-fact disagreements were more common than affectively negative behavior. Across time, unsupportive events declined and mixed events increased, whereas parents' individual parenting styles remained the same.

Fathers supported mothers more often than the reverse, probably because more mothers than fathers initiated action toward the child to which the other parent responded. Parental age, parental education, family income, and number of years married were not associated with coparenting behavior in this White, middle-class sample.

Using the naturalistic observations taken when the children were 15 months old, Belsky et al. (1995) tested the hypothesis that larger differences between parents on a number of demographic, personality, relational style, and childrearing attitude variables are associated with less supportive and more unsupportive coparenting. They further hypothesized that daily hassles moderate those associations. They found that greater relational style differences between parents in closeness were associated with more unsupportive parenting, which included both matter-of-fact disagreements and negatively emotionally charged interactions. Greater differences between parents in the personality styles of extroversion and interpersonal affect were associated with more unsupportive parenting that included negative affect. Greater differences between parents in the relational style anxiety were associated with less supportive coparenting. No associations emerged for differences in parental age, years of education, or childrearing attitude differences—the latter of which were not large. As predicted, daily hassles moderated the associations that emerged, such that higher levels of hassles were associated with more unsupportive parenting.

McHale (1995) used both self-report and observational data to determine whether parents' reports about their personal and marital adjustment or their observed behavior toward one another during an interview better predicted their coparenting behavior during observed interactions with their 8.5- or 11-month-old children. McHale found that the self-report instruments did not predict coparenting behavior, but observed marital interaction did. Parents' display of more troubled marital interaction predicted less functional coparenting behavior. Specifically, parents who enacted more conflict with each other during the couple interview were found to engage in more hostile–competitive behavior toward each other during play with their sons, and parents who displayed an unequal balance of power during the couple interview interacted unequally with their daughters. Usually, the parent who was less dominant in the couple interview was more dominant during play with the child.

The Blocks and their colleagues (Block, Block, & Morrison, 1981; Vaughn, Block, & Block, 1988) conducted a longitudinal study in which the extent of interparental agreement, measured using parents' responses to the Child Rearing Practices Report (CRPR; Block, 1965) when their children were 3 years old, predicted the children's adjustment at 4, 7, 11, 14, and 18 years of age, as well as their home environments 2.5 years after the CRPR was completed. Block et al. (1981) described the homes of agreeing parents as "congenial, productive centers in which consideration of others is evidenced and value is accorded to intellectual and cultural pursuits" (p. 968) and those of disagreeing parents as featuring "family discord and conflict; a cheerless, constricted atmosphere; [and] the possibility of discrimination based on race, religion, or social class" (pp. 968–969).

Block et al. (1981) found parental agreement to correlate differently with boys' and girls' adjustment, both concurrently with the CRPR at age 3 and longitudinally at ages 4 and 7. Agreement was associated with better adjustment in boys; among girls, however, agreement was associated with more undercontrolled behavior. The findings were not attributable to demographic differences and were replicated using a high school sample. Block et al. suggested that the gender-specific findings result from boys' greater vulnerability to parental discord, as indicated in studies of divorced families. This makes parental agreement particularly important to boys' adjustment, but not as important in determining girls' adjustment.

Vaughn et al. (1988) reported that the same pattern continued into the participants' adolescence. The undercontrolled behavior in girls, however, matured into "an openness of behavior" that helped the girls to become more socially and relationally competent. Vaughn et al. concluded that, over the long run, parental agreement was associated with competent behavior in both boys and girls, although this competence took different forms according to child gender.

In concluding this section, we mention a study that emphasizes the link between coparenting behaviors and child outcomes. Jouriles et al. (1991) studied 3- to 6-year-old boys' adjustment in nondivorced families. Based on maternal reports, they found that child-related disputes between parents were associated more strongly with child behavior problems than were general marital disagreement, general marital conflict, or child exposure to general marital conflict.

As previously reported, Camara and Resnick (1989) found several associations between coparenting and child outcomes to be significant in both divorced and nondivorced families. In addition, they found that, in two-parent families, interparental cooperation was positively associated with mother–child relationship quality, but not with father–child relationship quality. Clearly, further research is needed to determine how coparenting processes are linked with children's psychosocial competence.

COPARENTING AMONG AFRICAN-AMERICAN FAMILIES

Deal, Halverson, and Wampler (1989) noted that more research needs to be conducted with families other than those headed by the White, middle-class, college graduates who tend to make up the sample in many of the studies of coparenting relationships. They noted that people from other ethnicities and cultural groups may not share this group's opinions of optimum parenting, and have cultural ideals concerning childrearing that are unique to each specific group. This is the case with the group we studied—rural African-American families, many of whom live in poverty. We focused on this group in our studies because of the dearth of information available about this population and because of the special challenges that these families face. To date, very little attention has been given to understanding the ways in which rural poverty affects personal well-being, family functioning, and youth outcomes among African Americans. Most research about African-American families focused on those living in densely populated, urban inner cities. This focus does not acknowledge the diversity of African-American families and children nor the variety of ways in which they respond to poverty and economic stress. For rural African-American families, the challenge of overcoming the environmental obstacles associated with poverty and chronic economic stress is exacerbated by oppressive social structures (see Tickamyer & Duncan, 1990) and the lack of facilities and other services that are often available to urban families (Orthner, 1986).

In small towns and communities in the rural South, poverty rates are among the highest in the nation. Families are often faced with conditions similar to those in poor inner-city neighborhoods, including high crime rates, a large proportion of single-parent households, and the persistence of poverty from generation to generation (O'Hare & Curry-White, 1992). Parents must often hold several jobs to earn enough money to support their families (Brody, Stoneman, Flor, McCrary, Hastings, & Conyers, 1994). Educational problems, such as illiteracy, failure to complete high school, and school failure in general, are particularly serious for rural African-American children.

Despite these chronic problems, however, many of these children mature into emotionally healthy, competent people. They are the resilient children whom Rutter (1979) and Garmezy (1976, 1981) described. The strength of their rural Southern families may explain the adaptability of these children. The families often have strong extended kin networks that support members in need (Hawkes, Kutner, Wells, Christopherson, & Almirol, 1981), providing economic and instrumental assistance (Tienda & Angel, 1982), nurturance, socialization, and a cultural identity (Hawkes et al., 1981; Shimkin, Louie, & Frate, 1978). These patterns of family life were established in African societies and modified in response to enslavement in America (Sudarkasa, 1988), as reliance on family and extended kin networks supported African Americans through many social transitions. An expanded view of family processes that places transactions in the extended family context is therefore needed in the study of family processes among African Americans. This is particularly true for understanding the development of child competence because extended family members have frequent contact with children and play significant childrearing roles. In fact, Edwards (1976) and Lee (1984, 1985) found, in their qualitative studies, that close, supportive, extended family relationships were positively associated with African-American adolescents' school performance.

In this chapter, we present findings from ongoing projects, in which our laboratory staff observed and interviewed both two-parent and single-mother-headed, African-American families living in rural areas to identify the links from various family and parental characteristics to coparenting relationships. We, in turn, looked for associations between coparenting relationships and child outcomes. With our sample of single-mother-headed families, the coparenting relationships under study were cocaregiving relationships between each single mother and an extended family member, usually the child's maternal grandmother. In both studies, we collected self-report data from the participants, and in the study of two-parent families, we also made observational ratings of the parents' marital interactions. Data were also provided by the children's schools as part of the measurement of their development of competency.

Development of Research Methods and Assessments With the Assistance of Community Members

From the beginning of our projects, community leaders were involved in the decision-making process to help them feel as if they were part of the project and to make them comfortable in referring potential participants. The accurate assessment of the families in our study concerned us because most instruments used to evaluate family processes and individual outcomes were developed for use with and standardized on White, middle-class families. Accordingly, a focus group comprised of rural African-American community members was recruited to help develop culturally appropriate measures. Most of the group members served as peer agents for the Energy Education Program and the Expanded Food and Nutrition Program, two state agencies housed on the University of Georgia campus; some of these agents recommended other African-American community leaders for participation. The final focus group included 40 people from throughout Georgia who were representative of the population to be studied. The group addressed two issues, one of which concerned the development of valid self-report instruments. Each group member rated each instrument that we planned to use on a 5-point Likert-type scale ranging from 1 (*not appropriate*) through 3 (*appropriate*) to 5 (*very appropriate*) for rural African-American families. Those instruments with a mean rating of at least 3.5 were retained. Most of the instruments presented no validity problems to the focus group members. Some individual items were reworded for simplicity and clarity, according to the group members' suggestions, and a few were eliminated as irrelevant to African Americans.

The second issue concerned our plan to videotape family interactions. In past projects, we found the videotaping of these interactions to be essential to the close study of family relationships. The focus group suggested that this procedure be made as nonthreatening as possible by recording no interactions involving finances or other sensitive information. From a list of activities in which families were videotaped in past studies, the group selected game playing as the context that the families would consider most acceptable. In addition, during the first home visit, the project staff clearly explained the videotaping procedure and the reasons for its use, strongly emphasizing its confidentiality. The staff also gave particular attention to establishing rapport and putting the families at ease, which was emphasized throughout the project. The majority of the families freely cooperated with the taping.

To enhance rapport and cultural understanding, African-American students and community members served as the home visitors who collected data from the families. Prior to data collection, the visitors received 1 month of training in administering the self-report instruments and conducting the observational procedures.

Each of the studies we conducted involved family characteristics that predicted the quality of the coparenting relationship; the specific predictor variables we examined varied with the study and are described later. The coparental relationship, in turn, was used to predict a number of child outcomes, including parent–child relationship quality, academic performance, and psychosocial functioning.

Coparenting and Its Correlates in Two-Parent African-American Families

The studies pertaining to coparenting in two-parent households included 90 African-American families, each of which had a 9- to 12-year-old firstborn child who served as the target child in the studies. All of the families came from rural areas in Georgia and South Carolina, in which community populations were less than 2,500. An economic cross-section of families was represented in the sample.

Finances and Parent Psychological Functioning as Predictors of Coparenting. Earlier in this chapter, we described the special difficulties faced by African-American families living in the rural South, one of which is poverty. The stresses and strains associated with inadequate income can take a toll on parents' relationships with one another, thus affecting their ability to cooperate in rearing their children. To explore this possibility, we conducted a series of studies in which we examined the associations among family income, parents' personal functioning, the coparental relationship, and child outcomes. Because our sample included an economic cross-section of participants, income varied widely enough to enable us to examine these associations meaningfully.

Brody, Stoneman, Flor, McCrary, Hastings, & Conyers (1994) measured per capita income (as an indicator of family financial stress), parental depression, and parental optimism as predictors of coparenting quality. Coparenting was operationalized using four variables—the support (defined as communication and instrumental assistance) that the mother received from the father, the support that the father received from the mother, coparental conflict, and the quality of the parents' marital relationship (e.g., harmony, engagement, communication, and warmth)—and was evaluated through observation of spousal interactions. Although it has been suggested that child-related interactions between spouses are better predictors of child adjustment than are general marital interactions (see Belsky et al., 1995; McHale, 1995), Gable et al. (1995) noted that higher marital quality is associated with better parenting quality, which, in turn, is associated with better child adjustment; the converse is also true.

These coparenting variables, in turn, were hypothesized to be associated with *child self-regulation*, defined as a child's ability to set and attain goals, to plan actions and to consider their consequences, and to persist (Bandura, 1977). Self-regulation, in turn, was hypothesized to be associated with reading and mathematics performance in school and with externalizing and internalizing problems.

Higher per capita income was associated with less parental depression and more parental optimism. Depression and optimism were associated with all four coparenting measures, such that less depression and more optimism were associated with more support, higher marital quality, and less conflict. This configuration of coparenting variables was in turn associated with greater self-regulation on the part of the child. Greater self-regulation, in turn, was associated with better reading and mathematics performance and with fewer externalizing and internalizing problems. Thus, the quality of the coparental relationship was indirectly linked with the outcome variables through its association with child self-regulation.

In another study involving per capita income and parental education as predictors of child competence, Brody, Stoneman, and Flor (1995) included only interparental conflict as a measure of coparenting quality. They found higher per capita income to be associated with less interparental conflict and less conflict to be associated with greater child self-regulation and better academic achievement. In this study, the coparenting variable was directly associated with academic competence, as well as indirectly associated with it through self-regulation.

Parental Religiosity as a Predictor of Coparenting. In other studies conducted with our sample of rural, two-parent, African-American families, we used parental religiosity as a predictor of coparenting relationship quality, hypothesizing that higher religiosity is associated with more functional coparenting. Although Block et al. (1981) found that their measure of coparenting—parental agreement on childrearing values and practices—was negatively associated with what they termed "significant and genuine" religiosity in the home, different results emerge from our study for several reasons. First, our sample is entirely African American, whereas Block et al.'s sample was only 29% African American. Furthermore, the African-American families were entirely excluded from some analyses due to excessive missing data. This difference in racial composition between the samples is important because African Americans consistently manifest higher levels of religiosity than do Whites (Taylor, 1988), and religious participation is an important component of many African Americans' lives (McAdoo, 1983; Taylor, Thornton, & Chatters, 1987). In addition, the measures of coparenting that we use in our research differ from the one that Block et al. used. Finally, the procedures for gathering data differed between the two studies; the religiosity data in the Block et al. study were based on home visitors' impressions, whereas our data were gathered through reports from the participants themselves.

We measured religiosity by asking each parent to rate, on a 7-point scale, the frequency with which he or she attended church services during the previous year; the scale ranged from 0 (*never*) to 6 (*more than once a week*). The parents also rated the importance of their church attendance, on a scale ranging from 1 (*not very important*) to 5 (*very important*). Each parent's responses to these questions were multiplied, yielding a score for each parent on a dimension that we termed *formal religiosity.*

Brody, Stoneman, Flor, and McCrary (1994) used parents' formal religiosity to predict four coparenting variables: the support that the mother received from the father, the support the father received from the mother, coparental conflict, and the observed quality of the parents' marital interactions. The coparenting variables, in turn, were used to predict parent–child relationship quality and inconsistent parenting. With one exception (the association between mother's religiosity and support received from the father), formal religiosity was significantly associated with all four coparenting variables, such that greater formal religiosity was associated with less coparental conflict, more support, and higher marital quality. In turn, less conflict was associated with higher parent–child relationship quality and less inconsistent parenting; more support was associated with better parent–child relationships, and higher marital quality was associated with less inconsistent parenting.

In another study designed to describe the pathways among parental religiosity, coparenting, and child outcomes (Brody, Stoneman, & Flor, 1996), only interparental conflict was included as a coparenting measure, with per capita income and parental religiosity as the predictors. Only religiosity significantly predicted interparental conflict, such that more religious parents experienced less conflict. Interparental conflict, in turn, predicted self-regulation, which predicted academic competence, internalizing problems, and externalizing problems. Thus, the impact of interparental conflict on the child outcome measures was indirect through self-regulation.

It appears that the child's development of self-regulation is an important link between characteristics of the coparental relationship and child outcomes among rural, two-parent, African-American families. Although some direct links emerged between coparenting and outcome variables, self-regulation served as an indirect link in every study in which it was included.

Coparenting and Its Correlates in Single-Mother-Headed African-American Families

We next turned our attention to the study of cocaregiving between single, African-American mothers and extended family members, usually the mother's own mother. Proceeding with our research in this way enabled us to gather data concerning children's competence in a family form in which a considerable number of African-American children currently live. It also enabled us to determine whether the pattern of associations that emerged in our studies of families headed by married parents were similar or different in single-mother-headed families, in which the cocaregiver is someone other than a spouse.

To study these issues, 154 African-American, single-mother-headed families with a 6- to 9-year-old child were recruited from nonmetropolitan counties in Georgia, similar to those from which the two-parent families were recruited. Again, only counties in which 25% or more of the population was African American were sampled, in order to insure that a viable African-American community existed in the county. Of these 154 families, 75% had a per capita income of $3,300 or less, which, according to criteria established by the Census Bureau (U.S. Bureau of the Census, 1992), placed them below the poverty line.

As in our studies of two-parent families, we proposed that less adequate financial resources would be associated with more depression and less optimism among mothers. In this study, financial resources were measured using the mothers' responses to the "money for necessities," "general money," and "money for extras" subscales of Dunst and Leet's (1987) Family Resource Scale. These responses indicated the mothers' perceptions of the adequacy of their incomes.

In turn, we proposed mothers' depression and optimism as the indirect links through which perceptions of the adequacy of financial resources influence the relationships between mothers and the other family members who care for their children. In this study, the cocaregiver construct included two dimensions that we hypothesized to be linked to specific parenting practices: communication/support and conflict. We expected less depressed and more optimistic mothers to be more likely to communicate with co-caregivers and to elicit instrumental support on childrearing tasks.

Based on the data from our studies with two-parent families, we expected supportive and communicative cocaregiving to be the pivotal process con-necting earlier steps in the model to parenting practices. Earlier studies also documented the enhancement of effective parenting in African-American families by social support networks that provide both emotional and tangible help (Brody et al., 1995; Brody, Stoneman, Flor, McCrary, Hastings, & Conyers, 1994; Stevens & Duffield, 1986; Taylor & Roberts, 1995; Wilson, 1984). Particularly for single mothers, this enhancement is especially likely when a grandmother or other adult partner is involved in cocaregiving (Brown & Gary, 1988; Lewis, 1989). Brody, Stoneman, Flor, McCrary, Hastings, and Conyers (1994) and Wilson (1984, 1986) noted, however, that the extended caregiver network also holds the potential for dissension and strain. Contradictory and confusing messages from disagreeing caregivers stress the child's loyalties and complicate his or her attempts to discern order and predictability in the world. Under such circumstances, it is unlikely that the cocaregiver relationship provides support for effective parenting. In their predominantly White sample of families headed by married parents, Block et al. (1981) found that active participation by relatives in the socialization of the children in the study was associated with parental disagreement on childrearing attitudes, values, and practices. This suggests that, for those families, extended family cocaregiving was associated with less than optimum coparenting relationships. In our sample of single African Americans, how-ever, in which no fathers were present with whom the mothers could disagree and in which the extended family members make up the coparenting rela-tionship, the meaning and impact of extended family involvement in childrearing could well be different.

We next predicted that cocaregiver communication, support, and conflict would be associated with two variables that we expected to be associated with child outcomes: a childrearing style that we termed *no-nonsense parent-ing*, and mothers' involvement in their children's schools. Derived from Young's (1974) ethnographic analyses of African-American child socialization in rural Georgia, no-nonsense parenting consists of high levels of parental control, including the use of physical restraint and physical punishment, along with affectionate behaviors. This particular combination of parenting behaviors is intended to communicate to the child that the parent is vigilant and concerned for the child's welfare. The mothers in Young's ethnographic analyses believed that such parenting practices protected their children from dangerous surroundings and involvement in antisocial activity, while promoting the development of responsible behavior (cf. Allen, 1978; Bartz & Levine, 1978).

Both sociologists and psychologists suggested that parents' involvement in their children's schooling is a pivotal process through which parents influence their children's academic competence (Heyns, 1978). Intermittent contact with teachers allows parents to receive feedback about their children's academic performance and self-regulatory skills. In anticipation of future parent–teacher interaction, teachers become more likely to monitor the academic performance and classroom conduct of students whose parents are more involved in the schooling process (Epstein & Becker, 1982). The research, to date, consistently indicates that students whose parents are more involved in their schooling earn higher grades and have fewer self-control difficulties at school (Baker & Stevenson, 1986; Brody et al., 1995; Epstein, 1983; Reynolds, 1989; Stevenson & Baker, 1987). We measured school involvement by asking the children's teachers whether or not the children's mothers participated in school activities such as attending parent–teacher conferences, open houses, orientation meetings, or children's programs, or had volunteered to help with field trips or fund-raising projects.

We predicted both no-nonsense parenting and mothers' involvement in their children's schooling, in turn, to be indirectly linked with children's academic and psychosocial outcomes by facilitating the child's development of self-regulation. As we found in the studies of two-parent families, we expected self-regulation to be associated with greater academic success and fewer externalizing and internalizing problems.

Our findings revealed that perceptions of greater adequacy of financial resources were linked with less maternal depression and more maternal optimism. Less maternal depression was associated with less conflict in the cocaregiver relationship, but depression was not related to cocaregiver support or to parenting practices. Mothers who were more optimistic experienced greater support and less conflict in their relationships with cocaregivers. Greater cocaregiver support was linked with more use of no-nonsense parenting, and greater cocaregiver conflict was associated with less maternal involvement in children's schooling. More use of these parenting practices was associated with more self-regulation, which in turn was linked with greater academic and psychosocial competence.

CONCLUSIONS

The studies about coparenting summarized at the beginning of this chapter, as well as our own work with two-parent, African-American families, indicate that harmonious interactions among adults who share childrearing responsibilities are associated with parenting practices that enhance children's development. These associations emerged for both African-American and White married couples, as well as for single, African-American mothers who obtained childrearing assistance from extended family members. Like their children, parents have psychological and emotional needs as well as needs for practical assistance with the work involved in childrearing. When parents have their own needs for both emotional and instrumental support met by other adults, they have more personal resources from which to meet their children's needs for strong and loving parenting.

This need for support is particularly important for the single mothers in our own study, as 75% of them lived below the poverty line. The stresses associated with poverty place these families at particular risk for compromised functioning. Rutter (1985) proposed and empirical studies (Bretherton, Ridgeway, & Cassidy, 1990; Crockenberg, 1981; Morriset, Barnard, Greenberg, Booth, & Speiker, 1990) confirmed that the influence of protective factors is strongest under high-risk conditions. Thus, for single mothers, support offered by cocaregivers should be particularly likely to be associated with their engagement in vigilant, involved, childrearing practices, despite the stresses they encounter.

The creation and maintenance of supportive, involved, caregiving practices is important to children's development. Research provides useful information for the development of culturally sensitive educational programs and intervention strategies by identifying those family characteristics that enhance or detract from the development of well-functioning cocaregiving relationships among families of varying structure and ethnicity. This helps parents and other caregivers to provide their children with an optimum environment in which to grow and develop competence.

ACKNOWLEDGMENTS

The research reported in this chapter was supported by grants from the Spencer Foundation and the National Institute of Child Health and Human Development (Grant HD 30588).

REFERENCES

Allen, W. R. (1978). Black family research in the United States: A review, assessment, and extension. *Journal of Comparative Family Studies, 9*, 167–189.

Baker, D. P., & Stevenson, D. L. (1986). Mothers' strategies for children's school achievement: Managing the transition to high school. *Sociology of Education, 59*, 156–166.

Bandura, A. (1977). Self-efficacy: Toward a unifying theory of behavioral change. *Psychological Review, 84*, 191–215.

Bartz, K. W., & Levine, E. S. (1978). Child rearing by Black parents: A description and comparison to Anglo and Chicano parents. *Journal of Marriage and the Family, 40,* 709–719.

Belsky, J., Crnic, K., & Gable, S. (1995). The determinants of coparenting in families with toddler boys: Spousal differences and daily hassles. *Child Development, 66,* 629–642.

Block, J. H. (1965). *The child-rearing practices report.* Berkeley, CA: University of California, Institute of Human Development.

Block, J. H., Block, J., & Morrison, A. (1981). Parental agreement–disagreement on child-rearing orientations and gender-related personality correlates in children. *Child Development, 52,* 965–974.

Bretherton, I., Ridgeway, D., & Cassidy, J. (1990). Assessing internal working models of the attachment relationship: An attachment story completion task. In D. Cicchetti, M. Greenberg, & E. M. Cummings (Eds.), *Attachment in the preschool years* (pp. 273–308). Chicago: University of Chicago Press.

Brody, G. H., & Flor, D. (in press). Maternal resources, parenting practices, and child competence in rural, single-parent African American families. *Child Development.*

Brody, G. H., Stoneman, Z., & Flor, D. (1995). Linking family processes and academic competence among rural African American youths. *Journal of Marriage and the Family, 57,* 567–579.

Brody, G. H., Stoneman, Z., Flor, D., & McCrary, C. (1994). Religion's role in organizing family relationships: Family process in rural, two-parent African American families. *Journal of Marriage and the Family, 56,* 878–888.

Brody, G. H., Stoneman, Z., Flor, D., McCrary, C., Hastings, L., & Conyers, O. (1994). Financial resources, parent psychological functioning, parent co-caregiving, and early adolescent competence in rural two-parent African-American families. *Child Development, 65,* 590–605.

Brown, D. R., & Gary, L. E. (1988). Unemployment and psychological distress among Black American women. *Sociological Focus, 21,* 209–221.

Buchanan, C. M., Maccoby, E. E., & Dornbusch, S. M. (1991). Caught between parents: Adolescents' experience in divorced homes. *Child Development, 62,* 1008–1029.

Camara, K. A., & Resnick, G. (1989). Styles of conflict resolution and cooperation between divorced parents: Effects on child behavior and adjustment. *American Journal of Orthopsychiatry, 59,* 560–575.

Crockenberg, S. (1981). Infant irritability, mother responsiveness, and social support influences on the security of mother–infant attachment. *Child Development, 52,* 857–865.

Deal, J. E., Halverson, C. F., Jr., & Wampler, K. S. (1989). Parental agreement on child-rearing orientations: Relations to parental, marital, family, and child characteristics. *Child Development, 60,* 1025–1034.

Dozier, B. S., Sollie, D. L., Stack, S. J., & Smith, T. A. (1993). The effects of postdivorce attachment on coparenting relationships. *Journal of Divorce and Remarriage, 19*(3–4), 109–123.

Dunst, C. J., & Leet, H. E. (1987). Measuring the adequacy of resources in households with young children. *Child: Care, Health, and Development, 13*(2), 111–125.

Edwards, O. L. (1976). Components of academic success: A profile of achieving Black adolescents. *Journal of Negro Education, 45,* 408–422.

Epstein, J. L. (1983). Longitudinal effects of family–school–person interactions on student outcomes. In A. C. Kerckhoff (Ed.), *Research in sociology of education and socialization* (Vol. 4, pp. 101–127). Greenwich, CT: JAI.

Epstein, J. L., & Becker, H. J. (1982). Teachers' reported practices of parent involvement: Problems and possibilities. *Elementary School Journal, 83,* 103–113.

Gable, S., Belsky, J., & Crnic, K. (1995). Coparenting during the child's 2nd year: A descriptive account. *Journal of Marriage and the Family, 57,* 609–616.

Garmezy, N. (1976). The experimental study of children vulnerable to psychopathology. In A. Davids (Ed.), *Child personality and psychopathology: Current topics* (Vol. 2, pp. 171–216). New York: Wiley.

Garmezy, N. (1981). Children under stress: Perspectives on antecedents and correlates of vulnerability and resistance to psychopathology. In A. I. Rabin, J. Aronoff, A. M. Barclay, & R. A. Zucker (Eds.), *Further explorations in personality* (pp. 196–269). New York: Wiley.

Hawkes, G. R., Kutner, N. G., Wells, M. J., Christopherson, V. A., & Almirol, E. B. (1981). Families in cultural islands. In R. T. Coward & W. M. Smith (Eds.), *The family in rural society* (pp. 87–126). Boulder, CO: Westview Press.

Heyns, B. (1978). *Summer learning and the effects of schooling.* New York: Academic Press.

Jouriles, E. N., Murphy, C. M., Farris, A. M., Smith, D. A., Richters, J. E., & Waters, E. (1991). Marital adjustment, parental disagreements about child rearing, and behavior problems in boys: Increasing the specificity of the marital assessment. *Child Development, 62,* 1424–1433.

Lee, C. C. (1984). An investigation of psychosocial variables related to academic success for rural Black adolescents. *Journal of Negro Education, 53,* 424–434.

Lee, C. C. (1985). Successful rural Black adolescents: A psychosocial profile. *Adolescence, 20*(77), 129–142.

Lewis, E. (1989). Role strain in African-American women: The efficacy of social support networks. *Journal of Black Studies, 20,* 155–167.

Maccoby, E. E., Depner, C. E., & Mnookin, R. H. (1990). Coparenting in the second year after divorce. *Journal of Marriage and the Family, 52,* 141–155.

McAdoo, H. P. (1983). *Extended family support of Black single mothers: Final report to the National Institute of Mental Health.* Unpublished manuscript.

McHale, J. P. (1995). Coparenting and triadic interactions during infancy: The roles of marital distress and child gender. *Developmental Psychology, 31,* 985–996.

Morriset, C. E., Barnard, K. E., Greenberg, M. T., Booth, C. L., & Speiker, J. S. (1990). Environmental influences on early language development: The context of social risk. *Development and Psychopathology, 2,* 127–149.

O'Hare, W. P., & Curry-White, B. (1992). *The rural underclass: Examination of multiple problem populations in urban and rural settings.* Louisville, KY: Population Reference Bureau, University of Louisville.

Orthner, D. (1986, April). *Children and families in the South: Trends in health care, family services, and the rural economy* (Prepared statement for a hearing before the US House of Representatives Select Committee on Children, Youth, and Families, Macon, GA). Washington, DC: US Government Printing Office.

Reynolds, A. J. (1989). A structural model of first-grade outcomes for an urban, low socioeconomic status, minority population. *Journal of Educational Psychology, 81,* 594–603.

Rutter, M. (1979). Protective factors in children's responses to stress and disadvantage. In M. W. Kent & J. E. Rolf (Eds.), *Primary prevention of psychopathology: Vol. 3. Promoting social competence and coping in children* (pp. 49–74). Hanover, NH: University Press of New England.

Rutter, M. (1985). Resilience in the face of adversity: Protective factors and resistance to psychiatric disturbance. *British Journal of Psychiatry, 147,* 598–611.

Shimkin, D. B., Louie, G. J., & Frate, D. A. (1978). The Black extended family: A basic rural institution and a mechanism of urban adaptation. In D. B. Shimkin, E. M. Shimkin, & D. A. Frate (Eds.), *The extended family in Black societies* (pp. 25–148). The Hague, The Netherlands: Mouton.

Stevens, J. H., & Duffield, B. N. (1986). Age and parenting skill among Black women in poverty. *Early Childhood Research Quarterly, 1,* 221–235.

Stevenson, D., & Baker, D. (1987). The family–school relation and the child's school performance. *Child Development, 58,* 1348–1357.

Sudarkasa, N. (1988). Interpreting the African heritage in Afro-American family organization. In H. P. McAdoo (Ed.), *Black families* (2nd ed., pp. 27–43). Beverly Hills, CA: Sage.

Taylor, R. D., & Roberts, D. (1995). Kinship support and maternal and adolescent well-being in economically disadvantaged African-American families. *Child Development, 66,* 1585–1597.

Taylor, R. J. (1988). Structural determinants of religious participation among Black Americans. *Reveiw of Religious Research, 30,* 114–125.

Taylor, R. J., Thornton, M. C., & Chatters, L. M. (1987). Black Americans' perception of the sociohistorical role of the church. *Journal of Black Studies, 18,* 123–138.

Tickamyer, A. R., & Duncan, C. M. (1990). Poverty and opportunity structure in rural America. *Annual Review of Sociology, 16,* 67–86.

Tienda, M., & Angel, R. (1982). Headship and household composition among Blacks, Hispanics, and other Whites. *Social Forces, 61,* 508–531.

U. S. Bureau of the Census (1992, September). *Poverty in the United States, 1991.* Washington, DC: U.S. Department of Commerce.

Vaughn, B. E., Block, J. H., & Block, J. (1988). Parental agreement on child rearing during early childhood and the psychological characteristics of adolescents. *Child Development, 59,* 1020–1033.

Wilson, M. N. (1984). Mothers' and grandmothers' perspectives of parental behavior in three-generational Black families. *Child Development, 55,* 1333–1339.

Wilson, M. N. (1986). The Black extended family: An analytical consideration. *Developmental Psychology, 22,* 246–258.

Young, V. H. (1974). A Black American socialization pattern. *American Ethnologist, 1,* 415–431.

12

▼▼▼▼▼▼▼

Family Environmental Influences and Development: Illustrations From the Study of Undernourished Children

Theodore D. Wachs
Purdue University

Research about the nature and impact of family relations on development fits within the broader general area of the study of environmental influences. The systematic study of environmental influences on human behavior and development is a relatively recent scientific area of focus, dating from the early part of the present century (Wachs, 1992). Over the past century there has been an increasing emphasis on developing more complex conceptual frameworks that describe how the environment is structured and the processes whereby the environment influences variability in human behavior and development. Particularly within the past 15 years, with the increasing emphasis on contextual perspectives both in psychology in general (Hayes, 1993) and developmental psychology in particular (Reese, 1991), studies of family environment–development relations have also become increasingly influenced by contextual principles. In particular, the contextual principles of *openness* (development is probabilistic in nature) and *scope* (development occurs within a complex multidimensional multilevel web of influences) have become an integral part of environmental research and theory (Wachs & Shpancer, in press). At the same time, the nondeterministic aspects of classical contextualism, which sharply limit the possibility of generalizability of findings, have become particularly problematical to many developmental researchers (Reese, 1991). For environmentalists who are interested in the study of family influences, a strict contextual approach necessitates at least questioning whether we should expect invariant patterns of environment–development relations across different family contexts.

At present, the generalizability across different family contexts of the *content of environment* (specific domains of the environment that influence development, e.g., parental sensitivity and caregiver disciplinary practices) remains an open question. (For a review of this area see Wachs, 1996.) However, the study of environmental influences encompasses more than the study of content. In addition to content, the study of environmental influences also encompasses understanding the *processes of environmental action* (the means through which environmental variability relates to variability in development). What I show in the present chapter is that the processes underlying environmental influences at the level of the family may be generalizable across both different psychosocial and biosocial contexts.[1] At present, the bulk of developmental research is based on family studies using populations of adequately nourished children from developed Western countries (Schoepflin & Muller-Brettel, 1990). The specific question to be addressed in the present chapter is how well environmental action process mechanisms identified in studies with this population generalize to chronically undernourished or malnourished children living in non-Western, less-developed countries? To deal with this question I focus on the degree to which principles of environmental action identified in studies with adequately nourished children in Western developed countries can also be shown to be relevant to understanding developmental outcomes for undernourished children living in non-Western, less-developed countries.

ENVIRONMENTAL ACTION PROCESS MECHANISMS

Family Environmental Influences Operate Across a Wide Range

In his classic 1961 volume *Intelligence and Experience*, Hunt reviewed a half-century of research and came to the conclusion that the question of whether environment has an influence on development had been answered in the affirmative. For the most part this conclusion was accepted and expanded on by the vast majority of developmental researchers. However, in recent years this conclusion has been challenged by a small group of "predeterminist" researchers[2] who argue that only very extreme environments

---

[1]Whereas context is traditionally thought of in terms of sociocultural factors, contexts can also refer to stable individual characteristics that moderate how individuals perceive and react to external sociocultural factors. Hence, a child who is chronically malnourished can be viewed as being in a different biosocial context than a child who is adequately nourished, even if both are living in the same geographic area.

[2]The term *predeterminist* is used here in the sense used by Hunt (1961), namely that all development automatically unfolds as a function of genetically driven programs.

are relevant for development; nonextreme environments are viewed as essentially providing only random noise that contributes little to development (Rowe, 1994; Scarr, 1992). On empirical, methodological, and statistical grounds this viewpoint is very suspect. While a detailed summary of the multiple problems associated with this predeterminist viewpoint are beyond the scope of the present paper, a summary of these problems is listed in the following section. For detailed and referenced critiques see Baumrind (1993) and Wachs (1995a).

- *Methodological problems.* Conclusions based primarily on studies where environment is either assessed only as a residual term or via parent phenotype.
- *Statistical problems.* Low statistical power associated with indirect as opposed to direct measures of the environment.
- *Empirical problems.* Conclusion ignores a substantial body of infrahuman evidence showing how even nonextreme environmental manipulations can effect both central nervous system development and subsequent behavior; conclusion ignores multiple human studies showing how nonextreme family process variables can buffer (protect) the development of children who are at biological or psychosocial risk; conclusion ignores the influence of nonfamily nonextreme environmental factors, such as studies of school effects on cognitive performance.

In contrast to the threshold argument it seems clear that an overwhelming majority of evidence supports the position that environmental influences operate across a broad range (Wachs, 1996). Within this range more extreme environments can have a stronger influence than less extreme environments, but this in no way negates the salience of the family environment, even under what we consider to be normal rearing conditions.

Family Environment is Nested Within a Complex
Multilevel Structure

Although a large number of environmental variables has been identified as being salient for development (for a review see Wachs, 1992), it is clear from the pioneering work of Bronfenbrenner (1989) that we are not dealing with a fuzzy cloud of unrelated variables. Rather, as shown in Fig. 12.1, the environment operates as an interconnected multilevel dynamic system. This system encompasses proximal influences that impinge directly on the individual (e.g., the microsystem, which includes family environmental influences), the interconnection among these proximal systems (e.g., the mesosystem), as well as higher order environmental processes, which may not directly impinge on the individual, but which have the potential to influence individual development (e.g., exosystem, macrosystem; for a detailed description see Bronfenbrenner, 1989). In addition, each level of the environment

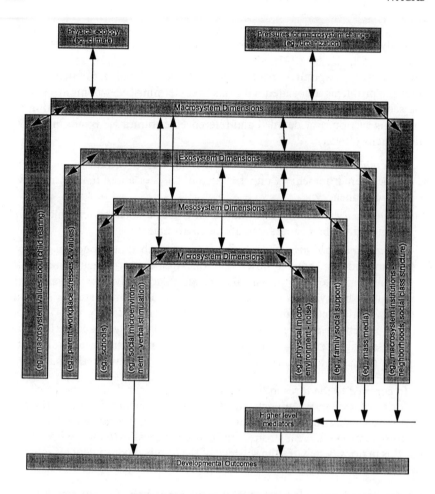

Double headed arrows refer to bidirectional levels of influence across the environment. Single headed arrows refer to direct or mediating influences of the environment upon development.

FIG. 12.1. The structure of the environment. From *The Nature of Nurture* by T. D. Wachs, 1992, Newbury Park, CA: Sage. Copyright © 1992 by Sage Publications. Reprinted by permission of Sage Publications.

is comprised of multiple subunits. For example, the microsystem is divided into both the physical and social domains (Wohlwill & Heft, 1987). The social microsystem can be further subdivided into a series of subdomains that are defined on the basis of source, modality, and characteristics of caregiver input (Bradley & Caldwell, 1995). Similarly, the physical microsystem can be divided into subdomains defined along such dimensions as the degree of stimulus salience and responsivity (Wachs, 1989) and spatial characteristics (Moore, 1987).

Although not clearly illustrated in Fig. 12.1 it is also important to recognize that different levels of the environment may systematically covary with each other. For example, children in lower quality day care are more likely to live in homes characterized by more stress and less parental involvement (Howes & Stewart, 1987). It is this covariance among different domains of the environment that defines levels of the environment such as the mesosystem. As shown in Fig. 12.1 there are three ways in which such an environmental system operates to influence development:

1. Higher levels of the environment will influence the nature of experiences encountered at more proximal levels, as in the case of culturally driven caregiver values influencing how parents view children, or when children should be taught specific skills (Goodnow, 1988). For example, culturally based beliefs about what types of behaviors should be encouraged in infants are mirrored in the types of interactions that infants have with their parents (Richman, Miller, & Levine, 1992). Similarly, level of ambient community violence was found to influence the parent's belief about the appropriateness of children's fighting and the degree to which parents believed they could control children's aggressive behavior; these belief systems in turn influenced the degree to which parents actually attempted to discourage the aggressive behavior of their children (Fry, 1988).

2. In addition to structuring the characteristics of lower level environmental influences, higher level environmental characteristics can also accentuate or attenuate the impact of more proximal family stimulation. For example, the relation of parent behaviors to children's cognitive and behavioral outcomes (Smith, Bradley, & McCarton, 1995) and to adolescent academic achievement (Steinberg, Lanborn, Dornbusch, & Darling, 1992) are moderated by the ethnic group membership of the parents. Higher level moderation of more proximal influences is not restricted just to the home environment. Based on cross-cultural data, Stevenson and Lee (1990) argued that culturally driven values concerning the importance of effort and education act to attenuate the impact on achievement of extremely crowded classrooms in Asian countries. Similarly, higher order moderation influences do not occur just for the microsystem. As shown by Goduka, Poole, and Aitki-Phenice (1992), relations between children's cognitive test scores and the exosystem factor of parental education level are moderated by even higher order macrosystem factors such as residence area.

3. Relations between different domains are bidirectional, both within and across levels. For example, parents clearly have the potential to influence the physical characteristics of the home environment within which their child lives (social microsystem influences physical microsystem). Going the other way, a consistent body of evidence also shows how physical microsystem characteristics, such as noise and crowding in the home, inhibit parents'

ability to provide developmentally appropriate environments for their child, as seen in lower levels of parental responsivity, vocalization and object scaffolding, which occurs when there are higher levels of noise and crowding in the home (physical microsystem influences social microsystem; Wachs, 1989). Bidirectionality also occurs across levels. For example, high social support (an exosystem dimension) can act to attenuate the detrimental impact of home crowding (microsystem) on behavior; however, over time high levels of crowding, in turn, act to attenuate the protective effects of social support (Lepore, Evans, & Schneider, 1991).

Environmental Influences Operate Across Time

Based on constructs from both the psychoanalytic and ethological domains, environmental researchers have had a long-standing interest in the question of whether very early family experiences, in and of themselves, can have long-term unalterable effects on subsequent behavior and development. With a few exceptions (e.g., environmental contributions to human binocular vision, Aslin, 1981 or to the development of phonological language features, Snow, 1987), previously dominant ideas about the unique importance of early environmental influences, as exemplified in such concepts as mother–infant bonding, have been tried and found to be wanting (Bornstein, 1989). In contrast to a simple sensitive-period hypothesis, the evidence currently indicates that the salience of a particular age period depends on the environmental parameters and the developmental outcomes under study, as well as on the nature of subsequent experiences encountered by the individual (Bornstein, 1989). For some developmental outcomes the impact of early experiences have a significant probability of being maintained in spite of changing circumstances later in life. As with the case of attachment this is particularly true when early parent–child relations help shape either the nature of later interpersonal relations or individual reactions to later experiences (Benoit & Parker, 1994). In contrast, for other outcomes the impact of later experiences may prove to be more salient than the impact of earlier experiences, as is most dramatically illustrated in the washout of early intervention effects when intervention follow-ups do not occur (Clarke & Clarke, 1989). Evidence is also available supporting the operation of a cumulative process, involving either the combined influence of early and later environmental influences, or the stability of environmental influences across time. In this latter case, development is a function of neither early nor later experiences, but rather of causal chain processes wherein early family experiences help to increase or to decrease the probability of certain types of later nonfamily experiences being encountered by the individual (Rutter, Champion, Quinton, Maughan, & Pickles, 1994). It is also important to emphasize that, rather than being mutually exclusive, all three patterns may be occurring simultaneously. For example, when predicting later general and school-age competence from proximal environmental assessments taken in infancy and again in middle childhood, Bradley, Caldwell, & Rock (1988) have shown that, for prediction of classroom behaviors, the salience of early environmental influences appears to be maintained even when statistically partialling out later experiences. For specific classroom competencies, later experiences appear to override the impact of earlier experiences, whereas for general competence the influences appear to be cumulative in nature.

Specificity of Environmental Action

One of the consequences of our increasing appreciation of the multidimensional nature of the environment has been a shift from a global to a specificity framework for understanding the processes underlying environmental influences. A global framework of environmental interaction (see Fig. 12.2) is based on the assumption that good aspects of the family environment will uniformly enhance all aspects of the development, whereas bad aspects will uniformly depress all aspects of development. Such a global framework underlies what Thomas and Chess (1980) have characterized as the "mal de la mère" syndrome, wherein all of a child's developmental problems are viewed as being caused by disturbances in the mother–child relationship. In contrast, a specificity framework (see Fig. 12.2) does not assume uniform environmental influences; rather, specificity is based on the proposition that different aspects of the environment act to influence different aspects of development (Wachs & Gruen, 1982).

Within a specificity framework individual dimensions of the family environment may act to facilitate, inhibit, or bear no relation to development, depending on the outcome variable under consideration. Specificity may occur across developmental domains as well as within subdomains of more general developmental domains. For example, aspects of maternal language stimulation have been found to uniquely predict toddler language skills but are unrelated to the level of toddler play; level of toddler play, in turn, is uniquely predicted by the quality of maternal play patterns that bear no relation to the level of toddler language (Tamis-LeMonda & Bornstein, 1994). Within the domain of early language development per se, development of new words is uniquely related to environmental indices encompassing the degree of exposure the child has to novel stimuli, whereas the child's functional use of language is uniquely related to indices of caregiver responsivity to the child's language (Wachs & Chan, 1986).

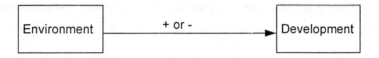

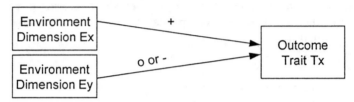

Conditional Specificity

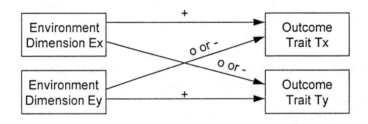

Strong Specificity

+ = positive influence
- = negative influence
o = no influence

FIG. 12.2. Global versus specificity models of environment action. From *The Nature of Nurture* by T. D. Wachs, 1992, Newbury Park, CA: Sage. Copyright © 1992 by Sage Publications. Reprinted by permission of Sage Publications.

Organism–Environment Covariance

Organism–environment covariance refers to the fact that certain biological or individual characteristics and certain environmental characteristics have a greater than chance probability of covarying with each other. One of the major contributions of behavioral genetic researchers has been to delineate the types of organism–environment covariance that may occur (Plomin, DeFries, & Loehlin, 1977).

The first type of organism–environment covariance that occurs is passive in nature. This type of covariance occurs when children receive both specific biological influences and specific environments from their parents. For example, to the extent that intelligence or education level has a heritable component, correlations between measures of parental intelligence and quality of their children's home environment (Gottfried & Gottfried, 1984) suggest the possibility of passive organism–environment covariance, in the sense that children of bright parents may inherit both genes predisposing toward higher intelligence and more stimulating environments from their parents.

The second type of covariance, *reactive organism–environment covariance*, refers to situations wherein children with specific characteristics have a greater probability of eliciting certain types of reactions from their parents. For example, children displaying overly intense or aggressive levels of behavior are more likely to elicit caregiver redirecting behaviors or parental punishment, whereas children displaying higher levels of passive or inactive behavior are more likely to elicit parental prompting (Bell & Chapman, 1986). Reactive covariance need not operate purely at the family level. As demonstrated by Olson (1992), antisocial children are much more likely to elicit long-term aggressive reactions from their classmates than are nonaggressive children.

Carried out over time, reactive covariance becomes a bidirectional transactional process wherein the child influences the environment and the environment, in turn, influences the child (Sameroff, 1989). Bidirectional transactional processes developing out of reactive covariance are seen in the work of Maccoby and colleagues (Maccoby, Snow, & Jacklin, 1984), showing that appropriate maternal teaching techniques can reduce the extent of children's difficult temperament but, over time, mothers get less and less involved with their difficult temperament children. A similar reactive covariance—bidirectional transactional process—is seen in the work of Patterson and Bank (1989), illustrating how escalating bidirectional fight cycles between parent and child can act to amplify disobedient behavior into actual conduct disorder.

Finally, there is *active covariance*. This process relates to situations wherein children with certain characteristics are more likely to seek out certain niches than are children without these characteristics. In spite of a good deal of theoretical emphasis on the importance of active covariance (Scarr & McCartney, 1983), there is remarkably little evidence on the actual operation of this process at the environmental level. One of the few examples is from the work of Gunnar (1994), who demonstrated that children with physiological patterns characteristic of high reactivity to novelty are less likely to seek out or engage other children in naturally occurring novel social situations.

Organism–Environment Interaction

One usage of the term organism–environment interaction refers to what Rutter (1983) called *additive coaction*, namely the operation of simultaneous multiple influences on development. The nature of this process is such that as the number of assessed influences increases, linear increases in our ability to predict specific outcomes occur. For example, available evidence shows a linear decline in children's IQ as the number of biological and environmental risk factors to which the child is exposed increases (Sameroff, Seifer, Baldwin, & Baldwin, 1993). Alternatively, as the number of protective factors in the child's family environment increases, high-risk children show significantly lower probabilities of displaying developmental deficits (Bradley et al., 1994).

Of greater theoretical interest is the question of whether nonlinear interactions occur between individual characteristics and the environment. Nonlinear interactions occur when a potential environmental factor influences development only for certain classes of individuals, or when relations between environment and development are multiplicative rather than additive for individuals with certain kinds of characteristics as in synergistic interactions (Rutter, 1983). These types of nonlinear interactions have the status in environmental theory similar to the status of top quarks in theoretical physics: theoretically important but very difficult to detect. The major reasons why nonlinear organism–environment interactions are so difficult to detect has been documented in a number of recent publications (McClelland & Judd, 1993; Wachs & Plomin, 1991). Identified problems include:

1. The atheoretical nature of most attempts to detect interaction (fishing expeditions); all too often the environmental or individual measures used are ones chosen for convenience rather than being specifically selected as likely to enter into interactions.

2. Use of insensitive (nonprecise) measures of organism and environment; the less precise the measure, the greater the error of measurement, and the less power available to actually detect interactions.

3. The lack of oversampling of extreme groups; this is particularly important when nonprecise measures are used. If extreme groups are used researchers may be able to get away with less precise measures, whereas if nonextreme groups are used then more precise environmental or individual measures are essential.

4. Low power found in most standard statistical tests of interaction, particularly when higher-order interactions are involved.

In spite of these difficulties, environmental researchers have been able to detect and replicate a number of organism–environment interactions (for a detailed review see Wachs, 1992). Available evidence indicates that there is significantly greater reactivity to stress for children with difficult temperaments (e.g., Crockenberg, 1987), high levels of stimulus sensitivity (Strelau, 1983) or insecure attachments (e.g., Sroufe & Egeland, 1991), as well as for children with biosocial risk histories including parental depression (Hammen et al., 1987) and parental schizophrenia (Walker, Downey, & Bergman, 1989). There is also a consistent body of evidence indicating that males are more adversely impacted than females by family environmental stress in the early years of life, whereas females are more reactive to stress in the adolescent years (Werner & Smith, 1992). Consistent evidence is also available indicating that children with externalizing behavioral characteristics have a higher probability of construing ambiguous stimuli as aggressive in nature than do nonaggressive children (Dodge, Coie, Pettit, & Price, 1990; Dodge, Pettit, McCluskey, & Brown, 1980). Some of these findings have been replicated cross-culturally. For example, the greater sensitivity of male infants to crowding has been replicated in Egypt (Wachs, Bishry, Sobhy, & McCabe, 1991), while the greater probability that aggressive boys will interpret neutral situations as aggressive in nature has been replicated in Japan (Tachibana & Hasegawa, 1986).

SUMMARY OF ENVIRONMENTAL ACTION PRINCIPLES

What has been documented up to the present is a number of the specific processes through which variability in family environment is translated into variability in children's development. These principles include the following:

1. Both extreme and nonextreme environmental influences act to influence development.
2. The environment is organized as a multilevel structure, such that the action of environmental influences at one level cannot be understood without reference to the nature of environmental influences at other levels.
3. The environment operates across time such that, depending on the outcome under consideration, early, later, or cumulative environmental influences may be most salient.
4. The environment operates in highly specific ways, such that different aspects of the environment are relevant for different aspects of development.
5. Environmental risk and protection factors covary with non-environmental risk and protective factors.
6. Contributions of the environment to development cannot be considered in isolation from the nature of the individual on whom the environment impacts.

The aforementioned principles of environmental action hold at the level of the family environment as well as at all other levels of the environment, at least for children living in Western developed countries. However, within a strict contextual framework, the generalizability of these principles for children living outside of Western developed countries is open to question. One test of the validity of a strict contextual framework is whether these same principles can also be shown to be operating as influences on the development of children living in a radically different context, namely chronically undernourished children living in non-Western, less-developed countries. Relevant data on this question are found in the following section.

CROSS-DOMAIN GENERALIZABILITY OF PRINCIPLES OF ENVIRONMENTAL ACTION

Nutritional Influences Operate Across a Wide Range

Although a clear majority of studies about nutrition and human development has involved populations with moderate to severe protein energy malnutrition, or clinical levels of micronutrient deficits such as anemia (Simeon & Grantham-McGregor, 1990), human nutritional researchers have been extremely careful not to explicitly assume a threshold model, wherein only clinical levels of nutritional deficits are related to deficits in human development. This caution is clearly warranted given recent results from studies of the relation between nutritional intake and development in Egyptian and Kenyan toddlers and school-age children who are chronically undernourished but are not clinically malnourished. While children in both countries were below the RDA (recommended daily allowance) in protein-energy intake, the level of protein-energy deficit was not sufficiently severe to reduce physical growth to a point indicating moderate to severe malnutrition (e.g., children were not wasted). Similarly, even though the majority of children in both countries were below the RDA for a number of trace minerals and vitamins, the level of micronutrient deficits were not sufficient to produce clinical signs (e.g., in both countries fewer than 10% of the sample were iron-deficient anemic). If nutrient deficits act only in a threshold manner, then we should expect to find no significant relation between developmental outcomes and level of intake of Egyptian and Kenyan children. However, consistent with the family environmental literature, studies of nutrition–behavior relations in these countries reveals that lower levels of energy intake are related to lower levels of toddler mental performance and symbolic play, and to less adequate patterns of social interaction and lower activity levels in the school-age years (Espinosa, Sigman, Neumann, Bwibo, & McDonald, 1992; Rahmanifar et al., 1993; Sigman, Neumann, Baksh, Bwibo, & McDonald, 1989; Sigman, Neumann, Jansen, & Bwibo, 1989; Sigman, McDonald, Neumann, & Bwibo, 1991; Wachs, 1993; Wachs et al., 1992). Higher levels of intake of animal source foods are related to higher levels of neonatal orientation and infant alertness, as well as to 5-year cognitive performance and higher activity levels in school-age children (Espinosa et al., 1992; Kirksey et al., 1991, 1994; Rahmanifar et al., 1993; Sigman, Neumann, Baksh et al., 1989; Sigman, Neumann, Jansen et al., 1989; Sigman et al., 1991). Intake of animal-source iron and zinc are related to infant alertness, Bayley MDI score, and school-age classroom behavior, while higher intake of B vitamins are related to faster neonatal habituation, higher levels of infant vocalization and alertness, and more toddler symbolic play (Kirksey et al., 1994; McCullough et al., 1990; Rahmanifar et al., 1993; Wachs, 1993; Wachs et al., 1995).

These data suggest a clear parallel between the environmental literature and the nutritional literature, in the sense that in neither domain is there strong evidence for a threshold model. Rather, both family environment and nutrition appear to operate across a wide range in terms of influencing human behavior and development.

Nutritional Influences Are Nested Within a Complex Multilevel System

As described previously, there is a consistent body of evidence illustrating how culturally driven beliefs and values can act to structure parent beliefs about children or parent emphasis on what behaviors should or should not be encouraged in children (Goodnow, 1988). Recent data also suggest parallels for this process in the human nutrition literature, though for the most part, available data is not at the family level per se. For example, recent data show that higher intake of animal-source foods by Egyptian female school-age children was associated with teachers rating these children as being less involved in the classroom (Wachs et al., 1995). This result is inconsistent both with our previous research showing a positive influence of animal-source foods and with other data from the same study showing that higher intake of animal-source foods was associated with teachers' ratings of females as displaying more classroom-directed attention seeking (e.g., asking the teacher questions about class material). These findings make sense only when we recognize the nature of Egyptian cultural expectations about the role of females. In traditional Egyptian culture, females are not supposed to seek attention (Fahmy, 1979). It is, therefore, not surprising to find that females who were rated by their teachers as being higher in classroom-directed attention seeking were also rated as being lower in classroom involvement ($r = -.51, p < .01$). Integrating higher order culturally driven expectations with proximal nutritional influences allows us to make sense out of what looks like a random finding; specifically, our results suggest that higher intake of animal-source foods increases females' classroom-directed attention seeking behavior, but this increase in attention seeking results in females being rated as less involved in the classroom, based on cultural expectations about what is appropriate female behavior in a school situation.

Examples of moderation by higher order contextual factors of proximal nutritional influences on behavior also appear in the literature. For example, Grantham-McGregor, Chang, Walker, & Powell (in press) have recently shown that providing food supplementation to Jamaican children results in more on-task behavior by children in some schools but either no effect or even less on-task behavior in other schools. The differences found are associated with contextual characteristics of the schools. Specifically, schools where supplemented children improved following food supplementation had individual rooms for each class, individual desks for each child, and the school was relatively quiet. Schools where children's performance deteriorated following supplementation were characterized by multiple classes in one room, multiple children at desks, and high levels of noise. Similar moderation effects also appear in supplementation studies done in Guatemala (Barrett, Radke-Yarrow, & Klein, 1982), wherein nutritional supplementation resulted in more prosocial behavior from children in certain villages and more aggressive behavior from children in other villages. Village differences in response to supplementation were associated with the harshness of ecological conditions in the different villages. These results suggest that the effects of nutritional supplementation increased the probability of occurrence of group-level predominant responses; which responses were predominant depended on ecologically driven characteristics such as harshness of climate or degree of chaos in the classroom.

Finally, we also see parallels in the human nutritional literature in regard to bidirectional influences. As noted earlier, it seems clear that the quantity and quality of nutritional intake can influence individual behavior and development. However, the adequacy of the child's diet can also be influenced not only by higher order contextual factors (e.g., percent of the family income earned by the mother or age of the primary caregiver of younger children, Engle, 1992), but also by individual characteristics such as the child's temperament. For example, available evidence indicates that fussy or difficult children are more likely to get a greater share of available food than are more calm, placid children (DeVries, 1984).

Once again we see parallels between results from the nutritional and environmental domains. In both domains higher order contextual influences act to structure and moderate the impact of more proximal nutritional and environmental influences; similarly, we see bidirectionality in influences, both within and across levels in both domains.

Nutritional Influences Operate Across a Background of Time

Parallel evidence for the dynamic interplay between early and later time periods can also be seen in the human nutrition literature, particularly for those studies where children with a history of early malnutrition received subsequent nutritional and psychosocial interventions. For example, the 15-point IQ difference favoring previously malnourished children who were subsequently reared in adoptive homes versus previously malnourished children who were reared in institutions illustrates how later positive contexts can overcome the effects of early-risk histories (Colombo, de la Parra, & Lopez, 1992). On the other hand, the significant and positive correlation between the later IQs of previously malnourished children and the length of time these children subsequently spent in more nutritionally and psychosocially advantaged family situations attests to the cumulative impact of interventions across time (Paine, Dorea, Pasquali, & Monteior, 1992). However, when previously malnourished children are adopted into later nutritionally and environmentally adequate circumstances, the degree of gain shown by these children is dependent on the level of early malnutrition originally encountered (Winick, Meyer, & Harris, 1975). These results clearly illustrate the potential long-term influence of early nutritional history. These overall findings from the nutritional literature clearly parallel the complex interrelationship of time and family environment shown earlier, again suggesting that simplified sensitive-period models do not do justice to the complex processes wherein both environment and biology operate to influence development across time.

Specificity Operates Across Cultures and for Nonenvironmental Influences

Evidence for the operation of specificity processes can also be demonstrated across different cultures. Based on data from research involving young children in Western developed countries, available evidence suggests that level of toddler vocalization is uniquely related to level of caregiver vocalization, while the degree of toddler distress is uniquely related to the degree to which caregivers respond to such distress. This specificity pattern has been replicated using a population of chronically undernourished Egyptian toddlers (Wachs, Bishry et al., 1993). Replication of patterns of specific environment–development relations for the United States and Japan has also been shown by Bornstein, Azuma, Tamis-LeMonda, & Ogino (1990).

While it would be tempting to speculate about the operation of specificity processes in nutrition–development relations (e.g., the high sensitivity of measures of discrimination learning to iron deficiency; Pollitt, 1993) such speculation would probably be premature at the present time. However, it is worth noting that some biological studies do suggest that such parallels may well exist. For example, Bendersky & Lewis (1994) reported that environmental risk indices are much more strongly predictive of early language development than are biological risk indices; in contrast, biological risk indices appear to be much stronger predictors of gross motor development than are environmental risk indices.[3]

From an environmental perspective, one of the most important implications of the operation of specificity has to do with the assessment of family environments. To the extent that specificity processes are operating, the use of global measures of the environment may well act to mask the role of specific family environmental influences by lumping together both predictive and nonpredictive aspects of the environment in a single score, which McCall & Applebaum (1991) called the "problem of infinite dilution" (p. 915). To the extent that nutritional specificity processes are also operating, it may be as important to assess the impact of specific nutrients as it is to use global measures such as energy intake (k-cal) as predictors.

Covariance Processes Also Operate at the Nutritional Level

Although evidence for the operation of active covariance at the nutritional level also is relatively scarce, theoretical formulations along these lines have been developed by nutritional researchers. Both the concepts of *nutritional adaptation* (adults reduce or increase their activity level to correspond to their level of nutritional intake, Scrimshaw & Young, 1989), and the concept of *functional isolation* (lower motor activity associated with malnutrition results in a child living in a relatively restricted environmental niche, Pollitt, Gorman, Engle, Martorell, & Rivera, 1993), are nutritional parallels to what was described previously as active organism–environment covariance.

In contrast, ample evidence is available on the operation of *passive organism (nutritional status)–environment covariance*. Children at risk for malnutrition are much more likely to also encounter a variety of environmental risk factors than are adequately nourished children, including both general (Powell & Grantham-McGregor, 1985) and specific (Cravioto & DeLicarde, 1972) psychosocial stimulation deficits. A similar pattern can be seen in the case of micronutrients. When Egyptian mothers are low in level of vitamin B6, not only do their neonates receive less of this critical nutrient (through lower levels of B6 in the mothers' breast milk), but they also receive less maternal responsivity and less effective maternal responsivity as a consequence of the mothers nutritional deficit (McCullough et al., 1990).

In terms of *reactive organism (nutritional status)–environment covariance*, previous research has shown how supplementation of previously malnourished children results in differential treatment of these children by their caregivers (e.g., Chavez & Martinez, 1984). However, until recently it was unclear whether the differential treatment could also be due to supplemen-

---

[3]Specificity processes may also underlie what behavioral genetic researchers have called nonshared environmental variance (Wachs, 1992).

tation also being given to the parents, which would suggest passive rather than reactive covariance. In a cross-cultural study designed to separate parent from child nutritional influences, measures were taken of both child and caregiver nutritional intake as well as of five caregiver behaviors. Hierarchical regression was used to test whether child intake, caregiver intake, or the combination of child and caregiver intake best predicted caregiver behaviors. For four out of five comparisons (there was no difference for speed of response to distress), the Egyptian data indicate that child intake was the primary predictor of caregiver behavior patterns, even after controlling for level of caregiver intake; a parallel pattern was shown in Kenya (Wachs et al., 1992). These results, indicating that changes in caregiver behaviors are a function of child rather than caregiver intake, illustrate the operation of reactive organism–environment covariance at the nutritional level.

The parallel findings in regard to the operation of organism–environment covariance for both the environmental and nutritional domains emphasize the importance of this process as a salient influence on development. Unfortunately, for the most part, both environmental and biological researchers have sought to minimize, rather than to highlight, the contributions of covariance to development through experimentally or statistically partialling out what is often regarded as *nuisance variance* (variance from domains other than what is the focus of study). Although it is always possible to do statistical or experimental partialling to separate out covarying influences, the fact that such statistical separation is possible does not always mean that it is necessarily desirable. If our goal is to understand the processes underlying individual differences in behavior and development, and if underlying processes covary, then we may be making a major mistake if we attempt to artificially separate what nature has joined together. If there is organism–environment covariance, it is as essential to interpret family environmental influences within the context of covarying biological (genetic or nutritional) parameters as it is to interpret biological influences within the context of covarying family environmental parameters. In this situation our unit of analysis should be neither the environment nor the biological status of the organism taken in isolation. Rather, our unit of analysis should be the degree and nature of covariance between family environmental factors and either biologically driven individual characteristics such as temperament, or direct biological measures such as nutritional intake or DNA sequence.

Organism–Environment Interaction Operates at the Nutritional Level

Evidence from recent multivariate studies clearly shows that combinations of nutritional and nonnutritional risk factors are significantly more likely to produce developmental deficits than are individual nutritional or nonnutritional risk factors taken in isolation (for a review see Wachs, 1995b).[4] Evidence for nonlinear nutrient–environment interactions, though rare, also can be found. One example showing evidence for both additive coactions and nonlinear interactions is found in research relating specific nutrients and environment to development of Egyptian toddlers (Wachs, Moussa et al., 1993). Through use of hierarchical regression, it is possible to test whether an additive coaction term (nutrition plus family environment) adds significant variance over and above the level of nutritional status per se; it is also possible to test whether a nonlinear interactive term (family nutrition × environment) adds significant predictive variance over and above that accounted for by the nutrient predictor or the additive coaction term taken in isolation. When predicting Bayley MDI scores, our results indicate additive coaction occurring between family caregiver's nonverbal response to toddler vocalization and toddler intake of energy, protein, fat, carbohydrates, animal k-cal, or animal protein. In contrast, for the prediction of symbolic play, our results reveal significant nonlinear interactions between family caregiver nonvocal response to vocalization and toddlers' intake of either animal k-cal or animal protein (Wachs, Moussa et al., 1993).

Again we find parallels between environmental research and results from studies of nutrition and development. In both domains we find evidence for both additive and nonadditive interactions between organism and environment. One of the critical conclusions from this parallel line of evidence reaffirms the conclusion previously made in regard to organism–environment covariance, namely that we cannot consider the influence of the family environment in isolation from the influence of the individual on whom the environment impinges. Specifically, it is no longer a question of which environment optimizes development, but rather of which environment is most appropriate for which individual. These parallels again suggest the importance of linkages between the study of family environmental influences and the study of influences from other domains including the genetic, biomedical, and nutritional.

CONCLUSIONS

In discussing the nature and characteristics of environmental influences on children's development, it is perhaps an understatement to say that the role environment plays in development is an extremely complex one. In order to

---

[4]Available evidence also indicates that there are nutrient-nutrient interactions, wherein deficits associated with a critical micronutrient (e.g., iron) are amplified when there are also deficits in other micronutrients that influence bioavailability of the critical micronutrients (e.g., iron can interact with calcium and vitamin C, Wachs, 1995b).

understand the nature of family environmental influences, it is important to encompass principles such as multiple levels of the environment, changes in the impact and nature of salient environmental influences over time, environmental specificity, and both covariance and interaction between individual and environment. While such complexity may not seem to fit our treasured notion of scientific parsimony, it is important to emphasize that parsimony does not mean the simplest explanation per se, but rather the simplest explanation that fits the available phenomena. The role of environmental influences on human development is a very complex one and requires explanatory models that honor this complexity.

While such complexity may seem to be quite discouraging, it is also important to remember that many of the underlying processes wherein variability in environment translates into variability in development (e.g., specificity, covariance, nonthreshold influences) generalize across both countries and populations, as illustrated in the parallel processes shown to influence both the development of adequately nourished children from Western developed countries and undernourished children from less-developed countries. In this sense we may conclude that the nature of environmental influences, while more complex than perhaps desired, are potentially more generalizable then we had believed possible.

The importance of the generalizability of family environmental processes across populations may be particularly critical when considering development of risk groups in the United States. Research on nutrition and development in advantaged countries, such as the United States, has been hampered by two misleading assumptions. The first is that malnutrition is not really a problem in developed countries; the second is that whereas some children in developed countries may be undernourished, malnutrition is an influence on development only at the extremes. The falsity of this latter assumption has been noted earlier in this chapter. In terms of the former assumption, a review from the Tufts University Center on Hunger, Poverty, and Nutrition Policy (Cook & Martin, 1995) clearly shows that, in terms of energy intake (K-cal), more than 1 million U.S. children fall below 70% of the recommended daily allowance—one standard deviation below the mean. Several million children living in poverty are below 70% of RDA of zinc intake while between 20%–25% of poor children in the United States may be suffering from iron deficiency. Given the high probability that chronic undernutrition covaries with environmental risk factors, it seems clear that research with children living in poverty in developed countries such as the United States needs to take account of both environmental and nutritional influences on children's development.

The aforementioned evidence also suggests the importance of multifocal rather than monofocal interventions, encompassing both nutritional and environmental parameters. The work of Grantham-McGregor and colleagues (Grantham-McGregor, Powell, Walker, Chang, & Fletcher, 1994) is exemplary in this regard, in terms of showing how stronger and more stable intervention effects occur when relatively low-cost interventions encompass both nutritional and environmental parameters. In designing multifocal intervention efforts for poverty populations in developed countries, I further argue that such efforts need to be based on the underlying mechanisms discussed in this chapter. For example, issues concerning what types of interventions are most effective for what types of outcomes, what ages might be most sensitive to combined nutritional and environmental interventions, what groups of children might be in greatest need of such intervention, or ways of tailoring specific interventions to specific groups of children, are among those that need to be considered in future intervention efforts with children at risk and their families. By utilizing intervention strategies that come from basic research on biological and environmental determinants of development we maximize the chances, not only of increasing collaborative research efforts among scientists from different domains, but also of developing research strategies that are optimal for children encountering multiple biological and family environmental risks.

ACKNOWLEDGMENTS

Collection of the Egyptian and Kenyan Nutritional Data reported in the chapter was supported by AID contracts DAN-1309-55-1070-002; DAN-1309-A009090.

REFERENCES

Aslin, R. (1981). Experiential influences and sensitive periods in perceptual development. In R. Aslin, J. Alberts, & N. Pedersen (Eds.), *Development of perception* (pp. 45–93). New York: Academic Press.

Barrett, D., Radke-Yarrow, N., & Klein, R. (1982). Chronic malnutrition and child behavior. *Developmental Psychology, 18*, 541–556.

Baumrind, D. (1993). The average expectable environment is not good enough. *Child Development, 64*, 1299–1317.

Bell, R., & Chapman, N. (1986). Child effects in studies using experimental or brief longitudinal approaches to socialization. *Developmental Psychology, 22*, 595–603.

Bendersky, M., & Lewis, M. (1994). Environmental risk, biological risk in developmental outcome. *Developmental Psychology, 30*, 484–494.

Benoit, D., & Parker, K. (1994). Stability and transmission of attachment across three generations. *Child Development, 65*, 1444–1456.

Bornstein, M. (1989). Sensitive periods in development. *Psychological Bulletin, 105*, 179–197.

Bornstein, M., Azuma, H., Tamis-LeMonda, C., & Ogino, M. (1990). Mother and infant activity and interaction in Japan and the United States. *International Journal of Behavioral Development, 13*, 267–288.

Bradley, R., & Caldwell, B. (1995). Caregiving and the regulation of child growth and development: Describing proximal aspects of caregiving systems. *Developmental Review, 15*, 38–55.

Bradley, R., Caldwell, B., & Rock, S. (1988). Home environment and school performance: A 10 year follow-up and examination of three models of environmental action. *Child Development, 59*, 852–867.

Bradley, R., Whiteside, L., Mundfrom, D., Casey, P., Kelleher, K., & Pope, S. (1994). Early indications of resilience and their relation to experiences in the home environments of low birth weight premature children living in poverty. *Child Development, 65*, 346–360.

Bronfenbrenner, U. (1989). Ecological systems theories. *Annals of Child Development, 6*, 187–249.

Chavez, A., & Martinez, C. (1984). Behavioral measurements of activity and children and their relation to food intake in a poor community. In E. Pollitt & P. Amante (Eds.), *Energy intake and activity* (pp. 303–321). New York: Liss.

Clarke, A., & Clarke, A. (1989). The later cognitive effects of early intervention. *Intelligence, 13*, 289–297.

Colombo, M., de la Parra, A., & Lopez, I. (1992). Intellectual and physical outcome of children undernourished in early life is influenced by later environmental conditions. *Developmental Medicine and Child Neurology, 34*, 611–622.

Cook, J., & Martin, K. (1995). Differences in nutrient adequacy among poor and nonpoor children. *Center on Hunger, Poverty and Nutrition Policy Monograph*. Medford, MA: Tufts University School of Nutrition.

Cravioto, J., & DeLicardie, E. (1972). Environmental correlates of severe clinical malnutrition and language development in survivors from kwashiorkor or marasmus (publication #251). Washington, DC: Pan American Health Organization.

Crockenberg, S. (1987). Predictors and correlates of anger toward and punitive control of toddlers by adolescent mothers. *Child Development, 58*, 964–975.

DeVries, M. (1984). Temperament and infant mortality among the Masai of East Africa. *American Journal of Psychiatry, 141*, 1189–1194.

Dodge, K., Coie, J., Pettitt, G., & Price, J. (1990). Peer status and aggression in boys groups. *Child Development, 61*, 1289–1309.

Dodge, K., Pettitt, G., McCluskey, C., & Brown, M. (1980). Social competency in children. *Monographs of the Society for Research in Child Development, 51*(Serial No. 213).

Engle, P. (1992, March). *Care and child nutrition*. Paper presented to the UNICEF International Nutrition Conference, New York.

Espinosa, M., Sigman, M., Neumann, C., Bwibo, N., & McDonald, M. (1992). Playground behaviors of school-age children in relation to nutrition, schooling and family characteristics. *Developmental Psychology, 28*, 1188–1195.

Fahmy, H. (1979). Changing women in a changing society: The study of emerging consciousness of young women in the city of Akhmin in upper Egypt. *Cairo Papers in the Social Sciences, 3*, 30–59.

Fry, D. (1988). Intercommunity differences in aggression among Zapotec children. *Child Development, 59*, 1108–1119.

Goduka, I., Poole, D., & Aitki-Phenice, L. (1992). A comparative study of Black South Africa children from three different contexts. *Child Development, 63*, 509–525.

Goodnow, J. (1988). Parents ideas, actions and feelings. *Child Development, 59*, 286–302.

Gottfried, A. E., & Gottfried, A. W. (1984). Home environment and cognitive development in young children of middle socioeconomic status families. In A. Gottfried (Ed.), *Home environment and early cognitive development* (pp. 57–116). Orlando, FL: Academic Press.

Grantham-McGregor, S., Chang, S., Walker, S., & Powell, C. (in press). Jamaican school feeding studies. In S. Grantham-McGregor (Ed.), *Health, nutrition and children's development and achievement*. Washington, DC: Pan American Health Organization.

Grantham-McGregor, S., Powell, C., Walker, S., Chang, S., & Fletcher, P. (1994). The longterm follow-up of severely malnourished children who participated in an intervention program. *Child Development, 65*, 428–439.

Gunnar, M. (1994). Psychoendocrine studies of temperament and stress in early childhood. In J. Bates & T. D. Wachs (Eds.), *Temperament: Individual differences at the interface of biology and behavior* (pp. 175–198). Washington, DC: American Psychological Association.

Hammen, C., Adrian, C., Gordon, D., Berge, D., Jaenicke, C., & Hiroto, D. (1987). Children of depressed mothers: Maternal strain and symptom predictors of dysfunction. *Journal of Abnormal Psychology, 96*, 190–198.

Hayes, S. C. (1993). Analytic goals and the varieties of scientific contextualism. In S. C. Hayes, L. J. Hayes, H. W. Reese, & T. R. Sarbin (Eds.), *Varieties of scientific contextualism* (pp. 11–27). Reno, NV: Context Press.

Howes, C., & Stewart, P. (1987). Child's play with adults, toys and peers: An examination of family and child care influences. *Developmental Psychology, 23*, 423–430.

Hunt, J. M. (1961). *Intelligence and experience.* New York: Ronald.

Kirksey, A., Rahmanifar, A., Wachs, T., McCabe, G., Bassily, N., Bishry, Z., Galal, O., Harrison, G., & Jerome, N. (1991). Determinants of pregnancy outcome and newborn behavior of a semirural Egyptian population. *American Journal of Clinical Nutrition, 49*, 657–667.

Kirksey, A., Wachs, T. D., Srinath, U., Rahmanifar, A., McCabe, G., Galal, O., Bassily, N., Bishry, Z., Yunis, F., Harrison, G., & Jerome, N. (1994). Relation of maternal zinc nutriture to pregnancy outcome and early infant development in an Egyptian village. *American Journal of Clinical Nutrition, 60*, 782–792.

Lepore, S., Evans, G., & Schneider, N. (1991). Dynamic role of social support in the link between chronic stress and psychological distress. *Journal of Personality and Social Psychology, 61*, 899–909.

Maccoby, E., Snow, M., & Jacklin, C. (1984). Children's disposition and mother child interactions at 12 and 18 months. *Developmental Psychology, 20*, 459–472.

McCall, R., & Applebaum, M. (1991). Some issues of conducting secondary analyses. *Developmental Psychology, 27*, 911–917.

McClelland, G., & Judd, C. (1993). Statistical difficulties of detecting interaction and moderator effects. *Psychological Bulletin, 114*, 376–390.

McCullough, A., Kirksey, A., Wachs, T. D., McCabe, G., Bassily, N., Bishry, Z., Galal, O., Harrison, G., & Jerome, N. (1990). Vitamin B-6 status of Egyptian mothers: Relation to infant behavior and maternal infant interactions. *American Journal of Clinical Nutrition, 51*, 1067–1074.

Moore, G. (1987). The physical environment and cognitive development in child care centers. In C. Weinstein & G. David (Eds.), *Spaces for children* (pp. 41–72). New York: Plenum.

Olson, S. (1992). Development of conduct problems and peer rejection in preschool children. *Journal of Abnormal Child Psychology, 20*, 327–350.

Paine, P., Dorea, J. G., Pasquali, J., & Monteior, A. M. (1992). Growth and cognition in Brazilian school children: A spontaneously occurring intervention study. *International Journal of Behavioral Development, 15*, 160–183.

Patterson, G., & Bank, L. (1989). Some amplifying mechanism for pathological processes in families. In M. Gunnar & E. Thelen (Eds.), *Systems in development: The Minnesota Symposium on Child Psychology* (Vol. 22, pp. 167–210). Hillsdale: Lawrence Erlbaum Associates.

Plomin, R., DeFries, J., & Loehlin, J. (1977). Geneotype environment interaction and correlation in the analysis of human development. *Psychological Bulletin, 84*, 309–322.

Pollitt, E. (1993). Iron deficiency and cognitive function. *Annual Review of Nutrition, 13*, 521–538.

Pollitt, E., Gorman, K., Engle, P., Martorell, R., & Rivera, J. (1993). Early supplementary feeding and cognition: Effects over two decades. *Monographs of the Society for Research in Child Development, 58*(Serial No. 17).

Powell, C., & Grantham-McGregor, S. (1985). The ecology of nutritional status and development of young children in Kingston, Jamaica. *American Journal of Clinical Nutrition, 31*, 1322–1331.

Rahmanifar, A., Kirksey, A., Wachs, T. D., McCabe, G., Bishry, Z., Galal, O., Harrison, G., & Jerome, N. (1993). Diet during lactation associated with infant behavior and caregiver infant interaction in a semi-rural Egyptian village. *Journal of Nutrition, 123,* 164–175.

Reese, H. (1991). Contextualism and developmental psychology. In H. Reese (Ed.), *Advances in child development and behavior, Vol. 23* (pp. 188–231). New York: Academic Press.

Richman, A., Miller, P., & LeVine, R. (1992). Cultural and educational variations in maternal responsiveness. *Developmental Psychology, 28,* 614–621.

Rowe, D. (1994). *The limits of family influence.* New York: Guilford.

Rutter, M. (1983). Statistical and personal interactions. In D. Magnusson & V. Allen (Eds.), *Human development: An interactional perspective* (pp. 295–320). New York: Academic Press.

Rutter, M., Champion, L., Quinton, D., Maughan, B., & Pickles, A. (1994). Understanding individual differences in environmental risk exposure. In P. Moen & G. Elder (Eds), *Examining lives in context* (pp. 61–96). Washington, DC: American Psychological Association.

Sameroff, A. (1989). General systems and the regulation of development. In M. Gunnar & E. Thelen (Eds.), *Systems and development* (pp. 219–238). Hillsdale: Lawrence Erlbaum Associates.

Sameroff, A., Seifer, R., Baldwin, A., & Baldwin, C. (1993). Stability of intelligence from preschool to adolesence. *Child Development, 64,* 80–97.

Scarr, S. (1992). Developmental theories of the 1990s. *Child Development, 63,* 1–19.

Scarr, S., & McCartney, K. (1983). How people make their own environments. *Child Development, 54,* 424–425.

Schoepflin, U., & Muller-Brettel, M. (1990). Scope and trends. *International Journal of Behavioral Development, 13,* 393–406.

Scrimshaw, N., & Young, V. (1989). Adaptation to low protein and energy intakes. *Human Organization, 48,* 20–30.

Sigman, M., McDonald, M., Neumann, C., & Bwibo, N. (1991). Prediction of cognitive competence in Kenyan children from toddlers nutrition, family characteristics and abilities. *Journal of Child Psychology and Psychiatry, 32,* 307–320.

Sigman, M., Neumann, N., Baksh, N., Bwibo, N., & McDonald, M. (1989). Relationship between nutrition and development in Kenya toddlers. *Journal of Pediatrics, 115,* 357–364.

Sigman, M., Neumann, C., Jansen, A., & Bwibo, N. (1989). Cognitive abilities of Kenyan children in relation to nutrition, family characteristics, and education. *Child Development, 60,* 1463–1474.

Simeon, D. T., & Grantham-McGregor, S. (1990). Nutritional deficiencies and children's behavior and mental development. *Nutrition Research Reviews, 3,* 1–24.

Smith, J., Bradley, R., & McCarton, C. (1995, April). *The HOME inventory: Reliability and prediction of child outcome across three racial-ethnic groups.* Paper presented at the meeting of the Society for Research in Child Development. Indianapolis, IN.

Snow, C. (1987). Relevance of the notion of a critical period to language acquisition. In M. Bornstein (Ed.), *Sensitive periods in development.* Hillsdale, NJ: Lawrence Erlbaum Associates.

Sroufe, A., & Egeland, B. (1991). Illustrations of person–environment interaction from a longitudinal study. In T. D. Wachs & R. Plomin (Eds.), *Conceptualization and measurement of organism–environment interaction* (pp. 68–86). Washington, DC: American Psychological Association.

Steinberg, L., Lanborn, S., Dornbusch, S., & Darling, N. (1992). Impact of parenting practices on adolescent achievement. *Child Development, 63,* 1266–1281.

Stevenson, H., & Lee, S. (1990). Contexts of achievement. *Monographs of the Society for Research in Child Development, 55*(Serial No. 221).

Strelau, J. (1983). *Temperament, personality and activity.* New York: Academic Press.

Tachibana, Y., & Hasegawa, E. (1986). Aggressive responsive of adolescents to a hypothetical frustrating situation. *Psychological Reports, 58,* 111–118.

Tamis-LeMonda, C., & Bornstein, M. (1994). Specificity in mother toddler language play relation across the second year. *Developmental Psychology, 30*, 283–292.

Thomas A., & Chess, S. (1980). *The dynamics of psychological development.* New York: Brunner/ Mazel.

Wachs, T. D. (1989). The nature of the physical micro-environment: An expanded classification system. *Merrill-Palmer Quarterly, 35*, 399–420.

Wachs, T. D. (1992). *The nature of nurture.* Newbury Park, CA: Sage.

Wachs, T. D. (1993). Multidimensional correlates of individual variability in play and exploration. In M. Bornstein & A. O'Reilly (Eds.), *The role of play in the development of thought* (pp. 43–54). San Francisco: Jossey-Bass.

Wachs, T. D. (1995a). Genetic and family influences on individual development: Both necessary, neither sufficient. *Psychological Inquiry, 6*, 161–173.

Wachs, T. D. (1995b). Relation of mild to moderate malnutrition to human development: Correlational studies. *Journal of Nutrition Supplement, 125*, 22455–22555.

Wachs, T. D. (1996). Environmental and intelligence: Current status future directions. In D. Detterman (Ed.), *Current topics in human intelligence* (Vol. 5, pp. 69–86). Norwood, NJ: Ablex.

Wachs, T. D., Bishry, Z., Moussa, W., Yunis, F., McCabe, G., Harrison, G., Swefi, I., Kirksey, A., Galal, O., Jerome, N., & Shaheen, F. (1995). Nutritional intake and context as predictors of cognition and adaptive behavior of Egyptian school age children. *International Journal of Behavioral Development, 18*, 425–450.

Wachs, T. D., Bishry, Z., Sobhy, A., & McCabe, G. (1991, April). *Sex differences in the relation of rearing environment to adaptive behavior of Egyptian toddlers.* Paper presented at the meeting of the Society for Research on Child Development. Seattle, WA.

Wachs, T. D., Bishry, Z., Sobhy, A., McCabe, G., Shaheen, F., & Galal, O. (1993). Relation of rearing environment to adaptive behavior of Egyptian toddlers. *Child Development, 67*, 586–604.

Wachs, T. D., & Chan, A. (1986). Specificity of environmental action as seen in physical and social environmental correlates of 3 aspects of 12 month infant's communication performance. *Child Development, 57*, 1464–1475.

Wachs, T. D., & Gruen, G. (1982). *Early experience and human development.* New York: Plenum.

Wachs, T. D., Moussa, W., Bishry, Z, Yunis, F., Sobhy, A., McCabe, G., Terome, N., Galal, O., Harrison, G., & Kirksey, A. (1993). Relations between nutrition and cognitive performance in Egyptian toddlers. *Intelligence, 17*, 151–172.

Wachs, T. D., & Plomin, R. (1991). *Conceptualization and measurement of organism–environment interaction.* Washington, DC: American Psychological Association.

Wachs, T. D., Sigman, M., Bishry, Z., Moussa, W., Jerome, N., Neumann, C., Bwibo, N., & McDonald, M. (1992). Caregiver child interaction patterns in two cultures in relation to nutrition. *International Journal of Behavioral Development, 15*, 1–18.

Wachs, T. D., & Sphancer, N. (in press). A contextual perspective on child environment relations. In D. Gorlitz, H. Harloff, J. Valsiner, & B. May (Eds.), *Children, cities and psychological theories.* Berlin: DeGruyter.

Walker, E., Downey, G., & Bergman, A. (1989). The effects of parental psychopathology and maltreatment on child behavior. *Child Development, 60*, 15–24.

Werner, E., & Smith, R. (1992). *Overcoming the odds: High risk children from birth to adulthood.* Ithaca, New York: Cornell University Press.

Winick, N., Meyer, K., & Harris, R. (1975). Malnutrition and environmental enrichment by early adoption. *Science, 190*, 1173–1175.

Wohlwill, J., & Heft, H. (1987). The physical environment and the development of the child. In I. Altman & J. Stokels (Eds.), *Handbook of environmental psychology* (pp. 282–328). New York: Wiley.

13

▼▼▼▼▼▼▼

Child and Family Outcomes Over Time: A Longitudinal Perspective on Developmental Delays

Barbara K. Keogh
Lucinda P. Bernheimer
Ronald Gallimore
Thomas S. Weisner
University of California, Los Angeles

BACKGROUND AND INTRODUCTION

This chapter is focused on outcomes for children with developmental delays and their families. Children with developmental delays identified in the preschool years present unique problems, as they often do not fit the usual diagnostic categories. The delays may be expressed as generalized slowness in reaching expected milestones, or by delays in specific areas, such as language or motor skills. Despite uncertainties about etiology and diagnosis, and the heterogeneity of problems identified by the term, there is increasing support for the category as a justification for providing early services for young children and families (Bernheimer, Keogh, & Coots, 1993; McLean, Smith, McCormick, Shakel, & McEvoy, 1991). It is clear, too, that families of children with developmental delays, as well as the children themselves, may benefit from services and support. Indeed, parents with children who have nonspecific delays face particular and sometimes excessive demands, including coping with the ambiguities and uncertainties of the children's conditions and futures.

Based on our work in Project CHILD, a 10-year longitudinal study of young children with developmental delays and their families, we argue that both children and families must be considered as meaningful units of analysis when assessing outcomes. We suggest further that outcomes for both children and families must be differentiated to address a range of conditions and problems and that time and setting effects must be taken into account. In our approach we have relied on theory and findings from different disciplines and professional perspectives, including the burgeoning research about risk and resilience, which has identified a number of child, family, and contextual conditions associated with different developmental outcomes for children (see Masten, Best, & Garmezy, 1990; Pianta, Egeland, & Sroufe, 1990; Rutter, 1990; Werner & Smith, 1989, 1992). Understandably, the focus in most developmental studies has been on the characteristics of children, and the literature on risk provides a solid basis for defining child outcomes. Less is known about the range of outcomes for families. While proximal and distal family characteristics have been investigated as contributors to children's development (Baldwin, Baldwin, & Cole, 1990; Caldwell & Bradley, 1994), family status and adaptive conditions have seldom been studied as outcomes themselves. How families function in response to a child with problems is critical to our understanding of developmental delay over time and, thus, deserves to be a major component in the study of outcomes.

Reactive-Stress Models of Family Adjustment

Historically, family adjustment to children with delays has been considered within a reactive, mental health model. A large literature suggests that families with children with developmental problems experience high levels of stress and family disruption (Boyce & Barnett, 1993; Hampson, Hulgus, Beavers, & Beavers, 1988; Longo & Bond, 1984; Minnes, 1988). Researchers have described the negative impact of a disabled child on the family, citing higher than expected rates of maternal depression (Carr, 1988; Trute, 1995), marital problems (Gabel, McDowell, & Cerreto, 1983) and sibling problems (Gath, 1973). A common generalization is that a problem child equates to a problem family.

A smaller, but growing, body of work questions this model of expected impairment (Boyce & Barnett, 1993), as well as the association between increased parental stress and family maladjustment or dysfunction (Dyson, 1991; Glidden, 1993; Hanson & Hanline, 1990; Sloper, Knussen, Turner, & Cunningham, 1991). In an effort to capture the variation among families of children with disabilities, researchers have turned their attention to more positive aspects of family life. For example, a number of investigators have examined social support networks that help sustain families by alleviating some of the demands involved in meeting the daily needs of children with disabilities (Dunst, Trivette, & Cross, 1986), and/or by providing general support that has positive psychological benefits for parents (Beresford, 1994; Shonkoff, Hauser-Cram, Krauss, & Upshur, 1992). With the exception of findings relating to stress, however, the specific effects of a delayed child on family functioning are seldom delineated, obscuring the interactions over time between child outcomes and family outcomes.

Without dismissing the added demands and potential stresses that a child with developmental problems poses for parents and siblings, we suggest that the stress model is inadequate for understanding family functioning and the effects on children. Baldwin et al. (1990) pointed out that ". . . proximal and distal risk variables differ from one another in the degree to which they directly impinge upon the child" (p. 257). In their study of stress-resistant families and children, they emphasized that distal variables (e.g., social class) are mediated by proximal variables that reflect a wide range of individual differences. The challenge is to identify the functional influences represented by proximal variables that operate within families. Thus, we propose an approach to the study of families and children with disabilities that emphasizes the adjustments and adaptations that make up the daily routines of family life.

A Proactive Approach to Family Functioning

Our thinking is consistent with contemporary views that treat families as proactive agents, not hapless victims of implacable social and economic forces. Families do not merely have an ecology and a routine of daily life. Rather, they actively create their family ecology and routines, taking into account many presses including the particular needs and demands of a child with problems. Through their management of everyday life families can affect the impact of their ecocultural circumstances on children's activities and development. To do so, they use whatever resources they have to arrange their daily lives, a process guided by their values and limited by ecological and other constraints, including economic considerations. From a mix of constraints, resources, and values, families attempt to construct a sustainable everyday routine (Weisner, Matheson, Bernheimer, & Gallimore, 1994). In our model, the adjustments families make to sustain the daily routine are called *accommodations* (Gallimore, Weisner, Kaufman, & Bernheimer, 1989).

Accommodation is defined as a family's functional responses or adaptations to the demands of daily life with a child with delays. Family accommodation is presumed to occur in response to both serious concerns and mundane problems of daily life, and does not require individual or family stress to be activated. There is no presumption that accommodation is intentional, that families are conscious of their activities, or that they see themselves as dramatically different or special. We emphasize that this approach to family functioning is not limited to families with children with developmental problems. All families construct daily routines, some of which appear to be orderly, and others somewhat haphazard or even chaotic. The daily routine captures the common stuff of family life, and is an expression of how families organize their lives, of what is done and what is not done (Bernheimer & Keogh, 1995). The content of the daily routine reflects the nature of the accommodations made in order to ensure some continuity of everyday family life and reflects both the cultural code and the family code as proposed by Sameroff (1994).

Every accommodation is presumed to have costs as well as benefits to each individual in the family, and to the family as a whole. To illustrate, intense and daily language therapy may improve a delayed child's speech, but may intrude on parents' time with siblings. Such an accommodation could be judged positive for the child, but both positive and negative for the parents or siblings. Developing and maintaining a workable daily routine of family life depends on parents making accommodations to sometimes-competing pressures, such as getting a child to inconveniently located or scheduled services when both parents work fulltime, distributing care of a child who requires constant monitoring, or balancing needs of a child with behavior problems against religious or social obligations. Accommodation is not assumed to be positive or negative in its effects on the family or child because the valence of an accommodation must be determined by its correlation with other variables. The goodness of accommodations depends on long-term outcomes for parents and siblings, as well as for children with delays.

In our work about family accommodations to childhood disability we have documented accommodations in ten different ecological and cultural domains, including those pertaining to health and safety, family subsistence, domestic chores, and social and emotional relationships. The accommodation domains are listed in Table 13.1. (More detailed descriptions of these domains may be found in Gallimore, Weisner, Bernheimer, Nihira, & Guthrie, 1993; Weisner, 1984.) As example of an accommodation, to incorporate a long commute to a special-needs program into a family routine, a mother might cut her paid work to part time but strike a deal with her employer to maintain a valued career path. The father might arrange to leave his job early to pick up a sibling from day care. Each of these functional tradeoffs and adjustments represents a family accommodation to childhood disability (Gallimore, Coots, Weisner, Garnier, & Guthrie, 1996).

The accommodations identified in our work in Project CHILD are consistent with findings from other researchers who have studied families' functional responses to children with problems. Based on their work with physically disabled children and their families, Sloper and Turner (1993) suggested that parent resources and coping strategies include material resources, employment, housing, social and family resources, social networks and support systems, family environment, and marital relationship; and psychological resources such as personality, control orientation and problem-solving, and help-seeking skills and strategies. In a comprehensive review of relevant literature, Beresford (1994) identified socioecological coping resources, which included social support, support from spouse, support from extended family and formal agencies, marital status, socioeconomic circumstances, and the family environment.

TABLE 13.1
Accommodation Domains and Examples

Family Subsistence
　　Hours worked; flexibility of work schedule; adequacy of financial resources; amount of
　　coverage provided by medical insurance
Services
　　Availability of services; eligibility for services; sources of transportation; amount of parent
　　involvement required
Home/Neighborhood Safety and Convenience
　　Safety and accessibility of play area; alterations in home (installation of locks, fences related
　　to safety concerns); choice of particular neighborhood
Domestic Workload
　　Amount of work which needs to be done; persons available to do it; amount of time spent
　　by different family members
Child Care Tasks
　　Complexity of child care tasks; presence of extraordinary child care demands (medical
　　problems, behavior problems); number and availability of caregivers
Child Peer Groups
　　Child's play groups (children with disabilities vs. typically developing children); amount
　　of parent supervision needed; role of siblings as playmates
Marital Roles
　　Amount of shared decision making regarding child with delays; degree to which child care
　　and household tasks are shared
Instrumental/Emotional Support
　　Availability and use of formal (church, parent groups) and informal (friends, relatives)
　　sources of support; costs of using support
Father/Spouse Role
　　Amount of involvement with child with delays; amount of emotional support provided
Parent Information
　　Reliance on professional vs. nonprofessional sources of information; amount of time and
　　effort spent accessing information

Note. From "Weaving Interventions into the Fabric of Everyday Life: An Approach to
Family Assessment," by L. P. Bernheimer and B. K. Keogh, 1995, *Topics in Early Childhood
Special Education, 15*, p. 423. Copyright © 1995 by PRO-ED, Inc. Reprinted with premission.

Thus, there is increasing consensus that a range of phenomena must be
considered in assessing and understanding the proactive role of families in
the lives of children with developmental problems. One such phenomenon
is the set of functional accommodations and adjustments needed to sustain
everyday family life. We argue that researching and assessing these accommodations contributes to planning and implementing interventions which
are appropriate and sustainable, as well as increases theoretical understanding of the developmental paths of children and families. We illustrate
this with selected findings from Project CHILD. In this chapter we will
describe outcomes for children and families when the children were 11 years
of age. We recognize that outcome is a relative marker because outcomes
may be defined at different times and operationalized in a variety of ways.

In this chapter we consider outcomes when the children with delays were nearing the transition from childhood to adolescence.

FINDINGS FROM PROJECT CHILD

As part of Project CHILD we have followed a group of 103 children with nonspecific delays from age 3 to age 11, documenting both child charac- teristics and family adaptations over time. Children were assessed with stand- ard developmental and cognitive measures at modal ages 3, 7, and 11; parents and teachers provided ratings of social, behavioral, and personal competen- cies and problems at comparable time intervals. Using an ecocultural model as a framework (Weisner, 1984), in-depth interviews with parents provided detailed information about family status over time, including the kind and intensity of accommodations and adjustments made in response to the child with delays.

Outcomes for Children

The children in our study were identified in their preschool years by pedia- tricians, teachers, regional center professionals, and parents, or combinations of these groups, as having mild to moderate nonspecific developmental de- lays. The children were all Euro-American from English-speaking, primarily middle-class families. Children with indications of profound retardation, sen- sory impairments, or those with known etiologies (e.g., genetic syndromes, maternal drug or alcohol abuse) were not included. The children presented puzzling and ambiguous pictures, and their problems frequently did not match the criteria for established diagnostic categories; treatment implica- tions were often unclear. The developmental profiles based on standard as- sessment techniques were often uneven, and the children's behavior was inconsistent. Yet, in the preschool years, both parents and professionals recognized that something was amiss, and that the children's behavior and development were not right.

The research literature about developmental delays suggests consistently that early signs of delay are associated with subsequent cognitive status, and cognitive level is clearly an outcome of importance. Correlation coefficients between DQ and IQ at different times ranging from .74 to .81 have been reported by investigators from various research groups (Bernheimer & Ke- ogh, 1988; Goodman, 1977; Stavrou, 1990; Truscott, Narrett, & Smith, 1994; VanderVeer & Schweid, 1974). Based on group data, there is also evidence that children with delays have more behavioral, social, and educational problems than do their normally developing peers (Keogh, Bernheimer, Haney, & Daley, 1989; Thompson, 1986). Importantly, however, there is evidence of considerable within-group variability or change in the status of individual children over time, some children improving in cognitive status, others showing decline over time (Stavrou, 1990; Truscott et al., 1994). Furthermore, there are wide differences in social or behavioral competencies and problems, differences that may, in part at least, be related to context or setting, and to the nature, timing, and intensity of interventions. These findings have implications for both research and clinical practice, and for the assessment of outcomes.

Data gathered when the children were age 11 included information from individually administered measures and tests and from parents' and teachers' responses to standardized and Project-developed scales. We tapped a range of developmental and behavioral domains derived in part from the school competence model proposed and tested by Masten, Garmezy, and their colleagues at the University of Minnesota (Masten et al., 1990). Domains assessed included: Health and Physical Growth; Independence-Autonomy; Cognition-Education; Conduct-Behavior; and Social Adjustment. Our findings confirmed that as a group the children continued to evidence cognitive delay. DQ-IQ means and standard deviations were 72.22 (15.34) at entry age 3, and 66.13 (20.37) at follow-up. Examination of within-group variations in cognitive scores over time indicated that almost 40% of the children changed at least one standard deviation from ages 3 to 11; the direction of change was predominantly one of decline. A random coefficient regression technique identified stable differences in rate of cognitive decline over the 8-year period (Keogh, Bernheimer, & Guthrie, 1997). Girls with delays of unknown etiology had the most stable cognitive scores, boys with evidence of perinatal stress had the least stable scores (Keogh & Bernheimer, 1995). Consistent with the cognitive findings, the majority of our children required special education services in elementary school (Keogh, Coots, & Bernheimer, 1995).

Adults' ratings of children's social-behavioral problems and competencies at age 11 confirmed that the children as a group had higher rates of problems when compared to normative expectations, based on nondelayed peers (Keogh & Bernheimer, 1996). However, at age 11 the strength of agreement between parents' and teachers' ratings varied according to the domain assessed. Where significant differences occurred, teachers tended to rate the children more favorably than did their parents. There were few differences in parents' ratings of boys and girls. On the majority of measures teachers rated boys as having higher problem scores and lower competence scores than girls. Parents' ratings were more highly correlated with children's cognitive scores for girls than for boys, but teachers' ratings of children's conduct were significantly associated with IQ for both.

As a whole, our findings are consistent with earlier literature about cognitive and personal-social outcomes for children with developmental delays, suggesting that early signs of developmental problems are reasonable predictors of subsequent problem status. We emphasize, however, that examination of patterns over time confirmed considerable variation among individual children in the degree and rate of cognitive change, and in their social-behavioral problems and competencies. Cognitive status did not necessarily predict personal social competence, and problems in one personal domain did not always generalize to problems in general. There were differences related to time, setting, and observers, suggesting the need to assess outcomes in different settings using a variety of techniques and at different times. Based on our findings, we underscore the importance of including a range of child attributes when assessing outcomes for children, especially when outcome data are used as the basis for placement and intervention decisions or for evaluating intervention effects.

Outcomes for Families

We proposed earlier in this chapter that families proactively accommodate to the needs of their members, including, but not limited to, a child with disabilities, and that these accommodations are reflected in the daily routine of the family. We suggest further that what families do to sustain the daily routine will often be only loosely coupled with outcomes for individual children, as families do not devote all their resources and activities to a single family member. Rather, a sustainable daily routine deals with intra- and extrafamilial interactions necessary for balancing available attention to, and investment in, individuals and to the family as a whole. Family members are in many ways in competition for emotional, social, and material resources, and a child with delays requires a balancing of that child's needs with the needs of others. This is not qualitatively different from the task facing all families. The nature and effectiveness of the balance between individual and family provides a way to consider family outcomes.

In this chapter we discuss two outcomes for families based on selected findings from Project CHILD. Both focus on accommodations, that is, on what families do in adapting to their child with delays, and on what these adaptations mean to them. Specifically, we consider the kind and number of accommodations families made over time, and the sustainability of the resulting daily routines. The findings reported here are based on data gathered when the children with delays were chronologically ages 3, 7, and 11.

Accommodations Over Time.   From preschool to late childhood, 93 families reported a substantial, statistically significant increase in the number of accommodations made: 749, 891, and 1,388 at ages 3, 7, and 11, respectively. Ratings of intensity, or how much effort families put into their accommodations, on the other hand, showed little change over the same period. The discrepancy between increased frequency and stable effort suggested that by late childhood families were spreading their adaptive efforts and energies across more domains (Gallimore et al., 1996). The findings are consistent with the expectation that some forms of family adaptation to childhood disability continue into early and late childhood and are not simply an early stage of grieving and adjustment. Accommodation continues because sustaining a daily routine is an enduring family project, not a transient stage in family life or child development (Weisner et al., 1994).

At all three child ages assessed, the frequency and intensity of family accommodations were not strongly tied to the usual family markers such as socioeconomic status (SES) or mothers' education. Rather, they were related to the characteristics of the children that most directly impacted the daily routine. Families who reported more accommodations were adapting to high-hassle children who had many problems and relatively poor everyday competencies. For example, one family's accommodations were related primarily to the behavior of an extremely difficult child who required constant monitoring because he was capable of injuring himself or of wreaking serious destruction. His mother commented when he was 3 years old, "Our house is set up around Michael. We still have a gate in here and there's a smaller area for him and he can function better, and it isn't that he's ever been destructive, it's just that he can't control himself." By late childhood, although he was still a high-hassle child, the deadbolts and gates required at age 3 were no longer needed. Parents reported he was now capable of many more things—he was more competent but also more troublesome. For example, he became so competent at using a computer the family bought for him that he managed to purchase a car through the internet. His family still needed to monitor closely his activities, but the nature of their accommodations had changed—less intense, more varied.

Michael and his family illustrate the generalization that different accommodations emerge in response to children's changing developmental competencies and problems. Our findings concur with the literature describing changing parental concerns over time (Dyson, 1993; Orr, Cameron, Dyson, & Day, 1993), and underscore the importance of designing interventions that are sensitive to family changes in response to developmental transitions. For example, the restructuring of child-family relationships in adolescence for normally developing children is well documented in the developmental literature. It seems likely that the influence of children's characteristics on family accommodations will be especially strong as children with delays enter adolescence and new issues of autonomy and independence become salient. Thus, the indices of family outcome will vary as a function of children's developmental age.

Sustainability. Based on our assumption that a family's sense of well-being depends in part on the sustainability of its daily routine, all Project CHILD families were grouped on sustainability of the daily routines constructed between child ages 3 and 7. *Sustainable routines* were ones that could be kept going day to day or quickly put back on an even keel using existing resources, such as family income, child services, social support, and psychological resources. *Unsustainable routines* were buffeted by constant changes and serious problems, sapped material and parental energy and time resources, or were incongruent with some fundamental value or goal of one or both parents. In general, the more sustainable a family's daily routine, the greater the sense of well-being parents reported.

Project CHILD fieldworkers familiar with the cases conducted extensive case reviews. During these reviews the fieldworkers were blind to conventional measures of child and family status. The case reviews produced a high degree of convergence on five exclusive classifications, each representing different degrees of sustainability: (a) Multiply Troubled, (b) Vulnerable but Struggling, (c) Improving, Increasingly Resilient, (d) Active but Less Satisfied, and (e) Satisfied, Stable. (See Weisner et al., 1994, for detailed description of methods and findings.) The Multiply Troubled families ($n = 8$) were illustrative of low sustainability and low sense of well-being. As an example, during one year, the T family was harassed by a neighbor involved in criminal activities, Mr. T was laid off, Mrs. T had severe emotional problems, and the 12-year-old sister was involved in frequent fights at school. There was little energy left over for Jimmy, the child with delays, who had severe behavior problems and required constant supervision. Life in Multiply Troubled families, as evidenced in the T family, was frequently chaotic, and the daily routine was driven by problems in several areas of living: paying the rent, finding or maintaining employment, marital situation, and child behavior.

Vulnerable but Struggling ($n = 15$) and Improving-Increasingly Resilient ($n = 22$) families reflected marginal sustainability and a moderate sense of well-being. Like the Multiply Troubled families, Vulnerable but Struggling families struggled with long-standing problems, often some of the same ones encountered by the Multiply Troubled. However, Vulnerable but Struggling families did not appear to be as overwhelmed as their more troubled counterparts. They somehow managed to sustain their everyday routine, often with a single resource such as strong religiosity, or a high-energy, positive, proactive parent. The Improving-Increasingly Resilient ($n = 22$) families were similar to the Vulnerable but Struggling group, with the exception that they perceived decreasing adaptive problems as their child grew older, and their daily routines changed accordingly.

Active but Less Satisfied ($n = 18$) and Satisfied-Stable ($n = 29$) families reflected the highest sustainability. Families considered Active but Less Satisfied adapted actively and fairly effectively over time, yet displayed an underlying attitude of dissatisfaction regarding characteristics surrounding the child with delays, for example, school placement and services, diagnosis or prognosis, or child's behavior problems. These parents often wondered if they were doing enough. Their routine was sustainable, however, and they had a moderate sense of well-being. In contrast, Satisfied-Stable families had an underlying attitude of satisfaction or contentment regarding their child's situation, their ongoing family adaptation, and the way the child's needs fit into the daily routine of the entire family. As an example, Mrs. O was a single mother of three who lived in a rural area with an acre of land and many animals. She considered it a perfect environment for raising children, and particularly appropriate for raising Megan, the child with delays. There were several families who lived near with children around the same age as the O children. Megan was included in all their activities. Mrs. O loved watching Megan run free with the neighborhood children, who seemed impervious to Megan's delays. In addition, she enjoyed a close relationship with the other parents.

The O family was representative of the Satisfied-Stable group because Mrs. O expressed a general sense of well-being and because her daily routine was very sustainable, largely because of the community support. In other Satisfied-Stable families the child had shown significant progress and was currently receiving minimal special education or other services. In other cases in which the child was high hassle or low functioning, the family had made significant accommodations and had created a smooth, workable routine.

When the children reached age 7, the family groups did not differ according to children's IQ, verbal and linguistic competence, or in the total number of child problems as perceived by the parents. This no-difference finding supported the notion of a loosely coupled relationship between family adaptation and the children's abilities, suggesting that there is no simple, direct pathway from child status to family adaptation status. Not surprisingly, the child characteristics that differentiated the groups were those likely to influence family adaptation, a finding congruent with an ecocultural model of family accommodation. Children in the Vulnerable but Struggling families were rated as having the highest hassle, or impact on the daily routine, whereas children in the Satisfied-Stable group had the lowest hassle ratings.

Importantly, the five family classifications were not simply proxies for SES (i.e., level of parental education, marital status, household composition such as single parents vs. couples), although there were differences in how such families were distributed across the groups. The Multiply Troubled group reported the lowest income, as well as the lowest level of parental education. The Less Satisfied group had the highest income, significantly higher than that for the Stable-Satisfied group. There were also significant differences among the groups in accommodation activity. The Less Satisfied families evidenced the most activity with regard to accessing services; the Multiply Troubled group reported the highest childcare workload.

When the children reached age 11, the families were again interviewed about their daily routines and accommodations. This provided a second opportunity to classify the families in terms of the sustainability of their daily routines. On the average, 40% of the families were placed in the same group both times. Two-thirds of the families remained in the same or moved into an adjacent group (e.g., Less Satisfied to Stable-Satisfied or to Vulnerable). The one outlying group was Multiply Troubled—only 1 of the original 7 families was troubled both times. Overall, this suggests a mix of stability and change in well-being over time. Family life, with and without a child with delays, is subject to change over time. These fluctuations work both ways. Families with many problems can, in time, be in a better place, and as our analysis indicated, some doing well now may not be so well fixed later.

The five family groups continued to be differentiated by income, with the Multiply Troubled families reporting the lowest income and the Less Satisfied the highest income. Children with the highest hassle ratings were in the Vulnerable and Multiply Troubled family groups, and children with the lowest hassle ratings were in the Satisfied-Stable group. In contrast to age-7 findings, at age 11 the total number of child problems also differentiated the groups, the children with the most problems were in the Multiply Troubled and Active-Less Satisfied groups. It was the latter group that showed the most accommodation activity across a broad range of dimensions, while the Multiply Troubled group showed the least. Importantly, at both ages family groups were not differentiated by children's cognitive-developmental test scores, but were associated with children's characteristics, which had a direct impact on sustaining the family's daily routine. Clearly, family activities and environments are important to children's well-being. However, the functional connections are complex and often uncertain, suggesting caution in drawing inferences about good or not-so-good families based on the characteristics of the children.

We recognize the potential problems and limitations in using this classification scheme as a tool for assessing family outcomes. The scheme has not been validated outside of our sample of families with children with delays, and the turnover of families across the five categories could be due to factors other than family adaptations to the children with delays. However, the five family groups allow us to view family status from the point of view of adaptation over time. They are not intended to be a rigid typology, but rather to provide assistance in understanding family responses to children with delays (Weisner et al., 1994). An essential aspect of our model is the recognition that families can and will change over time and across developmental periods. Thus, we underscore the need to be wary of family outcome measures that assume the status of a stable trait.

As we know from personal experience, family life is not a smooth, linear march toward a happy ending. The ups and downs most families experience somehow have to be captured in our assessments. We should not be surprised that over an 8-year period these families varied in their satisfaction with everyday life as well as with the nature and extent of the accommodations they made. Whether the lack of stability is due to the methods of classification or to reality, the case materials make clear that the families strongly perceived their lives as varying over time. Parents' own views of their circumstances reflected their uncertainty about the outcomes of their accommodation efforts, their changing understanding of their children's conditions, and the effects of being buffeted by other crises in their lives. However, considering both the number and nature of accommodations over time and the finding that the majority of parents were generally satisfied with their family status, our findings challenge the notion that children's problems are inexorably associated with family problems, and that family reactions are best described by a reactive stress model.

DISCUSSION AND IMPLICATIONS

We have addressed outcomes for families and children and have proposed that both must be systematically assessed if we are to understand the long-term implications of developmental problems. Our work has documented a broad range of outcomes for children with delays and their families. We acknowledge that generalizations from our findings are limited by the selective nature of our sample, but we argue that the functional accommodations comprising family life are inherent in every culture and every group. The kinds of adaptive problems faced by families with children with delays also occur in families without delayed children. To date we have focused on the impact of children's characteristics on family adaptations, showing that children's attributes and problems are but one contributor to the nature of family organization and functioning. We have also shown that children's outcomes and family outcomes are only loosely linked, such that a child with problems does not necessarily imply a problem family.

An important background issue in the study of outcomes for children and families has to do with definition. There are serious questions about what constitute appropriate goals for children with developmental delays, about the emphases and content of early intervention efforts, and about the content of program evaluations. Our findings confirm that early nonspecific delays signal the likelihood of continuing cognitive limitations, but underscore the variability in child status in social-behavioral areas. A comprehensive picture of a child with delays requires consideration of both problems and competencies in different domains and in different settings. This indicates the need for differentiated analyses of child attributes across a range of cognitive and personal-social areas and has implications for assessment, intervention, and evaluation of intervention effects. Because cognitive-language delays are salient characteristics in the identification of young children with developmental problems, the emphasis in assessment has logically focused on these domains, and a number of well-designed and well-tested measures are available for identification and diagnostic purposes (Bailey & Wolery, 1989). There are fewer comprehensive and well-documented approaches to assessing young children's social, affective, and behavioral competencies and problems. This limitation complicates comprehensive description of children's status in the early years. Clinicians working with young delayed children must often rely on observational data and adult reports when assessing those domains, information sources that are subject to a number of threats to validity and reliability (Keogh & Bernheimer, 1996). We emphasize, too, that children with delays, like other children, develop and change, thus mandating the need for continuity of assessment measures and data over time.

How to assess young children's social, behavioral, and affective functioning is a research topic with important practical applications. Consider the need to develop interventions that are sensitive to individual variations in children's abilities and needs. Consider the need to provide reliable evidence of intervention effects in order to ensure continuity of support for programs. The increasing emphasis on accountability requires that intervenors demonstrate the efficacy of their practices, thus underscoring the need for assessment techniques that provide solid data documenting child status across a range of attributes. Few would challenge the generalization that early intervention is positive. Still uncertain is what outcomes should be emphasized and how to document program effects in those domains.

Similarly, what is a good outcome for a family with a delayed child? Are family stability and peace of mind more important than intensive intervention with a delayed child? How are the needs of a single family member balanced against the needs of the family as a whole? We cannot assume that successful family outcomes necessarily lead to the best or most optimal outcomes for any single family member. Rather, for a family as a unit to have a good outcome it must sustain all members in a daily routine of life that creates and supports resilient responses to threat and challenge (Lancaster & Lancaster, 1983). As noted by Minuchin (1985), there are periods in family life when the child is not the stimulus for change but must share in the need to reorganize the system, either because external events or other members have rocked the established routine. Certainly, families with a child who has disabilities face added demands and stresses, but we argue that a reactive stress model does not capture the kind of functional adjustments and balances that families make. Thus, level of stress is a limited index of family outcome. In our view, more powerful outcome indicators are found in the functional accommodations families make in response to a child with disabilities.

A major question for researchers and clinicians who work with children with delays has to do with the nature of family–child relationships and the effects on both children's development and family environment (Caldwell & Bradley, 1994; Sameroff, 1994). If we assume that child and family outcomes are only loosely coupled, it follows that the outcomes for children cannot be assumed to be an index of the outcomes for families. The loose coupling assumption contrasts with some research and clinical perspectives that expect specific child outcomes to be strongly correlated with specific family environments (e.g., Caldwell & Bradley, 1984; Moos & Moos, 1986). Our view is that child outcomes are connected to family outcomes to the extent that the child can successfully participate in a sustainable, meaningful, and satisfying routine of family life. Thus, limited cognitive and communicative functions of children that do not disrupt the daily routine will not relate to family accommodations. High hassle levels, severe behavior problems, or other child characteristics will relate to family outcomes to the extent that they affect parents' efforts to sustain a routine. To date, our analyses have focused on the impact of child characteristics on family functioning. We are currently examining relationships between family practices and children's cognitive and personal-social development.

Some final points about research and clinical interventions with families deserve note. To date, much of the work on child and family outcomes has been driven by the search for effective intervention and treatment programs. Comparative evaluations of alternative programs inevitably have led to some implicit assumptions about good or better families. Many of these assumptions are as unexamined as the ones held in our culture about the ideal family, both now and historically. They are based on sociohistorically conditioned beliefs about the ideal family and about desirable developmental goals for children. In the middle decades of this century, for example, the cultural ideal of family life was defined as a working man, a homemaking woman, and their few children living in an isolated household buffered from the world at large by intimacy, romantic love, privacy, and comfort (Skolnick, 1993). Researchers are no more immune than their fellow citizens to these deep cultural models of how things ought to be. Underlying many studies of child and family outcomes lurks some version of this ideal model of the two-parent, small family. Thus, researchers have often fallen victim to the ideal, treating variations in family functioning as deviations, and defining deviations as pathology or dysfunction. This relates to the problems of defining family outcomes in terms of comfortable structural categories, such as divorce rate or marital harmony, rather than in terms of the satisfaction, sustainability, and meaningfulness of daily life.

Another deep but unexamined assumption in many discussions of outcomes is the American preoccupation with achievement—of differentiating self by ladder increments between how one is now and what one will be in some better future. Yet, in family life there is much of importance that does not easily fit into this conception. What families do every day does not and should not be expected to predict or cause some specific outcome for children.

Scarr (1985) argued that the construction of causal inferences from the web of parent–child correlations is fraught with logical and scientific problems. Her view infers the need for caution in defining outcomes for children based on specific family practices.

This does not negate the importance of family environments in children's lives. From a cross-cultural perspective it is clear that the ecocultural context and the family environment are major influences that shape children's development (Weisner, 1996). Recent developments in the disability field have underscored the need to expand the scope and content of research about families adapting to children with special needs. The 1989 legislation (Amendments to the Individual with Disabilities Education Act or IDEA) mandating development of individual family service plans (IFSP), codified the idea that families can be recruited as proactive agents in interventions for children with disabilities (Harbin, 1993). The wording of the legislation refers, according to Gallagher (1989), to "enhancing the capacity of families to meet the special needs" of their children with handicaps (p. 388). Put in these terms, family proactivity, or capacity to meet the needs of their children, is a vital indicator of family outcome. We propose that this capacity is best shown in the family's daily routine, and that understanding the organization of this routine provides direction for planning and implementing appropriate and workable interventions that enhance the probability of positive adaptations both for children and their families.

Generations of women and men have discovered, so history teaches, that constructing and sustaining a rhythm of daily life is a key to survival. We have operationalized this rhythm as the daily routine. Using the functional indicators of family adaptation—meaningfulness, congruence, and sustainability of the daily routine—we are impressed with the positive and proactive adjustments most families have made to ensure that their children, including their children with developmental problems, are able to function within cohesive and positive units. For the most part our children and their families are doing remarkably well.

REFERENCES

Bailey, D. B., & Wolery, M. (1989). *Assessing infants and preschoolers with handicaps.* Columbus, OH: Merrill.

Baldwin, A. L., Baldwin, C., & Cole, R. E. (1990). Stress-resistant families and stress-resistant children. In J. Rolf, A. S. Masten, D. Cicchetti, K. H. Nuechterlein, & S. Weintraub (Eds.), *Risk and protective factors in the development of psychopathology* (pp. 257–281). Cambridge, England: Cambridge University Press.

Beresford, B. A. (1994). Resources and strategies: How parents cope with the care of a disabled child. *Journal of Child Psychology and Psychiatry, 35,* 171–209.

Bernheimer, L. P., & Keogh, B. K. (1988). The stability of cognitive performance of developmentally delayed children. *American Journal of Mental Retardation, 92,* 539–542.

Bernheimer, L. P., & Keogh, B. K. (1995). Weaving interventions into the fabric of everyday life: An approach to family assessment. *Topics in Early Childhood Special Education, 15*(4), 415–433.

Bernheimer, L. P., Keogh, B. K., & Coots, J. J. (1993). From research to practice: Support for developmental delay as a preschool category of exceptionality. *Journal of Early Intervention, 17*, 97–106.

Boyce, G. C., & Barnett, W. S. (1993). Siblings of persons with mental retardation: A historical perspective and recent findings. In Z. Stoneman & P. Berman (Eds.), *Siblings of individuals with mental retardation, physical disabilities, and chronic illness* (pp. 145–184). Baltimore: Brookes.

Caldwell, B. M., & Bradley, R. H. (1984). *Home observation for measurement of the environment* (rev. ed.). Little Rock, AR: University of Arkansas.

Caldwell, B. M., & Bradley, R. H. (1994). Environmental issues in developmental follow-up research. In S. L. Friedman & H. C. Haywood (Eds.), *Developmental follow-up: Concepts, domains, and methods* (pp. 235–256). San Diego, CA: Academic Press.

Carr, J. (1988). Six weeks to twenty-one years old: A longitudinal study of children with Down's syndrome and their families. *Journal of Child Psychology and Psychiatry, 29*, 407–431.

Dunst, C. J., Trivette, C. M., & Cross, A. H. (1986). Mediating influences of social support: Personal, family, and child outcomes. *American Journal of Mental Deficiency 90*, 403–417.

Dyson, L. (1991). Families of young children with handicaps: Parental stress and family functioning. *American Journal on Mental Retardation, 95*, 623–629.

Dyson, L. (1993). Responses to the presence of a child with disabilities: Parental stress and family functioning over time. *American Journal on Mental Retardation, 98*, 207–218.

Gabel, H., McDowell, J., & Cerreto, M. C. (1983). Family adaptation to the handicapped infant. In S. G. Garwood & R. R. Fewell (Eds.), *Educating handicapped infants* (pp. 455–493). Rockville, MD: Aspen.

Gallagher, J. J. (1989). A new policy initiative: Infants and toddlers with handicapping conditions. *American Psychologist, 44*, 387–391.

Gallimore, R., Coots, J., Weisner, T., Garnier, H., & Guthrie, D. (1996). Family responses to children with early developmental delays, II: Accommodation intensity and activity in early and middle childhood. *American Journal on Mental Retardation, 101*, 215–232.

Gallimore, R., Weisner, T., Bernheimer, L. P., Nihira, K., & Guthrie, D. (1993). Family responses to young children with developmental delays: Accommodation activity in ecological and cultural context. *American Journal on Mental Retardation, 98*, 185–206.

Gallimore, R., Weisner, T., Kaufman, S., & Bernheimer, L. P. (1989). The social construction of ecological niches: Family accommodation of developmentally delayed children. *American Journal on Mental Retardation, 94*, 216–230.

Gath, A. (1973). The school-age siblings of mongol children. *British Journal of Psychiatry, 123*, 161–167.

Glidden, L. M. (1993). What we do *not* know about families with children who have developmental disabilities: Questionnaire on resources and stress as a case study. *American Journal on Mental Retardation, 97*, 481–495.

Goodman, J. F. (1977). Medical diagnosis and intelligence levels in young mentally retarded children: A follow-up study. *Journal of Mental Deficiency Research, 21*, 205–212.

Hampson, R. B., Hulgus, Y. F., Beavers, R. W., & Beavers, J. S. (1988). The assessment of competence in families with a retarded child. *Journal of Family Psychology, 2*, 32–53.

Hanson, M. J., & Hanline, M. F. (1990). Parenting a child with a disability: A longitudinal study of parental stress and adaptation. *Journal of Early Intervention, 14*, 234–248.

Harbin, G. L. (1993). Family issues of children with disabilities: How research and theory have modified practices in intervention. In N. J. Anastasiow & S. Hamel (Eds.), *At-risk infants: Interventions, families and research* (pp. 101–111). Baltimore: Brookes.

Keogh, B. K., & Bernheimer, L. P. (1995). Etiologic conditions as predictors of children's problems and competencies in elementary school. *Journal of Child Neurology, 10*(Supplement 1), S100–S105.

Keogh, B. K., & Bernheimer, L. P. (in press). Concordance between mothers' and teachers' perceptions and behavior problems of children with developmental delays. *Journal of Emotional and Behavior Disorders.*

Keogh, B. K, Bernheimer, L. P., & Guthrie, D. G. (1997). Stability and change over time in cognitive level of children with delays. *American Journal on Mental Retardation.*

Keogh, B. K., Bernheimer, L. P., Haney, M. P., & Daley, S. (1989). Behavior and adjustment problems of young developmentally delayed children. *European Journal of Special Needs Education, 4,* 79–90.

Keogh, B. K., Coots. J., & Bernheimer, L. P. (1995). A longitudinal study of school placement of children with non-specific developmental delays. *Journal of Early Intervention, 20,* 65–97.

Lancaster, J. B., & Lancaster, C. S. (1983). Parental investment: The hominid adaptation. In D. Ortner (Ed.), *How humans adapt: A biocultural odyssey* (pp. 333–399). Washington, DC: Smithsonian Institution Press.

Longo, D. C., & Bond, L. L. (1984). Families of the handicapped: Research and practice. *Family Relations, 33,* 57–65.

Masten, A. S., Best, K. M., & Garmezy, N. (1990). Resilience and development: Contributions from the study of children who overcome adversity. *Development and Psychopathology, 2,* 425–444.

McLean, M., Smith, B. J., McCormick, K., Shakel, J., & McEvoy, M. (1991). Developmental delay: Establishing parameters for a practical category of exceptionality. *DEC Position Paper.* Reston, VA: Council for Exceptional Children.

Minnes, P. M. (1988). Family resources and stress associated with having a mentally retarded child. *American Journal on Mental Retardation, 93,* 184–192.

Minuchin, P. (1985). Families and individual development: Provocations from the field of family therapy. *Child Development, 56,* 289–302.

Moos, B. S., & Moos, R. H. (1986). *Family environment scale manual* (2nd ed.). Palo Alto, CA: Consulting Psychologists Press.

Orr, R. R., Cameron, S. J., & Day, D. M. (1991). Coping with stress in families with children who have mental retardation: An evaluation of the Double ABCX model. *American Journal on Mental Retardation, 95,* 444–450.

Orr, R. R., Cameron, S. J., Dyson, L. A., & Day, D. M. (1993). Age-related changes in stress experienced by families with a child who has developmental delays. *Mental Retardation, 31,* 171–176.

Pianta, R. C., Egeland, B., & Sroufe, L. A. (1990). Maternal stress and children's development: Prediction of school outcomes and identification of protective factors. In J. Rolf, A. S. Masten, D. Cicchetti, K. Nuechterlein, & S. Weintraub (Eds.), *Risk and protective factors in the development of psychopathology* (pp. 215–235). Cambridge, England: Cambridge University Press.

Rutter, M. (1990). Psychosocial resilience and protective mechanisms. In J. Rolf, A. S. Masten, D. Cicchetti, K. H. Neuchterlein, & S. Weintraub (Eds.), *Risk and protective factors in the development of psychopathology* (pp. 181–214). Cambridge, England: Cambridge University Press.

Sameroff, A. (1994). Ecological perspectives on longitudinal follow-up studies. In S. L. Friedman & H. C. Haywood (Eds.), *Developmental follow-up: Concepts, domains, and methods* (pp. 45–64). San Diego, CA: Academic Press.

Scarr, S. (1985). Constructing psychology: Making facts and fables for our times. *American Psychologist, 40,* 499–512.

Shonkoff, J. P., Hauser-Cram, P., Krauss, M. W., & Upshur, C. C. (1992). Development of infants with disabilities and their families. *Monographs of the Society for Research in Child Development, 57*(6, Serial No. 230).

Skolnick, A. (1993). Changes of heart: Family dynamics in historical perspective. In P. A. Cowan, D. Field, D. A. Hansen, A. Skolnick, & G. E. Swanson (Eds.), *Family, self, and society: Toward a new agenda for family research* (pp. 43–68). Hillsdale, NJ: Lawrence Erlbaum Associates.

Sloper, P., Knussen, C., Turner, S., & Cunningham, C. (1991). Factors related to stress and satisfaction with life in families of children with Down Syndrome. *Journal of Child Psychiatry and Psychology, 32*, 655–676.

Sloper, P., & Turner, S. (1993). Risk and resistance factors in the adaptation of parents of children with severe physical disability. *Journal of Child Psychology and Psychiatry, 34*, 167–189.

Stavrou, E. (1990). The long-term stability of WISC-R scores in mildly retarded and learning-disabled children. *Psychology in the Schools, 27*, 101–110.

Thompson, R. J., Jr. (1986). Behavior problems in children with developmental and learning problems. *Monographs of the International Academy for Research in Learning Disabilities* (Serial No. 3). Ann Arbor, MI: University of Michigan Press.

Truscott, S. D., Narrett, C. M., & Smith, S. E. (1994). WISC-R reliability over time: Implications for practice and research. *Psychological Reports, 74*, 147–156.

Trute, B. (1995). Gender differences in the psychological adjustment of parents of young, developmentally disabled children. *Journal of Child Psychology and Psychiatry, 36*, 1225–1242.

VanderVeer, B., & Schweid, E. (1974). Infant assessment: Stability of mental functioning in young retarded children. *American Journal of Mental Deficiency, 79*, 1–4.

Weisner, T. S. (1984). Ecocultural niches of middle childhood: A cross-cultural perspective. In W. A. Collins (Ed.), *Development during middle childhood: The years from six to twelve* (pp. 335–369). Washington, DC: National Academy of Sciences.

Weisner, T. S. (1996). Why ethnography should be the most important method in the study of human development. In R. Jessop, A. Colby, & R. Shweder (Eds.), *Ethnography and human development* (pp. 305–324). Chicago: University of Chicago Press.

Weisner, T. S., Matheson, C., Bernheimer, L. P., & Gallimore, R. (1994). Creating meaningful, sustainable routines of everyday life: Family adaptation among families with children with delays (Technical Report No. 3). Los Angeles: UCLA, Sociobehavioral Research Group, Mental Retardation Research Center.

Werner, E. E., & Smith, R. S. (1989). *Vulnerable but invincible: A longitudinal study of resilient children and youth.* New York: McGraw-Hill.

Werner, E. E., & Smith, R. S. (1992). *Overcoming the odds: High risk children from birth to adulthood.* Ithaca, New York: Cornell University Press.

14
▼▼▼▼▼▼▼

Socialization of Cognition:
A Family Focus*

Irving E. Sigel
Educational Testing Service, Princeton, NJ

SOCIALIZATION OF COGNITION: A FAMILY FOCUS

The basic proposition of this research effort is that the family unit, however structured, provides the primal source of influence on the child's cognitive development as the only social unit wherein biogenetic and social factors merge. The family, in turn, is embedded in a larger, complex social network comprised of many significant individuals who provide an array of experiences that influence the child as the child influences others (Feiring & Lewis, 1987; Lewis, 1982; Sigel, 1991). In this chapter we examine the role the family plays as a provider of a social environment influencing cognitive development. Our particular focus is on parents' teaching behaviors, which are expressions of their beliefs as to how children come to achieve representational competence. Such competence provides the foundation for subsequent academic proficiency in reading and mathematics.

Developmental Transformations

The developmental transformations that guide our work concern the changing nature of the child's ability to transform experience into some symbolic mode (e.g., knowing that an object in its three-dimensional form is equiva-

---

*Portions of this chapter are reprinted from Sigel, Stinson, and Flaugher (1993). Reprinted with permission of Lawrence Erlbaum Associates.

lent to its representation in the form of a word, picture, or drawing). A child's understanding of symbolic representation is acquired through social experiences and reflects an understanding of the rule that an event of any kind can be transformed into some other form. This integration of cognitive shift is evidence of the child's understanding of the representational rule, a concept basic to intellectual development. Imagine what it would be like if we did not understand the idea that one instance can stand for or represent another. For example, knowing that a number can represent a value is a critical requisite for understanding mathematics.

Representational competence is an overarching term that encompasses three aspects: reconstruction of the past, anticipation or planning, and transcending the ongoing present. These competencies are hypothesized as requisites for cognitive functioning and evolve in the social context of the family. The family environment can influence the course of development of these competencies, which are biologically based, but socially triggered.

Generally speaking, exchanges between parents and children may be categorized into two broad areas: discipline-management events and teaching situations in which the parent engages the child in a wide array of social interactions (e.g., discussion of daily events and reading stories). The class of social interactions that are foci of this chapter are the nonmanagerial aspects of the interaction and in particular, the parents' role in promoting distancing in the child.

The term *distancing* is used as a metaphorical construct denoting psychological separation of the person from the immediate, ongoing present. The distancing metaphor suggests that individuals can cognitively project themselves into the past or into the future, transcending the immediate present. This process of distancing is conceptualized as critical in the development of representational thinking because it serves to activate the child's cognitive processes in the direction of various representational schema (Sigel, 1982). Distancing behaviors usually have a built-in demand quality, a demand for the child to respond. Most typically, they are in the form of a question that may be direct (e.g., "Why do you think the spoon didn't float?"); or indirect (e.g., "Tell me why the spoon didn't float."). They can vary in level from high to low or from abstract to concrete. High-level distancing strategies are typically open ended and place cognitive demands on the child to infer causality, draw inferences, and generate alternatives. Low-level distancing strategies are closed ended type questions that ask the child to name or describe objects and events. Distancing strategies are assumed to generate discrepancies between what is experienced and what is expected, creating disequilibrium in the listener. Disequilibrium promotes tension, which by its discomforting nature demands resolution. It is the resolution of the discrepancy that impels the individual to reconsider prior knowledge, reexamine assumptions, or try out alternatives and, in so doing, to restructure the ongoing cognitive schema.

The History of the Project

Given our premise that the child's cognitive development and comprehension of the representational rule evolve in the family context, our 10-year research program has asked the following questions: (a) What parent variables in this context impinge on and influence the course of representational competence? (b) What are the determinants of such parent belief-behaviors? and (c) What effect do these parent actions have on the child's use of the representational rule, generally, and on school achievement, specifically?

In our initial study we discovered that birth order and spacing are familial structural factors that result in differential parent interactions and consequences for children. For example, one-child families were found to differ from three-child families in terms of parents' beliefs about how children learn. The former favored adult instruction and guidance more than the latter, who expressed more beliefs in the self-regulatory capabilities of the child (Sigel, McGillicuddy-DeLisi, & Johnson, 1980). Spacing of children had little effect on parenting beliefs, but level of education was highly related to how parents thought children learn.

Families of Communication-Handicapped Children

The next phase of our efforts focused on examining parent beliefs and teaching behaviors with families in which the target child was communication handicapped (CH). The rationale for such a choice was that parents teach their children predominantly through verbal strategies. Due to their language impairment, however, communication-handicapped children might be limited in their opportunities to interact verbally within the family environment. Comparing children with a diagnosed language impairment to nonhandicapped children would thus provide a natural experiment, enabling us to evaluate the effects of parents' verbal teaching strategies. Moreover, communication-handicapped children comprise a unique group because deficient language development is identifiable (and potentially remediable) earlier than other learning disabilities. Language disorders are also among the most common, albeit most varied, developmental abnormalities, encompassing a wide range of expressive and receptive linguistic problems. The prevalence of communication disorders among students classified as having special educational needs has been estimated from 28% (Case & Leavitt, 1986) to 90.5% of the learning disabled (LD) population as a whole (Gibbs & Cooper, 1989).

Moreover, when educators were asked their views regarding the impact of communication disorders on academic performance, 66% noted their adverse effects on achievement (Bennett & Runyan, 1982).

The Nature of the Sample

For this phase of our research effort, 240 families were recruited from the Princeton, New Jersey, area through schools, speech clinics, and child study teams. Of this number, 120 had a communication-handicapped child between the ages of 3½ and 7½, and 120 were control families matched for age, sex, and birth order of target child and family structural variables such as parent education, income, and occupational status. Children included in the CH category were those who demonstrated various degrees of developmental language disorders with no evidence of nonlinguistic functioning deficits or auditory impairment. Intellectual functioning of all children was determined to be within normal limits.

Initial Results. Using observational data derived from videotaped interactions of parents and children in two contextually varied tasks (storytelling and paper folding), we found that parents' low-level distancing strategies, which were closed ended and didactic, offering children few options or alternatives, tended to relate negatively to children's cognitive functioning, particularly to reconstructive memory. Conversely, parents' use of high-level distancing strategies, which require the child to infer, compare, or abstract, were positively associated with children's memory for sentences and anticipatory imagery on a Piagetian task (Sigel, McGillicuddy-DeLisi, Flaugher, & Rock, 1983).

We found that obtained relationships between parental teaching strategies and child outcomes were clearly dependent on the task involved and on the child's communication status. Parents of CH, compared to NCH, children tended to use more low-level distancing strategies (Sigel, Stinson, & Flaugher, 1993). Even more intriguing was the related finding that the child's competence on a paper-folding task varied with the sex of the parent working with her or him, indicating that mothers' and fathers' teaching strategies differentially influenced children's spontaneous problem-solving capabilities (McGillicuddy-DeLisi & Sigel, 1991; Sigel et al., 1983).

The Follow-Up Study (5 Years Later). In the remaining section of this chapter, the focus will be on the Time 2 findings because they address the questions of relationship between early experience and later academic competence, as well as take advantage of significant changes due to therapeutic intervention with the communication handicapped children (CH). The sample of families participating in this study was a subsample of families who were enrolled in the Time 1 project, 5 years earlier. I was specifically interested in the school performance of the CH children because of the literature on the academic consequences of language impairment (McKinney, 1989). Seventy-eight, two-parent, middle-class families, 38 with a communication-handicapped child and 40 nonhandicapped (NCH) controls returned to ETS to participate in our follow-up study. As before, CH and NCH target children in the sample were matched for age, grade, sex of child, and family socio-economic status (SES).

Data Collection. As in Time 1, a structured parent interview was used which was comprised of 12 vignettes covering everyday situations parents typically encounter with children in this age group (McGillicuddy-DeLisi & Sigel, 1991). Vignettes were designed to tap similar content areas to those presented at Time 1, although situations were altered to make them more age appropriate. Based on earlier findings regarding the salience of context in parent–child interactions, interview items were categorized into knowledge domains to determine whether parents' beliefs and teaching behaviors differed among knowledge domains. Confirmatory factor analyses revealed the presence of three distinct content areas tapping the parents' beliefs regarding how children acquire knowledge about the physical world, self-knowledge, and social-moral knowledge. Subsequently, these three domains were labeled: *Physical Knowledge, Intrapersonal,* and *Moral/Social.*

Child Measures. While parents were interviewed, children were administered a series of subtests from the Woodcock-Johnson Psycho-Educational Battery (WJPB) to measure their broad cognitive ability and achievement in mathematics and reading. As a standardized assessment instrument, the WJPB has been widely commended for its technical excellence and exceptional reliability and concurrent validity (Kaufman, 1985).

Follow-Up Results (5 Years Later)

This section is presented in the following sequence: Hypotheses of the current investigation are reviewed, findings are presented and discussed, and implications for applicability of results are considered. On the basis of our theoretical premises and findings from earlier studies with younger children, we expected to find positive linkages between parents' reported use of distancing strategies and their beliefs that children learn through active participation in the learning process (Sigel, 1982). Conversely, it was expected that parents who favored authoritative teaching strategies such as telling the child what to do, with or without explanations, would most likely believe that children learn best through direct instruction. It was further hypothesized that beliefs about how children acquire knowledge would differ among parents of CH and NCH children because of the differential experiences with language and processing of receptive language, as well as the expressive nature of their childrearing experiences. We know from the literature that parents of language-impaired children tend to hold different views of their teaching and socialization roles and to manage their children differently than do parents of nonhandicapped children (Freeman, 1971; Laskey & Klopp, 1982; Sigel et al., 1983). Parents of CH children, for example, are significantly more likely to believe that their children acquire knowledge passively (e.g., through instruction and negative feedback) as opposed to actively (e.g., through their own experimentation and intellectual exploration) (Sigel et al., 1983). Studies of maternal communication patterns, for instance, have found that mothers tend to comment, expand on, or otherwise acknowledge what their language-disordered children say significantly less than do controls (Schodorf & Edwards, 1983).

According to distancing theory, representational thinking is stimulated by the degree of cognitive demand parents place on their children to reason, reflect, and generate their own solutions. Presumably, these parental efforts encouraging the child's intrinsic capacity for self-directed, as opposed to other-directed, learning are guided by beliefs in cognitive processes. Academic subjects such as math and reading, which require abstraction and transformation of information, should thus be positively associated with beliefs mediated by strategies that further the development of representational thought.

Mindful of these expectations, we now focus on the following findings:

- The nature of parents' beliefs and their distribution across knowledge domains.
- Comparisons of CH and NCH parents' self-reported beliefs relative to their own childrearing strategies.
- Relationships between parents' beliefs and children's math and reading achievement for the total group and separately for girls and boys.
- Connections between parents' self-reported beliefs and their teaching behaviors.
- Within-group comparisons of achievement among handicapped children who are still receiving therapy versus those who have been remediated.

The Nature of Parents' Beliefs

Based on prior investigations using a similar version of the structured Parent Interview (Sigel et al., 1983), we theorized that parents hold a variety of beliefs regarding how their children learn and become socialized. We also anticipated that the situational context of the parent–child interaction would be important to the types of beliefs expressed. Table 14.1 illustrates how these beliefs distribute themselves within each knowledge domain. From the

TABLE 14.1
Group (CH-NCH) Comparisons of Parents' Interview Beliefs

| Belief | Parents of CH Group (n = 38) | | Parents of NCH Group (n = 40) | | | |
	M	(SD)	M	(SD)	t	p
	Mothers					
Cognitive processes (PK)	.228	(.281)	.338	(.284)	1.71	.09
Cognitive processes (IP)	.351	(.337)	.500	(.311)	2.03	.05
Cognitive processes (M-S)	.379	(.242)	.509	(.282)	2.18	.03
Negative feedback (M-S)	.288	(.241)	.200	(.203)	1.75	.08
	Fathers					
Cognitive processes (M-S)	.295	(.230)	.489	(.285)	3.30	.001
Direct Instruction (M-S)	.299	(.220)	.186	(.224)	2.23	.03

Note. Domains: PK = Physical Knowledge. IP = Intrapersonal Knowledge. M-S = Moral-Social Knowledge.

table it is apparent that the beliefs parents report as rationales for their teaching efforts tend to vary among groups (CH and NCH) and within groups (mothers vs. fathers). For the most part, however, parents in all groups endorse beliefs in cognitive processes most frequently in the Intrapersonal and Moral-Social domains, but not in the Physical Knowledge domain where beliefs in direct instruction prevail. On the other hand, beliefs coded as activity (e.g., learning by doing) are rarely alluded to outside of the physical knowledge sphere, while positive and negative feedback beliefs are most frequently expressed in relation to socialization concerns.

As anticipated, the content of the learning domain clearly influences the types of beliefs elicited. However, we found that the following four major categories apparently account for 87% of all stated beliefs regarding how children learn: *cognitive processes, direct instruction,* and *positive and negative feedback.* These beliefs encompass the primary learning perspectives of parents as reported in the interview and basically represent two dichotomous views of how individuals acquire knowledge, internally or externally. Of these two perspectives, the former reflects a freedom dimension (i.e., cognitive processes) wherein children are encouraged to think and solve problems through their own reasoning and initiative, whereas the latter reflects an authoritative dimension characterized by directives, reinforcement, and control by the parent or adult authorities (i.e., direct instruction, positive and negative feedback). Subsequent analyses were based on these four representative beliefs, while the remainder were dropped or incorporated into another category.

Comparisons of CH and NCH Parents' Beliefs

To determine whether CH and NCH parents' beliefs differed significantly from each other, t tests were done on the mean proportions of responses of mothers and fathers within each domain. Table 14.1 shows the parental belief for mothers and fathers by CH and NCH group. Differences between the groups are more pronounced in the Moral-Social domain than in any other. As a group, parents of nonhandicapped children expressed significantly more beliefs in their children's ability to think or reason on their own in the Moral-Social domain than did the CH parents. CH fathers, in particular, were significantly ($p < .03$) more likely to think that children learn best by being told what to do than NCH fathers who were much more likely to encourage their children to draw their own conclusions ($p < .001$).

This tendency to view the child as capable of inferential thinking and autonomous problem solving was also significantly more characteristic of NCH mothers than their CH counterparts in the Intrapersonal domain of feelings ($p < .05$) but less apparent in the realm of Physical Knowledge ($p < .09$).

In summary, it is apparent from Table 14.1 that parents are significantly more likely to express different views about how children learn if they are rearing a handicapped child. Specifically, mothers and fathers of CH children appear to perceive them as needing more explicit direction and control than parents of NCH children, a finding that is consistent with our own data of 5 years ago as well as with the literature about families with problem children (Grolnick & Ryan, 1987; Mash, 1984).

CHILD ACHIEVEMENT IN RELATION TO PARENTS' BELIEFS AND TEACHING STRATEGIES

A central issue endemic to every study of parental beliefs is whether these beliefs are linearly related to the behaviors that are presumed to underlie these behaviors. The question was examined in two ways: one by the interview in which both beliefs and behaviors were elicited, and the other by observing the parents teaching the child a task.

First is a presentation of the correlations between parents' beliefs and parents' reports of their distancing strategies. Mean percentages of reported beliefs and teaching strategies were calculated and then correlated with the child's standardized achievement scores from the Woodcock-Johnson Psycho-Educational Battery (WJPB). Different patterns of associations emerged for each group, suggesting that the handicap status of the child and the gender of the parent each influence observed outcomes (see Table 14.2).

TABLE 14.2
Correlations Between Inteview Strategies, Beliefs, and Achievement

Parent Variables	Child Achievement			
	(CH Group) (n = 38)		(NCH Group) (n = 40)	
	Math	Reading	Math	Reading
		Mothers		
Strategies				
Distancing	−.13	−.15	.05	.28*
Rational authoritative	−.06	−.00	−.12	.13
Direct authoritative	.23	.15	.07	.18
Negative reinforcement	−.03	−.07	−.01	.06
Positive reinforcement	−.19	−.10	.16	.08
Beliefs				
Cognitive processes	−.13	−.17	.03	−.12
Direct instruction	.17	.20	.09	.30*
Negative feedback	−.08	−.10	.03	−.01
Positive feedback	−.01	.00	.04	−.19
		Fathers		
Strategies				
Distancing	.22	.41**	−.16	.11
Rational authoritative	.15	.23	.03	−.21
Direct authoritative	.06	−.10	.17	.08
Negative reinforcement	−.26	−.33**	.26	.08
Positive reinforcement	−.20	−.05	−.07	−.09
Beliefs				
Cognitive processes	.23	.39**	−.01	.10
Direct instruction	−.03	−.01	−.17	−.34**
Negative feedback	−.22	−.25	.22	.08
Positive feedback	−.16	−.30*	−.10	.01

*$p < .10$. **$p < .05$.

Turning first to the CH group, we found that fathers' preferences for particular teaching strategies, specifically distancing and negative reinforcement, are more highly associated with children's achievement than are mothers'. Additionally, fathers' orientation toward beliefs in cognitive processes are positively related to reading achievement among communication-handicapped children ($r = .39$, $p < .05$). This finding is noteworthy because it suggests the positive link between a father's commitment to helping the handicapped child think through everyday problems and that child's performance in an area requiring representational skills. Mathematics achievement among CH children, however, was not significantly associated with parents' overall belief orientation or their self-reported actions.

Conversely, in the NCH group, we find that fathers' preferred teaching strategies appear unrelated to child achievement while mothers' reported use of distancing is marginally ($p < .10$), but negatively, related to reading. Table 14.2 also reveals oppositional relationships between children's reading achievement and mothers' and fathers' endorsements of direct instruction beliefs. The more fathers believe in telling children what to do and how to do it, the lower their children's reading achievement scores ($r = -.34$, $p < .05$). Mothers' same belief statements, however, do not reach statistical significance for reading achievement ($r = .30$, $p < .10$). It may well be that gender differential patterns of parental behaviors relative to the same beliefs account for these oppositional correlations, or the nonhandicapped child may just respond more positively to directiveness from mothers than from fathers.

Differences Between the Self-Reported Behaviors and the Observed Behaviors in Teaching the Rope-Tying Task. There are two reasons for these discrepancies or contradictions. The first is that the self-report may be methodologically flawed because the request for reporting strategies was embedded in the discussion of beliefs and so may well have been a product of the total context. A second, and a more telling issue, follows this argument. In the actual teaching situation, the task was quite specific and unrelated to any other item in the interview. Had the parent been asked about teaching strategies equivalent to the knot-tying task, the belief–behavior relationship might have received responses consistent with the behavior.

These global bivariate results were somewhat perplexing in terms of their magnitude and limited findings of significance. Thus, further analyses were undertaken to address the following questions: Do the behavioral mechanisms by which beliefs are transmitted to the child vary according to domain and parent gender? Are the relationships between parents' beliefs and children's achievement what we would expect, given the literature on the differential socialization of boys and girls (Antill, 1988; Block, 1983)? Does CH children's therapy status (e.g., still in therapy vs. remediated) affect achievement outcomes?

Belief-Behavior Response Patterns. Based on inspection of frequency data in which parents' beliefs were paired with their reported behaviors (teaching strategies), it became clear that there is considerable variability in the behavioral expression of those beliefs. We also found that belief–behavior response patterns of parents in the CH group who hold the same beliefs, activate different teaching strategies depending on parent gender and knowledge domain. Parents apparently hold a few core beliefs that guide their interactions with children, but the operationalization of those beliefs is complex and highly variable. This discrepancy in prediction is revealing, because it suggests that beliefs may not transcend situations, but rather, may be task specific, not to be confused with situation specific. That is, a task has its own demand quality irrespective of the situation in which it is embedded. It may well be that parents believe that different classes of tasks require different teaching strategies, and parents are not that committed to a specific belief and teaching strategy. In fact, it was demonstrated that parents holding a similar belief may differ in how they tend to express it (Sigel, 1985, 1986).

Parental Beliefs in Relation to Girls' and Boys' Achievement

Consistent with earlier results, different patterns of associations for the CH and NCH groups, as well as for mothers and fathers with respect to the relationship between beliefs and academic achievement, were found. Moreover, when the sample was divided by gender, correlations indicate that parents' beliefs are differentially associated with girls' and boys' achievement (see Tables 14.3 and 14.4). For example, correlations of parents' beliefs and CH children's achievement are largely nonsignificant until child gender is

TABLE 14.3
Correlations Between CH Parents' Interview Beliefs and Child Achievement

	Math Achievement			Reading Achievement		
Parental Beliefs	Girls (n = 13)	Boys (n = 25)	Total (n = 38)	Girls (n = 13)	Boys (n = 25)	Total (n = 38)
	Mothers (n = 38)					
Cognitive processes (PK)	.07	.00	−.02	−.03	−.06	−.13
Direct instruction (PK)	−.16	−.08	−.10	−.02	−.01	−.00
Cognitive processes (IP)	.17	−.04	−.01	.14	−.01	−.00
Direct instruction (IP)	−.05	.25	.18	.16	.22	.18
Positive feedback (IP)	−.17	−.33*	−.26	−.34*	−.23	−.21
Cognitive processes (M-S)	.22	.19	−.21	−.15	−.19	−.22
Direct instruction (M-S)	−.10	.31	.18	−.16	.28	−.17
Negative feedback (M-S)	.23	−.18	−.07	.17	−.23	−.13
	Fathers (n = 38)					
Cognitive processes (PK)	−.07	.18	.13	.09	.24	.25
Direct instruction (PK)	.17	−.25	−.18	.15	−.20	−.21
Cognitive processes (IP)	−.17	.23	.14	.00	.24	.19
Direct instruction (IP)	.31	.00	.05	.24	.05	.06
Positive feedback (IP)	−.07	−.25	−.21	−.03	−.29	−.24
Cognitive processes (M-S)	.51**	.10	.17	−.64**	.07	.05
Direct instruction (M-S)	.12	.01	.04	−.06	.07	.05
Negative feedback (M-S)	−.58*	−.08	−.21	.54***	−.18	−.23

Note. PK = Physical Knowledge. IP = Intrapersonal Knowledge. M-S = Moral-Social Knowledge.
$*p \leq .10.$ $**p < .05.$ $***p < .01.$

TABLE 14.4
Correlations Between NCH Parents' Interview
Beliefs and Child Achievement

	Math Achievement			Reading Achievement		
Parental Beliefs	Girls (n = 14)	Boys (n = 26)	Total (n = 40)	Girls (n = 14)	Boys (n = 26)	Total (n = 40)
	Mothers (n = 40)					
Cognitive processes (PK)	.66***	.13	.27*	.59**	−.13	.04
Direct instruction (PK)	−.08	−.01	−.07	.10	.26	.21
Cognitive processes (IP)	.20	−.27	−.14	−.01	−.23	−.15
Direct instruction (IP)	.24	.13	.16	.39	.34*	.36**
Positive feedback (IP)	−.38	.14	−.02	−.26	−.00	−.09
Cognitive processes (M-S)	.12	−.06	−.01	.17	−.30	−.13
Direct instruction (M-S)	.10	−.26	−.18	.38	.03	.15
Negative feedback (M-S)	−.21	.07	.03	−.36	.15	−.01
	Fathers (n = 40)					
Cognitive processes (PK)	−.22	.11	.00	−.03	.09	.04
Direct instruction (PK)	−.10	−.32	−.28*	−.46*	−.17	−.23
Cognitive processes (IP)	.15	.36*	.29*	.06	.14	.11
Direct instruction (IP)	−.34	−.12	−.17	−.56**	−.01	−.21
Positive feedback (IP)	.13	−.32	−.19	.35	−.17	.01
Cognitive processes (M-S)	−.38	−.10	−.20	−.18	.17	.07
Direct instruction (M-S)	.02	.07	.05	−.22	−.25	−.24
Negative feedback (M-S)	.47*	.08	.22	.49*	−.10	.08

Note. PK = Physical Knowledge. IP = Intrapersonal Knowledge. M-S = Moral-Social Knowledge.
$*p < .10.$ $**p < .05.$ $***p < .01.$

taken into account (see Table 14.3). Then, significant linkages emerge which were previously obscured. Paternal beliefs that are significantly related to girls' achievement have little or no relation to boy's achievement.

The correlational findings for the NCH group show a similar gender-differential pattern of relationships, but they are not the same as those observed for the CH group (see Table 14.4). Mothers' cognitive process beliefs in the Physical Knowledge domain relate positively to girls' overall achievement, while fathers' beliefs in direct instruction relate negatively to girls' reading achievement in two out of three domains. These results are largely consistent with our theoretical expectations when gender is not included in the prediction. When gender is inserted into the equation our predictions are compromised. Apparently, parents exhibit different beliefs and consequent behaviors depending on the gender of the child. However, the positive correlation between paternal negative-feedback beliefs and girls' achievement is surprising given the literature that generally reports negative linkages between parental control and intellectual outcomes (Deci & Ryan, 1987). There may be a cross-gender effect that alters how girls perceive their fathers' limit-setting stance in moral or social areas. Perhaps preadolescent females view paternal restrictiveness in the Moral-Social domain as indicative of caring and involvement in their welfare, rather than as punitiveness.

Finally, as was the case in the CH group, the achievement of nonhandicapped male children minimally related to parents' beliefs at a significant level. The possible reason why boys and girls show such different patterns of correlations between their achievement and their parents' beliefs, given the nature of our data, may be that girls are socialized to be more dependent on what others think of them than are boys. We know from the literature (Block, 1983; Huston, 1983), for example, that sons are encouraged to be autonomous in their play and learning experiences, while daughters are rewarded for being empathetic and sensitive to others. Whatever the explanation, these gender-differential correlations are clearly indicative of the need to study outcomes in terms of sex of child.

Within-CH Group Achievement Differences. The reader will recall that our CH group consisted of children diagnosed as communication handicapped when enrolled in Study 1. Noting greater variability in test performance among CH children in the sample, a closer look was taken at this group, particularly as related to therapy status. Initially, all of these children were receiving some type of remedial help such as speech or language therapy. However, from our updated family histories, we knew that many of the children who had been previously diagnosed as language impaired were now mainstreamed or were no longer in therapy of any kind. The sample was divided into two groups: those who were still receiving language therapy ($n = 16$) and those whose handicap condition had been remediated ($n = 22$).

One-way ANOVAs comparing the mean standard scores on the WJPB Mathematics and Reading achievement subtests of children in the therapy CH group, the remediated CH group, and the nonhandicapped group were computed. On both WJPB tests of achievement, differences between groups were highly significant ($p < .000$). Post hoc analyses using Scheffe's tests indicated differences at the .05 level between achievement means of the CH therapy group and both other groups, suggesting that the CH-remediated group has largely attained achievement parity with their nonhandicapped classmates. These results would strongly suggest that CH children who remain in therapy beyond grade 3 are at greater risk for academic failure than children whose therapy is of shorter duration. It may be the case that these children were more seriously CH at the outset.

Family Belief Orientations

It seemed worthwhile, at this point, to address whether the ideological environment of the home (i.e., parents' combined beliefs about how children learn) differed as a function of the therapy status of the child. The reader recalls that differences were anticipated among parents' ideas regarding the course of children's intellectual development in the presence of a learning disability. When one-way ANOVAs were performed on mean proportions of reported parental beliefs ($N = 78$), we found significant between-group differences ($p < .006$) on endorsement of cognitive processes and near significant ($p < .06$) differences on endorsement of direct instruction. Post hoc analyses indicated that the family belief systems of both CH subgroups (therapy and remediated) were more similar to each other than not, and both groups were significantly different from families with nonhandicapped children. These results are provocative for several reasons. I would have expected that the developmental beliefs of parents of the remediated group would more closely approximate those of the NCH group when their children's achievement levels were equivalent. With a standardized mean of 115, both groups' academic performance fell in the high-average range. Yet, parents of children in the remediated group tend to endorse higher levels of beliefs in direct instruction than either of the other two groups. This is surprising given their children's demonstrated ability to transcend earlier learning deficits. Perhaps there is an enduring parental belief that these children are still communication handicapped despite academic evidence to the contrary. Such a view might be maintained because people tend to hold on to beliefs that are confirmed by their own experiences. An alternative explanation is that parents of children who were previously diagnosed as communication handicapped, but have now been remediated, believe that their directive orientation facilitated the process of catching up for their children. Conversely, it is conceivable that the directive orientation expressed by these parents characterizes their paramount beliefs about how children generally acquire knowledge, irrespective of handicap condition. This latter speculation, however, would need to be verified through data on parents' interactions with the CH child's siblings.

Parental Beliefs and Child Functioning

In the course of reviewing these results it became evident that three convergent phenomena were accounting for findings: mothers and fathers differ in the behavioral expression of their stated beliefs, boys' and girls' achievement is differentially related to the parenting beliefs and strategies of their parents, and CH children who have remediated deficits and those still in therapy differ significantly in achievement levels and family orientation.

Regarding the first point, our data indicate that the teaching strategies parents say they employ as they act on their beliefs tend to vary by learning domain and by sex of parent. Depending on the situational context, mothers and fathers report similar levels of core beliefs, but differ in their manner of behaviorally expressing them. In essence, the patterns that emerge reflect the complex reality of the socialization task faced by parents because each knowledge domain has its own demand quality. The process of helping a child learn to solve a mathematics problem, for instance, requires a different approach than that used to help the child cope with emotional distress or fear of failure. Moreover, fathers and mothers tend to take a different tack with their child even when their reported rationales (e.g., to get the child to think) are the same. Thus, although we find that parental beliefs and behaviors individually relate to academic outcomes of children, their relationship to each other tends to vary according to gender and knowledge domain. The belief-behavior connection cannot be accurately described as a linear phenomenon.

Relative to the relation of parents' beliefs to their children's performance, the correlational results demonstrate how important it is to view parent–child relationships through a gender-sensitive lens. The bivariate analyses indicate that preadolescent girls' and boys' achievement in the CH sample is differentially related to how their mothers and fathers think they learn, lending credence to the argument that socialization experiences of female and male children (handicapped or not) are dissimilar (Block, 1983).

Although a large body of literature has begun to accumulate about the sex-differentiated socialization emphases of parents (see review by Block, 1983), few researchers of learning-impaired children have attended to gender differences, often grouping boys and girls together as if their common handicap status overrode all other concerns.

Admittedly, the well-documented disproportionate number of males compared to females (4 to 1) in the learning disabled population has made gender-balanced sampling difficult. Nevertheless, there is evidence that girls in need of special education are, in fact, more intellectually handicapped than boys (Owen, 1978). Moreover, it appears that patterns of dysfunctional classroom behavior among learning disabled adolescents differ for girls and boys, much as they do among nonhandicapped students (Ritter, 1989). These data serve as further evidence of the methodological fallacy of minimizing, or even ignoring, gender differences when investigating performance levels among LD children. However, the specific family socialization processes set in motion by parental beliefs about handicapped sons and daughters remain elusive until more opportunities become available to observe parent and child interactions in a variety of contexts.

On the basis of the literature, it is clear that the socialization goals of mothers and fathers differ: Fathers tend to be concerned with the child's acquisition of instrumental, cognitive skills, while mothers have been shown to assume responsibility for moral-social learning (Block, 1983). Yet, how do these differentiated socialization roles play themselves out when the child is handicapped? How are the traditional sex-typed socialization patterns, such as emphasizing independence for male but not for female children, altered in the presence of a language handicap? These are just a few of the questions raised by these findings that point out the importance of incorporating both child gender and handicap status into future research efforts.

The final point concerns the within-CH group differences stemming from the therapy status of the child. The persistent problem of sample heterogeneity has often frustrated research efforts seeking to build a generalizable fund of knowledge about learning impairments (Speece, McKinney, & Appelbaum, 1985). Thus, the discovery of a more severely disabled subsample of children within our CH group is consistent with findings of other longitudinal studies focusing on characteristics of learning disabled students. For many of these children, a learning disability represents a chronic, seriously handicapping condition that results in persistent academic underachievement if unremediated via special education in the primary grades (McKinney, 1989). Moreover, the disparity in achievement between children who require special educational services beyond grade 3 and their nonhandicapped peers has been reported to increase developmentally (McKinney, 1989). This pattern of achievement disparity was clearly evident within our subsamples of remediated and nonremediated CH children who were both diagnosed as language impaired 5 years ago.

SUMMARY AND CONCLUSIONS

Longitudinal research about children with learning disabilities is rare and, subsequently, there has been a lack of understanding about how individual differences in cognitive functioning develop and change through the elementary school years or how they contribute to academic failure (Kavale, 1988). My colleagues and I have sought to provide such longitudinal information on how school achievement of children with early-diagnosed communication handicaps relates to the learning orientations of their parents. As a group, parents of handicapped children were consistent in maintaining their perceptions of the child as a passive learner, while parents of nonhandicapped preadolescents were more likely to view their child as capable of drawing his or her own conclusions. Highly significant CH–NCH group differences in parental beliefs concerning how the child acquires moral-social concepts indicate that parents of communication-handicapped children are more likely to give advice and tell their children what to do in interpersonal situations than are parents of the NCH group. Given the age of these children and the fact that over half (22) of the CH group are no longer in therapy of any kind, it is surprising that there does not appear to be a shift toward beliefs supporting the child's autonomy (e.g., encouraging the child's own decision-making capabilities) as has been observed among parents of nonhandicapped preadolescents (Power & Shanks, 1989). It may well be that despite academic remediation, parents continue to perceive their children as handicapped in social interactions and their socialization efforts may reflect this concern.

Gibbs and Cooper (1989) labeled a diagnosis of communication disorder "practically synonymous" with a learning disability. While the majority of the CH children in our sample overcame initial deficits in receptive and expressive language and caught up to the achievement levels of their peers, more than one-third did not. Why is this so? One explanation lies in the diffuse nature of diagnoses of speech and language disorders. There are a variety of syndromes involving impairment in communication, which vary widely in terms of severity and duration (Speece et al., 1985). However, it may well be that opportunities for effective intervention reside within the context of the family, specifically in terms of parents' learning orientations and how they act on them.

Since the advent of Public Law 94-142, parents have increasingly been included in the special education process, and the salience of their roles as teachers and language facilitators has been recognized (Sigel et al., 1983). Our data indicate that intervention agents working with families of CH children would do well to investigate parents' belief systems regarding the handicapped child's learning capabilities. Parents of CH children in our sample maintained their directive orientation despite changes in their children's age and handicap status. Yet, there is accumulating evidence in the LD field that impaired learners may require more, rather than less, encouragement to be independent thinkers and problem solvers (Martin & Henderson, 1989). These findings, relative to distancing theory, have clearly shown that parents whose socialization practices enhance the child's opportunities to think, anticipate, imagine, and actively engage in the learning experience positively influence their children's representational competence and academic achievement.

ACKNOWLEDGMENTS

Part of the research reported in this paper was supported by the National Institute of Child Health and Human Development Grant No. R01-HD10686 to Educational Testing Service, National Institute of Mental Health Grant No. R01-MH32301 to Educational Testing Service, and Bureau of Education of the Handicapped Grant No. G007902000 to Educational Testing Service.

Thanks to Jim Wertsch for his encouragement to pursue this task, to Rod Cocking for acquainting me with the literature on language development and to Linda Kozelski for her preparation of the manuscript.

REFERENCES

Antill, J. (1987). Parents' beliefs and values about sex roles, sex differences, and sexuality. In P. Shaver & C. Hendrick (Eds.), *Sex and gender* (pp. 294–328). Beverly Hills, CA: Sage.

Bennett, C. W., & Runyan, C. M. (1982). Educators' perceptions of the effects of communication disorders upon educational performance. *Language, Speech and Hearing Services in Schools, 13*, 260–263.

Block, J. H. (1983). Differential premises arising from differential socialization of the sexes: Some conjectures. *Child Development, 54*, 1335–1354.

Case, E. J., & Leavitt, A. (1986). *Mental health project, P.L. 94-142: 1985–86 evaluation report.* Albuquerque, NM: Albuquerque Public Schools.

Deci, E. L., & Ryan, R. (1987). The support of autonomy and the control of behavior. *Journal of Personality and Social Psychology, 53*, 1024–1037.

Feiring, C., & Lewis, M. (1987). The child's social network: Sex differences from three to six years. *Sex Roles: A Journal of Research, 17*, 621–636.

Freeman, M. A. (1971). A comparative analysis of patterns of attitudes among mothers of children with learning disabilities, and mothers of children who are achieving normally. *Dissertation Abstracts International, 31*, 5125.

Gibbs, D. P., & Cooper, E. B. (1989). Prevalence of communication disorders in students with learning disabilities. *Journal of Learning Disabilities, 22*, 60–63.

Grolnick, W. S., & Ryan, R. M. (1987). Autonomy in children's learning: An experimental and individual difference investigation. *Journal of Personality and Social Psychology, 52*, 890–898.

Huston, A. (1983). Sex-typing. In P. H. Mussen (Series Ed.) & E. M. Heatherington (Vol. Ed.), *Handbook of child psychology, Vol. 4. Socialization, personality, and social development* (4th ed., pp. 387–467). New York: Wiley.

Kaufman, A. (1985). Review of the Woodcock-Johnson Psychoeducational Battery. In J. V. Mitchell (Ed.), *Ninth mental measurement yearbook* (Vol. 2, pp. 1762–1765). Lincoln, NE: University of Nebraska Press.

Kavale, K. A. (1988). The long-term consequences of learning disabilities. In M. C. Wang, H. J. Wallberg, & M. C. Reynolds (Eds.), *The handbook of special education: Research and practice* (pp. 303–344). Oxford, England: Pergamon.

Laskey, E., & Klopp, K. (1982). Parent–child interactions in normal and language disordered children. *Journal of Speech and Hearing Disorders, 47*, 7–18.

Lewis, M. (1982). The social network systems: Toward a general theory of social development. In T. Field (Ed.), *Review of human development, Vol. 1* (pp. 180–213). New York: Wiley.

Martin, C. E., & Henderson, B. B. (1989). Adult support and the exploratory behavior of children with learning disabilities. *Journal of Learning Disabilities, 22*, 67–68.

Mash, E. J. (1984). Families with problem children. In A. Doyle, D. Gold, & D. S. Moskowitz (Eds.), *Children in families under stress: New directions for child development* (No. 24). San Francisco: Jossey-Bass.

McGillicuddy-DeLisi, A. V., & Sigel, I. E. (1991). Family environments and children's representational thinking. In S. Silvern (Ed.), *Advances in reading/language research, Vol. 5: Literacy through family, community and school interaction* (pp. 63–90). Greenwich, CT: JAI.

McKinney, J. D. (1989). Longitudinal research on the behavioral characteristics of children with learning disabilities. *Journal of Learning Disabilities, 22*, 141–150.

Owen, F. W. (1978). Dyslexia—Genetic aspects. In A. L. Benton & D. Pearl (Eds.), *Dyslexia: An appraisal of current knowledge.* New York: Oxford University Press.

Power, T. G., & Shanks, J. A. (1989). Parents as socializers: Maternal and paternal views. *Journal of Youth and Adolescence, 18,* 203–220.

Ritter, D. R. (1989). Social competence and problem behavior of adolescent girls with learning disabilities. *Journal of Learning Disabilities, 22,* 460–461.

Schodorf, J., & Edwards, H. (1983). Comparative analysis of parent–child interactions with language-disordered and linguistically normal children. *Journal of Communication Disorders, 16,* 71–83.

Sigel, I. E. (1982). The relationship between parental distancing strategies and the child's cognitive behavior. In L. M. Laosa & I. E. Sigel (Eds.), *Families as learning environments for children* (pp. 47–86). New York: Plenum.

Sigel, I. E. (1985). A conceptual analysis of beliefs. In I. E. Sigel (Ed.), *Parental belief systems: The psychological consequences for children* (pp. 347–371). Hillsdale, NJ: Lawrence Erlbaum Associates.

Sigel, I. E. (1986). Reflections on the belief–behavior connection: Lessons learned from a research program on parental belief systems and teaching strategies. In R. D. Ashmore & D. M. Brodzinsky (Eds.), *Thinking about the family: Views of parents and children* (pp. 35–65). Hillsdale, NJ: Lawrence Erlbaum Associates.

Sigel, I. E. (1991). Representational competence: Another type? In M. Chandler & M. Chapman (Eds.), *Criteria for competence: Controversies in the conceptualization and assessment of children's abilities* (pp. 189–207). Hillsdale, NJ: Lawrence Erlbaum Associates.

Sigel, I. E. (1992). The belief–behavior connection: A resolvable dilemma? In I. E. Sigel, A. V. McGillicuddy-DeLisi, & J. Goodnow (Eds.), *Parental belief systems: The psychological consequences for children* (2nd ed., pp. 433–456). Hillsdale, NJ: Lawrence Erlbaum Associates.

Sigel, I. E., & Cocking, R. R. (1977). Cognition and communication: A dialectic paradigm for development. In M. Lewis & L. A. Rosenblum (Eds.), *The origins of behavior, Vol. 5: Interaction, conversation, and the development of language* (pp. 207–226). New York: Wiley.

Sigel, I. E., McGillicuddy-DeLisi, A. V., Flaugher, J., & Rock, D. A. (1983). *Parents as teachers of their own learning disabled children* (ETS RR 83–21). Princeton, NJ: Educational Testing Service.

Sigel, I. E., McGillicuddy-DeLisi, A. V., & Johnson, J. E. (1980). *Parental distancing, beliefs and children's representational competence within the family context* (ETS RR 80-21). Princeton, NJ: Educational Testing Service.

Sigel, I. E., Stinson, E. T., & Flaugher, J. (1993). Family process and school achievement: A comparison of children with and without communication handicaps. In R. E. Cole & D. Reiss (Eds.), *How do families cope with chronic illness?* (pp. 95–120). Hillsdale, NJ: Lawrence Erlbaum Associates.

Speece, D. L, McKinney, J. D., & Appelbaum, M. I. (1985). Classification and validation of behavioral subtypes of learning disabled children. *Journal of Educational Psychology, 77,* 67–77.

15

▼▼▼▼▼▼▼

Synergies in the Families
of Gifted Children

Nancy M. Robinson
University of Washington

This chapter addresses family contributions to talent development in gifted children and the ways in which myths, methods, and facts coalesce. In contrast to other populations described in this volume, gifted children are not usually considered at risk, and their families can often call on resources that are unavailable to at-risk populations. Even so, gifted children are not risk free.

I examine, briefly, definitions of giftedness and sources of information about families of gifted children; I describe common social attitudes and myths about such families; and I mention some evidence about the educational and social backgrounds of many—certainly not all—such families. In this chapter, I describe commonalities with marginalized groups in the ways in which gifted children and their families are generally regarded and treated. Finally, I describe a study of gifted and nongifted siblings that illustrates the ways in which myths and stereotypes can lead even rational investigators astray.

DEFINITIONS OF GIFTEDNESS

Definitions of giftedness vary widely. Because of the burden on schools to meet children's educational needs, academic abilities have traditionally been the focus of concerns about gifted children. Currently, however, attention is being paid to a much wider set of talent domains (Gagné, 1995; Gardner, 1983; Sternberg & Davidson, 1986). A confusing set of terminologies clouds the issues. For example, many authors (e.g., Feldman, 1986) speak of gift-edness in the sense of general (or "omnibus") ability, or at least the ability to reason at an advanced level in one or more broad intellectual domains such as verbal or mathematical reasoning. Such authors reserve the term *talents* for abilities in discrete, specialized fields such as chess, sports, or music. For others, however (e.g., Feldhusen, 1995; Gagné, 1995), advance-ment in aptitude domains constitutes giftedness while talents represent de-veloped manifestations of those aptitudes after learning, training, and practicing have occurred.

Even within populations identified by traditional means such as intelli-gence tests, there is no consensus about levels of measured ability above which a child is considered gifted or exceptionally gifted. Instead, the matter tends to be defined contextually in terms of needs as, for example, the definition stated in a report from the U.S. Department of Education, *National Excellence: A Case for Developing America's Talent* (1994): "These (gifted) children and youth exhibit high performance capability in intellectual, crea-tive, and/or artistic areas, possess an unusual leadership capacity, or excel in specific academic fields. They require services or activities not ordinarily provided by the schools" (p. 26).

Distinctions are also made between the promise represented by giftedness in children and the expertise exhibited by gifted adults. In children, giftedness is represented in large part by rapidity of development in one or more domains; in adults, actual accomplishments are the criteria. With few excep-tions, most often those rare child prodigies who exhibit remarkable musical talents, the performance of gifted children is precocious for its rate and to some extent its nature, but does not reach standards that would be seen as excellent in adult performance. Eminent adults are rare and special, but far too often taken as the defining case for giftedness, leading many parents and educators to underestimate the abilities of the very bright children they know.

A high level of ability alone does not automatically translate into gifted-ness. A traditional view of giftedness focuses on high performance on tests of general intelligence (e.g., Hollingworth, 1942; Terman, 1925), because it is taken as an index of the ability to acquire new kinds of skills, concepts, and insights (Sternberg, 1984). Continued high performance even on such limited indices demands continued optimal development—development that does not proceed in a vacuum. Without opportunity, encouragement, and practice, such potential giftedness can be diminished. Opportunities for learn-ing are essential (Bloom, 1985; Feldman, 1986) and a high degree of moti-vation or what Renzulli (1978) called "task commitment" (p. 184), is equally critical. So, too, is a degree of creativity seen as flexibility, fluency, or the willingness to take intellectual risks. Children's upbringing environments set the stage for the realization of these characteristics.

SOCIAL ATTITUDES AND MYTHS ABOUT GIFTED
CHILDREN AND THEIR FAMILIES

A decided ambivalence characterizes the position accorded gifted children and their families in contemporary American society. Despite respect, albeit sometimes grudging respect, for their achievement, negative stereotypes of gifted children abound (the elite or stuck-up, the nerd or geek, the bookworm, the smart-aleck or know-it-all, the emotionally vulnerable) as do negative stereotypes about their parents (the have-it-alls, the want-it-alls, the pushy ones). Moreover, the asynchronies in development that typify gifted children—especially the normal discrepancies among cognitive, social, emotional, and motor developmental levels—may be seen as faults, as in, "If you're so gifted, why can't you remember to tie your shoes?"

Gifted children are regarded with some awe but also with suspicion, as though they had stolen more than their share of resources. Even as young children, they are expected to be not only grateful but responsible for giving back, as, for example, by providing leadership in regular classrooms that are almost always underchallenging and by serving as teaching assistants for their classmates. In effect, our society strongly marginalizes gifted children as a group and tends to ignore their needs, especially their need for an educational program that matches the pace and level of their intellectual development. Advanced instruction in specific areas of talent such as music, art, dance, or chess is almost never provided in public schools—unlike talent in team sports (especially for boys), in which a high level of expertise is trained in the school setting and for which honors abound for high performance. Like members of ethnically marginalized groups, therefore, gifted and talented students experience risks for underachievement and other psychological ills that are costly not only for them but also for the society at large. Although as a group they appear psychologically healthy, especially during the years prior to and after adolescence (Robinson & Noble, 1991), theirs is certainly not a risk-free existence.

DEMOGRAPHICS OF THE FAMILIES
OF GIFTED CHILDREN

For a number of reasons, gifted children coming from economically disadvantaged and ethnically minority families, as well as those for whom English is a second language, are more likely to be overlooked than gifted children from mainstream, advantaged homes. Efforts to identify such hidden gifted children have been moderately successful (e.g., Baldwin, 1995; Feiring, Louis, Ukeje, & Lewis, 1997; Ford, 1994), especially when accompanied by broadened and somewhat relaxed definitions of giftedness. Nevertheless, the evidence points strongly to a relationship between giftedness and family advantage (Albert, 1980; Oden, 1942). Looking at the eminent, Simonton (1994), found about 80% coming from professional-level homes.

To cite our own work, parents who responded to community-wide invitations to identify children with advanced abilities, tend themselves to have advanced educational backgrounds. In one study (Robinson, Abbott, Berninger, & Busse, 1996), intensive efforts in a wide range of community settings elicited nominations of 778 math-talented young children in preschools and kindergartens. Despite a wide range, the average educational level of fathers and mothers of the nominees was 17.0 and 16.3 years respectively, and was 17.4 and 16.9 years for the parents of the children who qualified as math precocious on the basis of subsequent test scores. Similarly, a group of fathers and mothers who identified early talking toddlers averaged 16 years of education (Robinson, Dale, & Landesman, 1990). Parents of the school-age siblings to be described in more detail in a following section also had, on average, completed college education, with fathers of two gifted children averaging more than 17 years of education, those with one gifted child averaging about 16.5 years, and those of nongifted children 15.8 years. In each group, mothers had only slightly less education than fathers.

For several reasons, the demographics of school children identified as gifted are seldom described. First, as we have seen, there are severe problems of definition and terminology. If giftedness cannot be "diagnosed," then its epidemiology is difficult to describe. Even more powerful, however, the fact that these children come from educationally advantaged homes is a sore point, and becomes a handicap in securing appropriate educational services.

SOURCES OF DATA ABOUT FAMILIES
OF GIFTED CHILDREN

The sources of data about family influences on gifted children are varied, and each has its problems. The first studies were *biographical retrospectives* about the lives of persons who, by the time the data were reconstructed, were already eminent and were usually deceased (e.g., Cox, 1926; Goertzel, Goertzel, & Goertzel, 1978; McCurdy, 1957). Those studies are directed toward eminence, not childhood giftedness, and are biased by the styles and expectations of the original biographers themselves. More recently, the biographical method was applied by Bloom (1985) and his colleagues to the study of young adults who were world-class achievers in one of six areas, but were still young enough that their parents and teachers could be interviewed. The biographical method yields interesting hypotheses but tends to reveal a good deal more about eminence than about giftedness.

Interviews with family members are also subject to subtle biases. Most interview-driven investigations with families of gifted children (e.g., Ballering & Koch, 1984; Hackney, 1981; Peterson, 1977; Sunderlin, 1981) have been nonstructured and the interviewers have not been blind as to either the family composition or the original hypotheses. As we will see with regard to the effects of having a gifted sibling, interview studies tend to yield conclusions at some variance with those derived from more objective approaches.

Questionnaires have their limitations, but they also have potentially broader coverage and, if well constructed, somewhat greater protection from the expectations of the investigators. Parents, teachers, and the children themselves are the usual respondents. They have, for example, been asked to describe self-concept and adjustment status (e.g., Chamrad, Robinson, & Janos, 1995), especially in conjunction with special-program participation (e.g., Colangelo & Brower, 1987). Thousands of children have been followed up after participating in the various Talent Searches in which they have taken a test such as the SAT as seventh graders (e.g., Lubinski & Benbow, 1994). Generally speaking, the picture of the family drama has been less extreme when this method is employed than when families are interviewed.

Experience sampling is a fascinating way to get at the subjective issues involved in living the life of an able person, inside or outside the home. Csikszentmihalyi and his colleagues (Csikszentmihalyi, Rathunde, & Whalen, 1993) are major practitioners of this method. In their study, teenagers wore beepers for a week at a time. When alerted by the beepers, they recorded information about their setting, their companions (if any), their activities, how involved and satisfied they felt, and so forth.

Observational studies of parent–child interaction are almost nonexistent. Robinson, Dale, & Landesman (1990) included some brief mother–child interaction sequences in a longitudinal study of children who were precocious talkers as toddlers. Subsequently, Crain-Thoreson and Dale (1992) found that toddler interest while being read to was our best predictor of reading skills at age 4½ years. We had also tried to code dinner table interaction but these 20-month-old children, talkers though they were, were simply too young to be included.

FAMILY FACTORS

Family Factors that Help to Produce Bright Children

There is, of course, truth to the argument that gifted children tend to come from homes where parents are bright and are able and willing to devote time and attention to the welfare of their children (Kulieke & Olszewski-Kubilius,

1989; Robinson, 1993). In most of these families the level of language usage is high, usually there are two parents who provide adult models with productive lives, doors are opened to educational and other opportunities, health care and nutrition are assured, and there is enough money to run the affairs of the family in an orderly fashion and to make some choices.

This family picture is clearly not characteristic of all gifted children, however. Numerous projects funded by the only federal research resources earmarked for this population, the Javits grants, have discovered many gifted children living in poverty and coming from families that nobody would have guessed could produce them. Money is certainly not the most important variable here. Far more important are issues such as the organization and stability of the home and the existence of someone who cares very much and who monitors, supports, and focuses the child's efforts (VanTassel-Baska, 1989b).

Parents of gifted children typically report a high level of parental involvement with their children (Kulieke & Olszewski-Kubilius, 1989; Olszewski, Kulieke, & Buescher, 1987; Silverman & Kearney, 1989). They spend more time with the children and read to them much more often (even after they can read to themselves), than comparable families without gifted children (Karnes, Shwedel, & Steinberg, 1984). Mothers of gifted children are more frequently homemakers (VanTassel-Baska, 1983), although this trend may be changing (see Gottfried, Gottfried, Bathurst, & Guerin, 1994). Indeed, Thomas (1984) found that fathers of precocious readers worked, on average, 10 fewer hours per week than fathers of other children.

For example, Gottfried et al. (1994) followed from birth a group of about 130 children. Among this group, those who at age 8 scored 130 or higher on a WISC-R came from more enriched environments and homes of higher socioeconomic and educational status. Their parents were also more involved, responsive, and nurturing in the children's academic endeavors. From almost everything we know about child development, families of gifted children tend to provide a healthy start.

It is also worth mentioning that gifted children themselves play a role in shaping the favorableness of their environments. The same study by Gottfried et al. (1994) found gifted children making more demands of their parents—asking more questions and asking for more challenges, and getting more answers and opportunities—than did nongifted children. Such findings are fully in line with the concept described by Plomin and Daniels (1987), as well as other behavioral geneticists, of nonshared environments; that is, those factors that make experiences within a single setting, such as a family, different for different family members. Family influence is not a one-way street; parents influence children but children also influence parents and other family members in reciprocal cycles.

Family Factors That Help to Promote High Achievement

When it comes to motivation and attainment, even during childhood and adolescence, it is clear that some families do a better job of supporting children than do others. Parents whose children achieve well in school have consistently been identified as active in their roles, fostering not only general development but independence and individuation. Czikszentmihalyi and his colleagues (Csikszentmihalyi et al., 1993) have delineated what they call *complex families*, those who provide firm bonds of connection and support among family members as well as encouragement for each member to develop individuality by seeking out new challenges and opportunities. These authors have shown that teenagers who are freshman in high school and show talent in any of a number of areas are much more likely to stay with and develop that talent over a period of years if they come from complex families than those who come from families that the authors term *integrated* (supportive and consistent but no push toward individuation) or *differentiated* (less supportive but with greater push toward individuation). "Complex family environments breed . . . individuals who habitually react to a boring situation by seeking stimulation and challenge and to an anxiety-provoking one by increasing skills" (p. 157). Put a different way, following the family configurations described by Baumrind (1971), parents with *authoritative* styles breed children who are more likely to reach high, those with *laissez-faire* styles breed smart children who do not accomplish much, those with *authoritarian* patterns (high control, high demand) are likely to produce children with high achievement, high degrees of conformity, and lack of originality (Nichols, 1964; Olszewski et al., 1987).

High goals are an essential component of high achievement (see, e.g., MacKinnon, 1965) and yet gifted children who set high goals are often accused of perfectionism, as though it were a disease endemic to high IQ (Adderholt-Elliott, 1987). Clearly, some goalsetting is wholesome, as when children set high-level goals, pursue them with commitment and satisfaction, and can live with themselves if the effort does not in fact pay off as envisioned. Some goalsetting is detrimental, as when children feel driven to meet the standards of others, avoid activities in which they cannot be instant experts, and feel defeated if actual performance falls short of imagined heights. These processes have been little studied in gifted children, but only with high aspirations do people develop the motivation to invest, work very hard to develop expertise, weather frustration, and celebrate attainment.

Although paths to high achievement may not be clear, the high number of gifted students trapped in the pernicious grip of underachievement is tragic (Rimm, 1986). Although there are many paths to underachievement, including subtle learning disabilities that may be difficult to detect in gifted children, chronic underchallenge in educational settings is clearly one major culprit. Its effects can occur not only directly through boredom and lack of incentive to develop effective work habits and study skills, but indirectly through distorted views of one's own intellectual powers and realization of hollow victories. Underchallenged gifted children fall heir to what Dweck (1986) called an entity theory of intelligence, in which one's gift will seem diminished if one has to work hard, versus an incremental view, which views ability as the product of hard work. Equally powerful, however, are parents who themselves are underachievers or who expect too little of their children and create an atmosphere of conflict and hostility in the home. These factors can easily sap the determination of children, gifted or not, producing patterns of underachievement that are all the more tragic in children whose potential for achievement is so great (Rimm, 1986).

Family Factors That Tend to Promote Creativity

Creativity has many meanings (Sternberg, 1988) and, like giftedness, is defined differently for children and adults. Generally speaking, creativity in children is taken to mean fluidity in thinking, escape from the conventional, and ability to come up with original ideas and connections. The creative adult is, on the other hand, expected to have produced original work worthy of note.

With regard to children and youth regarded as creative, family backgrounds contrast in interesting ways with those of children who are bright but conventional. Parents of creative children tend to pursue their own interests and agendas (Albert, 1978), are less child centered and more accepting of children's nonconventional behavior (Getzels & Jackson, 1961), and are more likely to exhibit tense, distant, and less harmonious relationships with each other (Olszewski et al., 1987). Albert and Runco (1986) cite several factors as related to creativity, including early independence training (especially for boys), a sense of discontent, a sense of this child's being special, and hostility or indifference between the parents. As the result of these factors, the children experience both greater stress and a wider variety of models than those from conventional families. Perhaps, then, creativity reflects children's attempts to channel the emotional stress engendered by dysfunctional families into more rewarding activities. There is also an interesting association of highly creative writers, in particular, with bipolar affective disorder in both themselves and other family members (Andreason, 1987), but this phenomenon appears to be specific to a restricted subgroup of the creative.

Family Factors That Tend to Promote Eminence

When one looks at the lives of the eminent, additional factors emerge (Simonton, 1988, 1994). The most prominent factor is being male rather than female. Personality and character traits play a part, as do having marginal rather than mainstream social status and, indeed, luck. Moreover, according to Simonton, significant factors lie outside the family and reside in the political scene, including eras of violence (which may enhance the creativity of young adults but destroy that of children), geography and national values, the availability of patrons, and so on.

With regard to family factors, however, some writers, such as Albert (1978) have pointed to stressful "wobbles" that challenge the young person but don't overwhelm the family, which remains intact although stressed. Early parental loss is a repeated finding (Albert, 1980; Albert & Runco, 1986; VanTassel-Baska, 1989a). Kerr (1985) found many eminent women coming from homes with "at least one ineffectual, absent, deceased, or irresponsible parent" (p. 63). Presumably, the youngster has to grow up fast but is not alone, with at least one parent (Bloom, 1985) or grandparent (Sheldon, 1954), or sometimes an older sibling (McCurdy, 1957; Wallace, 1990) devoting emotional resources to the child and maintaining high expectations. Whether because the first born assumes leadership responsibility in the family, gains more than his or her share of both adult attention and monetary resources (the rules of primogeniture), or other factors, eminent political leaders and other high achievers are more often first born than the laws of probability would predict (Albert, 1980). They are also much more often male than female.

CONSEQUENCES OF HAVING A GIFTED SIBLING

So far, we have described families as consisting mainly of parents and target children, with little consideration of sibling relationships. It has long been thought that special stresses arise when one or more, but not all, of the children in a family are considered gifted. The children may, for example, compare themselves to each other (e.g., Bank & Kahn, 1982; Dunn, 1988) and family resources may be concentrated on the higher achieving child, who is not always the inherently most talented child (Bloom, 1985). Parents may expect too much or too little of the nonidentified (but possibly gifted) child (Brody, Stoneman, & McCoy, 1992; McHale & Pawletko, 1992) and, in fact, the giftedness of a younger child with a gifted older sibling may not even be recognized by the parents (Haensly, 1993).

Of course, there are potential assets to having a gifted sibling. In the interests of fairness, parents may encourage different kinds of competencies in different children, leaning over backwards to be even-handed. Moreover, the gifted children themselves may serve as role models, tutors, and relatively mature and insightful friends. Wallace (1990) focused on the powerful role sometimes played by siblings in creative lives, describing in detail the relationship of Dorothy Wordsworth to William and pointing to the collaborative lives of the brothers Grimm, Montgolfier, and Wright, as well as the Bronte siblings.

When my colleagues and I began, in the late 1980s, to plan our investigation, we found a literature that clearly emphasized the stresses attendant on having a gifted sibling. All sibling studies published at that time consisted of informal observations, case studies, and interviews with families of at least one gifted child (Hackney, 1981; Peterson, 1977; Sunderlin, 1981).

Interviewing parents about their first- and second-born children, for example, Cornell (1983) found that those who perceived a child as gifted were prouder of and felt closer to him or her and described their nongifted children as less mindful of social rules, more shy, and more easily upset. The latter descriptions were also more negative than those of parents of two nongifted children. Pfouts (1976, 1980) described 50 pairs of brothers. In 37 pairs, both boys had IQs well above average; in the others, only one did. She concluded that academic competition affected the relationships in both groups and produced hostility and low self-esteem in the less gifted child, but that two gifted brothers were most competitive of all. Similarly, other interview studies (Ballering & Koch, 1984; Cornell & Grossberg, 1986, 1989) painted equally negative pictures of sibling relationships.

When questionnaires have been involved in studies of siblings, the picture has been somewhat more positive, but these have been few. Colangelo and Brower (1987) compared 25 pairs of gifted–nongifted siblings at least 5 years after initial school placement. While the gifted children scored significantly higher in academic self-esteem, the pairs did not differ on general self-esteem. Renzulli and McGreevy (1986), also looking at effects of differential placement of siblings, in this case twins, found that the only pairs with different outcomes were identical twins who had been differentially placed. These studies had, however, not yet been published when we started our work. On the basis of the literature, therefore, we expected a series of negative outcomes for nongifted siblings in mixed pairs, and following the work of Pfouts (1976, 1980), we expected negative outcomes in pairs with two gifted children as well.

Because our study has been previously described (Chamrad et al., 1995), only essential details will be outlined here. To simplify matters, we restricted our sample to 378 triads composed of a mother and her only two children, both in grades 3 through 8. We focused on preadolescents because of the evidence that adolescence is a particularly vulnerable era for gifted youngsters

(Robinson & Noble, 1991). Mean ages were 9.8 years for younger siblings and 12.4 years for older siblings. We initially used eligibility of the children for special programs to constitute groups with zero, one, or two gifted members—a 16-cell model balanced for giftedness, birth order, gender, and gender-match of siblings. Interestingly, it took us considerably longer to recruit pairs with two gifted boys than any other group; parents who declined the invitation because of explicit fears about sibling competitiveness were almost all mothers of two gifted boys.

Families came to our laboratory in groups of three to five triads, with mothers and children answering questionnaires independently. The measures were grouped into three categories: child's cognitive abilities and achievement level (both measured directly and rated by the mothers), child's adjustment, and sibling relationship. The measures, some published and some specific to this study, have been detailed by Chamrad et al. (1995).

The results using the school-based criteria did not support our original expectations in any way. Except for the variables directly connected with the children's academic ability (test scores, maternal ratings, and self-perception of scholastic competence), all of which were consistent with school designations, there were no other differences by group membership.

Eventually, we realized that we were looking under the wrong lamppost because our real focus was on within-family interactions. We reconstituted our groups, using a median split of the principal component analysis of mothers' perceptions of the children's mental abilities to look at family issues as defined by families themselves. The median split was justified by the fact that, initially, the groups represented 50% gifted and 50% nongifted children by school designation.

Reconstituting the groups yielded more interesting data: 23 of the 48 ANOVAs yielded significant effects at the .05 level. We were generous with our alpha level because the study was exploratory. In nearly every case, the findings in the nongifted dyads were less positive than findings for the both-gifted dyads, with one-gifted dyads (either older or younger) tending to fall at intermediate levels. This finding suggests both that giftedness itself is a more powerful variable than giftedness of sibling, and that having a gifted sibling is better than not having one. When dyads having one or two gifted members were compared with those without a gifted member, in no instance did they appear disadvantaged.

Subsequent regression analyses yielded similar results. Wherever we could, we summarized variables by means of a principal components analysis. In this analysis, we simultaneously took into account age, gender, and giftedness of child and of sibling. Disregarding findings that had to do only with age, gender, or their interaction, again the findings are decidedly not negative (as we had originally predicted), but are positive. While most of the findings relate to giftedness of the child (as rated by the mother), there are some effects for siblings of gifted children, and they consistently suggest that it is certainly not a liability, and perhaps is an asset, to have a gifted sibling.

For example, for younger siblings, the presence of a gifted sibling is associated with decreased anxiety; mothers rated their younger children who had older gifted siblings as more attractive and better behaved, and described them in general by more positive adjectives than younger children without gifted siblings. For older children with a gifted sibling, similarly, mothers saw greater social competence, better behavior, and fewer behavior problems, and described the children by more positive adjectives than did mothers of older children whose younger siblings were not seen as gifted.

With regard to the quality of the sibling relationship, the results are even more consistently positive. Compared with nongifted children, gifted children tended to view their siblings in a more positive light, whether or not the siblings were gifted. Gifted older children seemed to take a more explicitly benevolent attitude toward siblings than did gifted younger children. Mothers confirmed the positive role of both older and younger siblings' giftedness on the relationship and suggested that, if the younger was gifted, the older child created fewer hassles. More effects in this set of variables related, again, to the giftedness of the child being rated than to the giftedness of the sibling.

Our findings generally confirm the expected advantage in adjustment for gifted children as well. Interestingly, ratings of athletic competence suggested a compensatory role, with both older and younger gifted subjects seeing themselves as less athletic than did the nongifted subjects.

What does all this suggest? We can only speculate, of course, but we are certainly led to wonder whether giftedness of sibling does not become the socially acceptable scapegoat for a number of normal family tensions, just as giftedness of the child is commonly blamed for a variety of psychosocial issues in spite of a large, redundant body of research attesting to the healthy adjustment of gifted children as a group. Of course, there were children in our sample whose adjustment and relationships were far from perfect, but this was true in all groups. The explanations for family issues are always complex, and we can be misled by glib assumptions.

SUMMARY

In summary, the various facets of giftedness may come from somewhat different sources. First, there are familial patterns not described in this chapter that suggest strong genetic influences. Second, however, genes do not operate in a vacuum. To raise bright children, families need to do all those things that we know promote healthy child development and cognitive growth. Third, to raise high achieving children, parents need to add elements of high expectations and differentiation to their basically warm, supportive relationships. They need to help their children to be self-directed and, in addition, to find areas of interest and talent, and to become highly invested in activities relevant to them. Fourth, if parents want to raise eminent children, it is helpful to live in the right place at the right time, to keep their children out of wars, to endure just enough, but not too much, hardship, and to elect one of the parents to die young. Furthermore, it helps if the parents start by being highly talented, even eminent, themselves.

By and large, the pictures of these families, as a group, are positive. The research reported here was not directed at those families who produce lower-achieving or bright, but not happy children, although certainly such families exist within this population as they do within any other. While our research and that of others has shown that the negative stereotypes of both gifted children and their siblings are just that—negative stereotypes—there is much work to be done to explain just what families do that makes the most difference in outcomes for their children.

ACKNOWLEDGMENTS

The study of siblings reported in this paper was funded in part by the National Institute of Mental Health, Grant No. MH39932. The author is indebted to her colleagues in that work, Diana Chamrad and Paul Janos.

REFERENCES

Adderholt-Elliott, M. (1987). *Perfectionism: What's bad about being too good?* Minneapolis, MN: Free Spirit.

Albert, R. S. (1978). Observations and suggestions regarding giftedness, familial influence and the achievement of eminence. *Gifted Child Quarterly, 28*, 201–211.

Albert, R. S. (1980). Family positions and the attainment of eminence: A study of special family positions and special family experiences. *Gifted Child Quarterly, 24*, 87–95.

Albert, R. S., & Runco, M. A. (1986). The achievement of eminence: A model of exceptional boys and their parents. In R. J. Sternberg & J. E. Davidson (Eds.), *Conceptions of giftedness* (pp. 332–357). New York: Cambridge University Press.

Andreason, N. C. (1987). Creativity and mental illness: Prevalence rates in writers and their first-degree relatives. *American Journal of Psychiatry, 144*, 1288–1292.

Baldwin, A. Y. (1995). The seven-plus story: Developing hidden talent among students in socioeconomically disadvantaged neighborhoods. *Gifted Child Quarterly, 38*, 80–84.

Ballering, L. D., & Koch, A. (1984). Family relations when a child is gifted. *Gifted Child Quarterly, 28*, 140–143.

Bank, S. P., & Kahn, M. D. (1982). *The sibling bond.* New York: Basic Books.

Baumrind, D. (1971). Current patterns of parental authority. *Developmental Psychology Monographs, 4*(1, Part 2).

Bloom, B. (Ed.). (1985). *Developing talent in young people.* New York: Ballantine.

Brody, G. H., Stoneman, Z., & McCoy, J. K. (1992). Associations of maternal and paternal direct and differential behavior with sibling relationships: Contemporaneous and longitudinal analyses. *Child Development, 63,* 82–92.

Chamrad, D. L., Robinson, N. M., & Janos, P. M. (1995). Consequences of having a gifted sibling: Myths and realities. *Gifted Child Quarterly, 39,* 135–145.

Colangelo, N., & Brower, P. (1987). Gifted youngsters and their siblings: Long-term impact of labeling on their academic and personal self-concepts. *Roeper Review, 10,* 101–103.

Cornell, D. G. (1983). Gifted children: The impact of positive labeling on the family system. *American Journal of Orthopsychiatry, 53,* 322–335.

Cornell, D. G. (1989). Child adjustment and parent use of the term "gifted." *Gifted Child Quarterly, 33,* 59–64.

Cornell, D. G., & Grossberg, I. N. (1986). Siblings of children in gifted programs. *Journal for the Education of the Gifted, 9,* 253–264.

Cornell, D. G., & Grossberg, I. N. (1989). Parent use of the term "gifted" correlates with family environment and child adjustment. *Journal for the Education of the Gifted, 12,* 218–230.

Cox, C. M. (1926). *Genetic studies of genius, Vol. 2: The early mental traits of three hundred geniuses.* Stanford, CA: Stanford University Press.

Crain-Thoreson, C., & Dale, P. S. (1992). Do early talkers become early readers? Linguistic precocity, preschool language, and emergent literacy. *Developmental Psychology, 28,* 421–429.

Csikszentmihalyi, M., Rathunde, K., & Whalen, S. (1993). *Talented teenagers: The roots of success and failure.* Cambridge, England: Cambridge University Press.

Dunn, J. (1988). *The beginnings of social understanding.* Cambridge, MA: Harvard University Press.

Dweck, C. S. (1986). Motivational processes affecting learning. *American Psychologist, 41,* 1040–1048.

Feiring, C., Louis, B., Ukeje, I., & Lewis, M. (1997). Early identification of gifted minority kindergarten students in Newark, New Jersey. *Gifted Child Quarterly, 41*(3), 13–19.

Feldhusen, J. F. (1995). Talent development: The new direction in gifted education. *Roeper Review, 18,* 92.

Feldman, D. H. (1986). *Nature's gambit.* New York: Basic Books.

Ford, D. Y. (1994). The recruitment and retention of African-American students in gifted education programs: Implications and recommendations, *Research-Based Decision Making Series* (No. 9406). Storrs, CT: National Research Center on Gifted and Talented.

Gagné, F. (1995). From giftedness to talent: A developmental model and its impact on the language of the field. *Roeper Review, 18,* 103–111.

Gardner, H. (1983). *Frames of mind.* New York: Basic Books.

Getzels, J., & Jackson, P. (1961). Family environments and cognitive style: A study of the sources of highly intelligent and of highly creative adolescents. *American Sociological Review, 26,* 251–260.

Goertzel, M., Goertzel, V., & Goertzel, T. (1978). *Three hundred eminent personalities.* San Francisco: Jossey-Bass.

Gottfried, A. W., Gottfried, A. E., Bathurst, K., & Guerin, D. W. (1994). *Gifted IQ: Early developmental aspects (The Fullerton Longitudinal Study).* New York: Plenum.

Hackney, H. (1981). The gifted child, the family, and the school. *Gifted Child Quarterly, 25,* 51–54.

Haensly, P. A. (1993, February). *Development of giftedness among siblings: A case study of differences and familial microsystems.* Paper presented at the Esther Katz Rosen Symposium, Lawrence, KS. (ERIC Document Reproduction Service No. ED 362 319).

Hollingworth, L. S. (1942). *Children above 180 IQ Stanford-Binet: Origins and development.* Yonkers-on-Hudson, NY: World Book.

Karnes, M. B., Shwedel, A. M., & Steinberg, D. (1984). Styles of parenting among parents of young, gifted children. *Roeper Review, 6,* 232–235.

Kerr, B. (1985). *Smart girls, gifted women.* Columbus, OH: Ohio Publishing.

Kulieke, M. J., & Olszewski-Kubilius, P. (1989). The influence of family values and climate on the development of gifted children. In J. L. VanTassel-Baska & P. Olszewski-Kubilius (Eds.), *Patterns of influence on gifted learners: The home, the self, and the school* (pp. 40–59). New York: Teachers College Press.

Lubinski, D., & Benbow, C. P. (1994). The study of mathematically precocious youth: The first three decades of a planned 50-year study of intellectual talent. In R. F. Subotnik & K. D. Arnold (Eds.), *Beyond Terman: Contemporary longitudinal studies of giftedness and talent* (pp. 255–281). Norwood, NJ: Ablex.

MacKinnon, D. W. (1965). Personality and the realization of creative potential. *American Psychologist, 20,* 273–281.

McCurdy, H. G. (1957). The childhood pattern of genius. *Journal of the Elisha Mitchell Scientific Society, 73,* 448–462.

McHale, S. M., & Pawletko, T. M. (1992). Differential treatment of siblings in two family contexts. *Child Development, 63,* 68–81.

National excellence: A case for developing America's talent. (1993). Washington, DC: Office of Educational Research and Improvement, U.S. Office of Education.

Nichols, R. C. (1964). Parental attitudes of mothers of intelligent adolescents and the creativity of their children. *Child Development, 35,* 1041–1049.

Oden, M. H. (1942). The fulfillment of promise: 40-year follow-up of the Terman gifted group. *Genetic Psychology Monograph, 77,* 3–93.

Olszewski, P., Kulieke, M. J., & Buescher, T. (1987). The influence of family environment on the development of talent: A literature review. *Journal for the Education of the Gifted, 11,* 6–28.

Peterson, D. C. (1977). The heterogeneously gifted family. *Gifted Child Quarterly, 21,* 396–411.

Pfouts, J. H. (1976). The sibling relationship: A forgotten dimension. *Social Work, 21,* 200–204.

Pfouts, J. H. (1980). Birth order, age spacing, I.Q. differences, and family relations. *Journal of Marriage and the Family, 42,* 517–521.

Plomin, R., & Daniels, D. (1987). Why are children within the family so different from each other? *The Brain and Behavioral Sciences, 10,* 1–16.

Renzulli, J. S. (1978). What makes giftedness? Reexamining a definition. *Phi Delta Kappan, 60,* 180–184, 261.

Renzulli, J. S., & McGreevy, A. M. (1986). Twins included and not included in special programs for the gifted. *Roeper Review, 9,* 120–127.

Rimm, S. B. (1986). *Underachievement syndrome: Causes and cures.* Watertown, WI: Apple Publishing.

Robinson, N. M. (1993). Identifying and nurturing gifted, very young children. In K. A. Heller, F. J. Mönks, & A. H. Passow (Eds.), *International handbook of research and development of giftedness and talent* (pp. 507–524). Oxford, England: Pergamon.

Robinson, N. M., Abbott, R. D., Berninger, V. W., & Busse, J. (1996). The structure of abilities in math-precocious young children: Gender similarities and differences. *Journal of Educational Psychology, 88,* 341–352.

Robinson, N. M., Dale, P. D., & Landesman, S. (1990). Validity of Stanford–Binet IV with linguistically precocious toddlers. *Intelligence, 14,* 173–186.

Robinson, N. M., & Noble, K. D. (1991). Psycho-social adjustment of gifted children. In M. G. Wang, M. C. Reynolds, & H. J. Walberg (Eds.), *Handbook of special education: Research and practise, Vol. 4* (pp. 23–36). New York: Pergamon.

Sheldon, P. M. (1954). The families of highly gifted children. *Marriage and Family Living, 16,* 59–67.

Silverman, L. K., & Kearney, K. (1989). Parents of the extraordinarily gifted. *Advanced Development Journal, 1,* 41–56.

Simonton, D. K. (1988). *Scientific genius: A psychology of science.* Cambridge, England: Cambridge University Press.

Simonton, D. K. (1994). *Greatness: Who makes history and why.* New York: Guilford.

Sternberg, R. J. (1984). Toward a triarchic theory of human intelligence. *Behavioral and Brain Sciences, 7,* 269–316.

Sternberg, R. J. (Ed.). (1988). *The nature of creativity.* Cambridge, England: Cambridge University Press.

Sternberg, R. J., & Davidson, J. E. (Eds.). (1986). *Conceptions of giftedness.* Cambridge, England: Cambridge University Press.

Sunderlin, A. (1981). Gifted children and their siblings. In B. S. Miller & M. Puce (Eds.), *The gifted child, the family and the community* (pp. 100–106). NY: Walter.

Terman, L. (1925). *Genetic studies of genius, Vol. 1: Mental and physical traits of a thousand gifted children.* Stanford, CA: Stanford University Press.

Thomas, B. (1984). Early toy preferences of 4-year-old readers and nonreaders. *Child Development, 55,* 424–430.

VanTassel-Baska, J. (1983). Profiles in precocity: The 1982 Midwest Talent Search finalists. *Gifted Child Quarterly, 27*(3), 129–144.

VanTassel-Baska, J. L. (1989a). Characteristics of the developmental path of eminent and gifted adults. In J. L. Van Tassel-Baska & P. Olszewski-Kubilius (Eds.), *Patterns of influence on gifted learners: The home, the self, and the school* (pp. 146–162). New York: Teachers College Press.

VanTassel-Baska, J. L. (1989b). The role of the family in the success of disadvantaged gifted learners. In J. L. VanTassel-Baska & P. Olszewski-Kubilius (Eds.), *Patterns of influence on gifted learners: The home, the self, and the school* (pp. 60–86). New York: Teachers College Press.

Wallace, D. B. (1990). Sibling relationships in creative lives. In M. J. A. Howe (Ed.), *Encouraging the development of exceptional skills and talents* (pp. 71–88). Leicester, England: British Psychological Society.

Author Index

Subject Index

A

Ability, definition of gifted children, 310
Absence, parental and divorce, 34
Abuse, antisocial behavior in children, 210, 211
Academic achievement
  age differences and HOME inventory measurement, 146-147
  coparenting in rural African-American families, 235, 239
  constructive reactions to anger, 98
  social and family influences on development of child competence, 176, 178
Academic performance
  age differences and HOME inventory measurement, 146
  definition of gifted children, 309
  family belief systems, 302
  family relationship effects on behavior outside of the family, 208–212
Accommodation, family functioning, 271
Achievement
  child and parental beliefs/teaching, 294–304
  children with developmental delays and family functioning, 283
  family factors that promote, 315–316
Active covariance, impact on child development, 253, 259, see also Covariance
Adaptation
  child and steady state effects, 15
  families with children with developmental delays, 276–277
Additive coaction, child development, 253–254
  nutritional influences, 262
Adjustment, child
  coparenting, 230–231, 235
  consequences of having a gifted sibling, 320

divorce, 34, 48
Adolescence
  early and development, 54
  accommodation with children with developmental delays, 277, 280
  competence and family systems approach in study, 57
  coparenting style in divorced families, 228, 229
Advanced instruction, see Teaching
Advice, social competence in child-peer interactions, 93–95
Affect management
  family-peer interactions, 96–99
  parent-child play and social competence, 92–94
African-American families, coparenting
  development of research methods and assessments, 233–234
  single-mother-headed families, 237–239
  two-parent families, 234–237
Age, differences and HOME inventory relation to child development, 144–150
Aggression
  children in Israeli Domestic Violence study, 220
  coparenting in divorced families, 228
  peer-child interactions, 13
Amelioration patterns, maternal foraging and primate infants, 82
Anger, child–peer interactions, 98
Anxiety
  consequences of having a gifted sibling, 320
  coparenting styles between married parents, 230
Arousal, modulation in young primates, 77–79

337